Hitoshi Okuda was famous in Japanese amateur manga (*doujinshi*) under a pen name long before he made his professional debut. He studied under Nobuteru Yuki

The All-New Tenchi Muyô!
Volume 7: Picture Book
Action Edition

STORY AND ART BY HITOSHI OKUDA

English Adaptation/Fred Burke
Translation/Aisei Japanese Language Services, Inc.
Touch-up Art & Lettering/Curtis Yee
Design/Hidemi Sahara
Editor/Shaenon K. Garrity

Managing Editor/Annette Roman
Director of Production/Noboru Watanabe
Vice President of Publishing/Alvin Lu
Sr. Director of Acquisitions/Rika Inouye
VP of Sales & Marketing/Liza Coppola
Publisher/Hyoe Narita

© 2001 HITOSHI OKUDA © AIC/VAP • NTV. Originally published in Japan in 2001 by KADOKAWA SHOTEN PUBLISHING CO., LTD.,
Tokyo. English translation rights arranged with KADOKAWA SHOTEN PUBLISHING CO., LTD., Tokyo.
New and adapted artwork and text © 2005 VIZ Media, LLC.
The ALL-NEW TENCHI MUYÔ! logo is a trademark of VIZ Media, LLC. All rights reserved.
The stories, characters and incidents mentioned in this publication are entirely fictional. For purposes of publication in
English, the artwork in this publication is generally printed in reverse from the original Japanese version.

Printed in Canada.

Published by VIZ Media, LLC
P.O. Box 77010
San Francisco, CA 94107

Action Edition
10 9 8 7 6 5 4 3 2 1
First printing, October 2005

For advertising rates or media kit, e-mail advertising@viz.com

www.viz.com
store.viz.com

PARENTAL ADVISORY
THE ALL NEW TENCHI MUYÔ! is rated T for Teen
and is recommended for ages 13 and up. It contains
fantasy violence and mild sexual humor.

VIZ GRAPHIC NOVEL

THE ALL-NEW TENCHI MUYŌ!

PICTURE BOOK

STORY AND ART BY
HITOSHI OKUDA

CONTENTS

Chapter 1: Omen

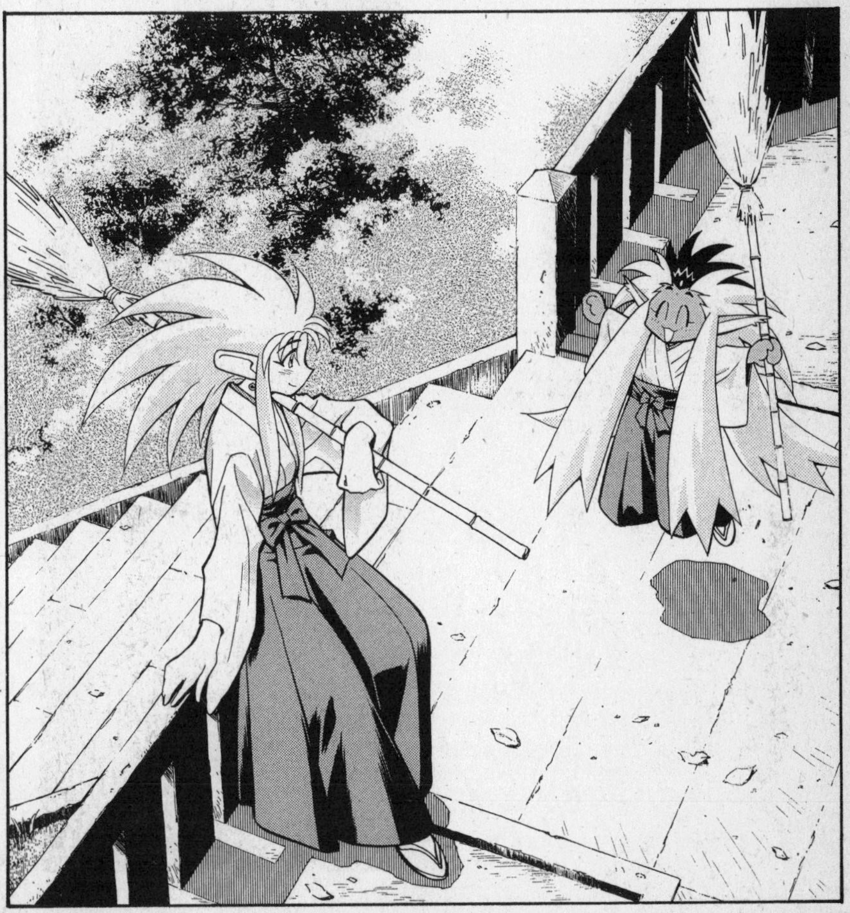

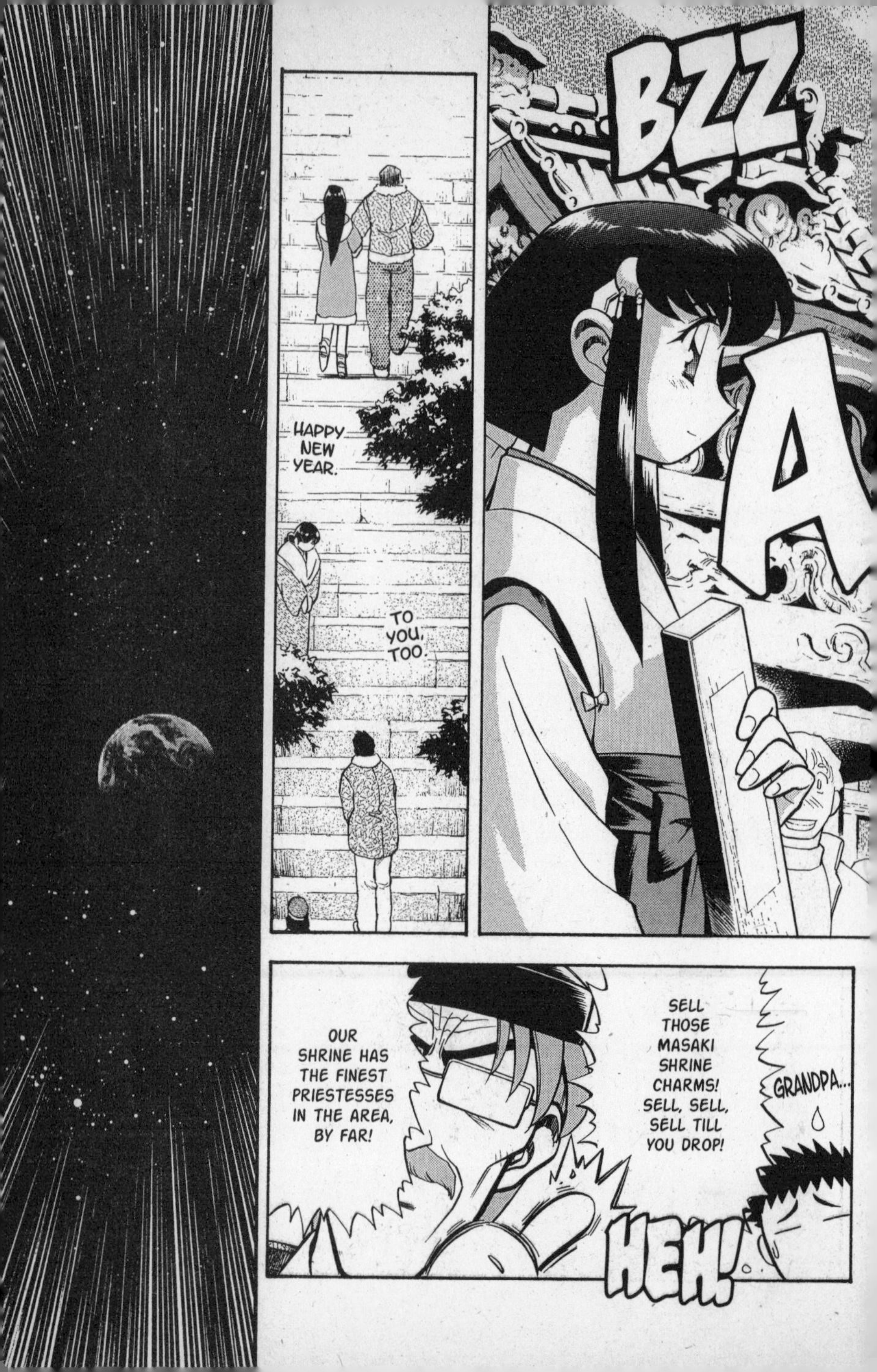
HAPPY NEW YEAR.
TO YOU, TOO.
BZZ
A
OUR SHRINE HAS THE FINEST PRIESTESSES IN THE AREA, BY FAR!
SELL THOSE MASAKI SHRINE CHARMS! SELL, SELL, SELL TILL YOU DROP!
GRANDPA...
HEH!

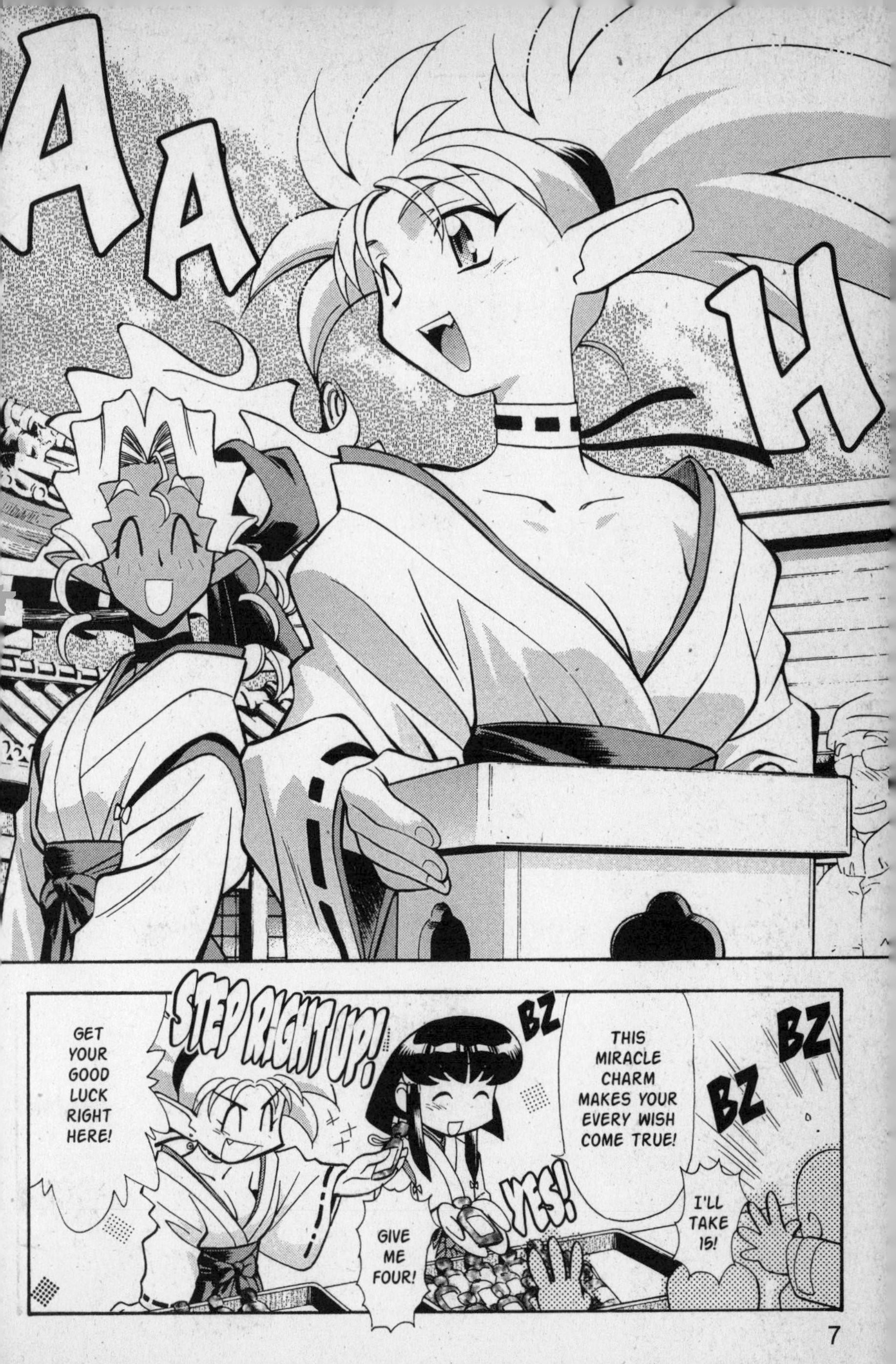
AAAH
GET YOUR GOOD LUCK RIGHT HERE!
STEP RIGHT UP!
BZ
THIS MIRACLE CHARM MAKES YOUR EVERY WISH COME TRUE!
BZ
BZ
YES!
GIVE ME FOUR!
I'LL TAKE 15!

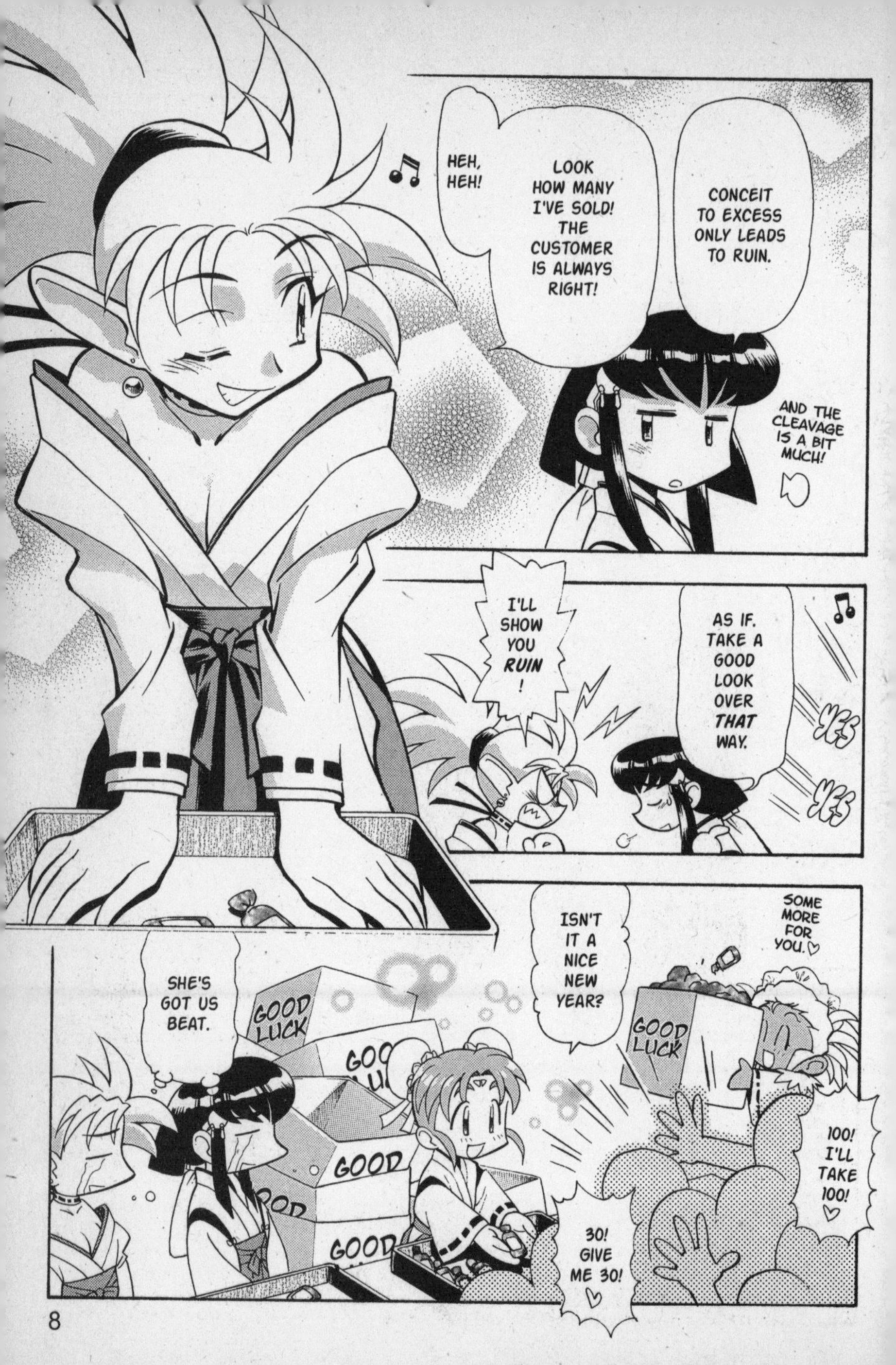
HEH, HEH!
LOOK HOW MANY I'VE SOLD! THE CUSTOMER IS ALWAYS RIGHT!
CONCEIT TO EXCESS ONLY LEADS TO RUIN.
AND THE CLEAVAGE IS A BIT MUCH!
I'LL SHOW YOU *RUIN*!
AS IF. TAKE A GOOD LOOK OVER *THAT* WAY.
YES
YES
SHE'S GOT US BEAT.
GOOD LUCK
ISN'T IT A NICE NEW YEAR?
SOME MORE FOR YOU.♡
GOOD LUCK
100! I'LL TAKE 100! ♡
30! GIVE ME 30! ♡

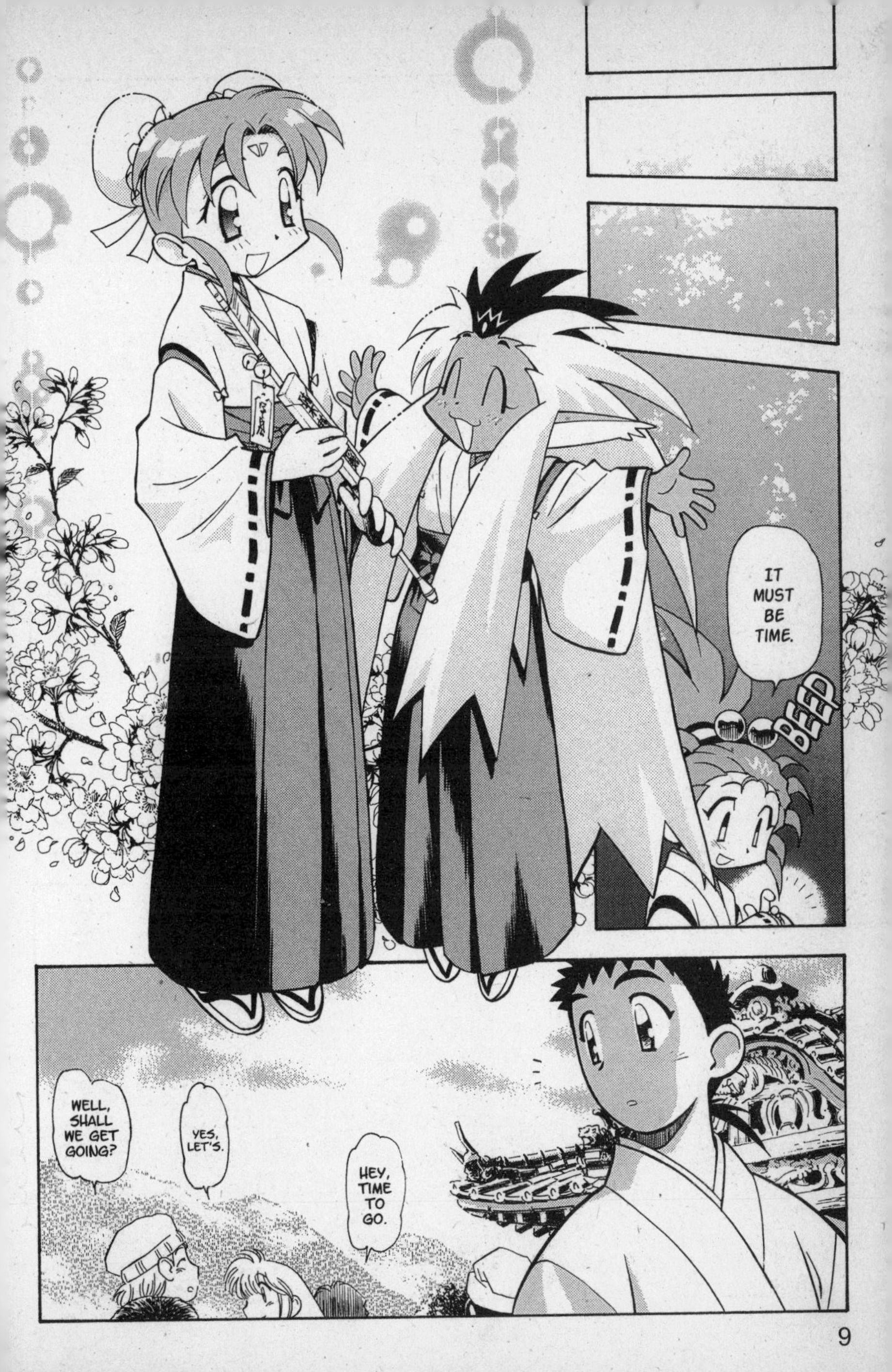
IT MUST BE TIME.
BEEP
WELL, SHALL WE GET GOING?
YES, LET'S.
HEY, TIME TO GO.

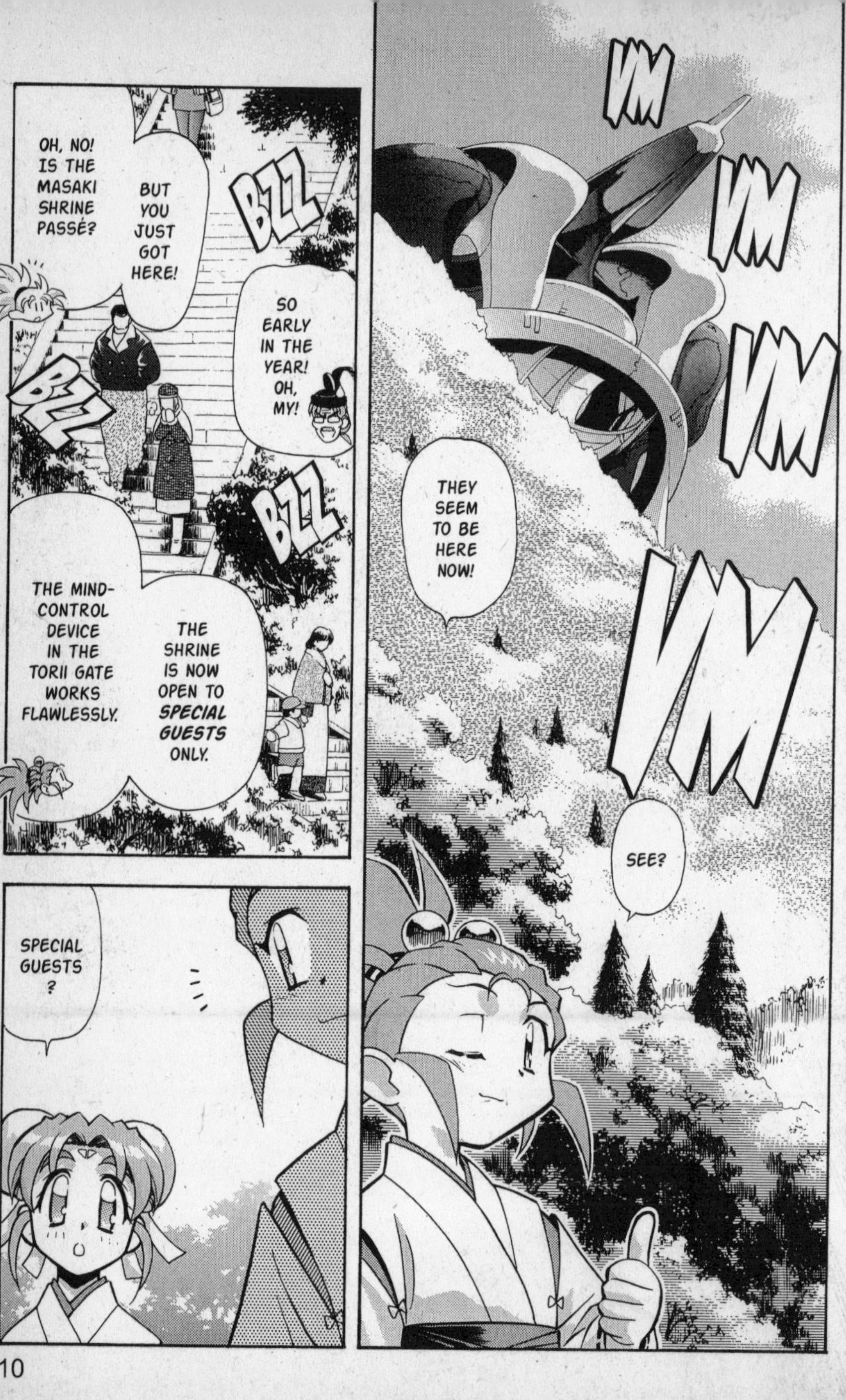
OH, NO! IS THE MASAKI SHRINE PASSÉ?
BUT YOU JUST GOT HERE!
BZZ
BZZ
SO EARLY IN THE YEAR! OH, MY!
BZZ
THE MIND-CONTROL DEVICE IN THE TORII GATE WORKS FLAWLESSLY.
THE SHRINE IS NOW OPEN TO *SPECIAL GUESTS* ONLY.
SPECIAL GUESTS?
VM
VM
VM
THEY SEEM TO BE HERE NOW!
VM
SEE?

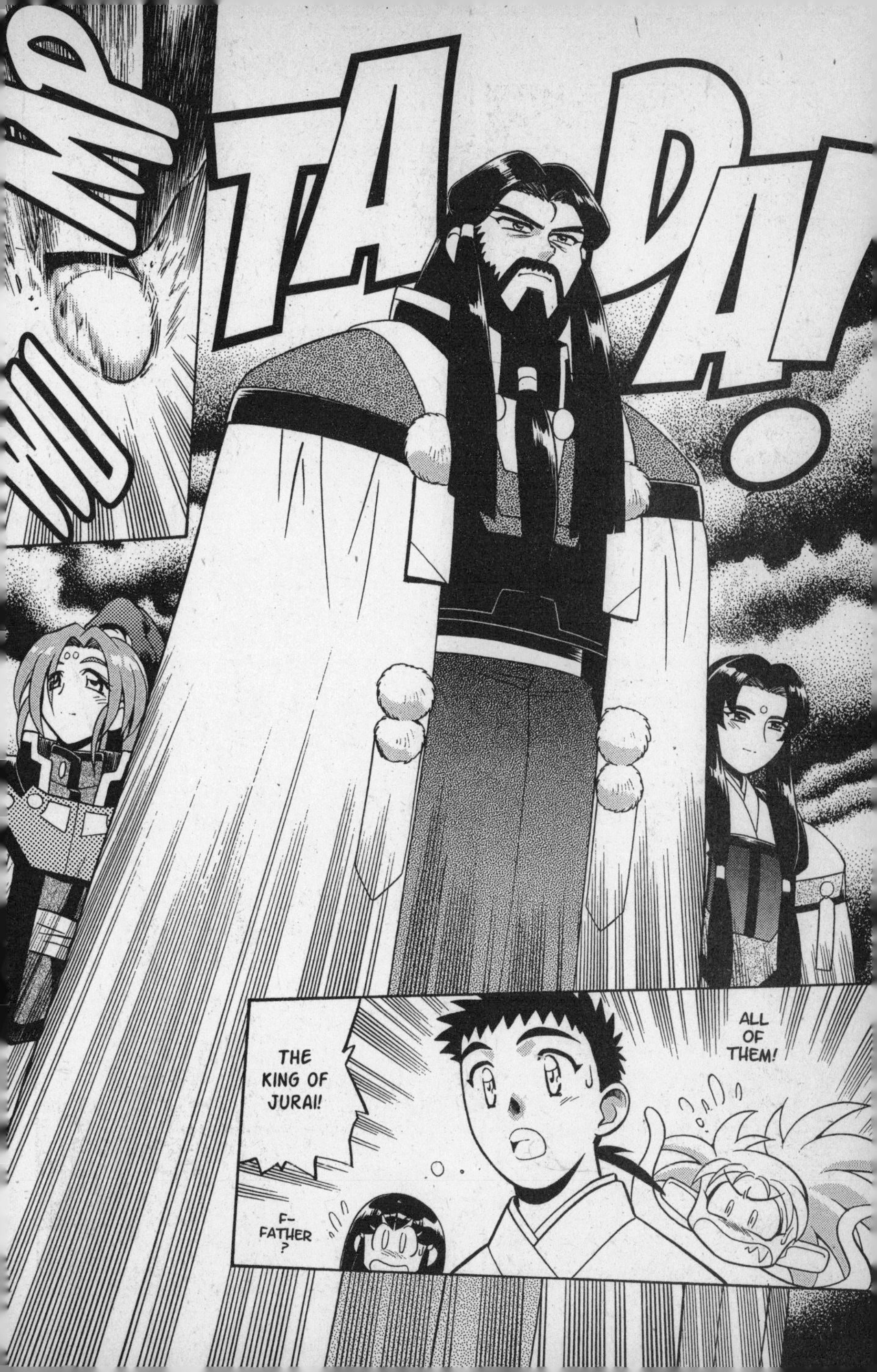
WHUMP
TA-DA!
THE KING OF JURAI!
F-FATHER?
ALL OF THEM!

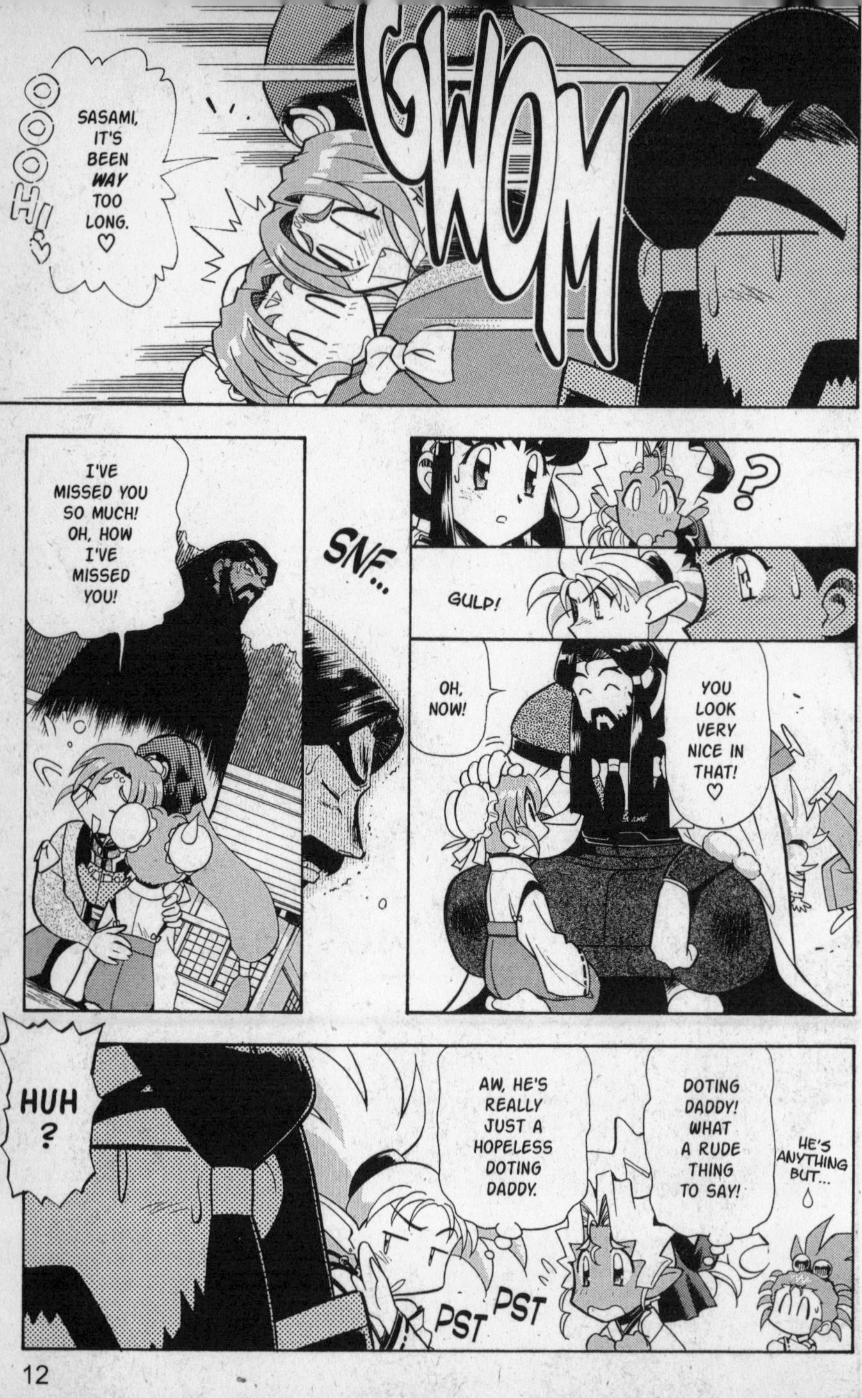
SASAMI, IT'S BEEN *WAY* TOO LONG. ♡
OOOH! ♡
GWOM
I'VE MISSED YOU SO MUCH! OH, HOW I'VE MISSED YOU!
SNF...
?
GULP!
OH, NOW!
YOU LOOK VERY NICE IN THAT! ♡
HUH ?
AW, HE'S REALLY JUST A HOPELESS DOTING DADDY.
DOTING DADDY! WHAT A RUDE THING TO SAY!
HE'S ANYTHING BUT...
PST PST

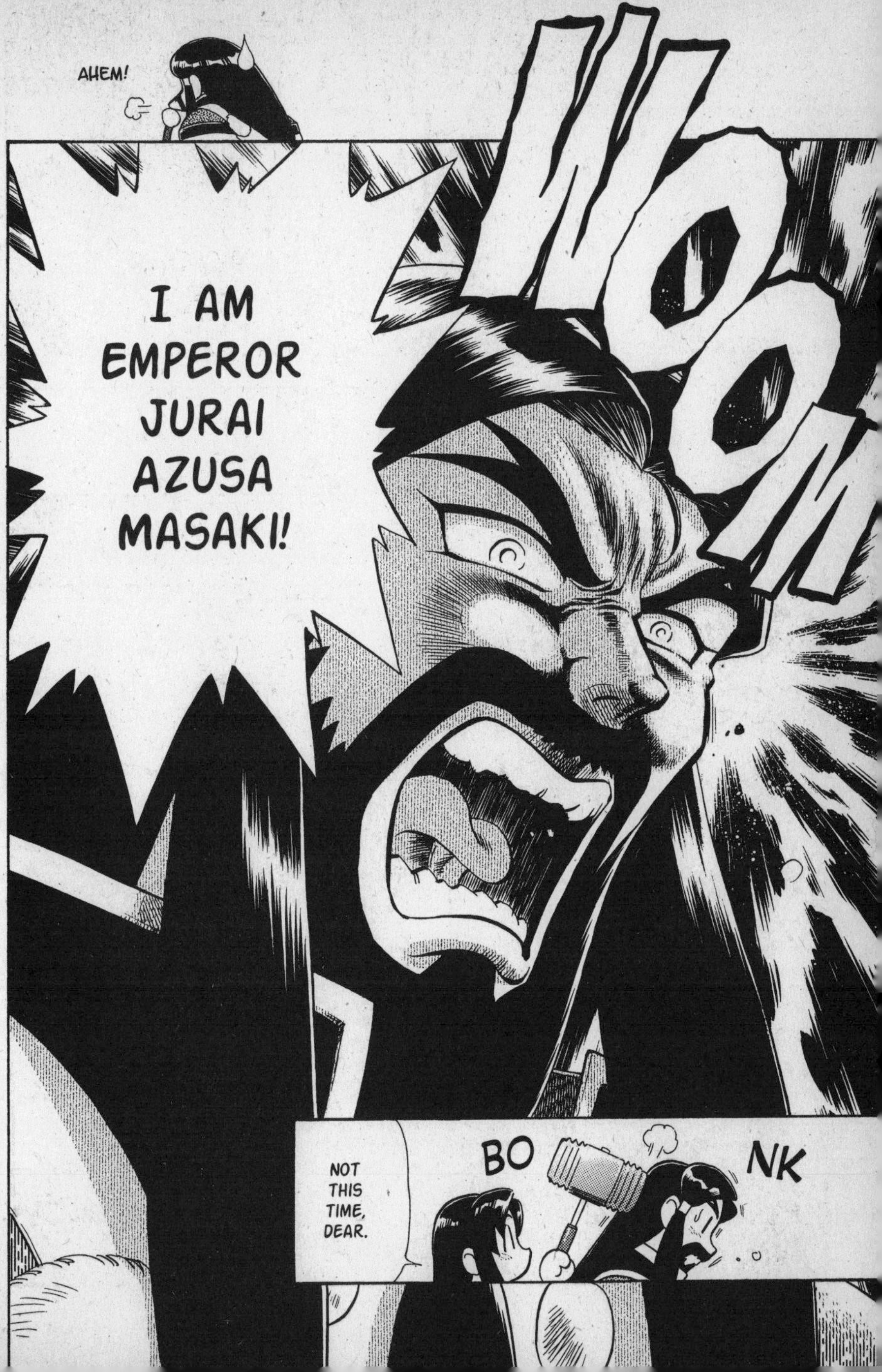
AHEM!
I AM EMPEROR JURAI AZUSA MASAKI!
WHOOM
NOT THIS TIME, DEAR.
BO
NK

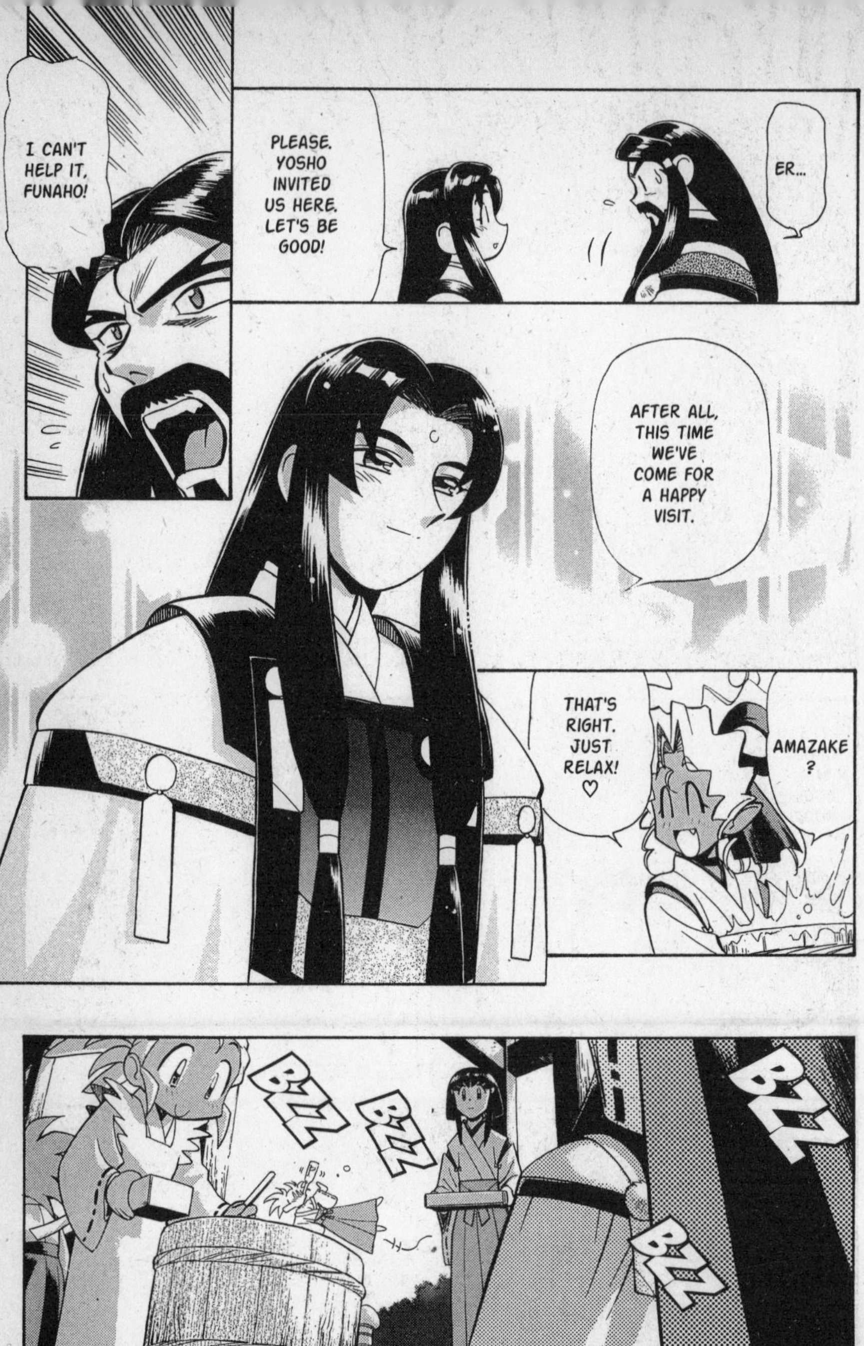
I CAN'T HELP IT, FUNAHO!
PLEASE. YOSHO INVITED US HERE. LET'S BE GOOD!
ER...
AFTER ALL, THIS TIME WE'VE COME FOR A HAPPY VISIT.
THAT'S RIGHT. JUST RELAX! ♡
AMAZAKE?
BZZ
BZZ
BZZ
BZZ

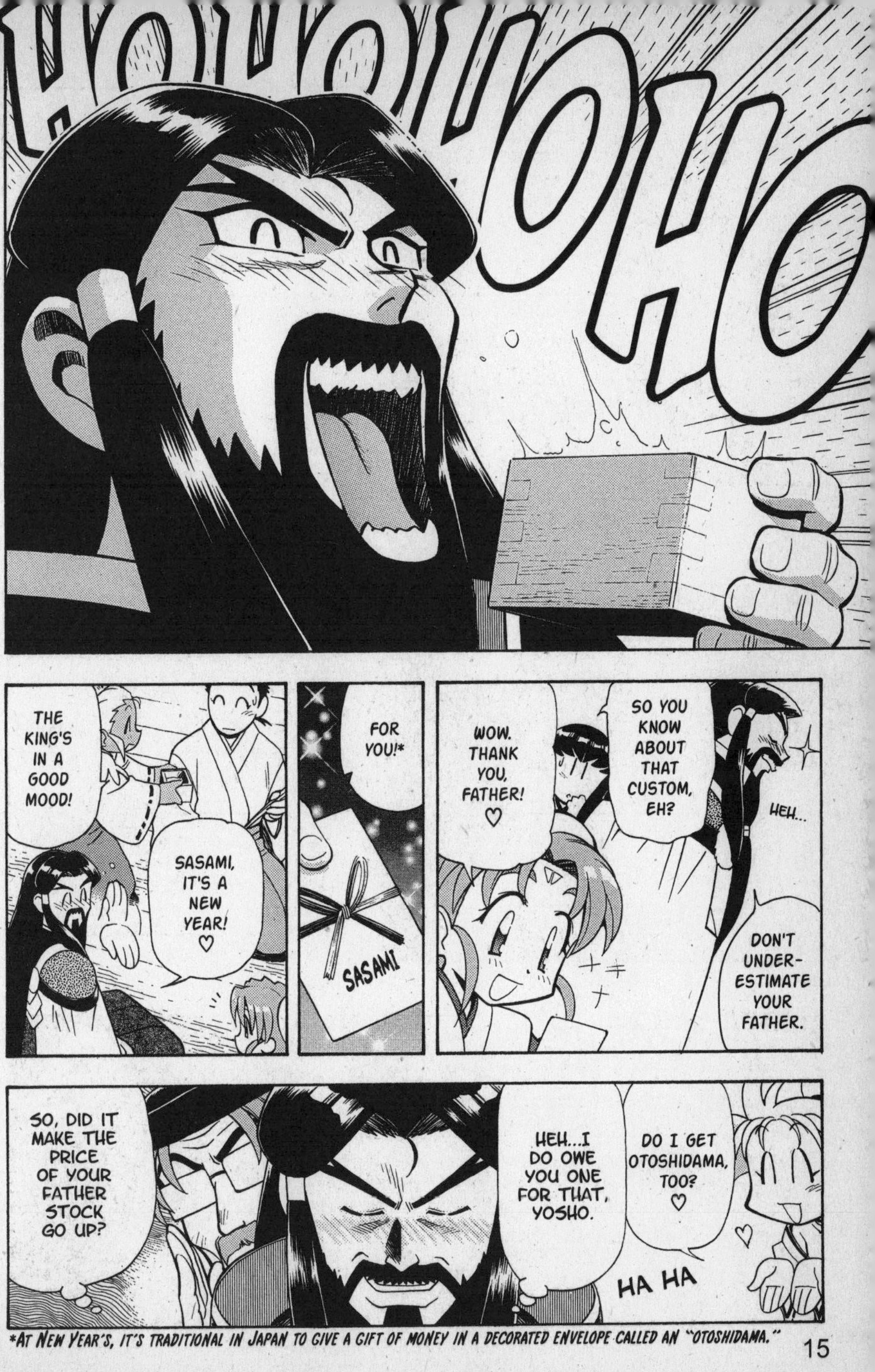
HOHOHOHOHOHO!
THE KING'S IN A GOOD MOOD!
SASAMI, IT'S A NEW YEAR! ♡
FOR YOU!*
SASAMI
WOW. THANK YOU, FATHER! ♡
SO YOU KNOW ABOUT THAT CUSTOM, EH?
HEH...
DON'T UNDER-ESTIMATE YOUR FATHER.
SO, DID IT MAKE THE PRICE OF YOUR FATHER STOCK GO UP?
HEH...I DO OWE YOU ONE FOR THAT, YOSHO.
DO I GET OTOSHIDAMA, TOO? ♡
HA HA

*At New Year's, it's traditional in Japan to give a gift of money in a decorated envelope called an "otoshidama."

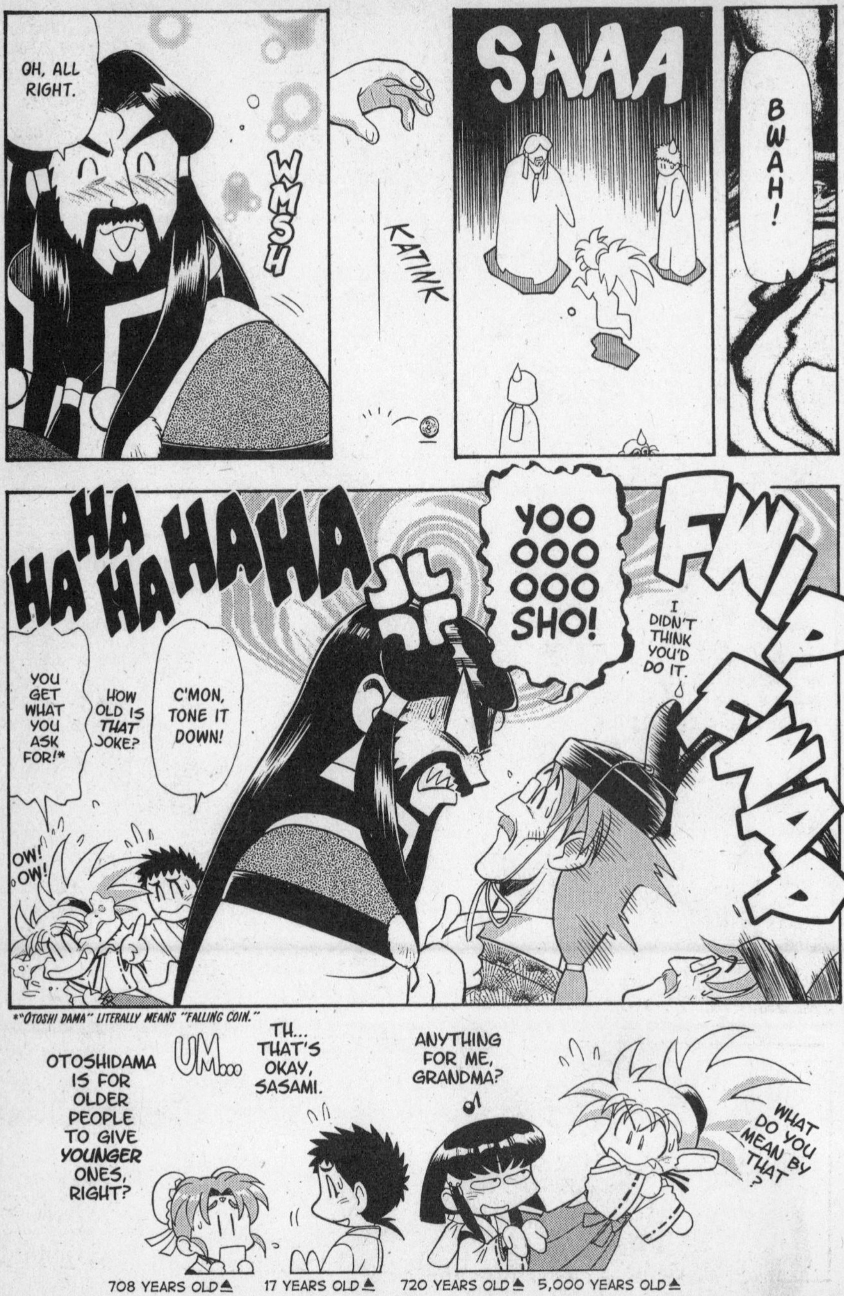
OH, ALL RIGHT.
WMSH
KATINK
SAAA
BWAH!
HA HA HA HA HAHA
YOU GET WHAT YOU ASK FOR!*
HOW OLD IS THAT JOKE?
C'MON, TONE IT DOWN!
OW! OW!
YOO OOO OOO SHO!
I DIDN'T THINK YOU'D DO IT.
FWIP FWAP
OTOSHIDAMA IS FOR OLDER PEOPLE TO GIVE YOUNGER ONES, RIGHT?
UM...
TH... THAT'S OKAY, SASAMI.
ANYTHING FOR ME, GRANDMA?
WHAT DO YOU MEAN BY THAT?
708 YEARS OLD
17 YEARS OLD
720 YEARS OLD
5,000 YEARS OLD

*"OTOSHI DAMA" LITERALLY MEANS "FALLING COIN."

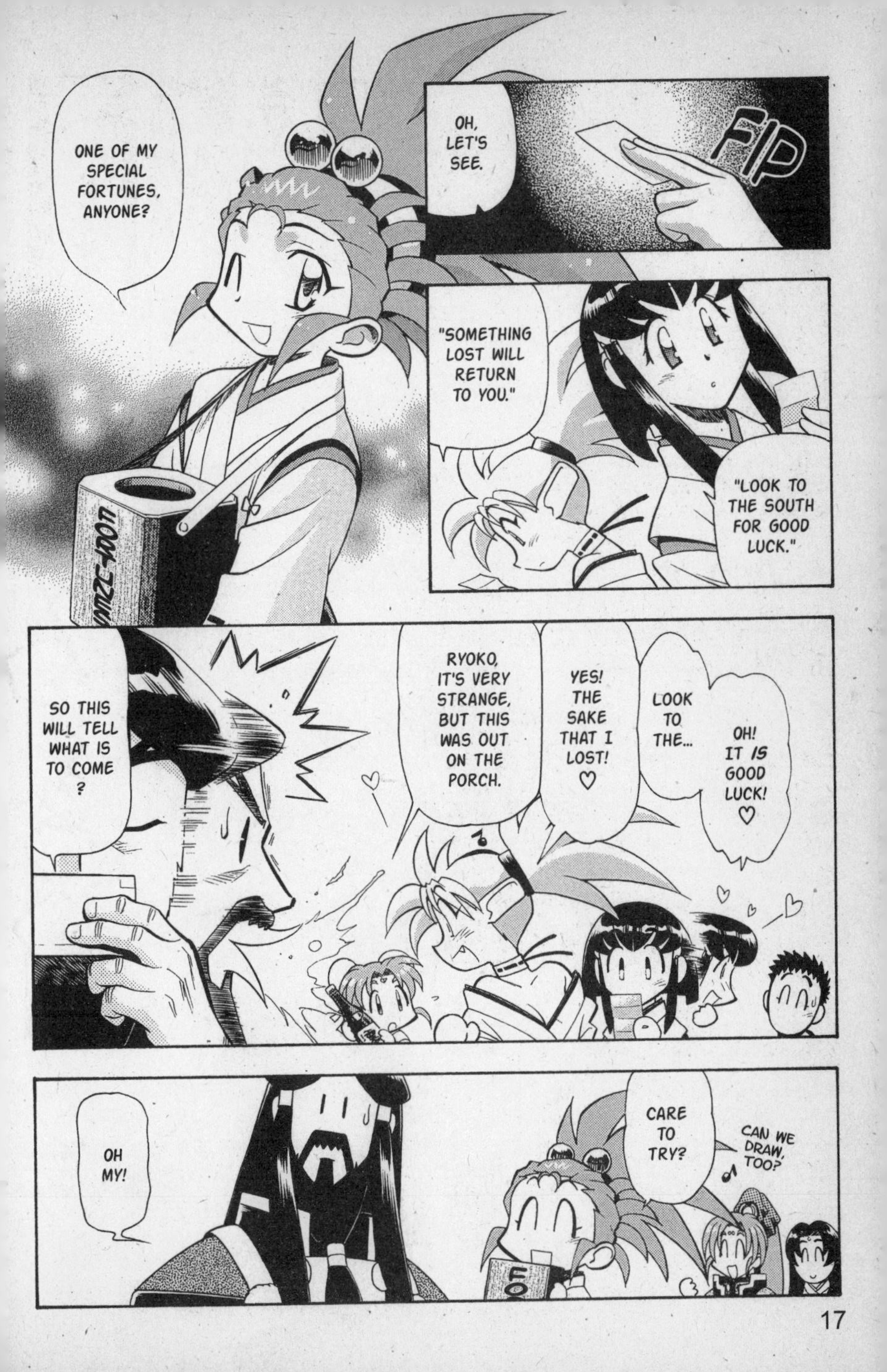
ONE OF MY SPECIAL FORTUNES, ANYONE?
OH, LET'S SEE.
FIP
"SOMETHING LOST WILL RETURN TO YOU."
"LOOK TO THE SOUTH FOR GOOD LUCK."
SO THIS WILL TELL WHAT IS TO COME ?
RYOKO, IT'S VERY STRANGE, BUT THIS WAS OUT ON THE PORCH.
YES! THE SAKE THAT I LOST! ♡
LOOK TO THE...
OH! IT IS GOOD LUCK! ♡
OH MY!
CARE TO TRY?
CAN WE DRAW, TOO?

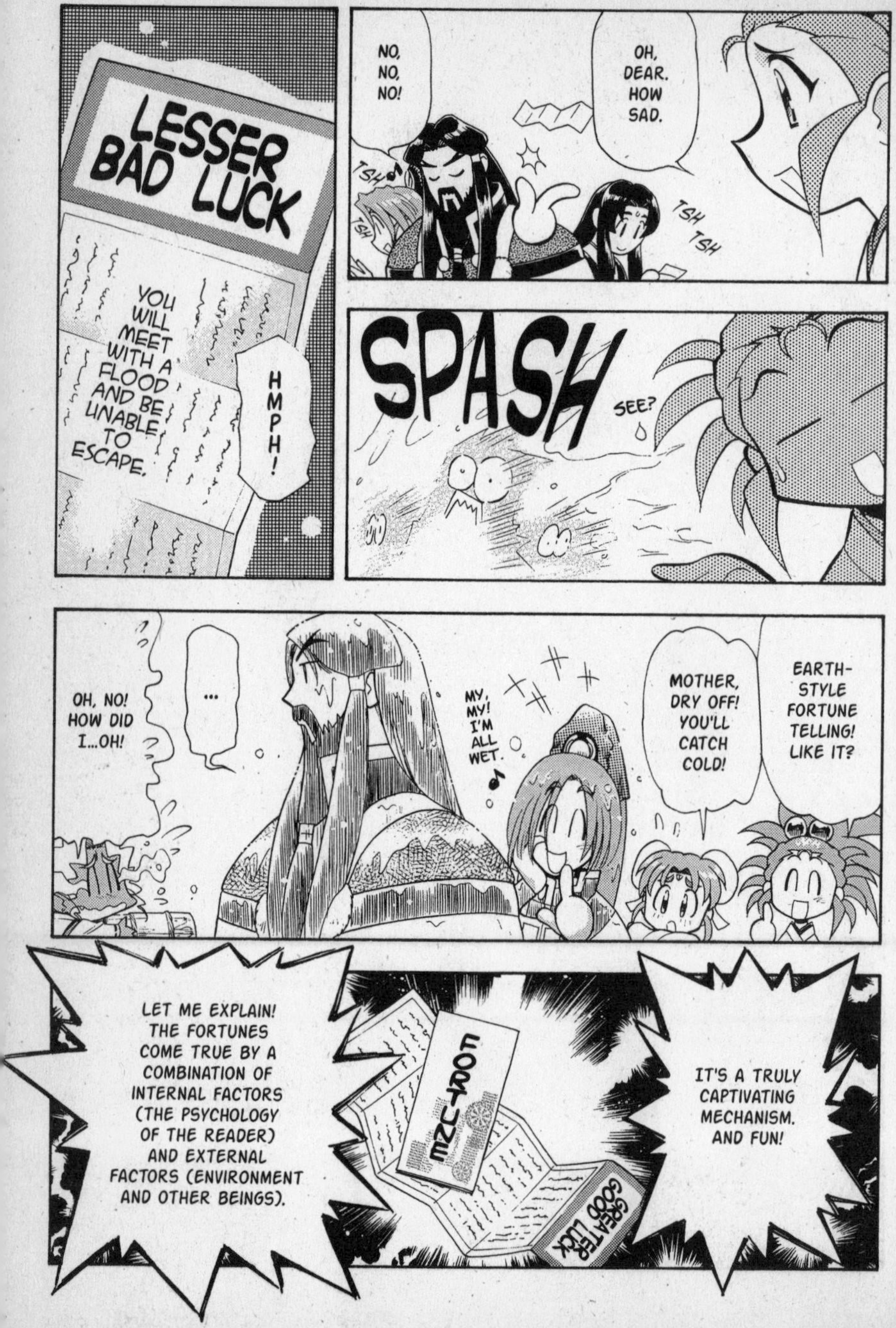
LESSER BAD LUCK
YOU WILL MEET WITH A FLOOD AND BE UNABLE TO ESCAPE.
HMPH!
NO, NO, NO!
TSH
TSH
OH, DEAR. HOW SAD.
TSH TSH
SPASH
SEE?
OH, NO! HOW DID I...OH!
...
MY, MY! I'M ALL WET.
MOTHER, DRY OFF! YOU'LL CATCH COLD!
EARTH-STYLE FORTUNE TELLING! LIKE IT?
LET ME EXPLAIN! THE FORTUNES COME TRUE BY A COMBINATION OF INTERNAL FACTORS (THE PSYCHOLOGY OF THE READER) AND EXTERNAL FACTORS (ENVIRONMENT AND OTHER BEINGS).
FORTUNE
GREATER GOOD LUCK
IT'S A TRULY CAPTIVATING MECHANISM. AND FUN!

HMPH!

FIP FAP

FIP FAP

[SIGH] ALL DRY

JUST LIKE A DOG.

A BASE GAME FOR A VILE WORLD. HMPH!

HONEY, HONEY! ♥

WHAT'S THE BIG DEAL WITH FORTUNES, ANYWAY? ▽

HOW DO I LOOK? ♥

MODERATE GOOD LUCK

DRESS IN THE GARB OF A TEMPLE GIRL, AND YOUR HEART WILL ALSO GROW YOUNG. ♥

...WHAT DO YOU THINK, DEAR?

IS IT A BIT MUCH?

UM... SO, TELL ME...

THAT WAS NO SHRINE VIRGIN, THAT WAS MY WIFE!

?

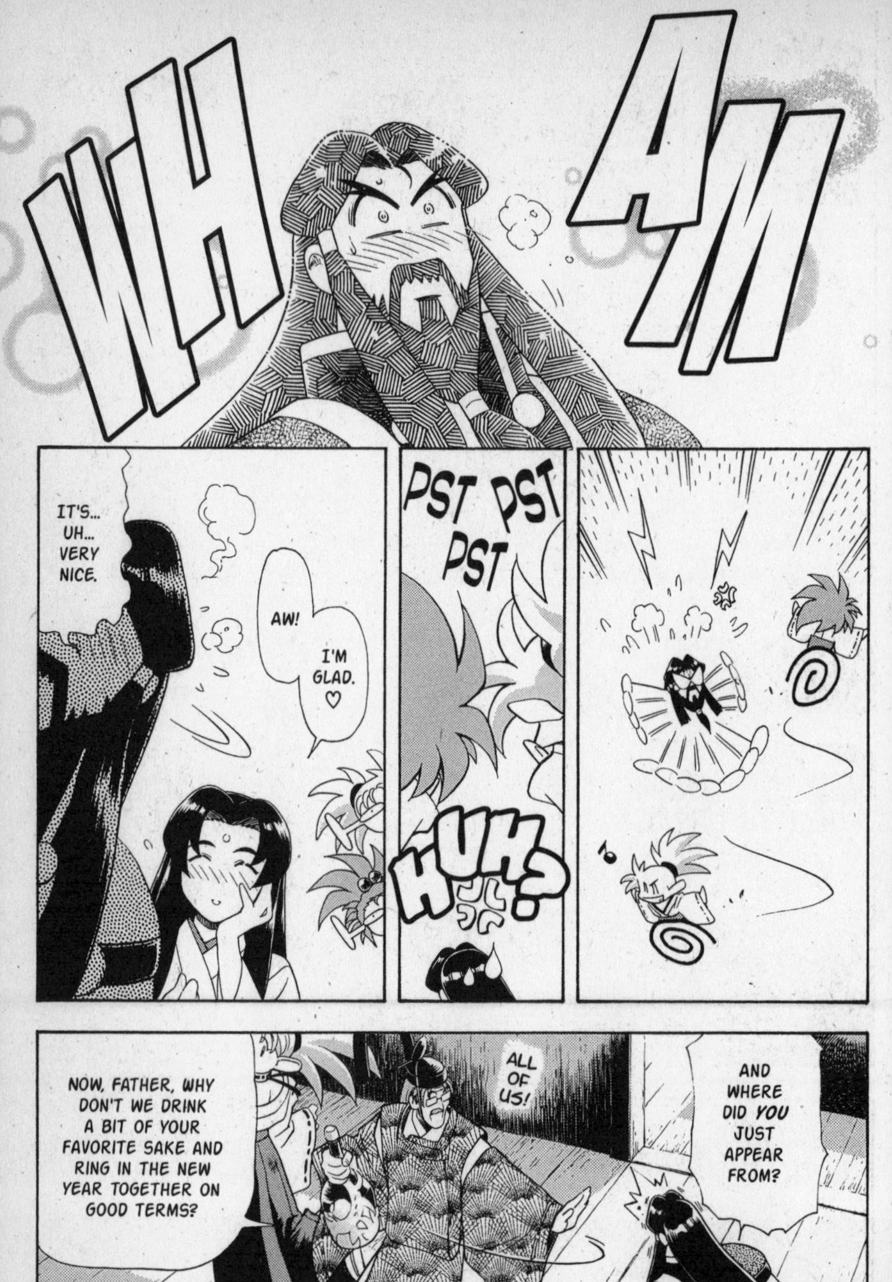
WAH
AN
IT'S... UH... VERY NICE.
AW! I'M GLAD. ♡
PST PST PST
HUH?
NOW, FATHER, WHY DON'T WE DRINK A BIT OF YOUR FAVORITE SAKE AND RING IN THE NEW YEAR TOGETHER ON GOOD TERMS?
ALL OF US!
AND WHERE DID *YOU* JUST APPEAR FROM?

BANG
CHANG
BANG
CHANG

IT'S YOUR FAULT FOR MAKING OFF LIKE THAT.

WHY DON'T YOU THINK OF YOUR DUTY AS FIRST PRINCE OF JURAI?

YO HO HO AND A...

THANKS TO YOU, AYEKA AND SASAMI ARE... CURSED.

SO IT'S ABOUT THAT, EH?

OH, TENCHI...I SEEM TO HAVE DRUNK TOO MUCH.

AYEKA!

HEH HEH HEH

RMB RMB

TENCHI! I CHALLENGE YOU TO A *DUEL!*

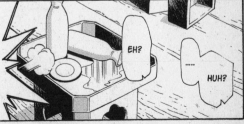

EH?

.....

HUH?

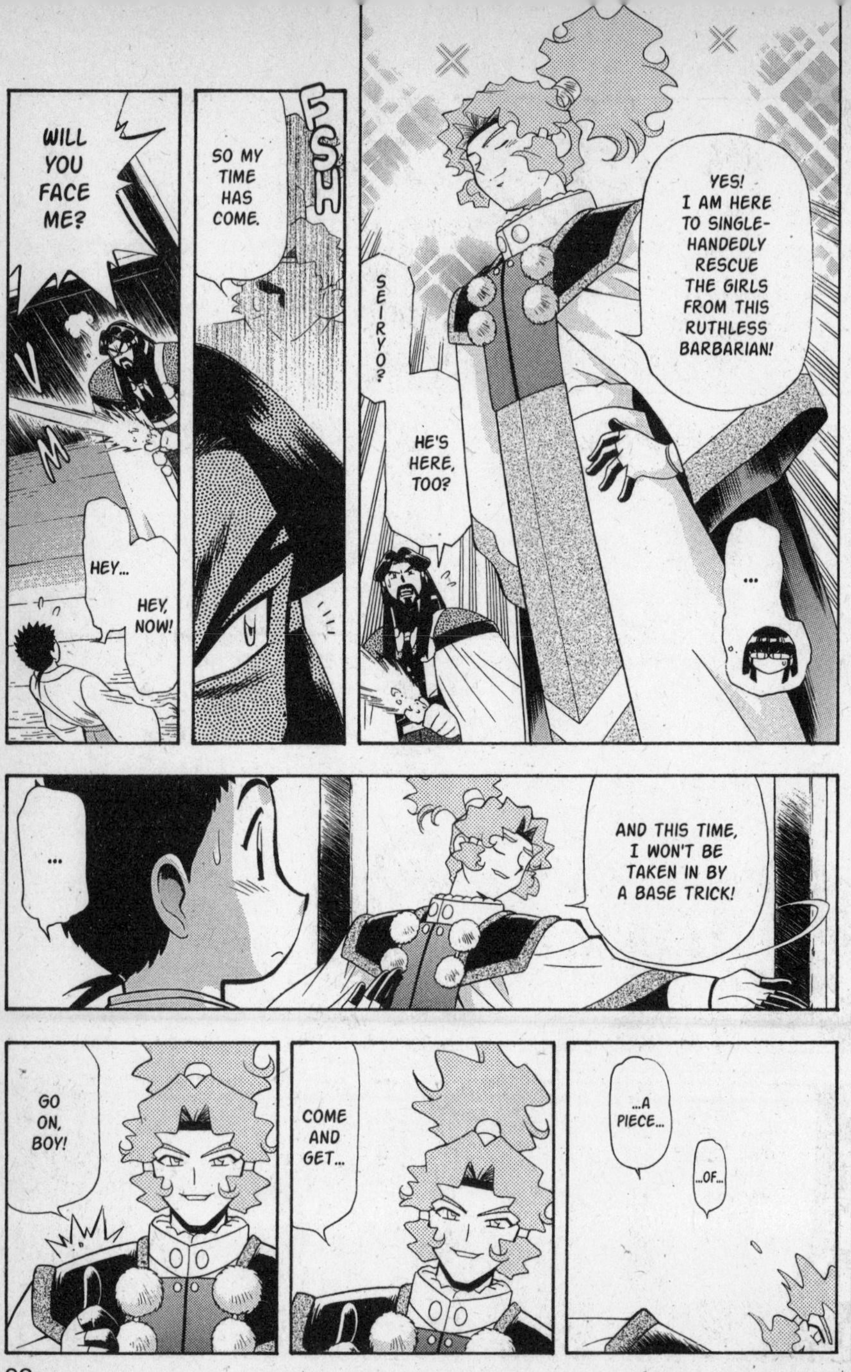
WILL YOU FACE ME?
VM
HEY...
HEY, NOW!
FSH
SO MY TIME HAS COME.
SEIRYO?
HE'S HERE, TOO?
YES! I AM HERE TO SINGLE-HANDEDLY RESCUE THE GIRLS FROM THIS RUTHLESS BARBARIAN!
...
...
AND THIS TIME, I WON'T BE TAKEN IN BY A BASE TRICK!
GO ON, BOY!
COME AND GET...
...A PIECE...
...OF...

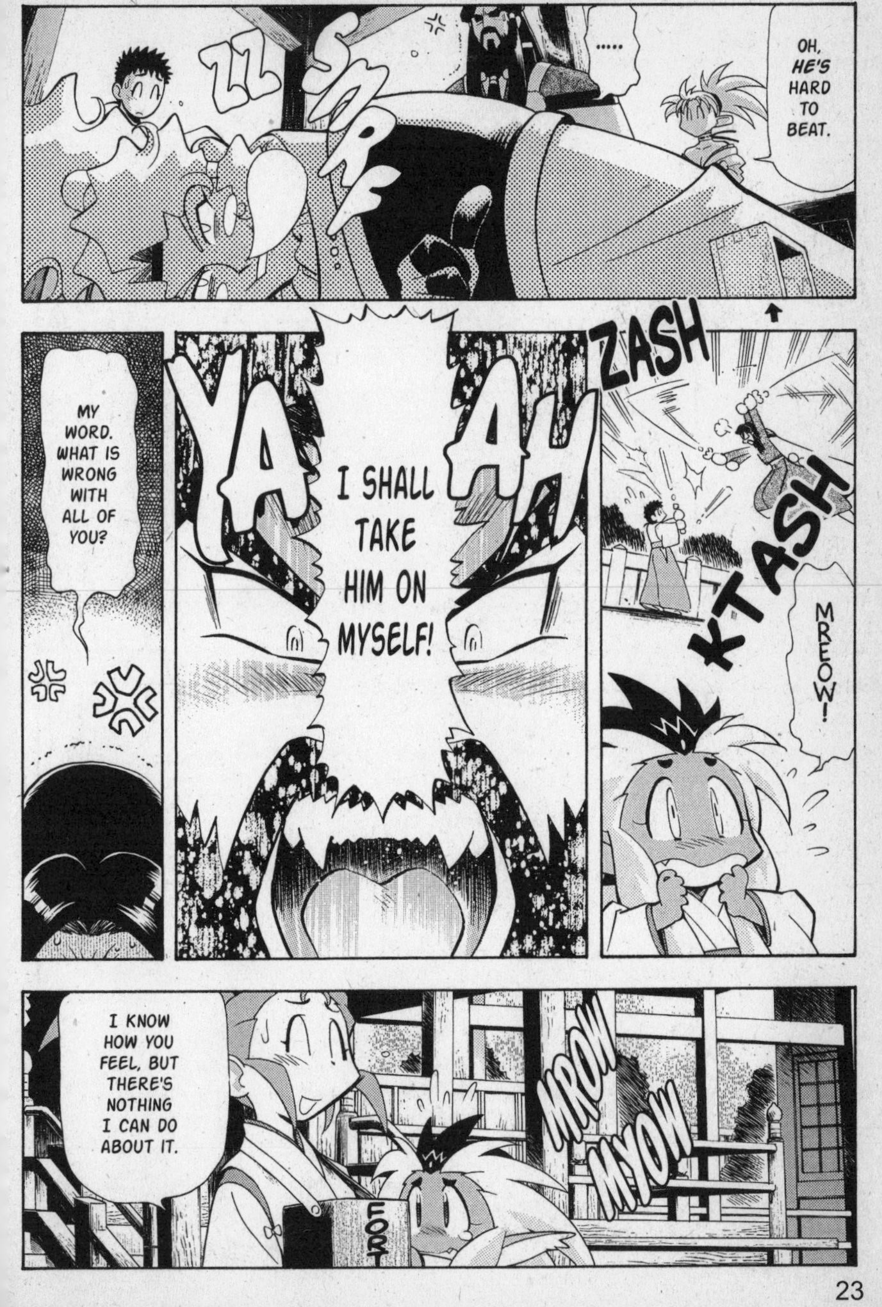
ZZ
SNORF
.....
OH, HE'S HARD TO BEAT.
MY WORD. WHAT IS WRONG WITH ALL OF YOU?
YA AH
I SHALL TAKE HIM ON MYSELF!
ZASH
KTASH
MREOW!
I KNOW HOW YOU FEEL, BUT THERE'S NOTHING I CAN DO ABOUT IT.
MROW
MYOW

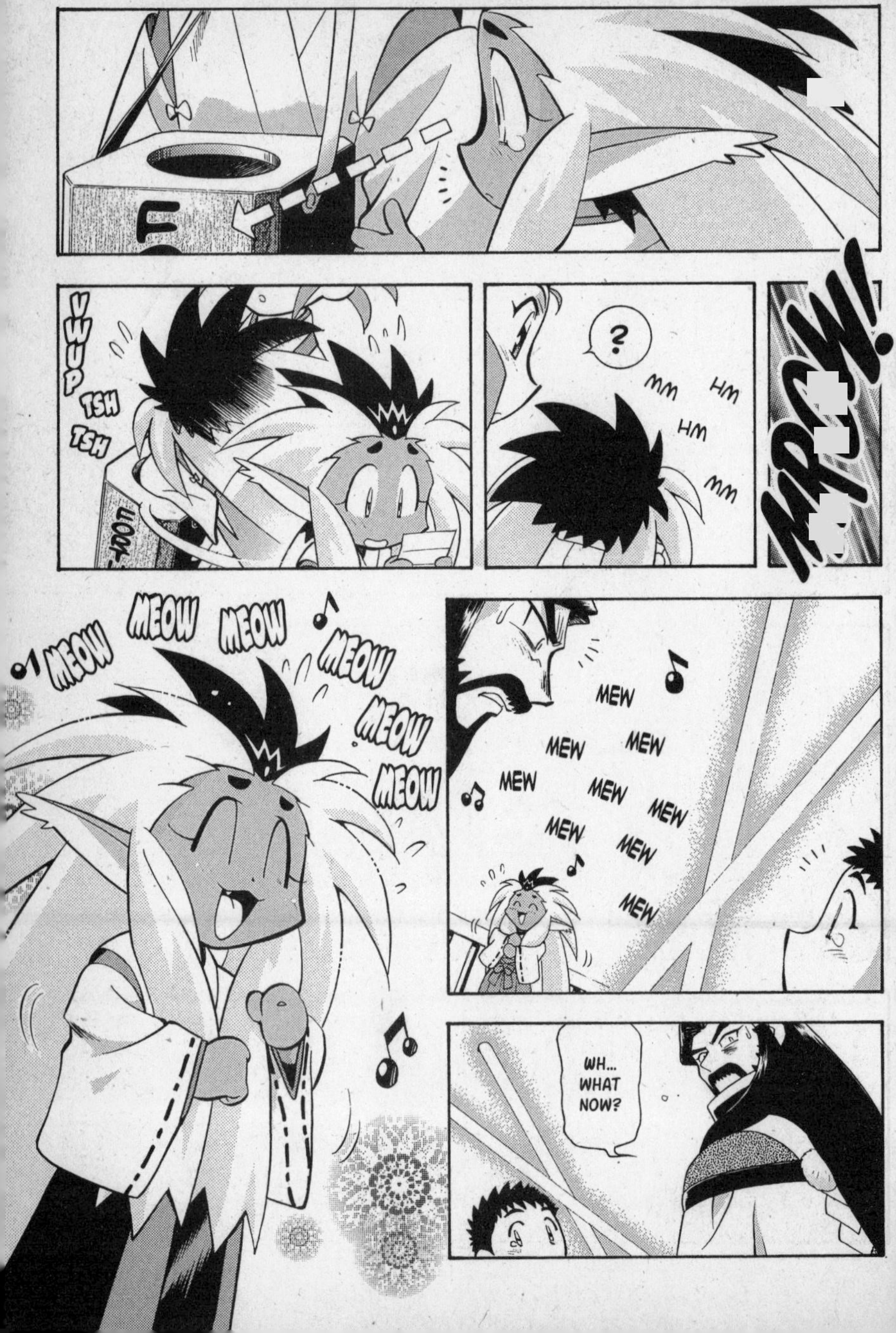
VWUP
TSH
TSH
?
MM
HM
HM
MM
MRROW!
MEOW
MEOW
MEOW
MEOW
MEOW
MEOW
MEW
MEW
MEW
MEW
MEW
MEW
MEW
MEW
MEW
MEW
WH... WHAT NOW?

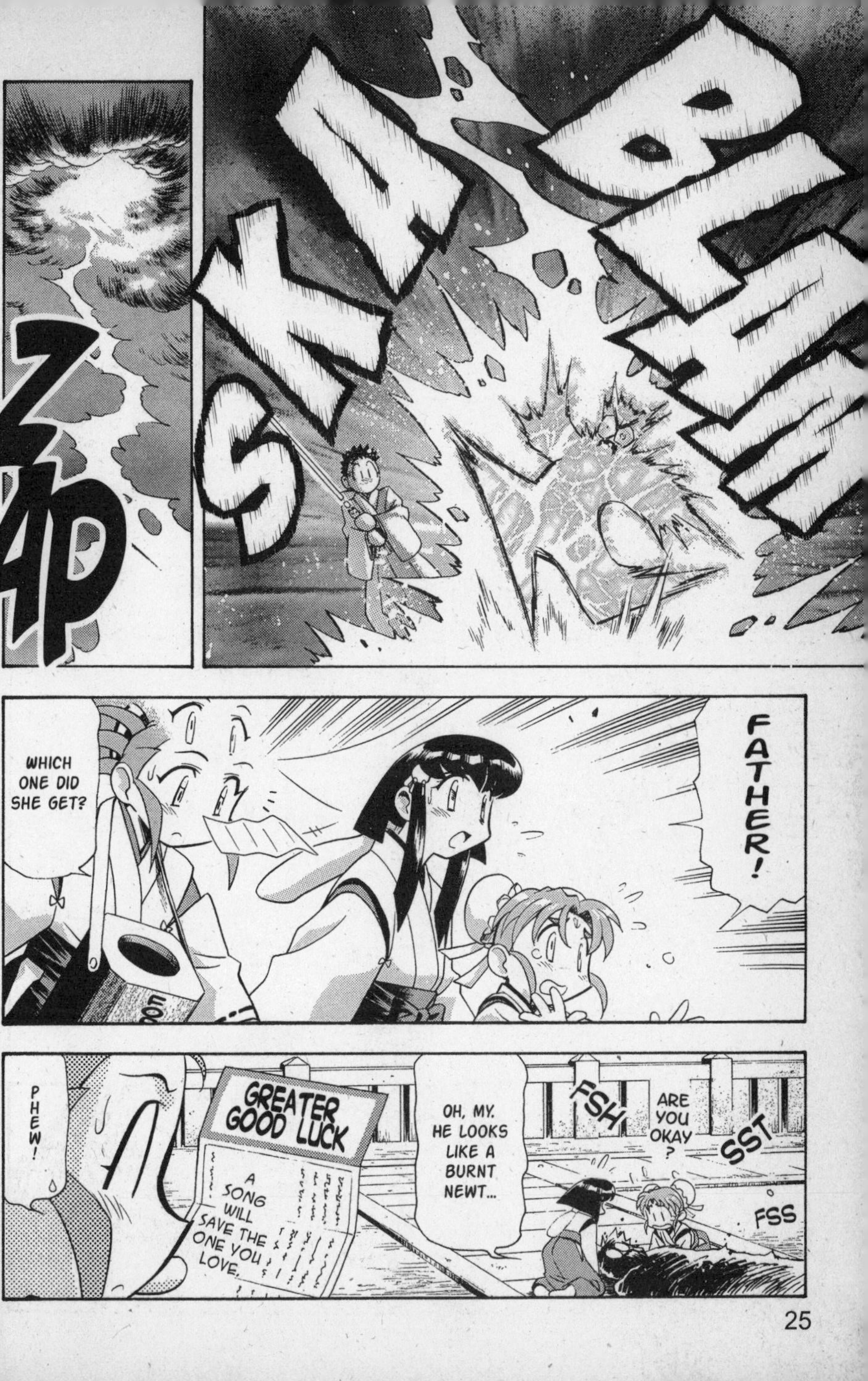
ZAP
WHICH ONE DID SHE GET?
FATHER!
PHEW!
GREATER GOOD LUCK
A SONG WILL SAVE THE ONE YOU LOVE.
OH, MY. HE LOOKS LIKE A BURNT NEWT...
FSH
ARE YOU OKAY?
SST
FSS

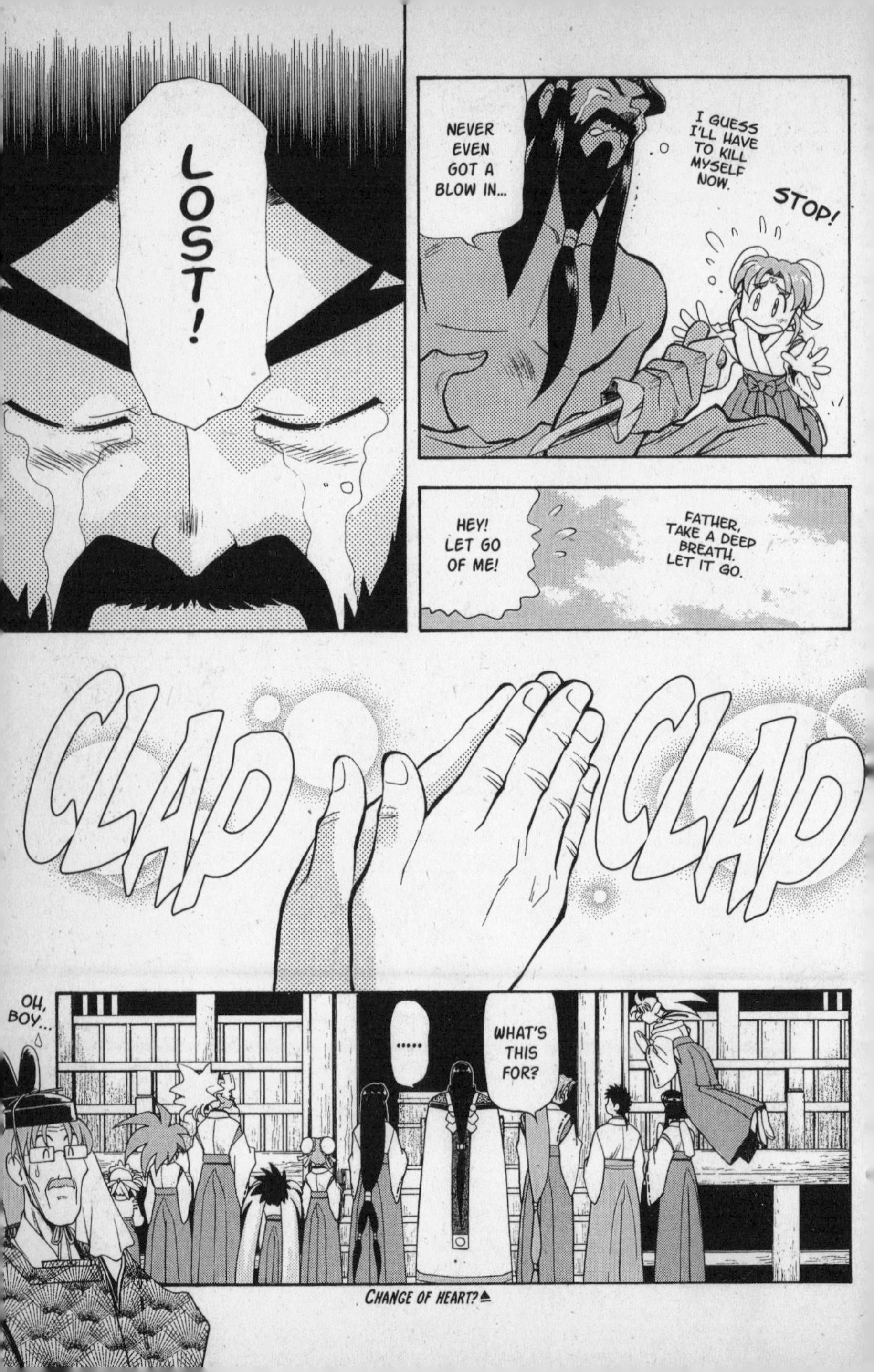
LOST!
NEVER EVEN GOT A BLOW IN...
I GUESS I'LL HAVE TO KILL MYSELF NOW.
STOP!
HEY! LET GO OF ME!
FATHER, TAKE A DEEP BREATH. LET IT GO.
CLAP CLAP
OH, BOY...
......
WHAT'S THIS FOR?
CHANGE OF HEART?

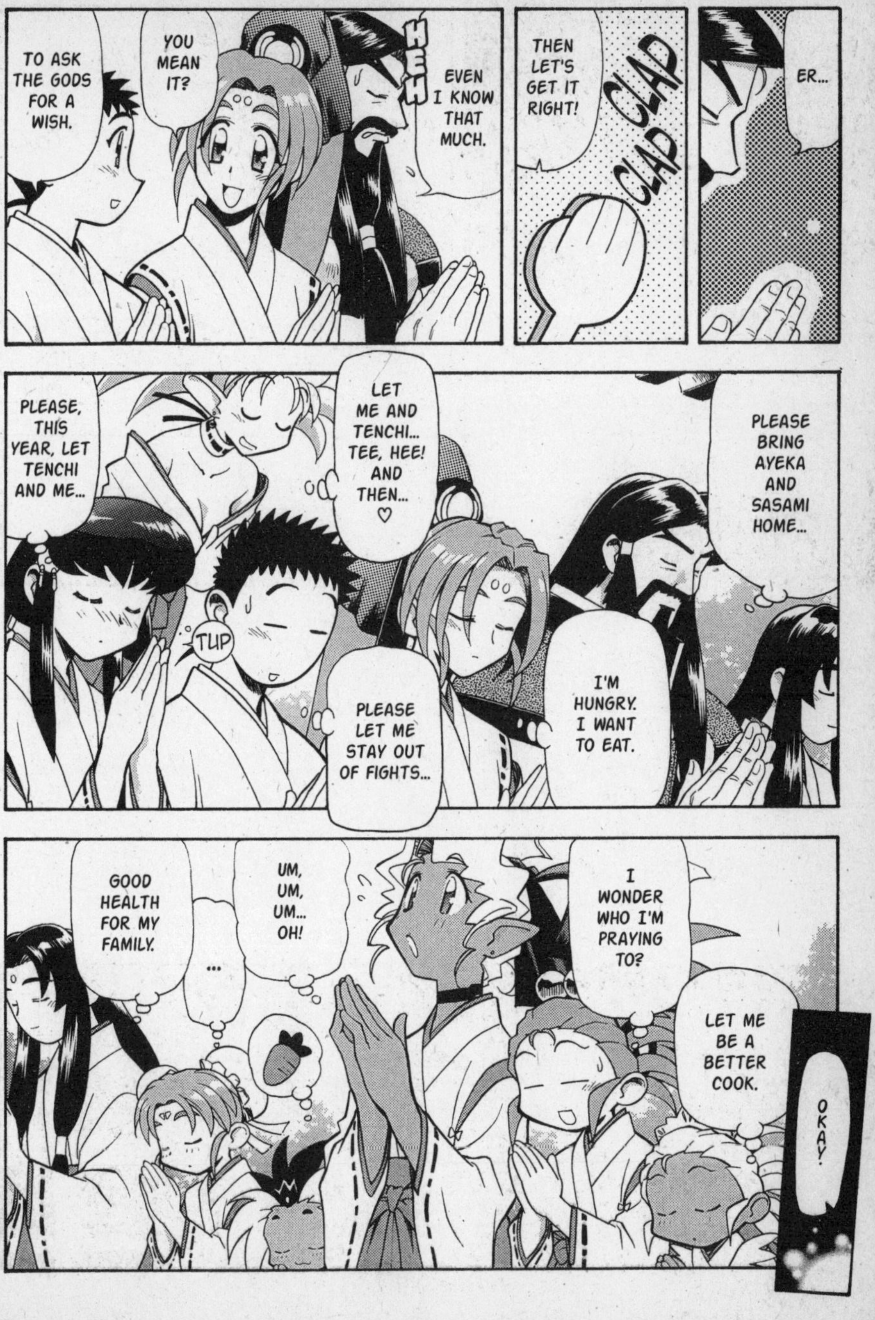
TO ASK THE GODS FOR A WISH.
YOU MEAN IT?
HEH HEH
EVEN I KNOW THAT MUCH.
THEN LET'S GET IT RIGHT!
CLAP CLAP
ER...
PLEASE, THIS YEAR, LET TENCHI AND ME...
LET ME AND TENCHI... TEE, HEE! AND THEN... ♡
PLEASE BRING AYEKA AND SASAMI HOME...
TUP
PLEASE LET ME STAY OUT OF FIGHTS...
I'M HUNGRY. I WANT TO EAT.
GOOD HEALTH FOR MY FAMILY.
...
UM, UM, UM... OH!
I WONDER WHO I'M PRAYING TO?
LET ME BE A BETTER COOK.
OKAY!

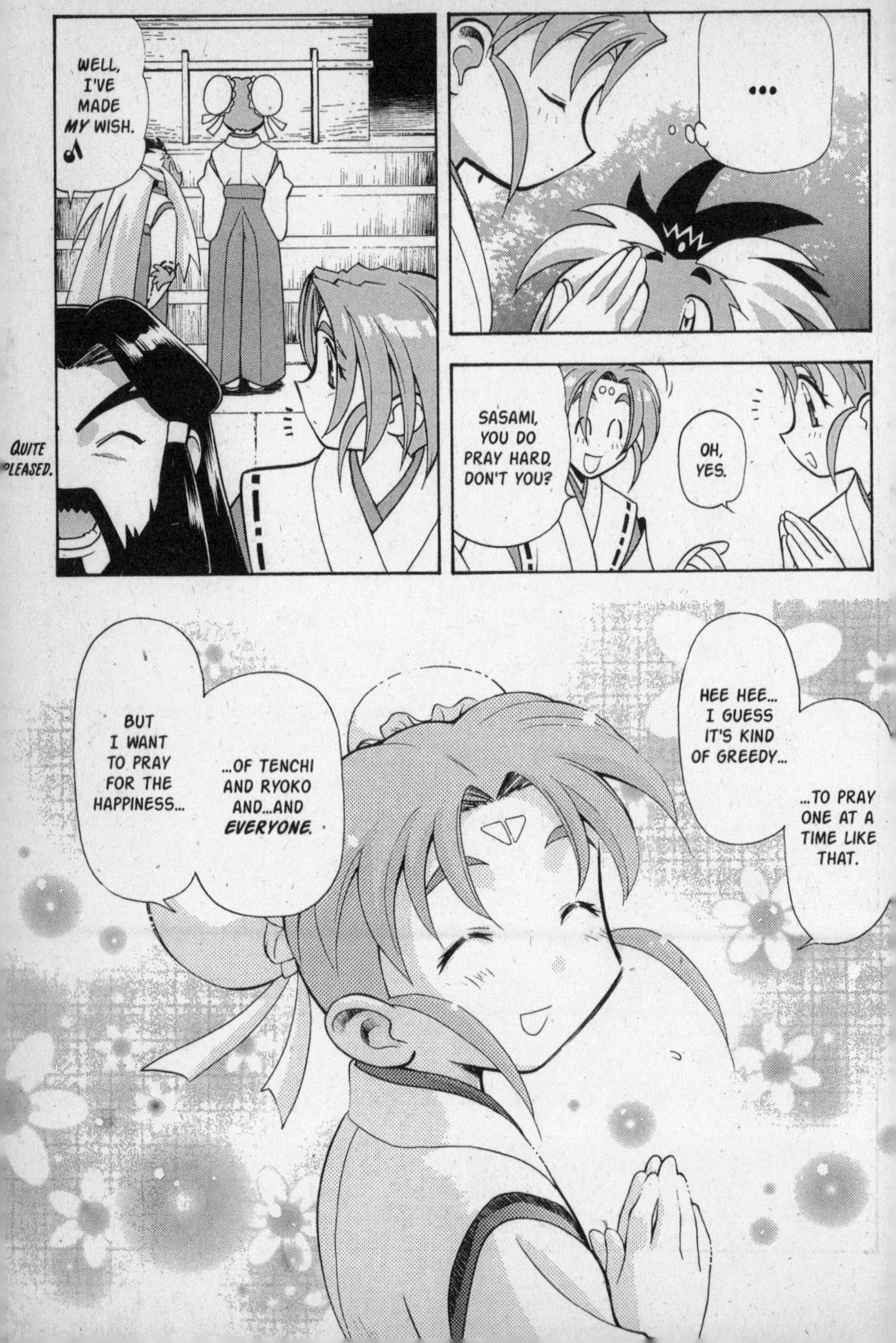
WELL, I'VE MADE MY WISH. ♪
QUITE PLEASED.
...
SASAMI, YOU DO PRAY HARD, DON'T YOU?
OH, YES.
BUT I WANT TO PRAY FOR THE HAPPINESS...
...OF TENCHI AND RYOKO AND...AND EVERYONE.
HEE HEE... I GUESS IT'S KIND OF GREEDY...
...TO PRAY ONE AT A TIME LIKE THAT.

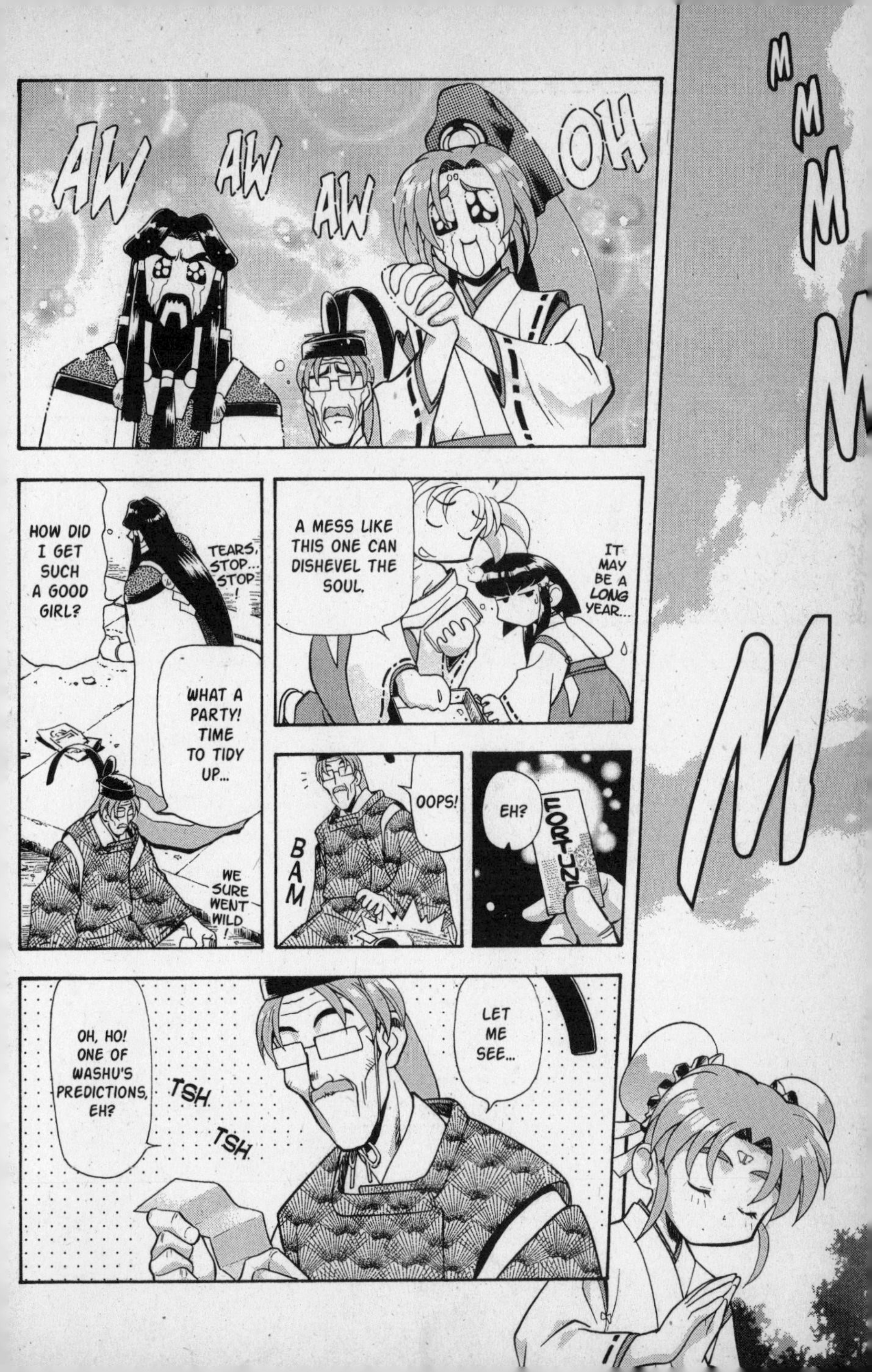
AW
AW
AW
OH
HOW DID I GET SUCH A GOOD GIRL?
TEARS, STOP... STOP!
WHAT A PARTY! TIME TO TIDY UP...
WE SURE WENT WILD!
A MESS LIKE THIS ONE CAN DISHEVEL THE SOUL.
IT MAY BE A LONG YEAR...
BAM
OOPS!
EH?
FORTUN
OH, HO! ONE OF WASHU'S PREDICTIONS, EH?
TSH
TSH
LET ME SEE...
MMMMM

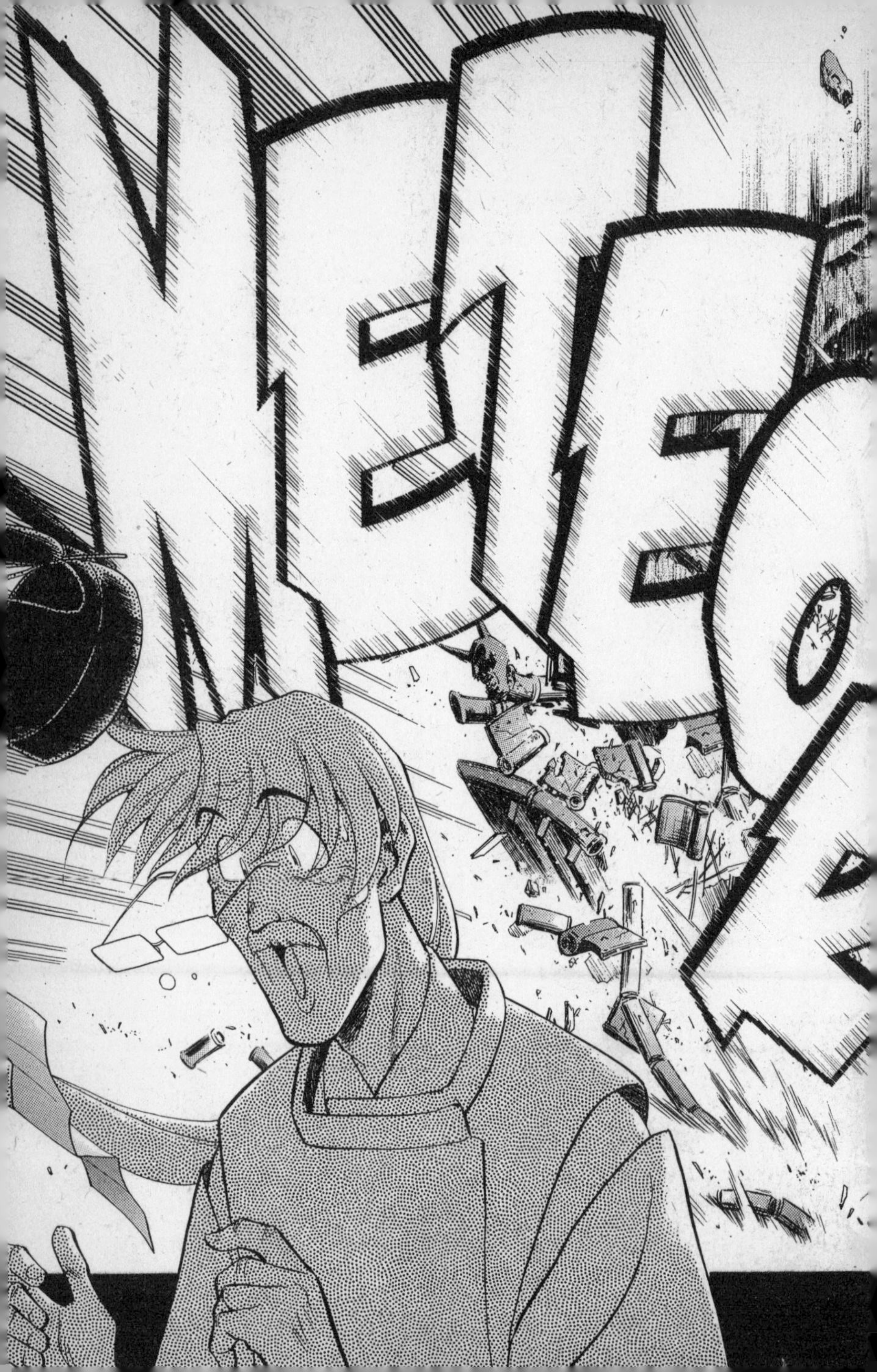

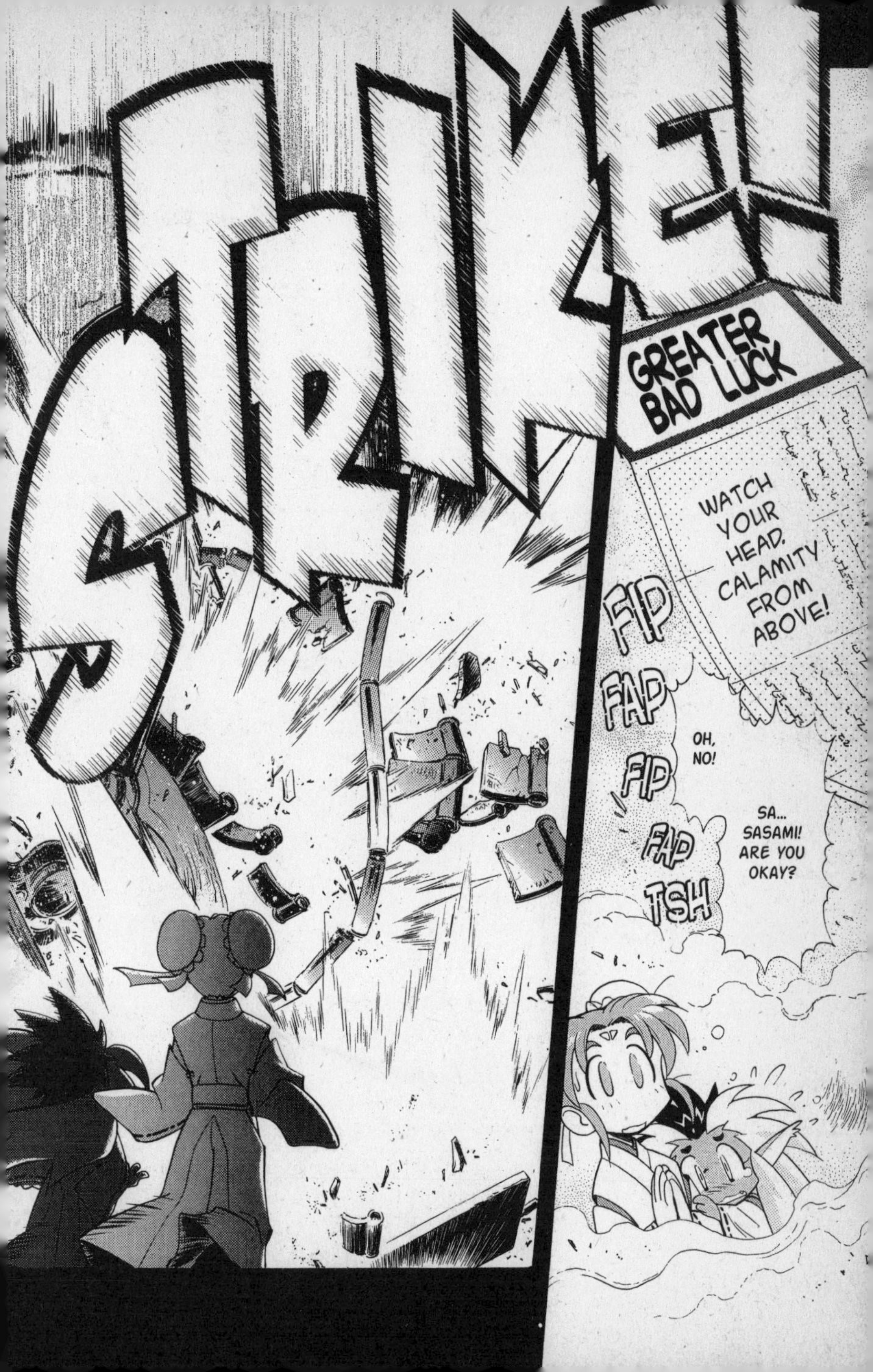
STRIKE!
GREATER BAD LUCK
WATCH YOUR HEAD. CALAMITY FROM ABOVE!
FIP
FAP
FIP
FAP
TSH
OH, NO!
SA... SASAMI! ARE YOU OKAY?

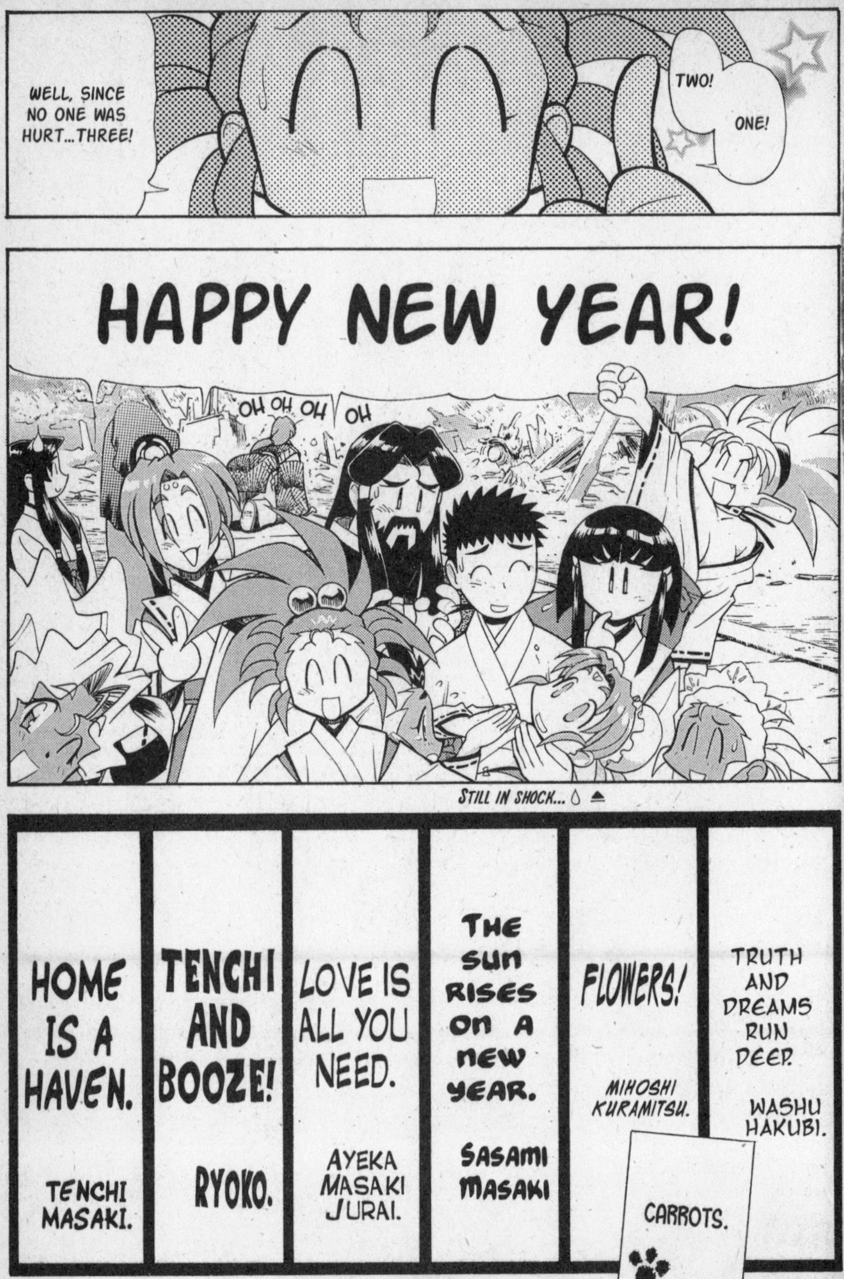
WELL, SINCE NO ONE WAS HURT...THREE!
TWO!
ONE!
HAPPY NEW YEAR!
OH OH OH OH
STILL IN SHOCK...
HOME IS A HAVEN.
TENCHI MASAKI.
TENCHI AND BOOZE!
RYOKO.
LOVE IS ALL YOU NEED.
AYEKA MASAKI JURAI.
THE SUN RISES ON A NEW YEAR.
SASAMI MASAKI
FLOWERS!
MIHOSHI KURAMITSU.
TRUTH AND DREAMS RUN DEEP.
WASHU HAKUBI.
CARROTS.

Chapter 2: Capture

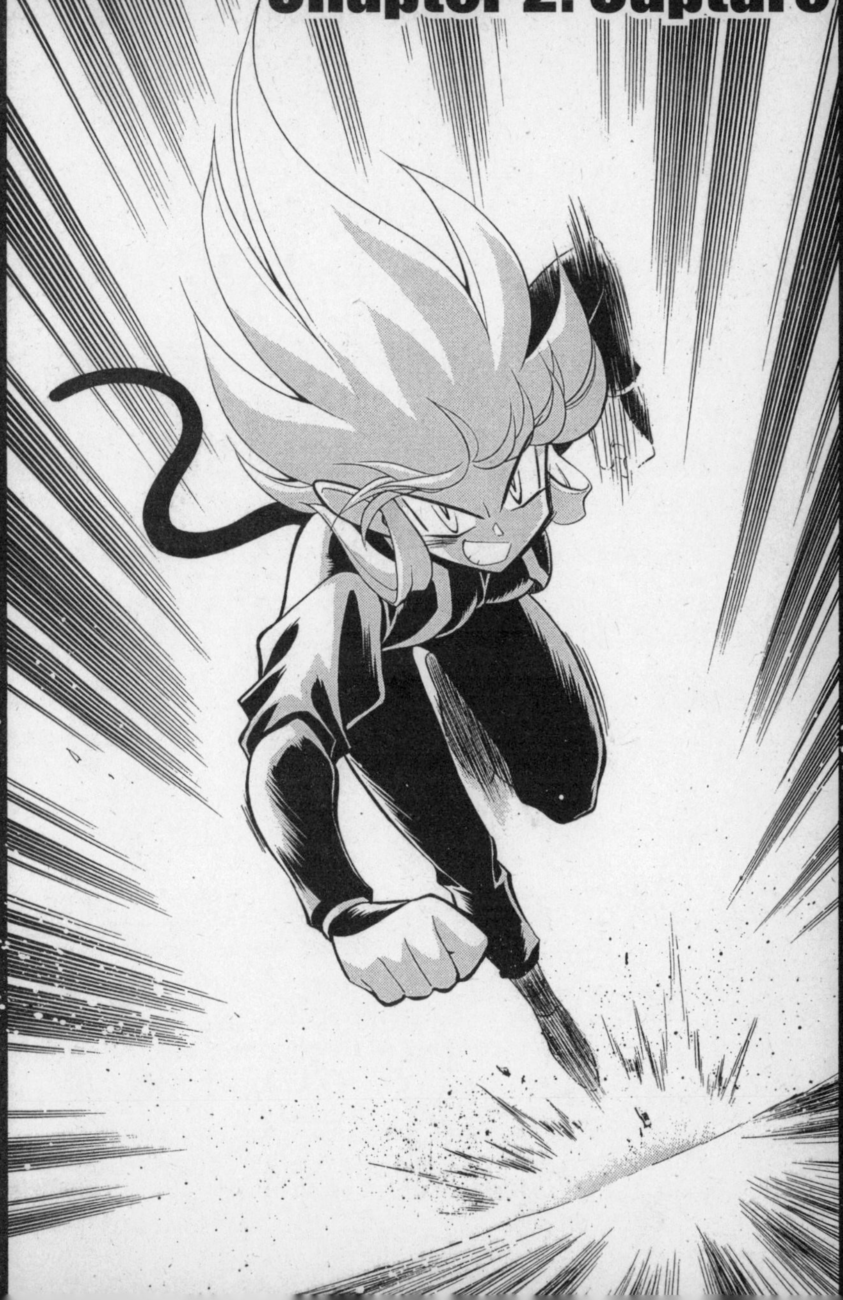

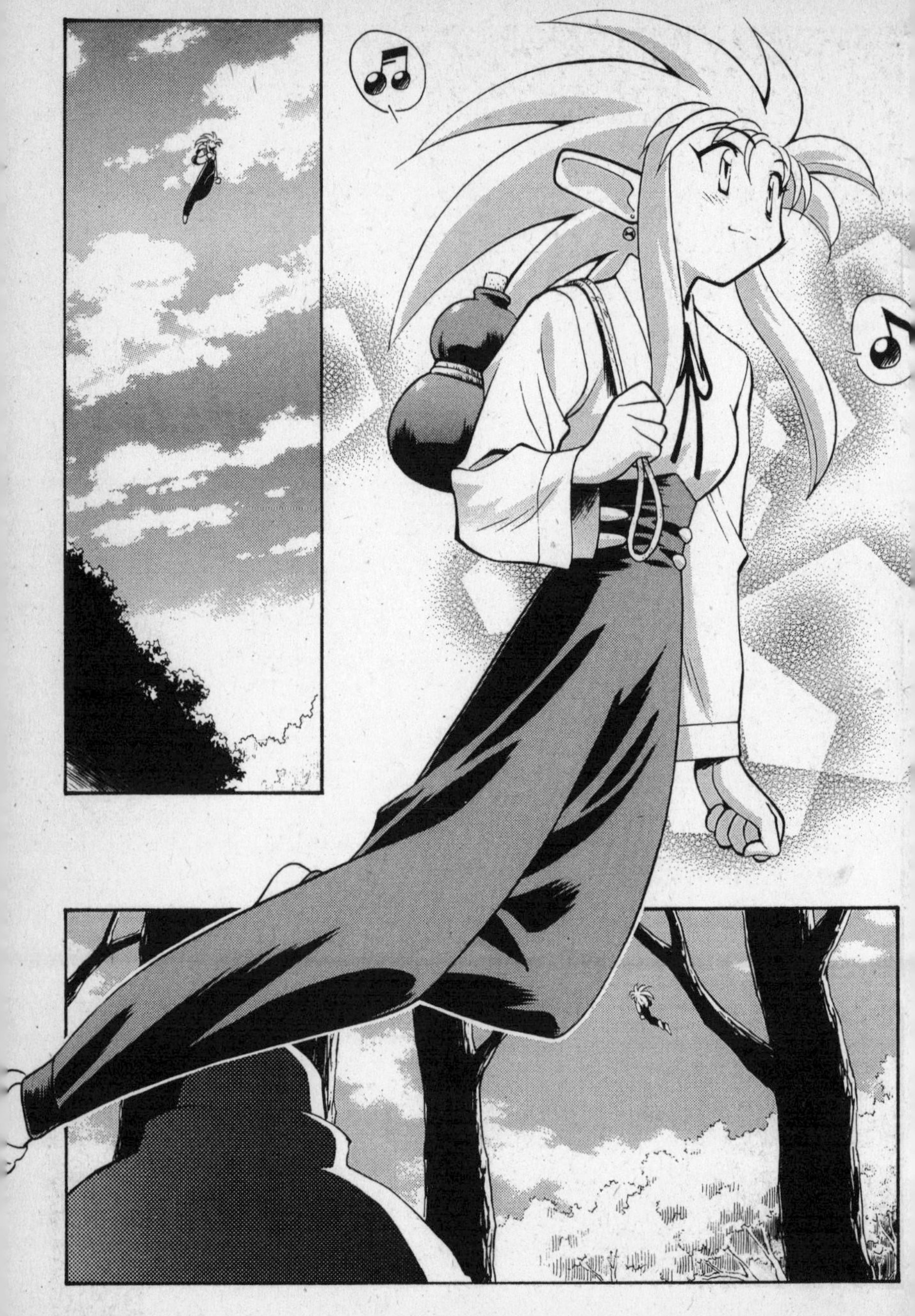

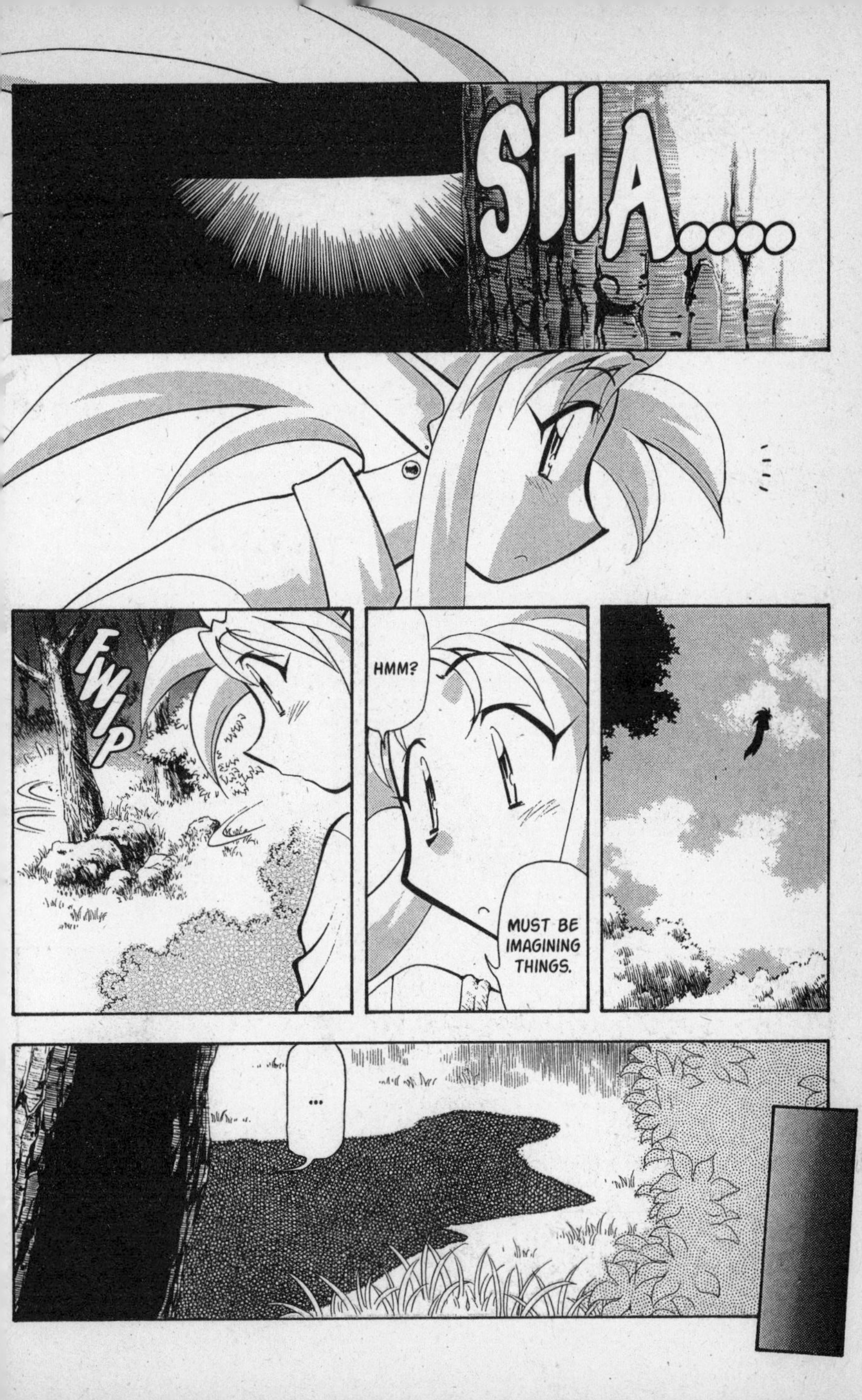
SHA....
FWIP
HMM?
MUST BE IMAGINING THINGS.
...

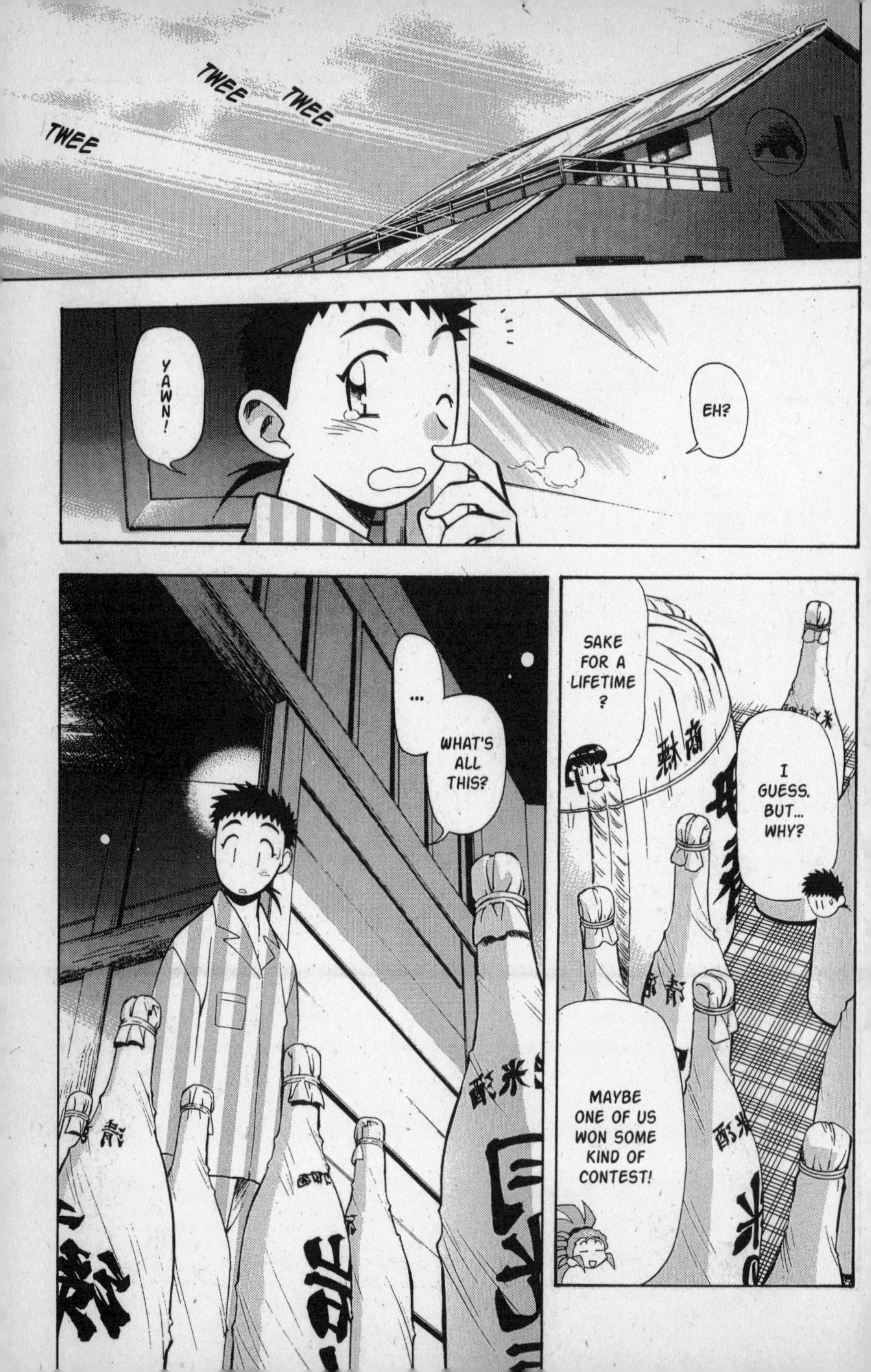
TWEE
TWEE
TWEE
YAWN!
EH?
... WHAT'S ALL THIS?
SAKE FOR A LIFETIME?
I GUESS. BUT... WHY?
MAYBE ONE OF US WON SOME KIND OF CONTEST!

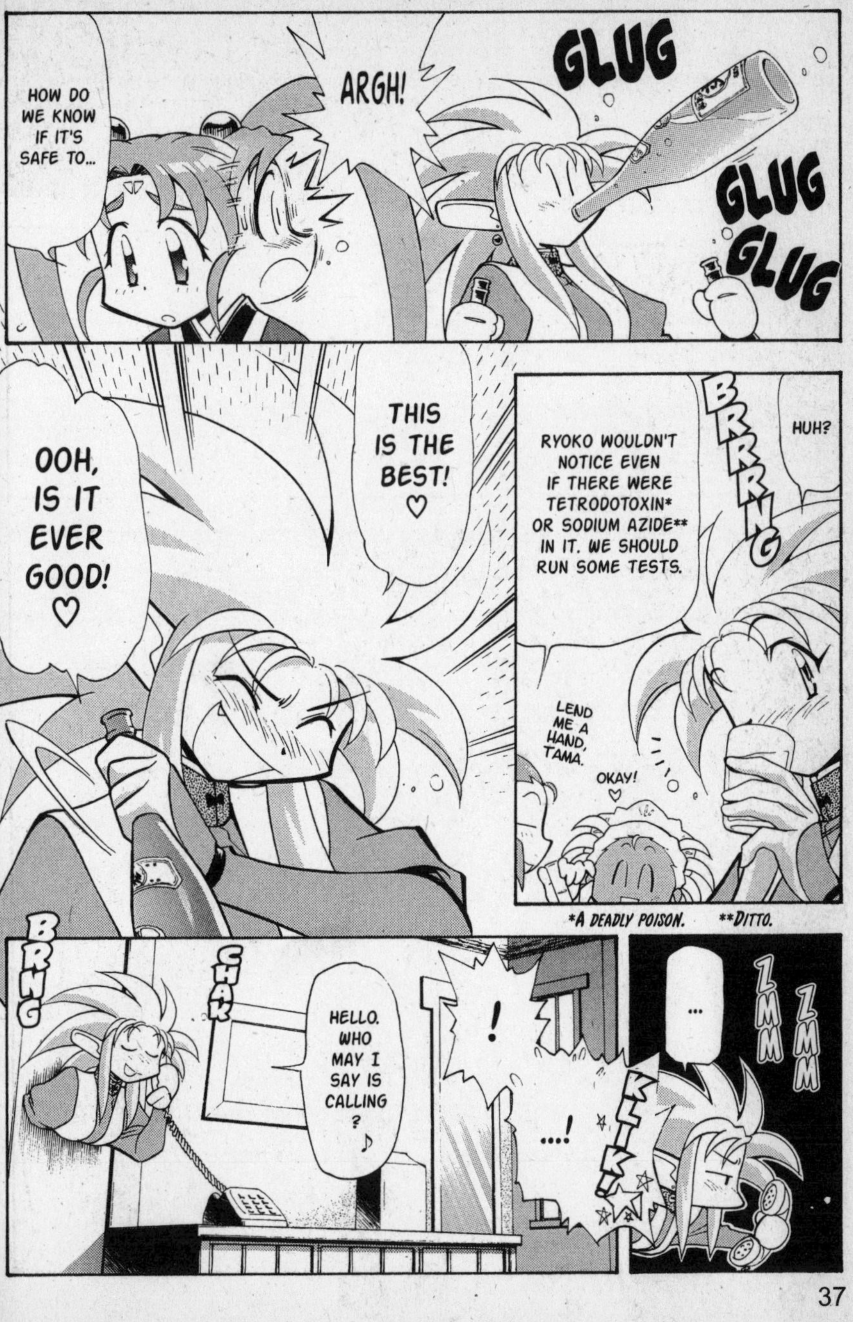
HOW DO WE KNOW IF IT'S SAFE TO...
ARGH!
GLUG
GLUG
GLUG
OOH, IS IT EVER GOOD! ♡
THIS IS THE BEST! ♡
RYOKO WOULDN'T NOTICE EVEN IF THERE WERE TETRODOTOXIN* OR SODIUM AZIDE** IN IT. WE SHOULD RUN SOME TESTS.
BRRRNG
HUH?
LEND ME A HAND, TAMA.
OKAY! ♡
*A DEADLY POISON. **DITTO.
BRNG
CHAK
HELLO. WHO MAY I SAY IS CALLING? ♪
!
...!
...
KLIK!
ZMM
ZMM

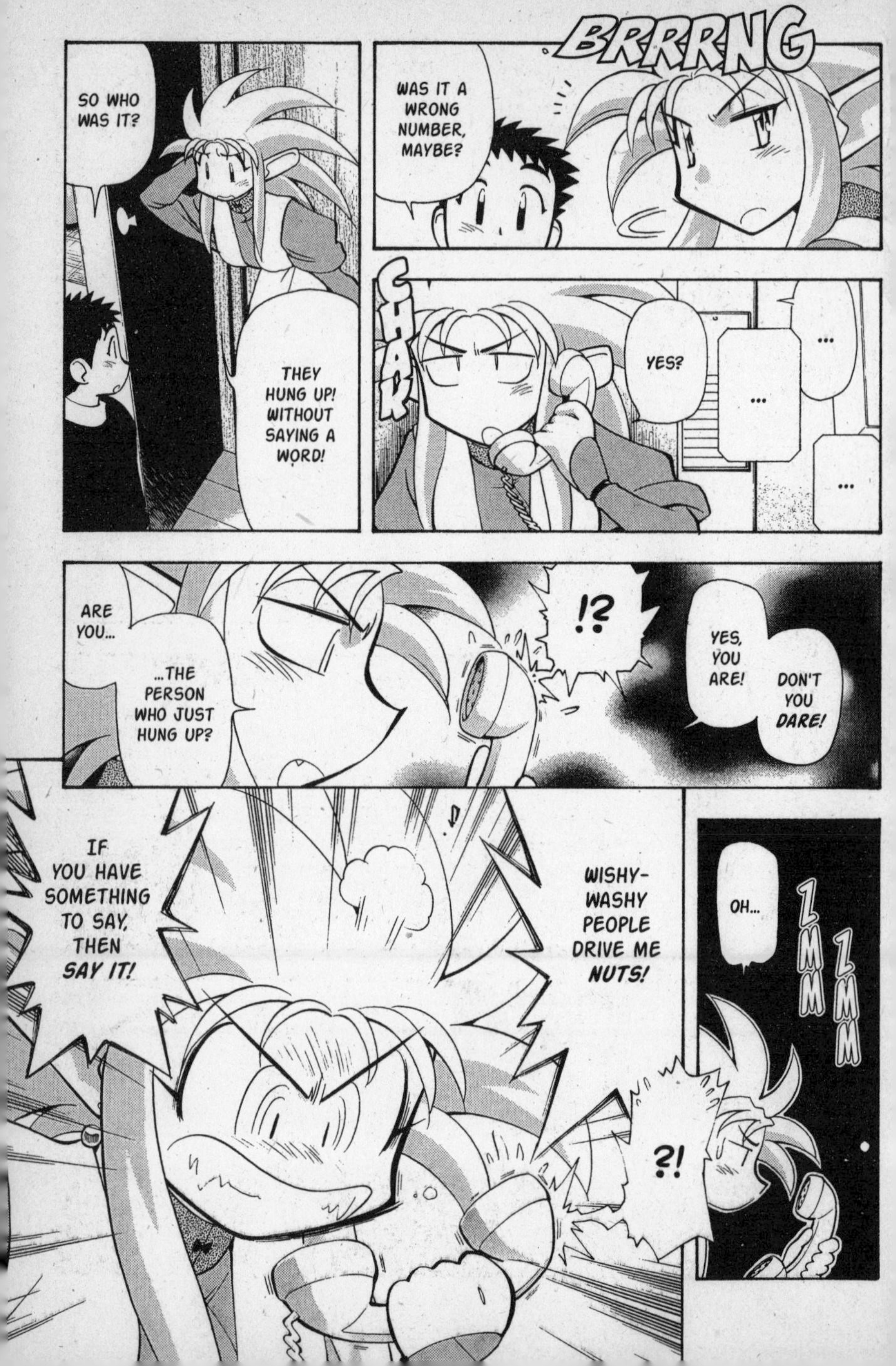
SO WHO WAS IT?
THEY HUNG UP! WITHOUT SAYING A WORD!
BRRRNG
WAS IT A WRONG NUMBER, MAYBE?
CHAK
YES?
...
...
...
ARE YOU...
...THE PERSON WHO JUST HUNG UP?
!?
YES, YOU ARE!
DON'T YOU DARE!
IF YOU HAVE SOMETHING TO SAY, THEN SAY IT!
WISHY-WASHY PEOPLE DRIVE ME NUTS!
?!
OH...
ZMM
ZMM

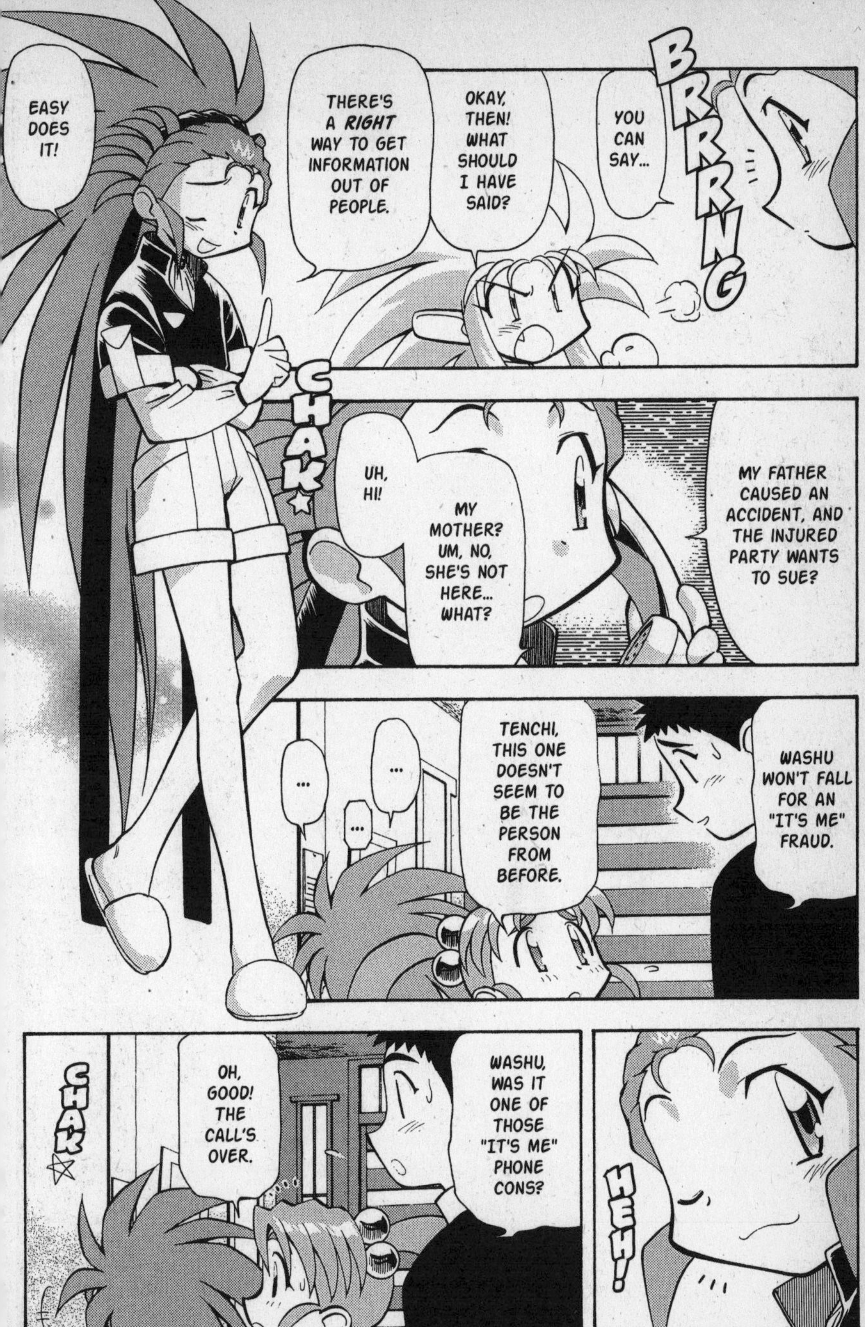
EASY DOES IT!
THERE'S A *RIGHT* WAY TO GET INFORMATION OUT OF PEOPLE.
OKAY, THEN! WHAT SHOULD I HAVE SAID?
YOU CAN SAY...
BRRRNG
CHAK
UH, HI!
MY MOTHER? UM, NO, SHE'S NOT HERE... WHAT?
MY FATHER CAUSED AN ACCIDENT, AND THE INJURED PARTY WANTS TO SUE?
...
...
...
TENCHI, THIS ONE DOESN'T SEEM TO BE THE PERSON FROM BEFORE.
WASHU WON'T FALL FOR AN "IT'S ME" FRAUD.
CHAK
OH, GOOD! THE CALL'S OVER.
WASHU, WAS IT ONE OF THOSE "IT'S ME" PHONE CONS?
HEH!

BY THE TIME I WAS DONE, HE AGREED TO WIRE MONEY TO THE BANK OF MY CHOICE!

CLP CLP CLP CLP CLP CLP

WOW! NICE WORK!

NEVER TRY TO CON A CON ARTIST... I MEAN, A GENIUS!

MEANWHILE...

LOOK AT THIS!

10 MILLION YEN WERE WIRED INTO OUR BANK, SISTER!

OH! THANKS BE TO GOD!

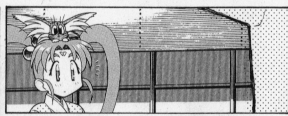

OOF!

UMPH!

EEEK!

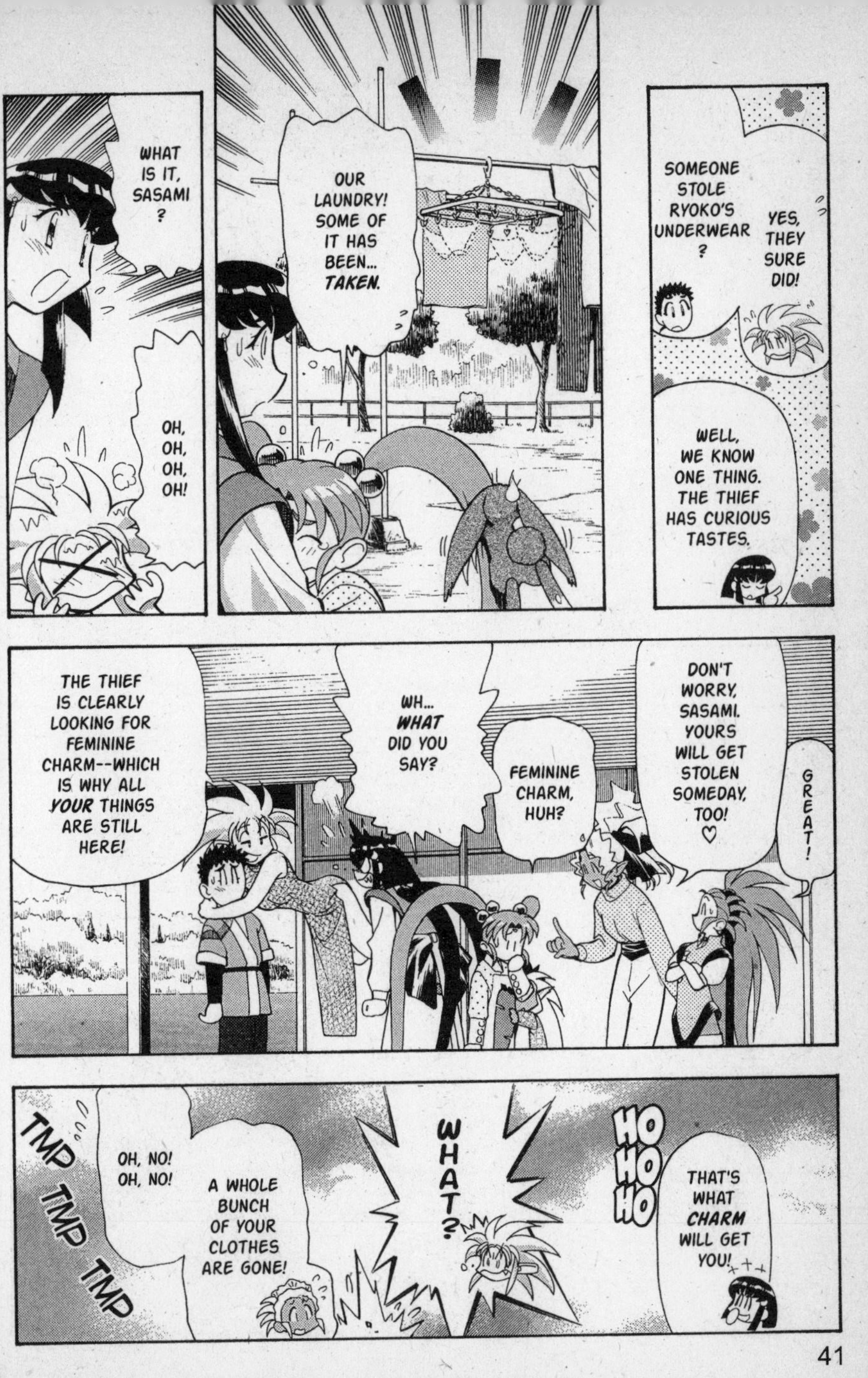
WHAT IS IT, SASAMI?
OH, OH, OH, OH!
OUR LAUNDRY! SOME OF IT HAS BEEN... *TAKEN.*
SOMEONE STOLE RYOKO'S UNDERWEAR?
YES, THEY SURE DID!
WELL, WE KNOW ONE THING. THE THIEF HAS CURIOUS TASTES.
THE THIEF IS CLEARLY LOOKING FOR FEMININE CHARM--WHICH IS WHY ALL *YOUR* THINGS ARE STILL HERE!
WH... *WHAT* DID YOU SAY?
FEMININE CHARM, HUH?
DON'T WORRY, SASAMI. YOURS WILL GET STOLEN SOMEDAY, TOO! ♡
GREAT!
TMP TMP TMP
OH, NO! OH, NO!
A WHOLE BUNCH OF YOUR CLOTHES ARE GONE!
WHAT?
HO HO HO
THAT'S WHAT *CHARM* WILL GET YOU!

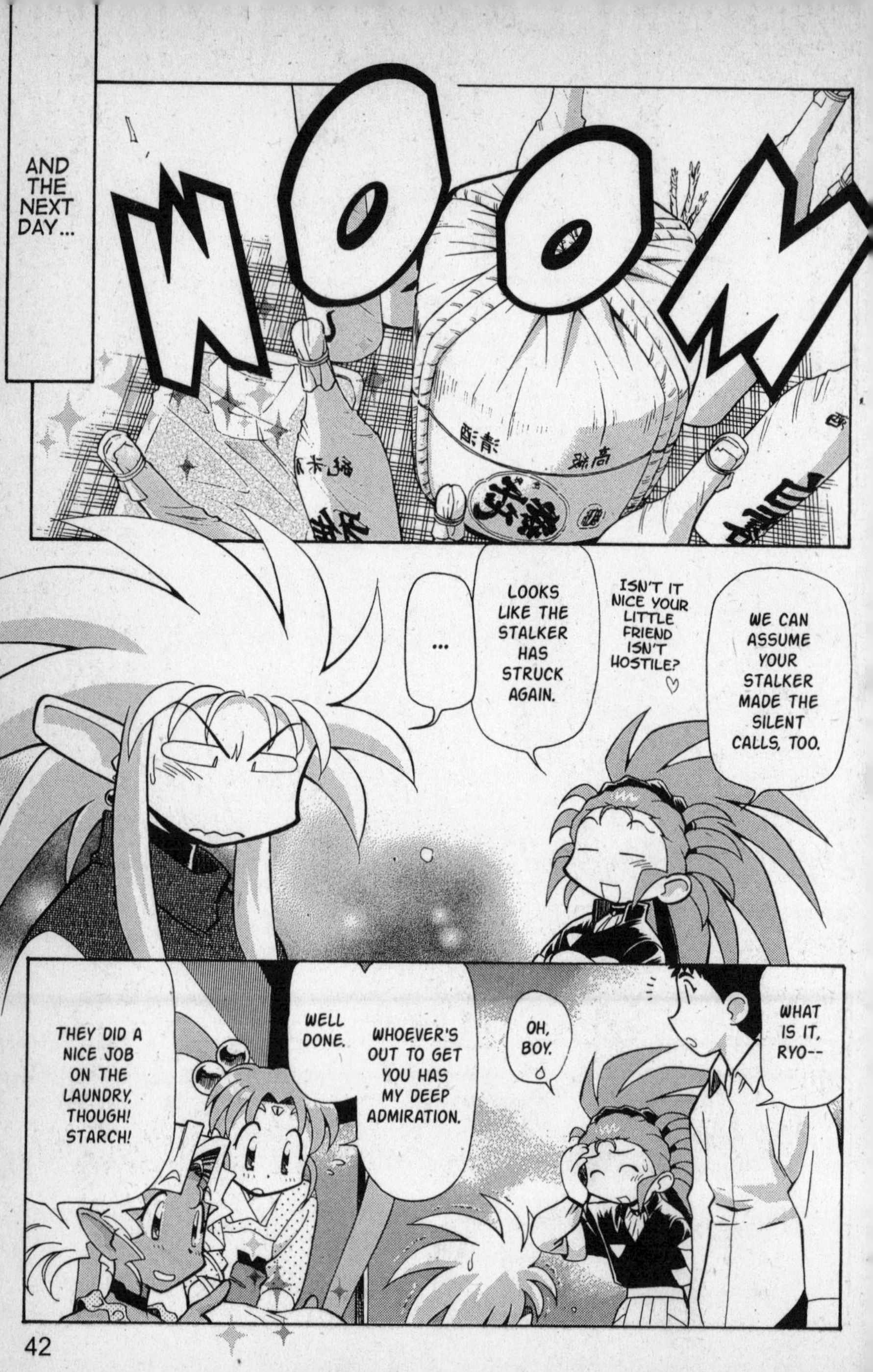
AND THE NEXT DAY...
WOOM
...
LOOKS LIKE THE STALKER HAS STRUCK AGAIN.
ISN'T IT NICE YOUR LITTLE FRIEND ISN'T HOSTILE? ♡
WE CAN ASSUME YOUR STALKER MADE THE SILENT CALLS, TOO.
THEY DID A NICE JOB ON THE LAUNDRY, THOUGH! STARCH!
WELL DONE.
WHOEVER'S OUT TO GET YOU HAS MY DEEP ADMIRATION.
OH, BOY.
WHAT IS IT, RYO--

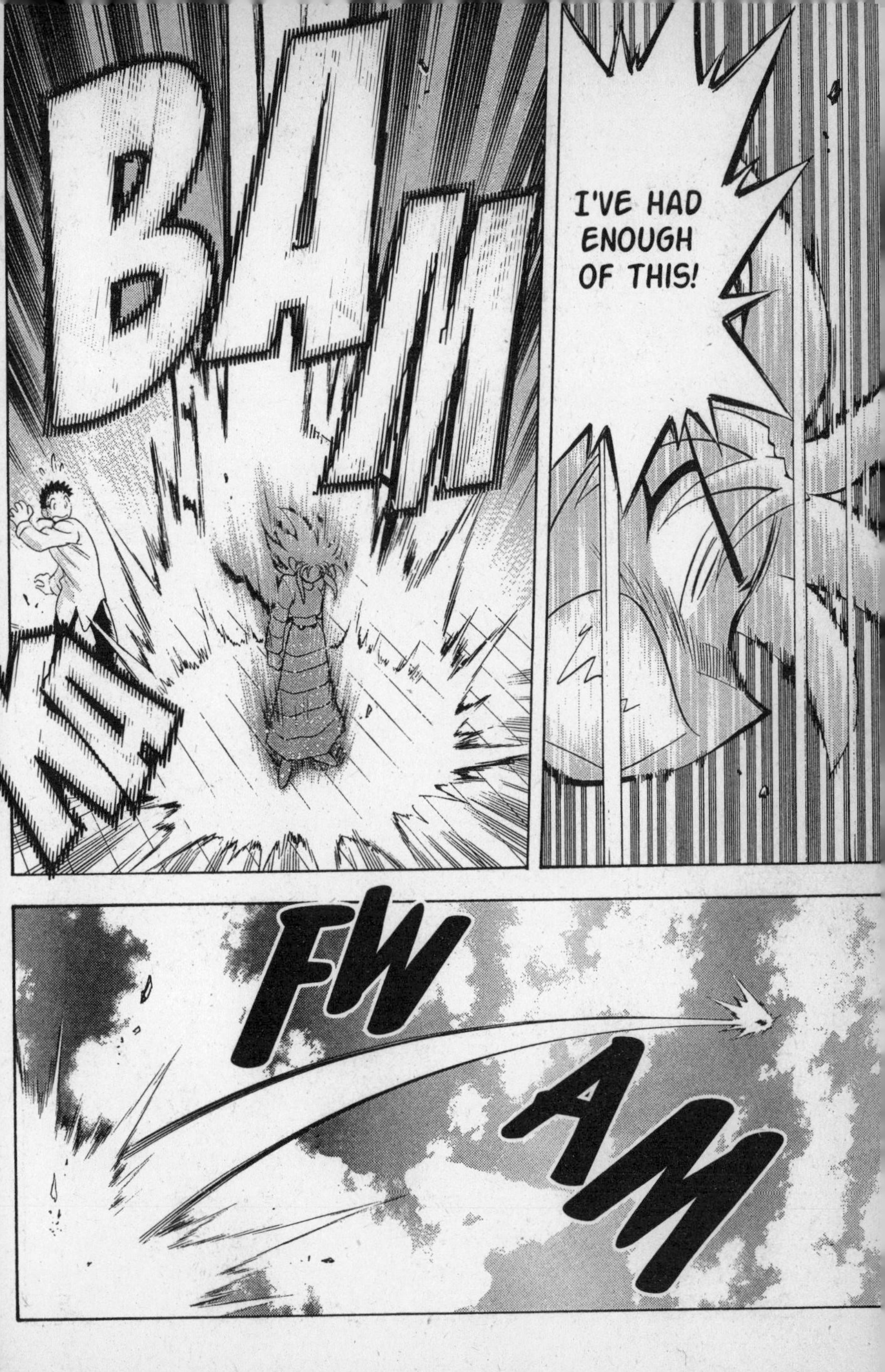
I'VE HAD ENOUGH OF THIS!
FWAM

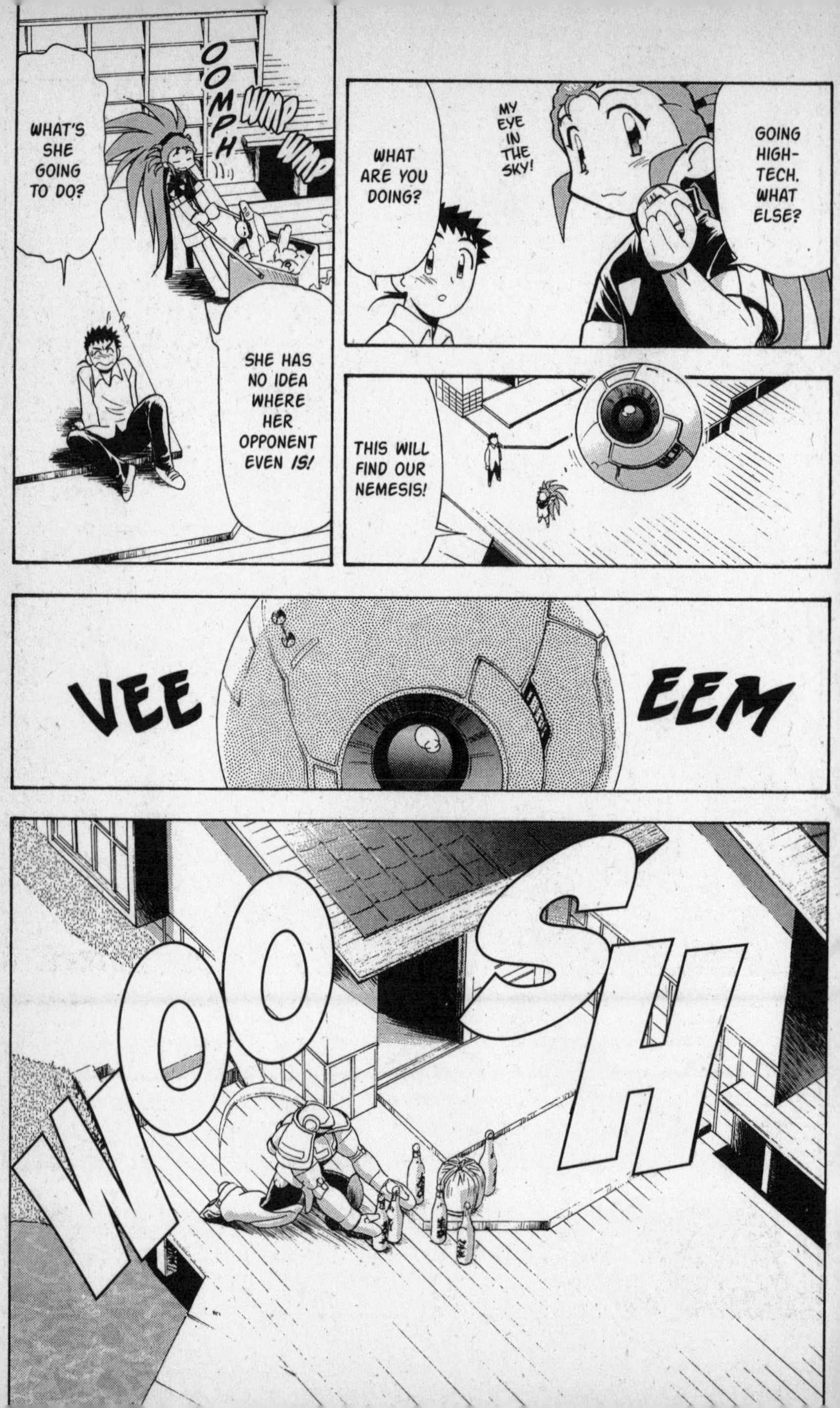
WHAT'S SHE GOING TO DO?
OOMPH
WMP WMP
SHE HAS NO IDEA WHERE HER OPPONENT EVEN *IS*!
WHAT ARE YOU DOING?
MY EYE IN THE SKY!
GOING HIGH-TECH. WHAT ELSE?
THIS WILL FIND OUR NEMESIS!
VEE EEM
WOOSH

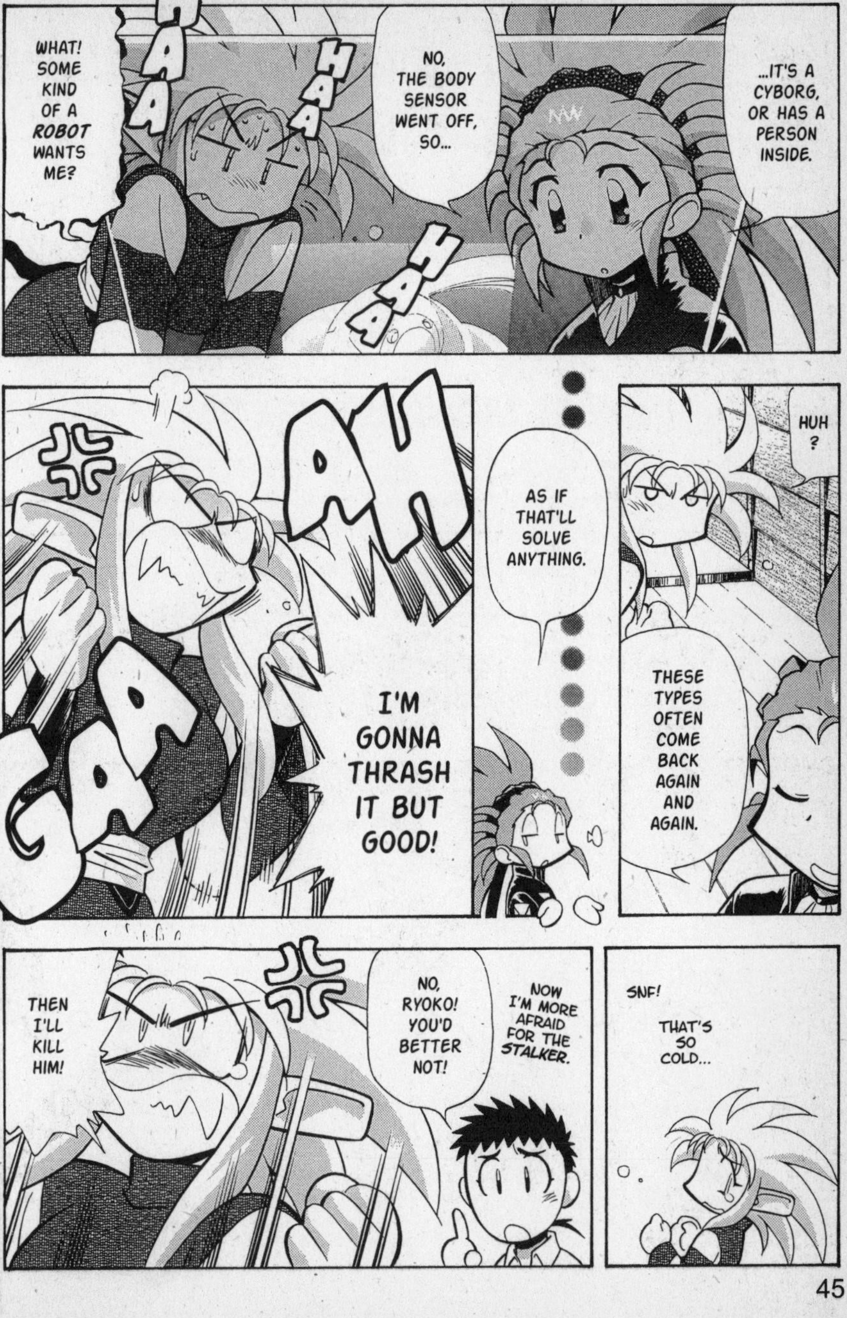
HA
HA
HA
WHAT! SOME KIND OF A ROBOT WANTS ME?
HA
HA
HA
NO, THE BODY SENSOR WENT OFF, SO...
...IT'S A CYBORG, OR HAS A PERSON INSIDE.
GRAA
AH
I'M GONNA THRASH IT BUT GOOD!
AS IF THAT'LL SOLVE ANYTHING.
HUH?
THESE TYPES OFTEN COME BACK AGAIN AND AGAIN.
THEN I'LL KILL HIM!
NO, RYOKO! YOU'D BETTER NOT!
NOW I'M MORE AFRAID FOR THE STALKER.
SNF!
THAT'S SO COLD...

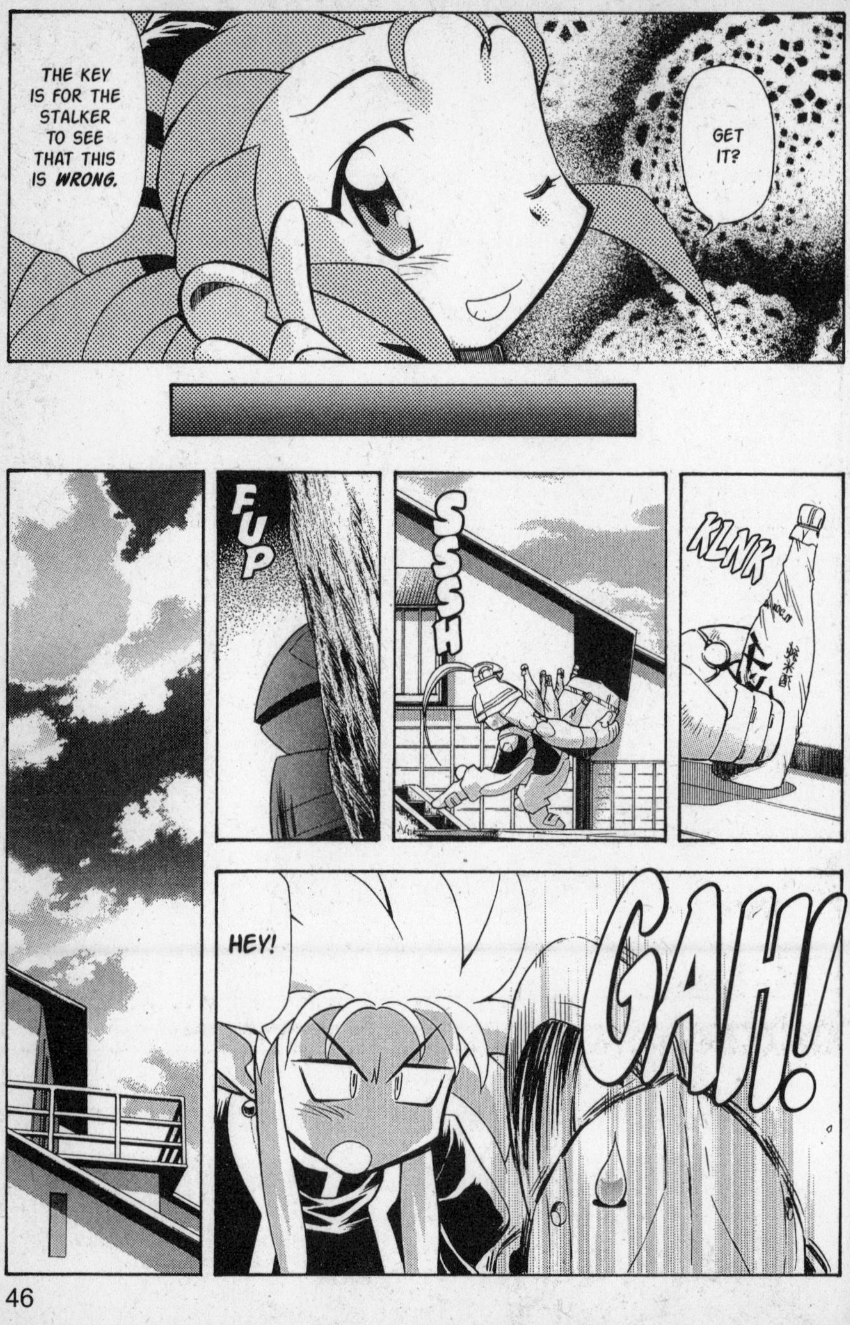

THE KEY IS FOR THE STALKER TO SEE THAT THIS IS *WRONG.*
GET IT?
FUP
SSSH
KLNK
HEY!
GAH!

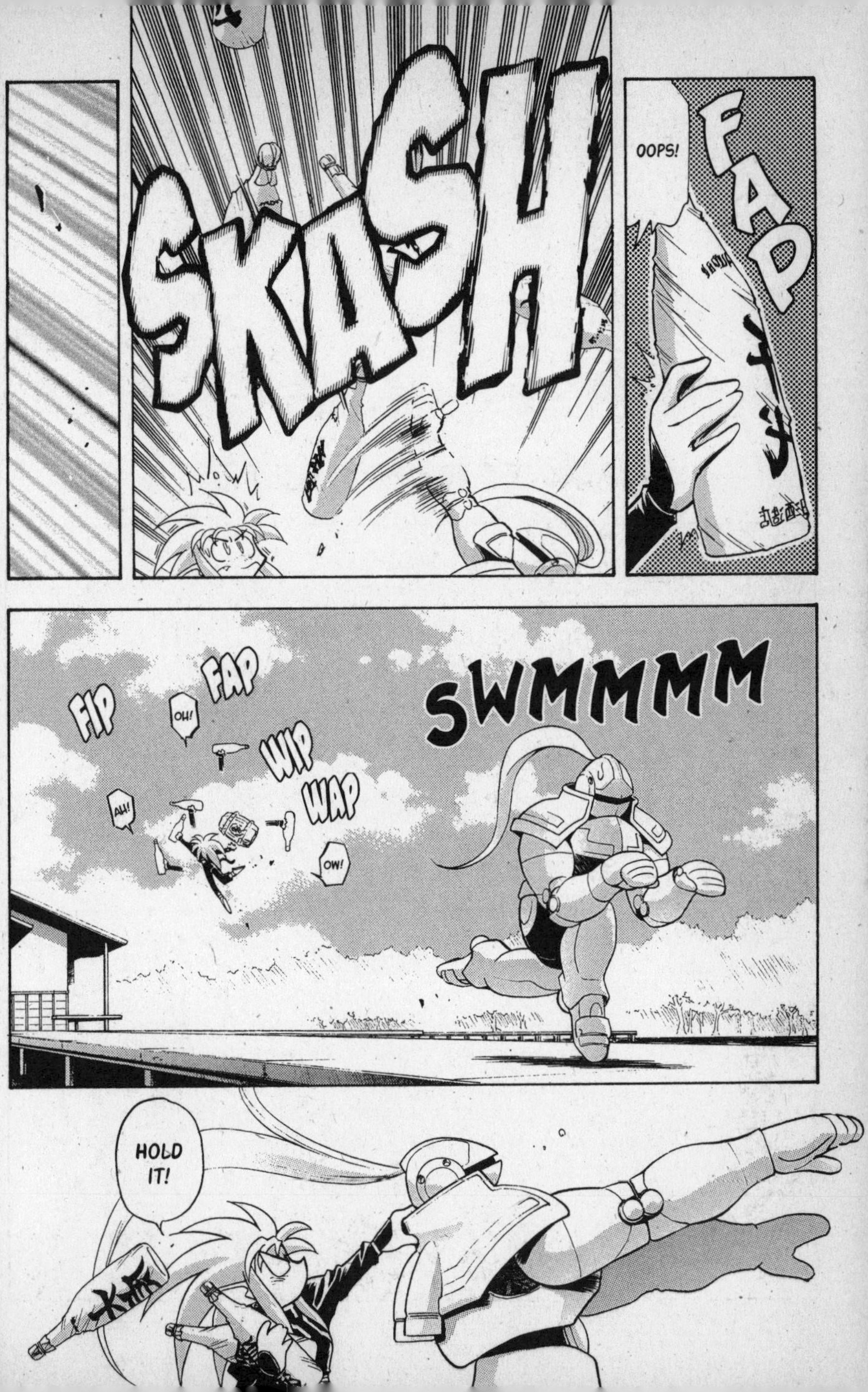
SKASH
OOPS!
FAP
FIP
OH!
FAP
AH!
WIP
WAP
OW!
SWMMMM
HOLD IT!

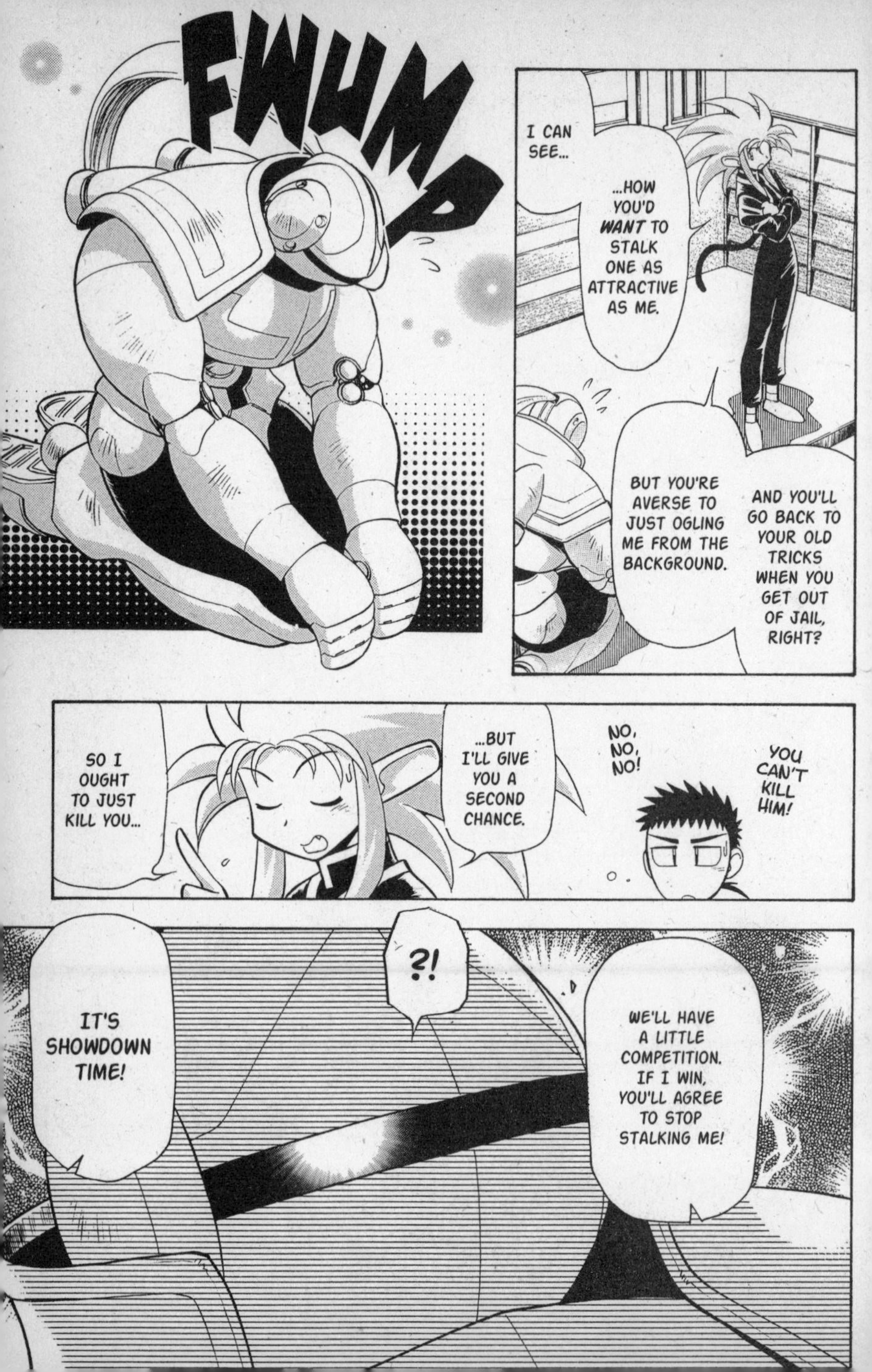
FWUMP
I CAN SEE...
...HOW YOU'D *WANT* TO STALK ONE AS ATTRACTIVE AS ME.
BUT YOU'RE AVERSE TO JUST OGLING ME FROM THE BACKGROUND.
AND YOU'LL GO BACK TO YOUR OLD TRICKS WHEN YOU GET OUT OF JAIL, RIGHT?
SO I OUGHT TO JUST KILL YOU...
...BUT I'LL GIVE YOU A SECOND CHANCE.
NO, NO, NO!
YOU CAN'T KILL HIM!
IT'S SHOWDOWN TIME!
?!
WE'LL HAVE A LITTLE COMPETITION. IF I WIN, YOU'LL AGREE TO STOP STALKING ME!

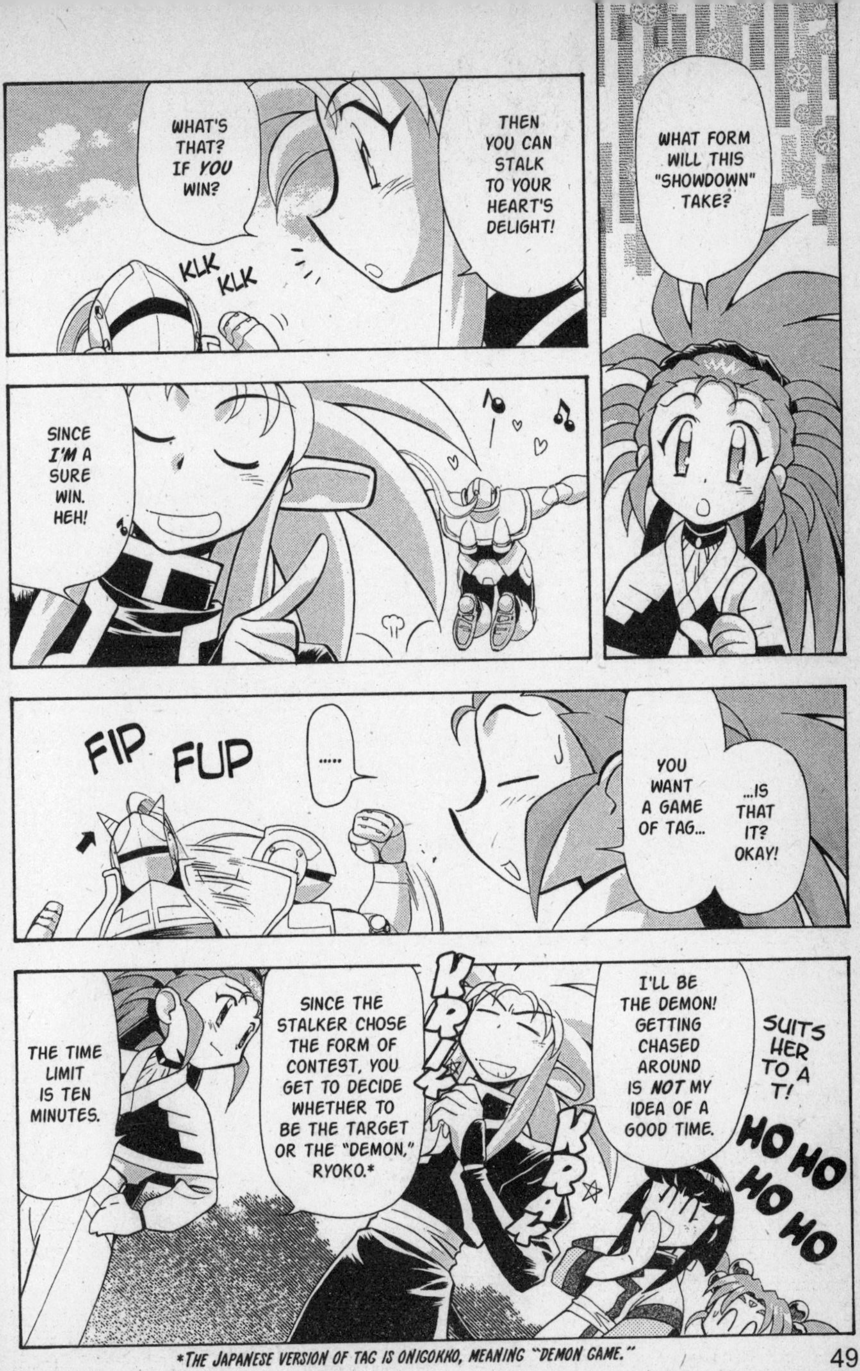
WHAT'S THAT? IF *YOU* WIN?
KLK KLK
THEN YOU CAN STALK TO YOUR HEART'S DELIGHT!
SINCE *I'M* A SURE WIN. HEH!
WHAT FORM WILL THIS "SHOWDOWN" TAKE?
FIP FUP
.....
YOU WANT A GAME OF TAG...
...IS THAT IT? OKAY!
THE TIME LIMIT IS TEN MINUTES.
SINCE THE STALKER CHOSE THE FORM OF CONTEST, YOU GET TO DECIDE WHETHER TO BE THE TARGET OR THE "DEMON," RYOKO.*
KRIK
I'LL BE THE DEMON! GETTING CHASED AROUND IS *NOT* MY IDEA OF A GOOD TIME.
KRAK
SUITS HER TO A T!
HO HO HO HO HO HO

*THE JAPANESE VERSION OF TAG IS ONIGOKKO, MEANING "DEMON GAME."

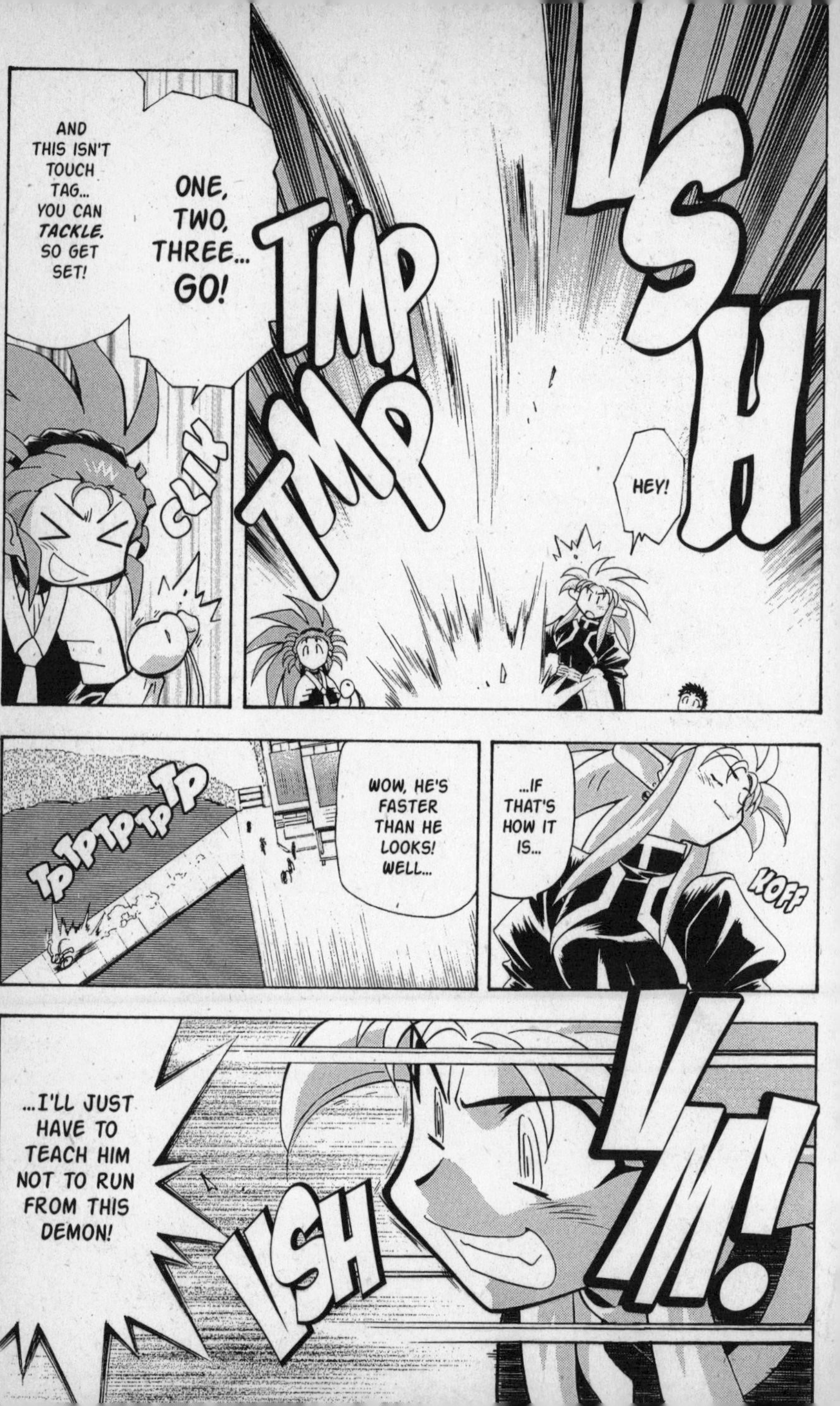
AND THIS ISN'T TOUCH TAG... YOU CAN *TACKLE.* SO GET SET!
ONE, TWO, THREE... GO!
CLIK
TMP TMP
SH
HEY!
TP TP TP TP TP TP
WOW, HE'S FASTER THAN HE LOOKS! WELL...
...IF THAT'S HOW IT IS...
KOFF
...I'LL JUST HAVE TO TEACH HIM NOT TO RUN FROM THIS DEMON!
ISH

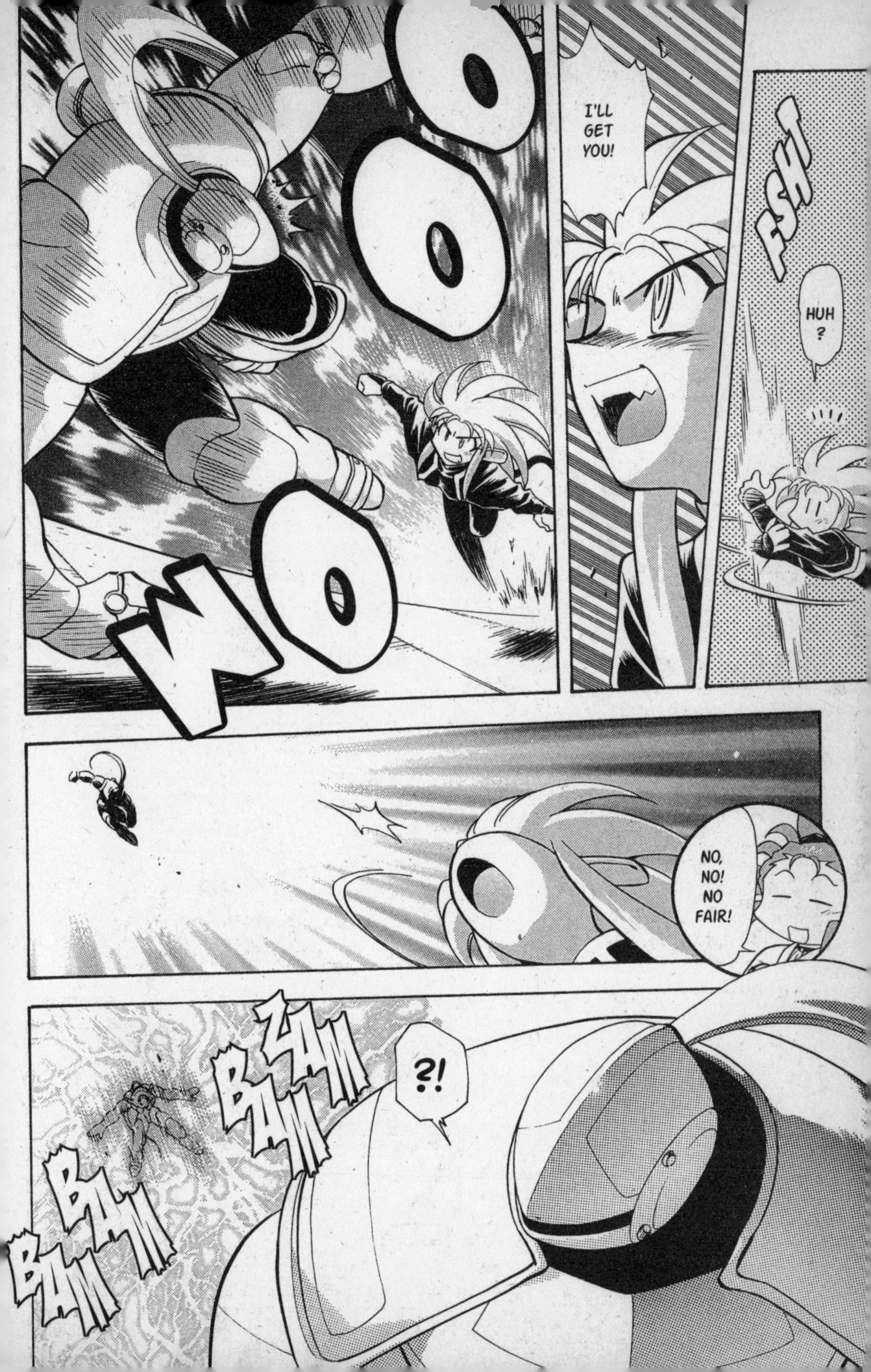
WOOO
I'LL GET YOU!
FSHT
HUH?
NO, NO! NO FAIR!
BAM
BAM
BAM
ZAM
?!

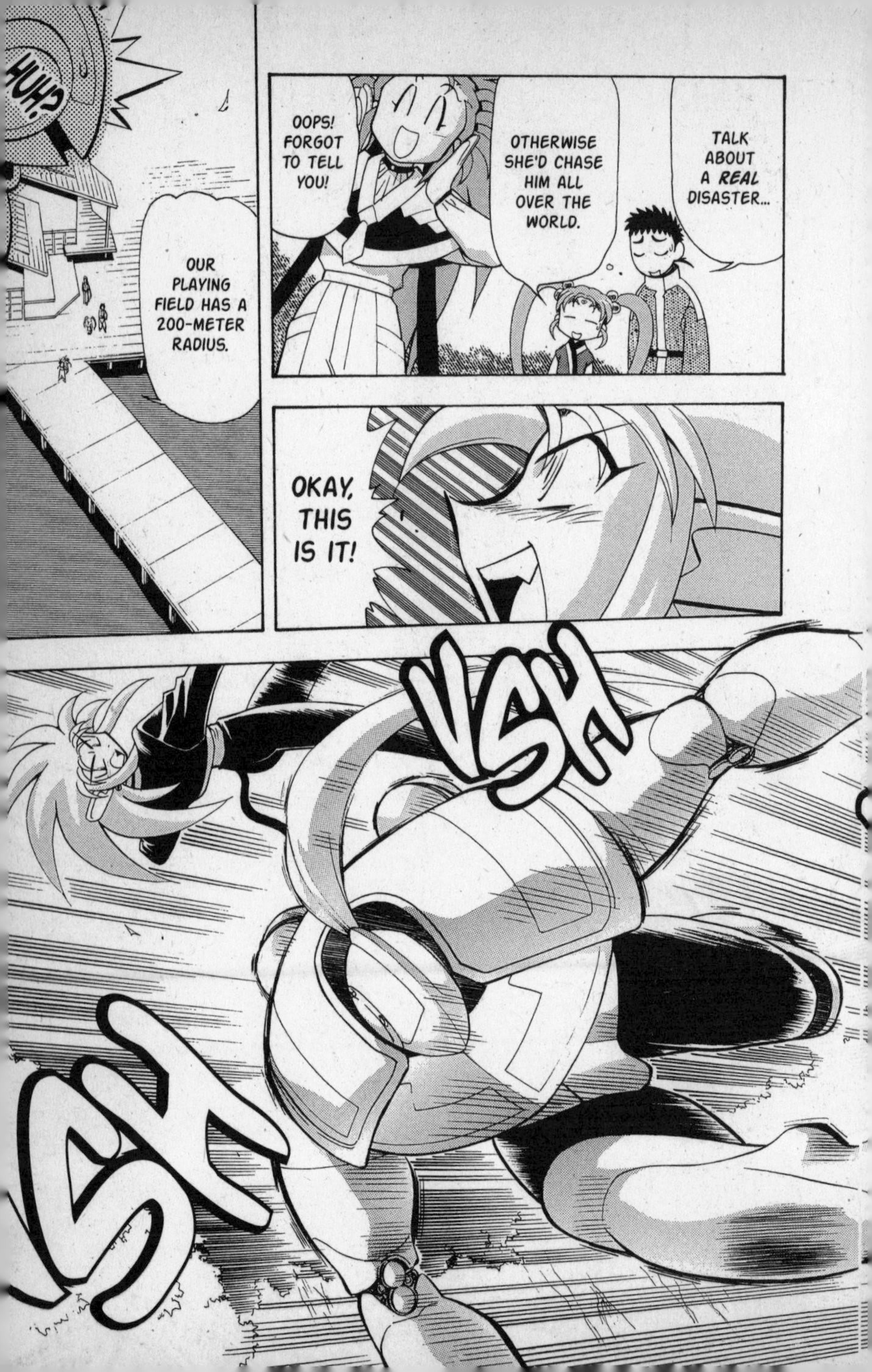
HUH?
OUR PLAYING FIELD HAS A 200-METER RADIUS.
OOPS! FORGOT TO TELL YOU!
OTHERWISE SHE'D CHASE HIM ALL OVER THE WORLD.
TALK ABOUT A *REAL* DISASTER...
OKAY, THIS IS IT!
VSH
SH

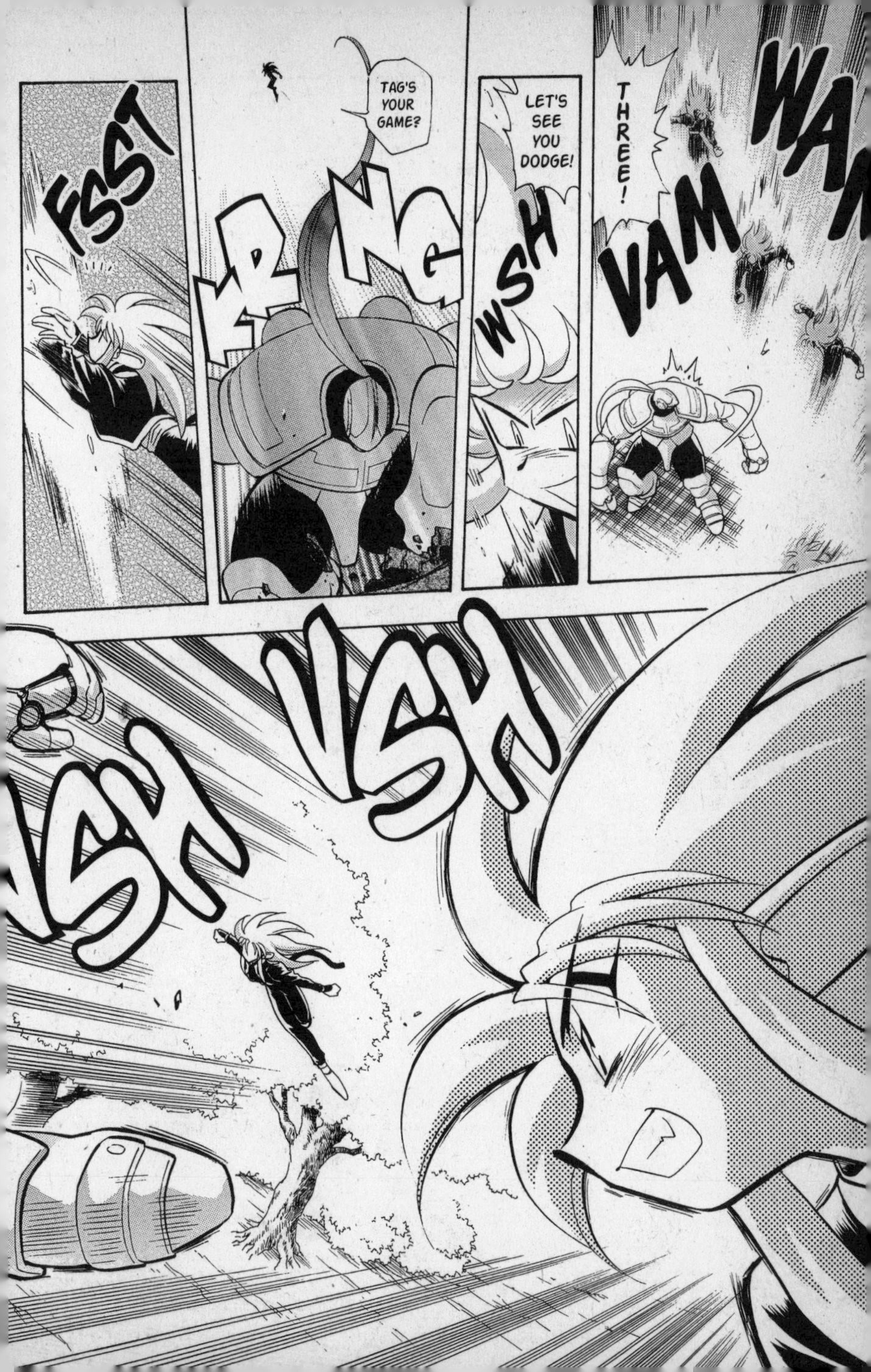
FSST
TAG'S YOUR GAME?
KRANG
LET'S SEE YOU DODGE!
WSH
THREEE!
VAM
WSH
WSH

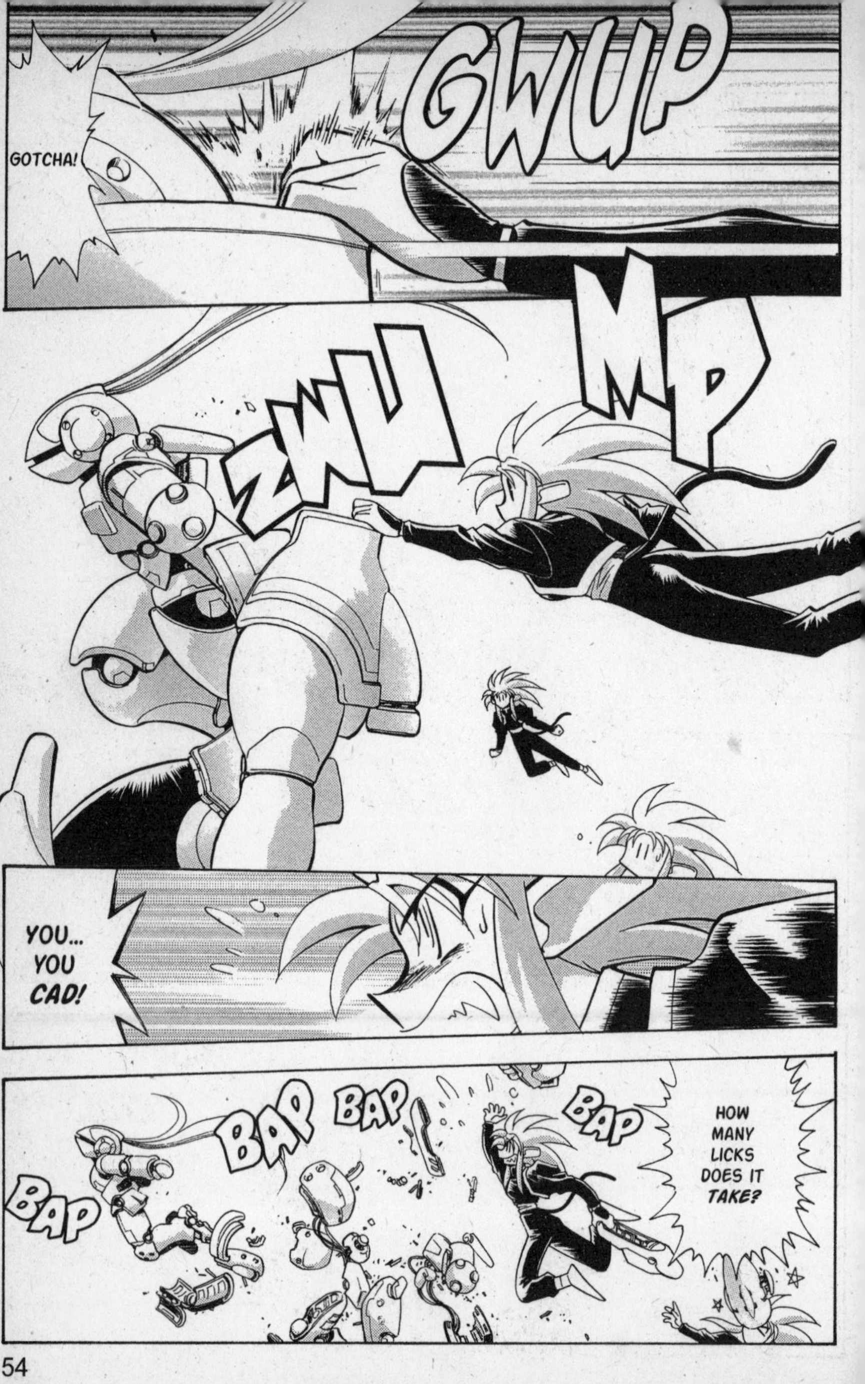
GWUP
GOTCHA!
ZNUMP
YOU... YOU CAD!
BAP
BAP
BAP
BAP
HOW MANY LICKS DOES IT TAKE?

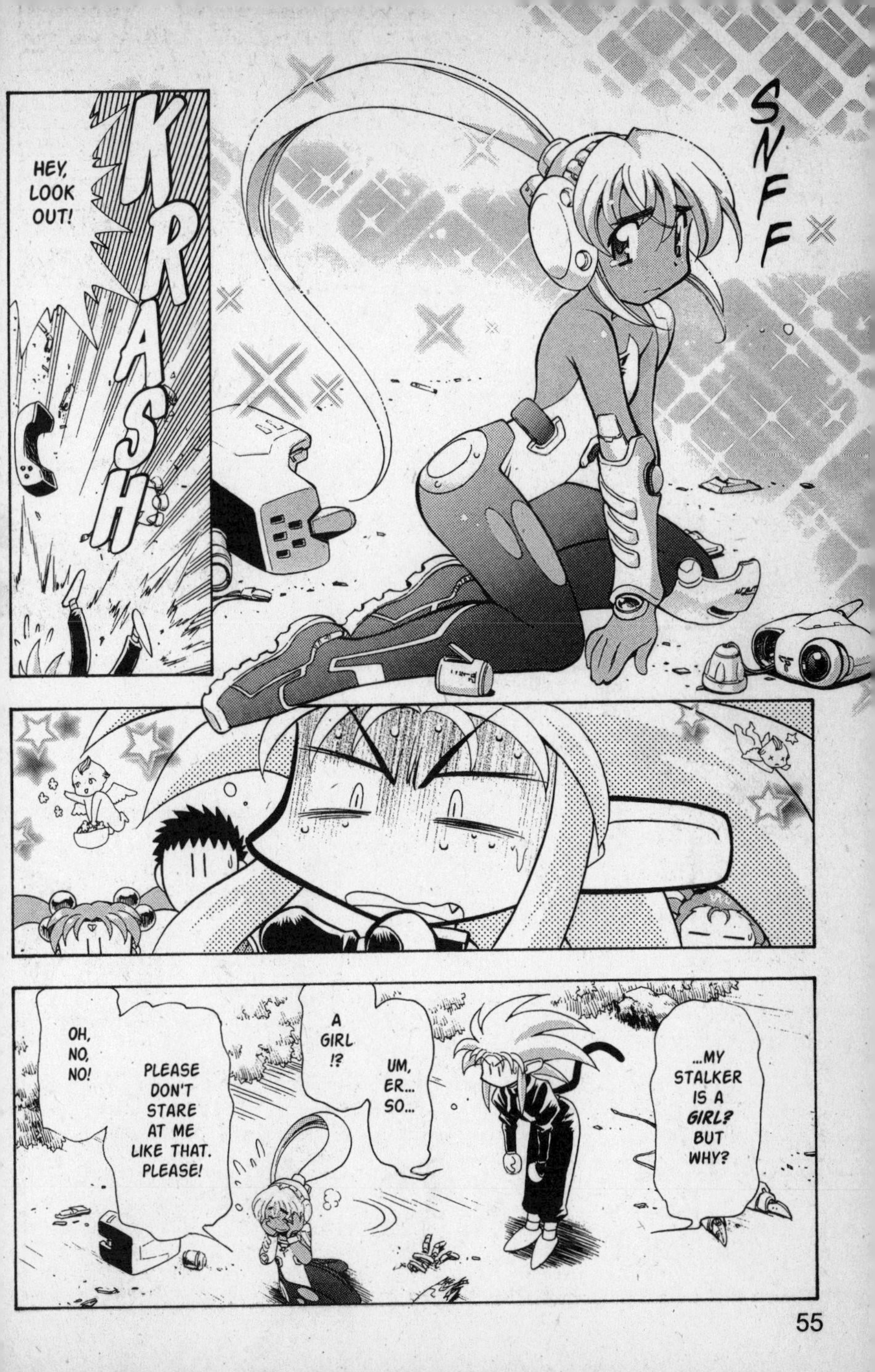
HEY, LOOK OUT!
KRASH
SNFF
OH, NO, NO!
PLEASE DON'T STARE AT ME LIKE THAT. PLEASE!
A GIRL!?
UM, ER... SO...
...MY STALKER IS A *GIRL?* BUT WHY?

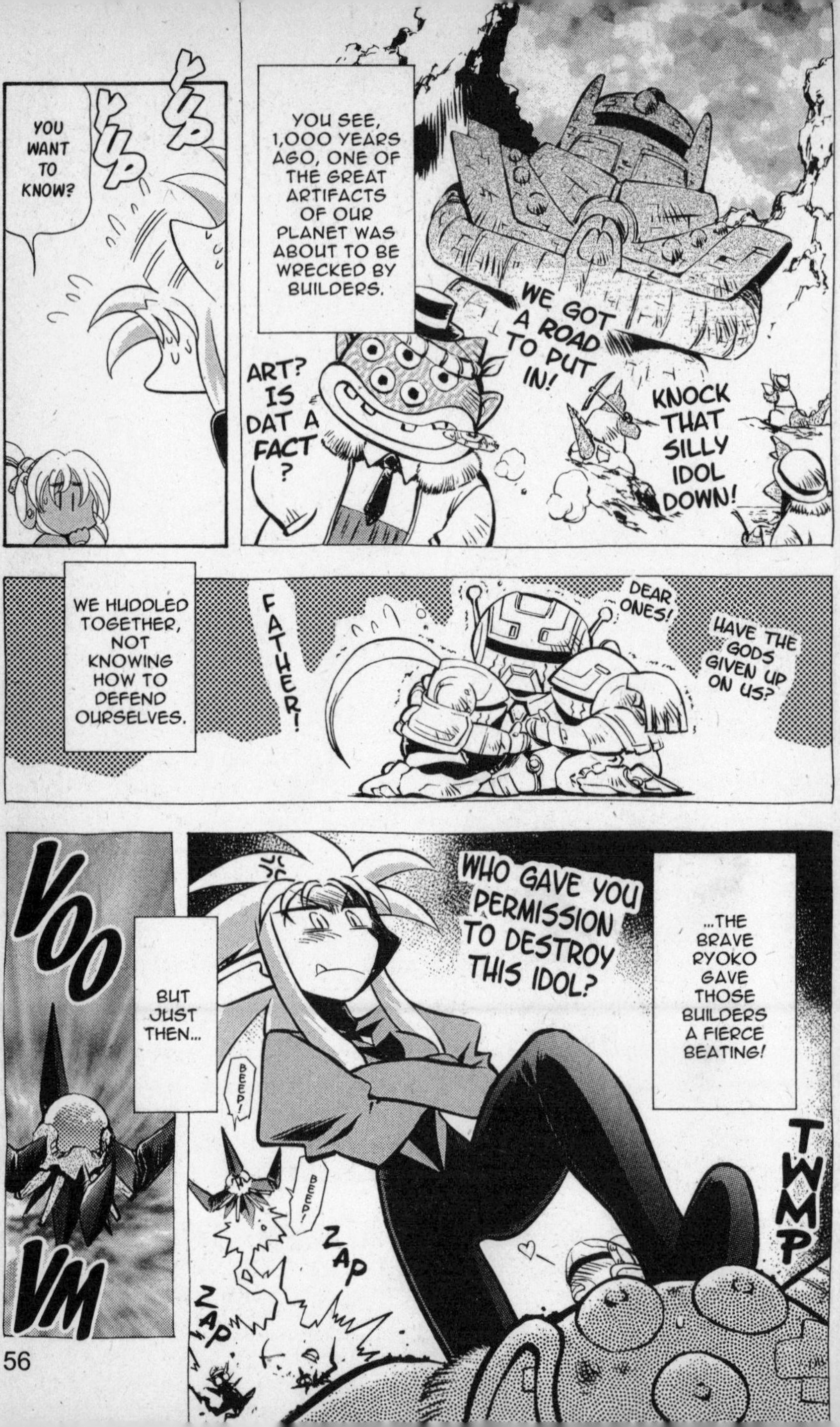
YUP YUP
YOU WANT TO KNOW?
YOU SEE, 1,000 YEARS AGO, ONE OF THE GREAT ARTIFACTS OF OUR PLANET WAS ABOUT TO BE WRECKED BY BUILDERS.
ART? IS DAT A FACT?
WE GOT A ROAD TO PUT IN!
KNOCK THAT SILLY IDOL DOWN!
WE HUDDLED TOGETHER, NOT KNOWING HOW TO DEFEND OURSELVES.
FATHER!
DEAR ONES!
HAVE THE GODS GIVEN UP ON US?
VOO
VM
BUT JUST THEN...
WHO GAVE YOU PERMISSION TO DESTROY THIS IDOL?
...THE BRAVE RYOKO GAVE THOSE BUILDERS A FIERCE BEATING!
BEEP!
BEEP!
ZAP
ZAP
TWMP

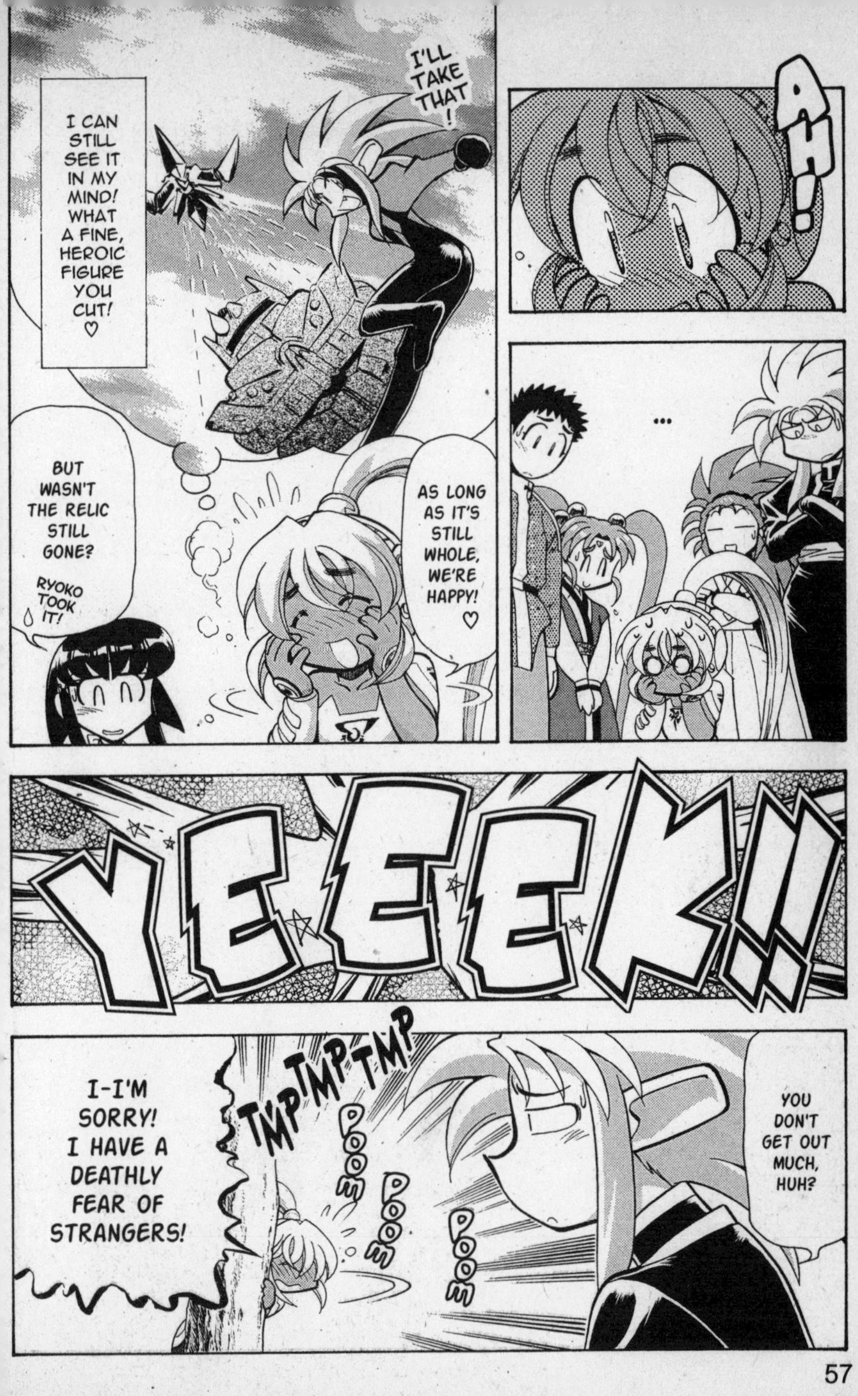
I CAN STILL SEE IT IN MY MIND! WHAT A FINE, HEROIC FIGURE YOU CUT! ♡
I'LL TAKE THAT!
BUT WASN'T THE RELIC STILL GONE?
RYOKO TOOK IT!
AS LONG AS IT'S STILL WHOLE, WE'RE HAPPY! ♡
AH!!
...
YEEEK!!
I-I'M SORRY! I HAVE A DEATHLY FEAR OF STRANGERS!
TMP TMP TMP TMP
POOM POOM POOM
YOU DON'T GET OUT MUCH, HUH?

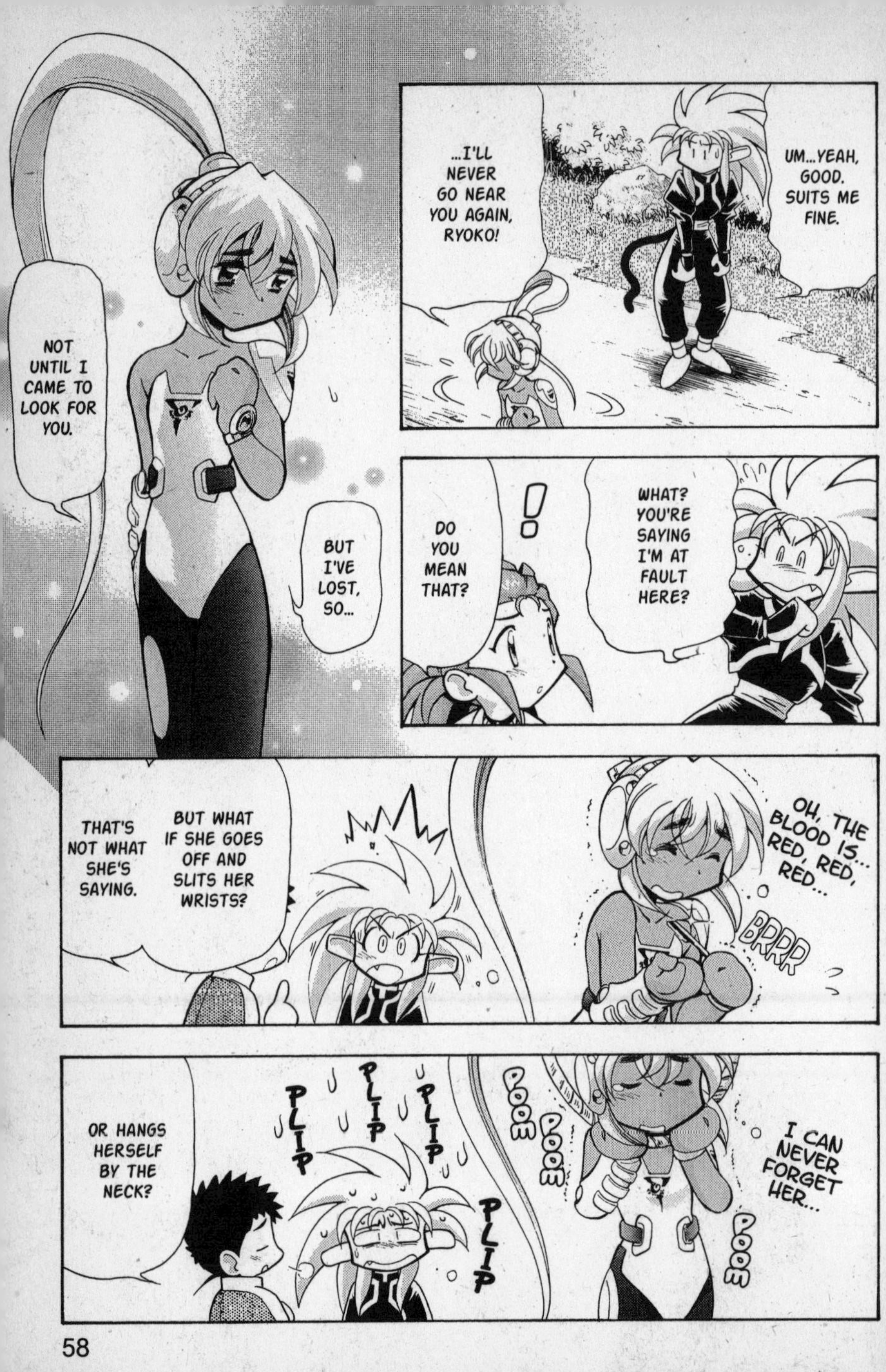
NOT UNTIL I CAME TO LOOK FOR YOU.
BUT I'VE LOST, SO...
...I'LL NEVER GO NEAR YOU AGAIN, RYOKO!
UM...YEAH, GOOD. SUITS ME FINE.
!
DO YOU MEAN THAT?
WHAT? YOU'RE SAYING I'M AT FAULT HERE?
THAT'S NOT WHAT SHE'S SAYING.
BUT WHAT IF SHE GOES OFF AND SLITS HER WRISTS?
OH, THE BLOOD IS... RED, RED, RED...
BRRR
OR HANGS HERSELF BY THE NECK?
PLIP
PLIP
PLIP
POOM
POOM
POOM
I CAN NEVER FORGET HER...
PLIP
POOM

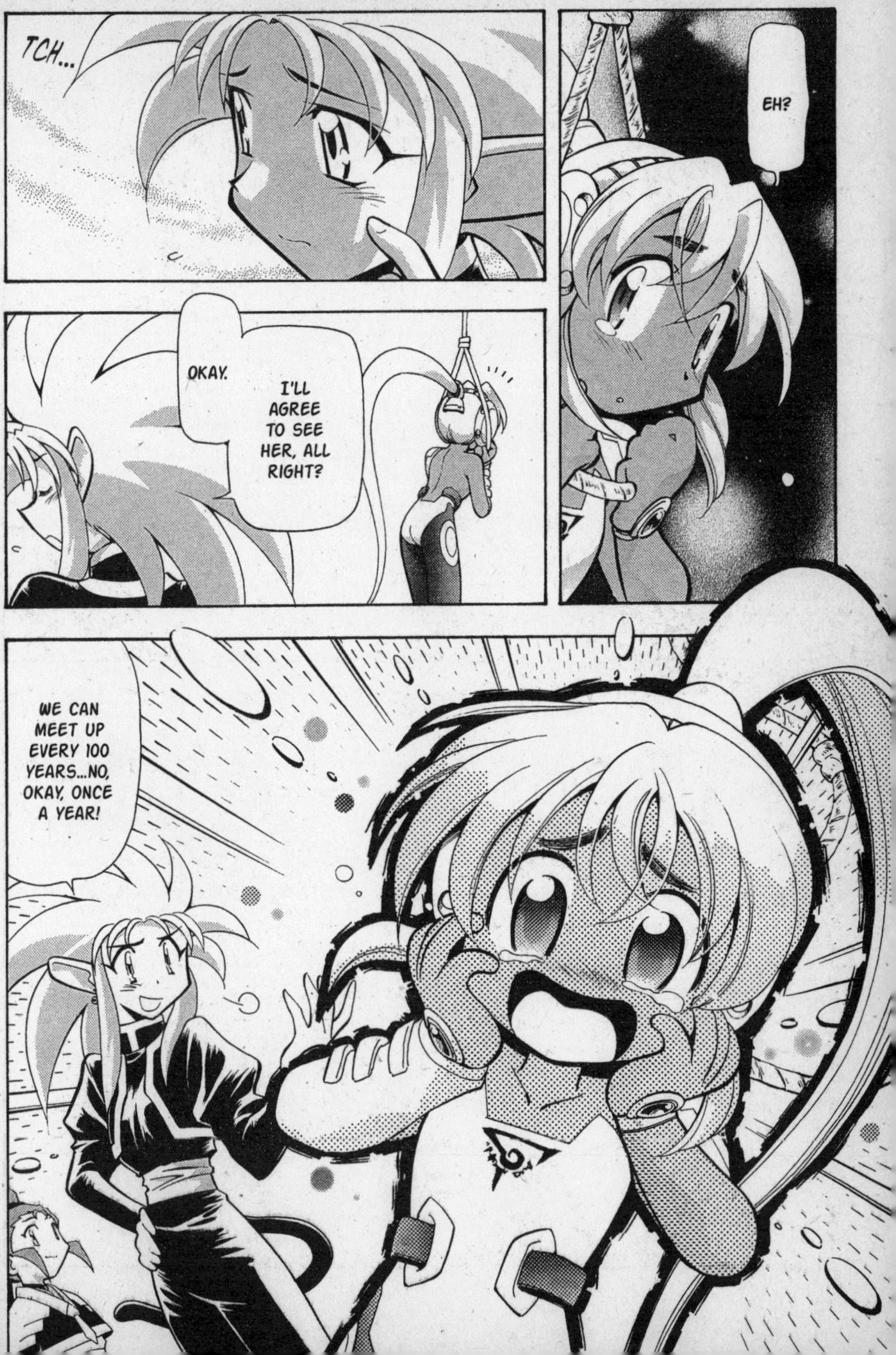
TCH...
OKAY.
I'LL AGREE TO SEE HER, ALL RIGHT?
EH?
WE CAN MEET UP EVERY 100 YEARS...NO, OKAY, ONCE A YEAR!

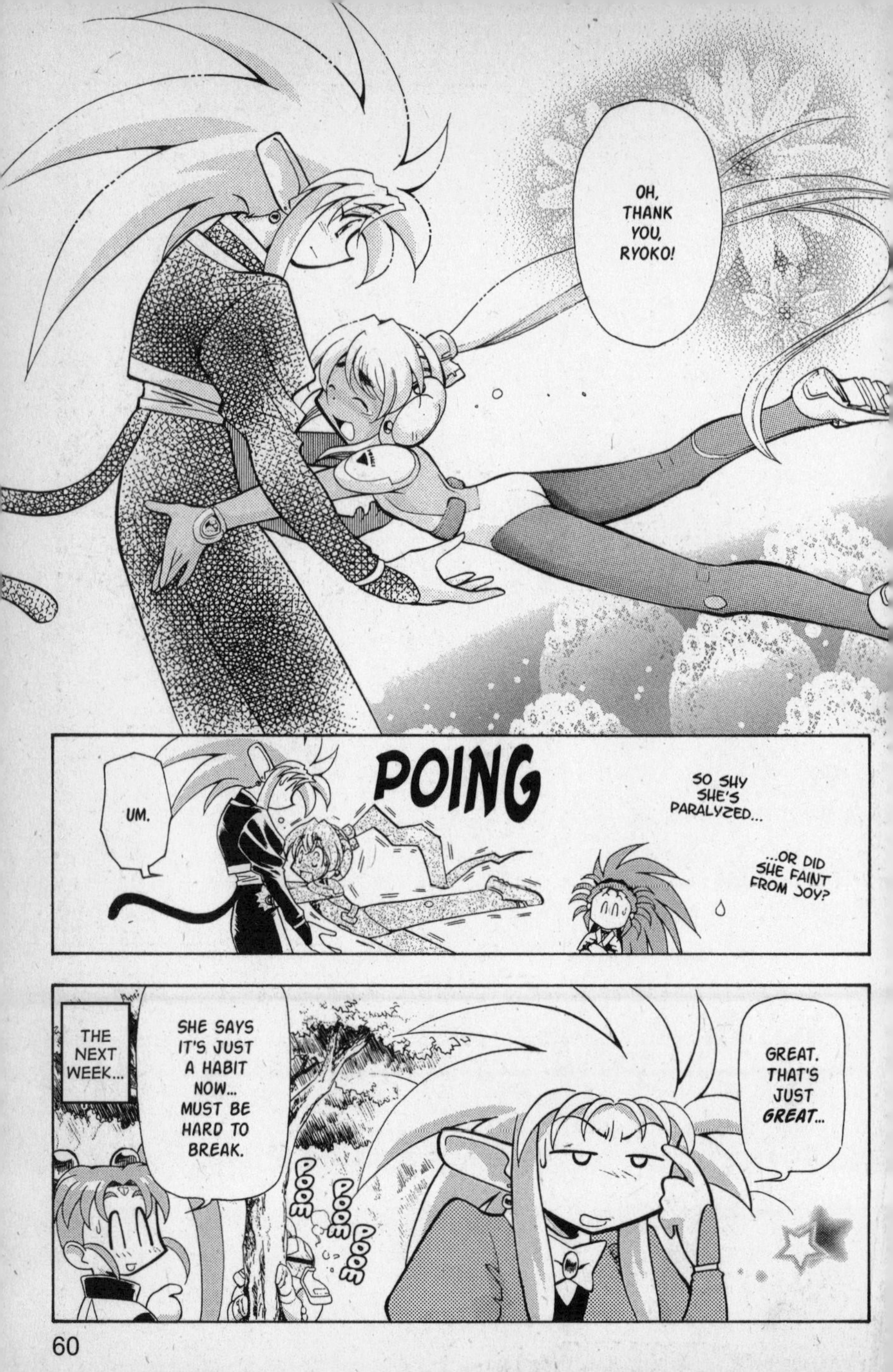
OH, THANK YOU, RYOKO!
UM.
POING
SO SHY SHE'S PARALYZED...
...OR DID SHE FAINT FROM JOY?
THE NEXT WEEK...
SHE SAYS IT'S JUST A HABIT NOW... MUST BE HARD TO BREAK.
POOF POOF
POOF POOF
GREAT. THAT'S JUST **GREAT**...

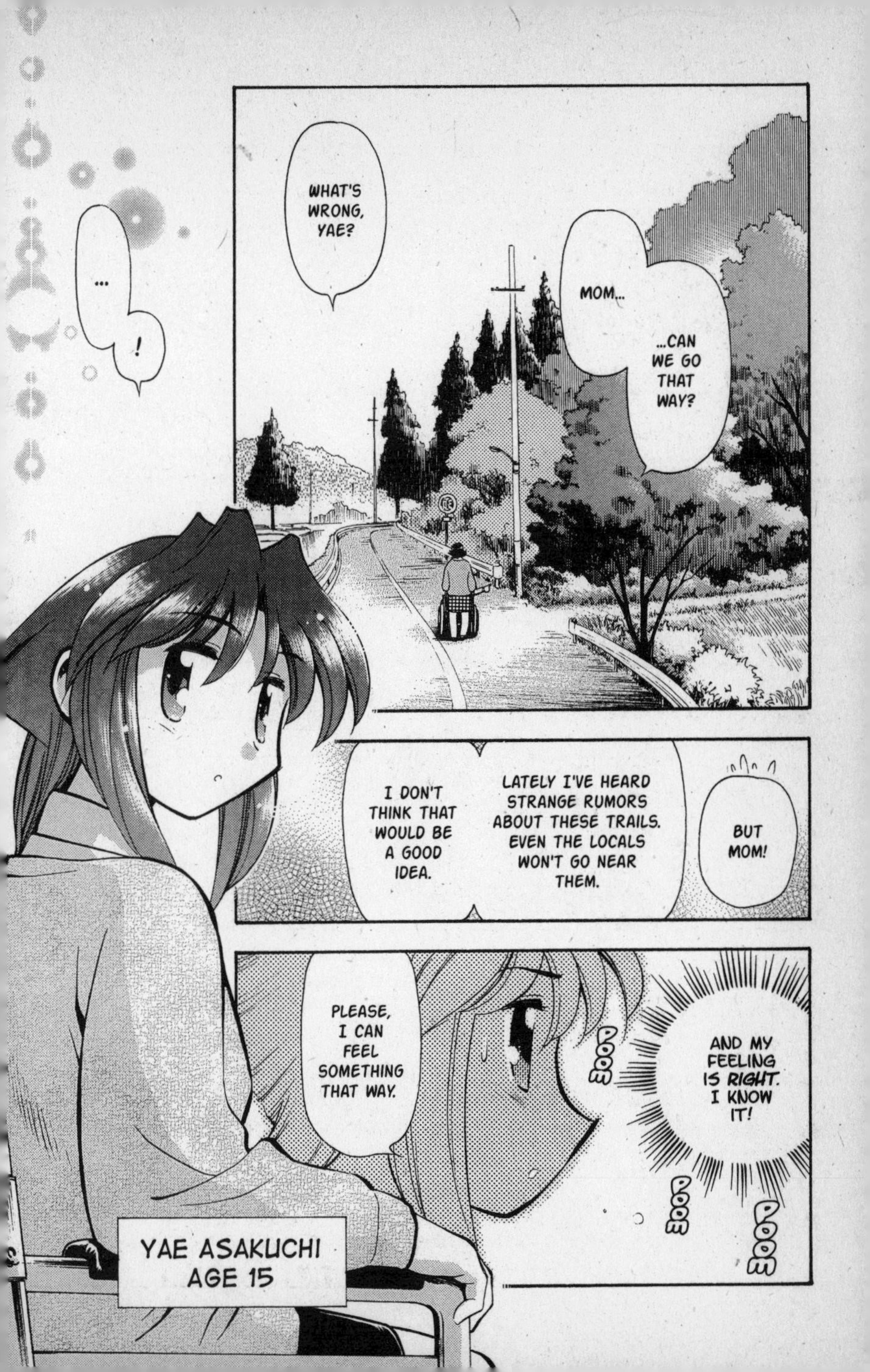
...
!
WHAT'S WRONG, YAE?
MOM...
...CAN WE GO THAT WAY?
I DON'T THINK THAT WOULD BE A GOOD IDEA.
LATELY I'VE HEARD STRANGE RUMORS ABOUT THESE TRAILS. EVEN THE LOCALS WON'T GO NEAR THEM.
BUT MOM!
PLEASE, I CAN FEEL SOMETHING THAT WAY.
DOOM
AND MY FEELING IS RIGHT. I KNOW IT!
DOOM
DOOM
YAE ASAKUCHI
AGE 15

Chapter 3: Shackles

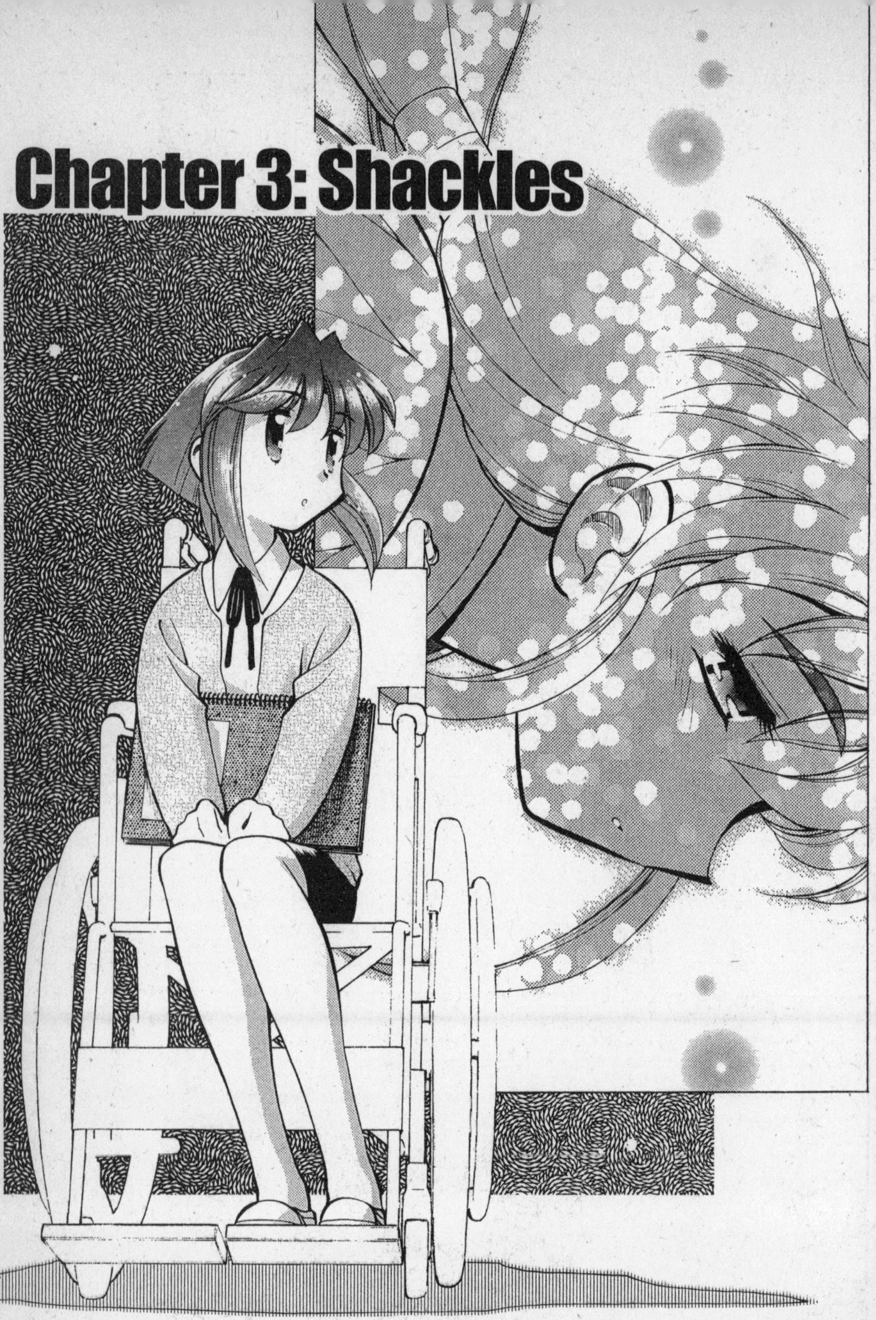

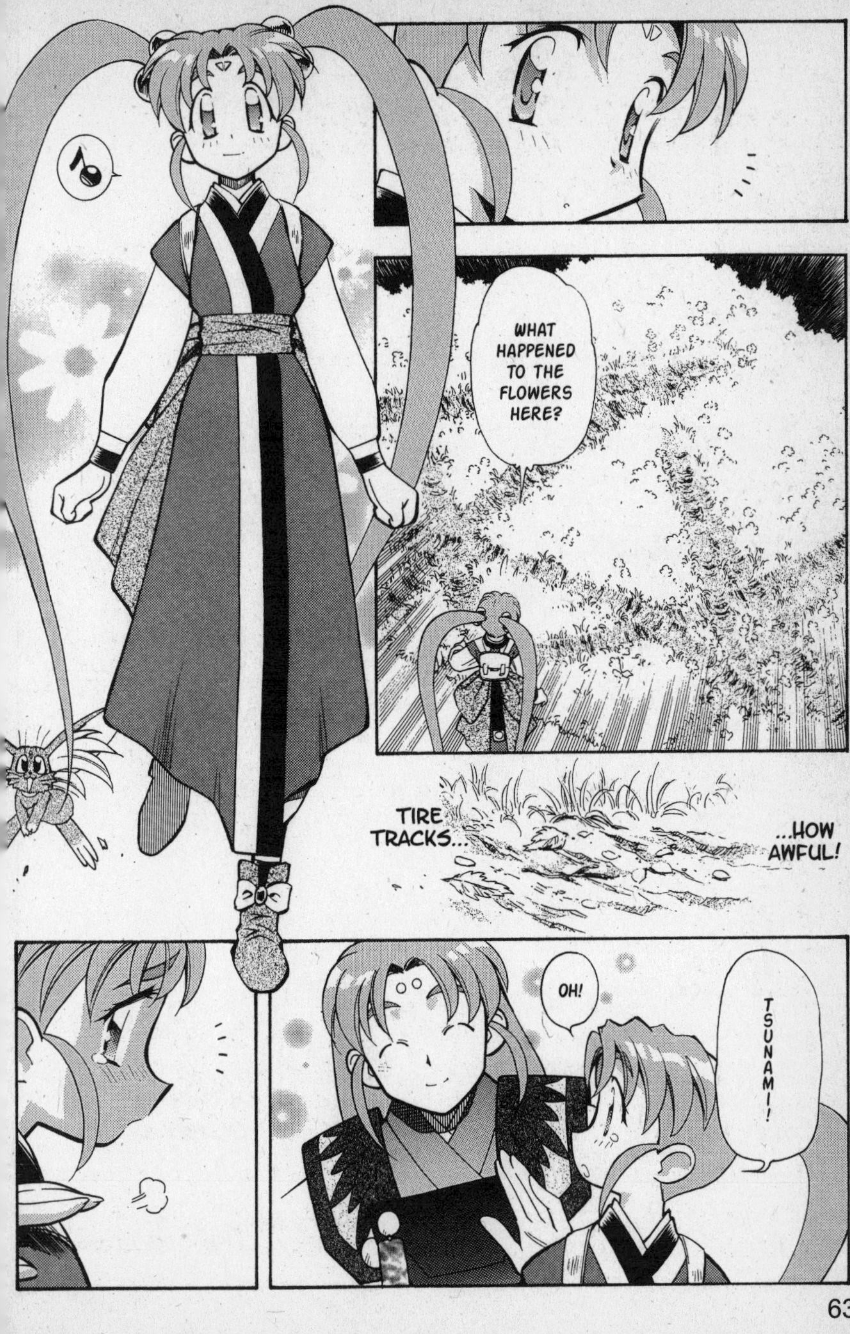
WHAT HAPPENED TO THE FLOWERS HERE?
TIRE TRACKS...
...HOW AWFUL!
OH!
TSUNAMI!

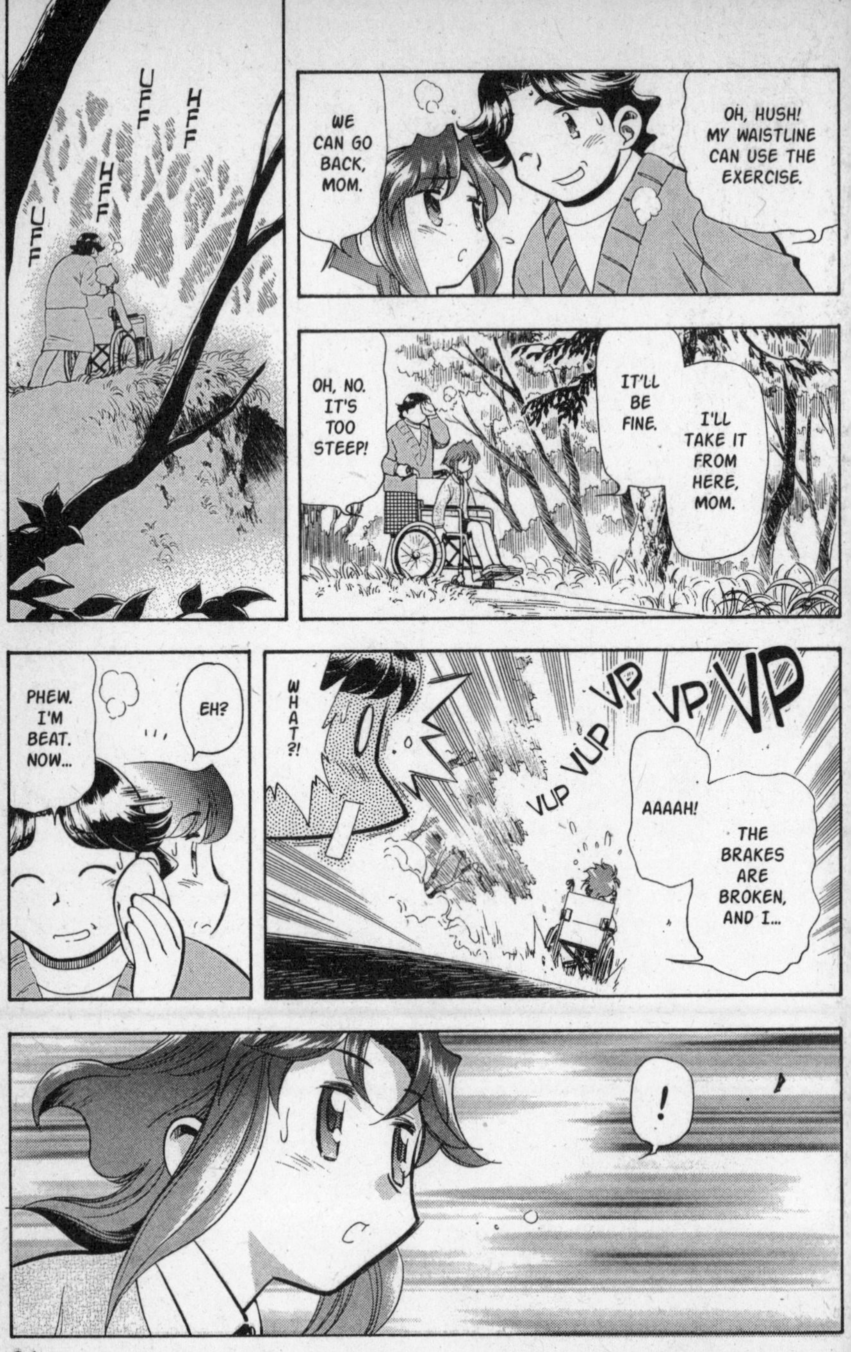
UFF
HFF
UFF
HFF
WE CAN GO BACK, MOM.
OH, HUSH! MY WAISTLINE CAN USE THE EXERCISE.
OH, NO. IT'S TOO STEEP!
IT'LL BE FINE.
I'LL TAKE IT FROM HERE, MOM.
PHEW. I'M BEAT. NOW...
EH?
WHAT?!
VUP
VUP
VUP
VP
VP
VP
AAAAH!
THE BRAKES ARE BROKEN, AND I...
!

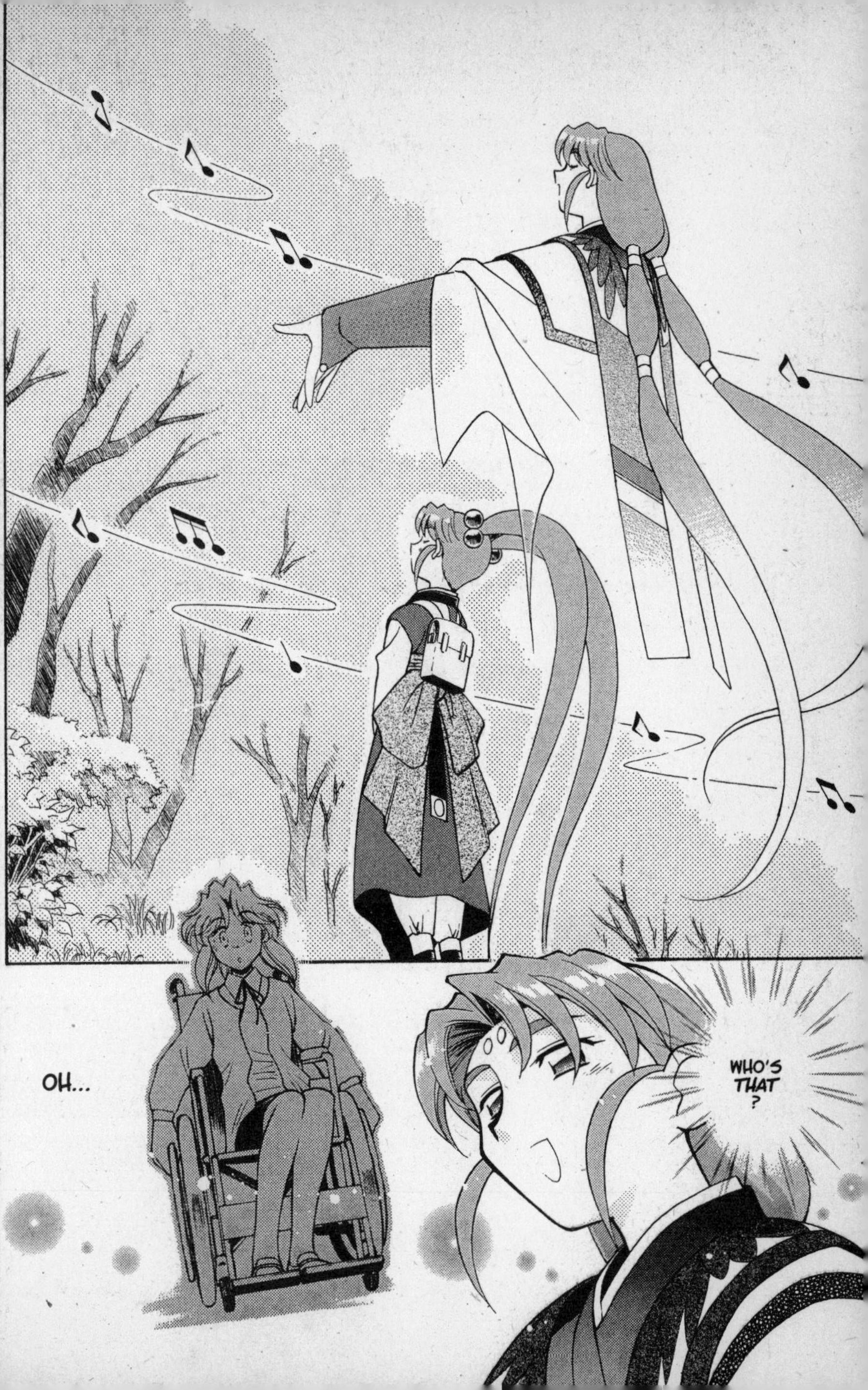
OH...
WHO'S THAT ?

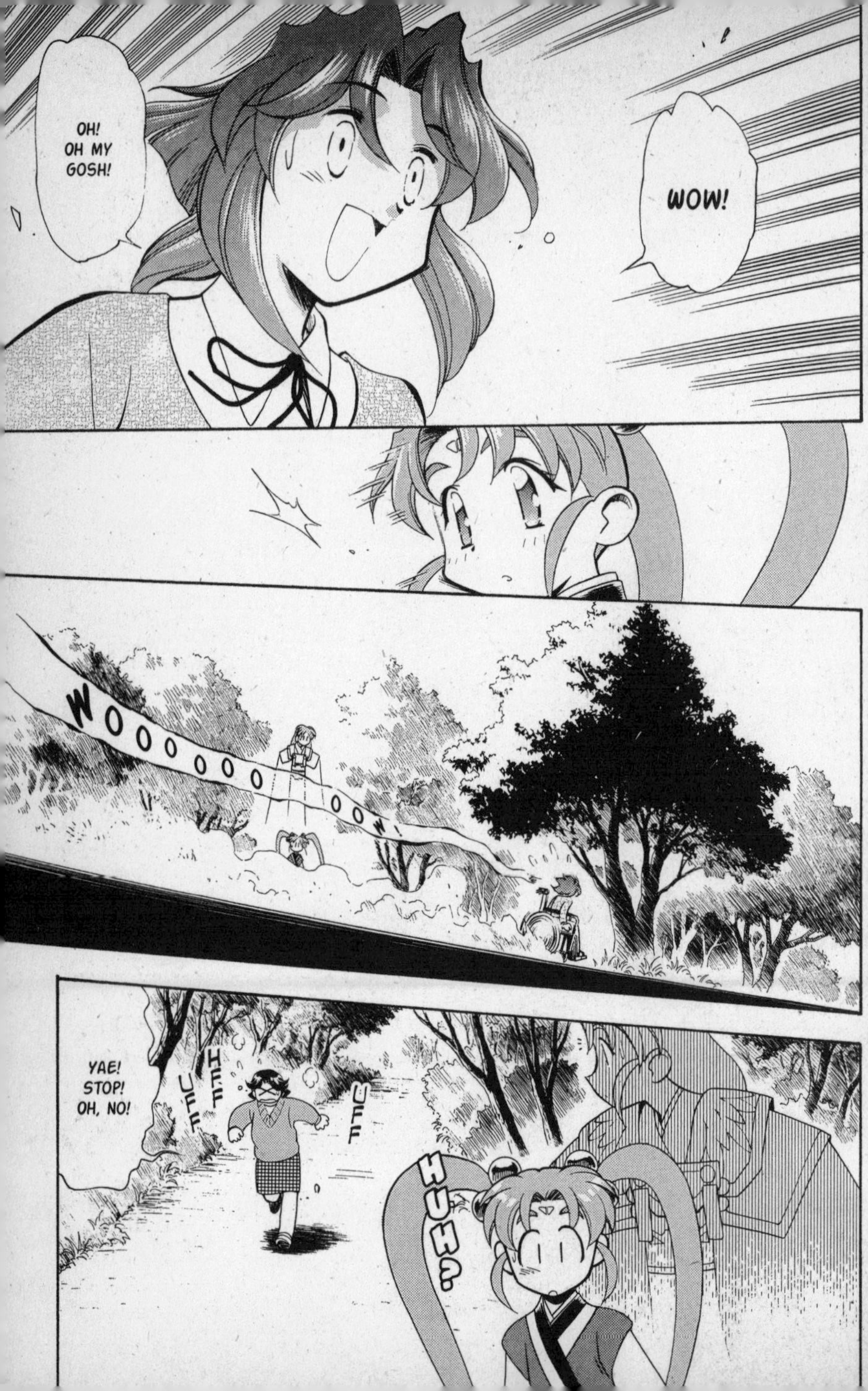
OH! OH MY GOSH!
WOW!
WOOOOOOOOOW!
YAE! STOP! OH, NO!
UFF
HFF
UFF
HUH?

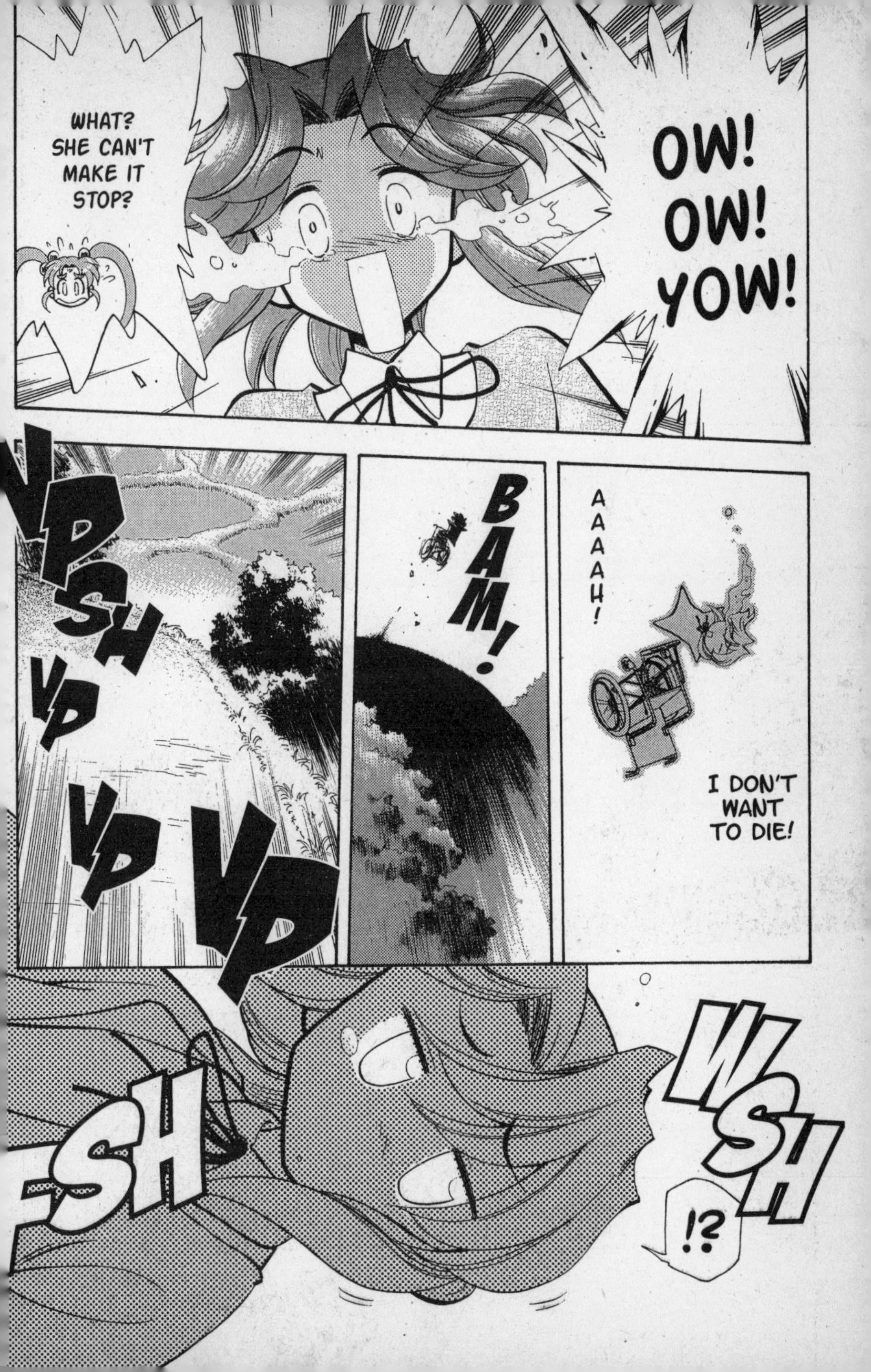
WHAT? SHE CAN'T MAKE IT STOP?
OW! OW! YOW!
VPSH
VP
VP
VP
BAM!
AAAAAH!
I DON'T WANT TO DIE!
SH
WSH
!?

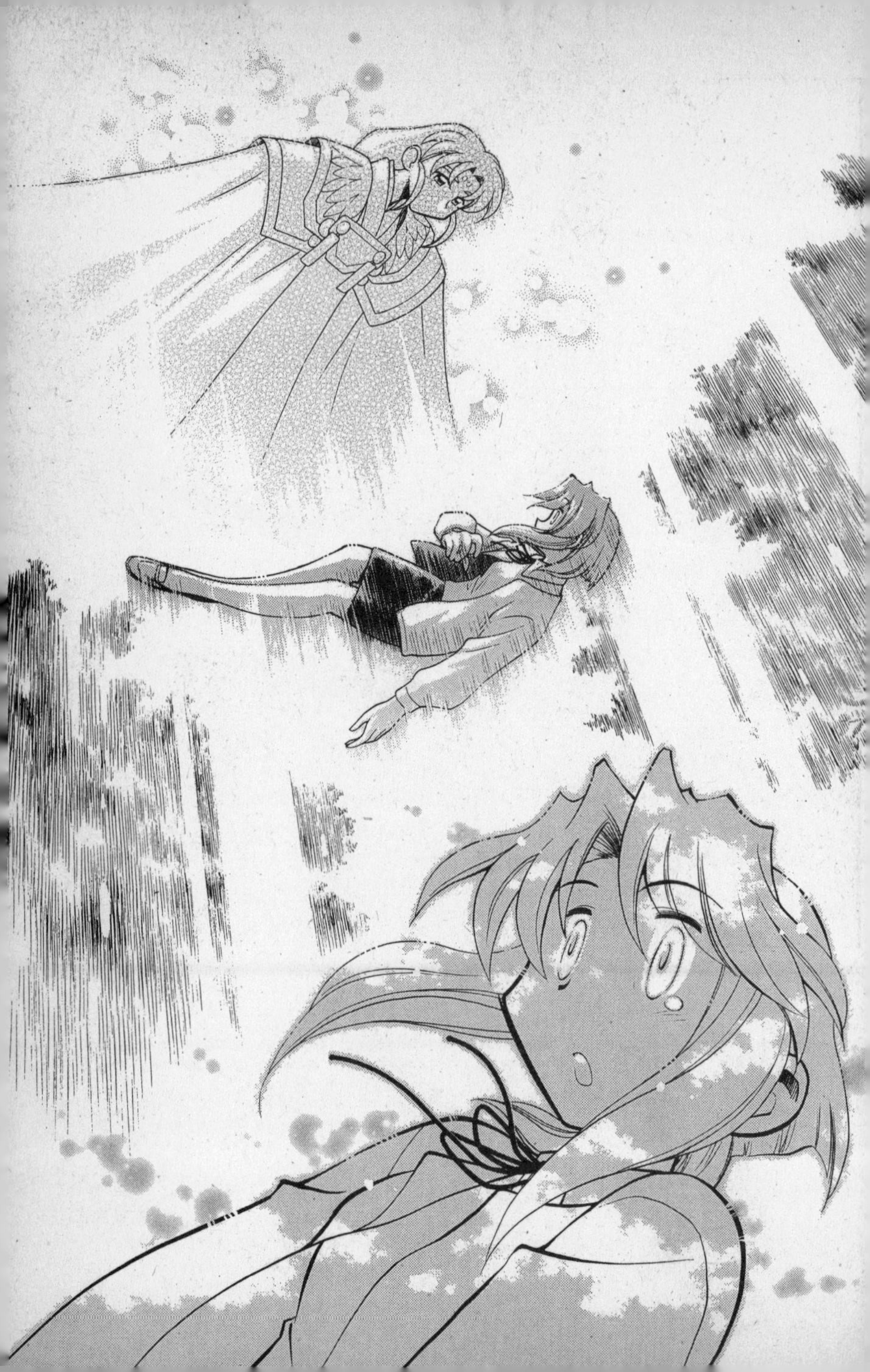

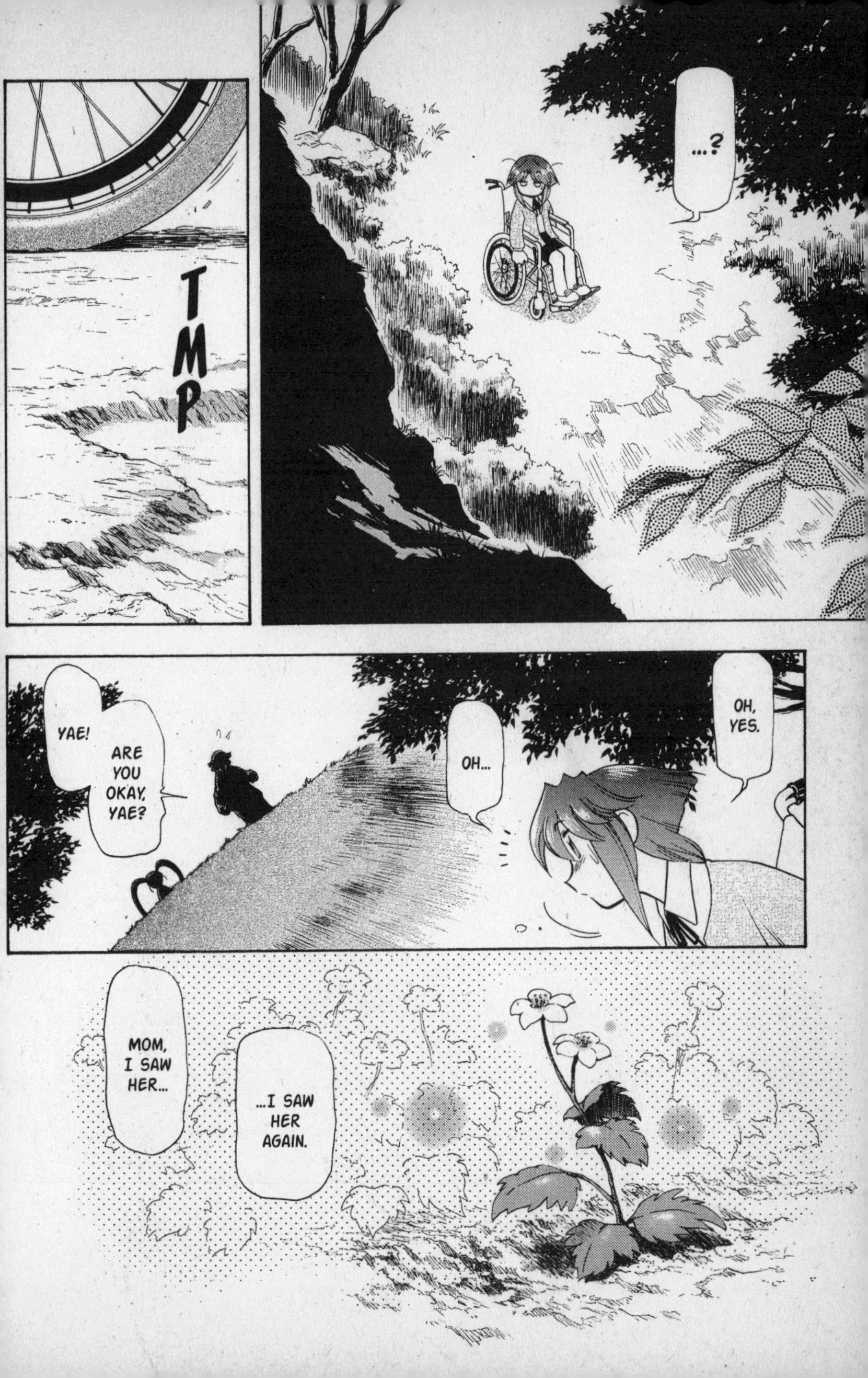
TMP
...?
YAE!
ARE YOU OKAY, YAE?
OH...
OH, YES.
MOM, I SAW HER...
...I SAW HER AGAIN.

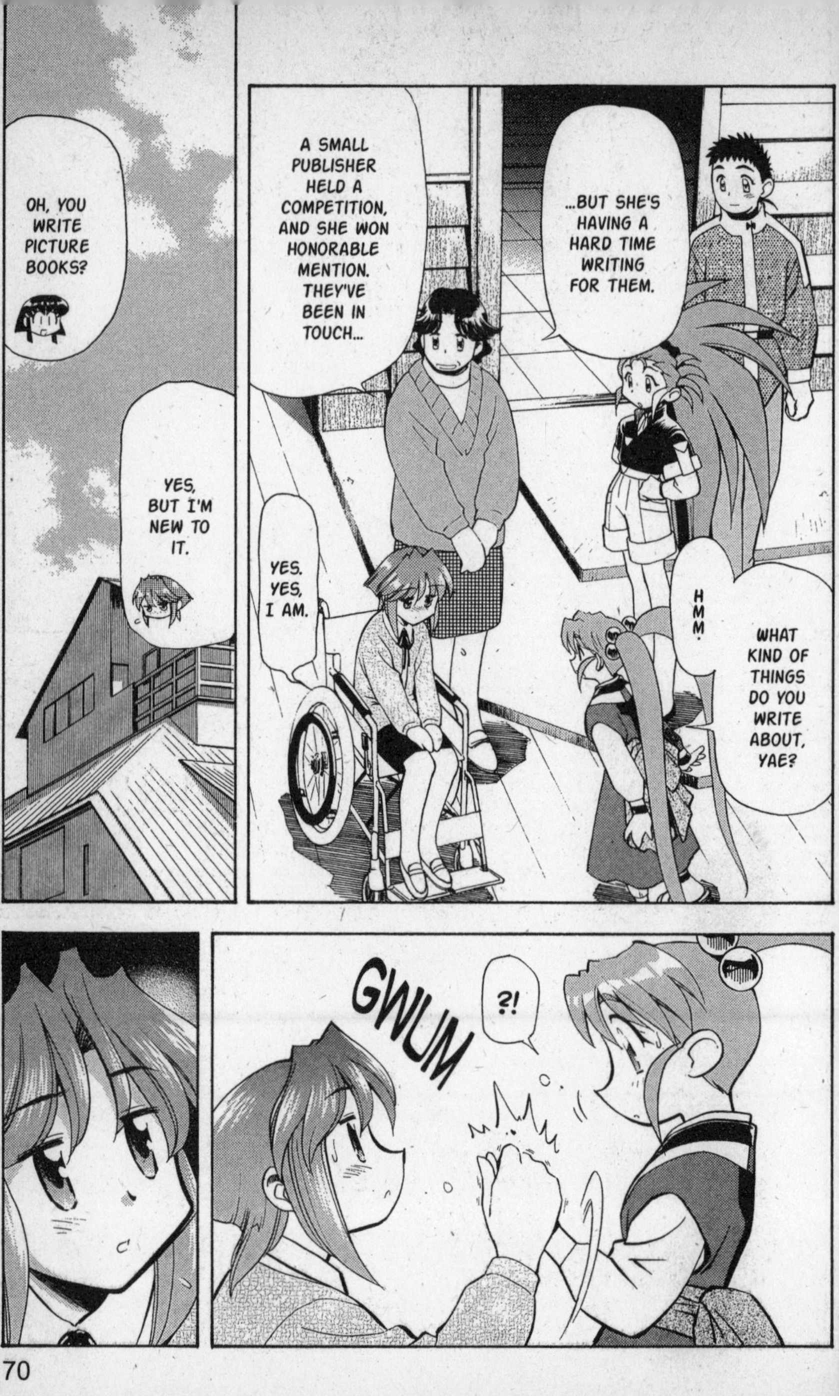
OH, YOU WRITE PICTURE BOOKS?
YES, BUT I'M NEW TO IT.
A SMALL PUBLISHER HELD A COMPETITION, AND SHE WON HONORABLE MENTION. THEY'VE BEEN IN TOUCH...
...BUT SHE'S HAVING A HARD TIME WRITING FOR THEM.
YES. YES, I AM.
HMM.
WHAT KIND OF THINGS DO YOU WRITE ABOUT, YAE?
GWUM
?!

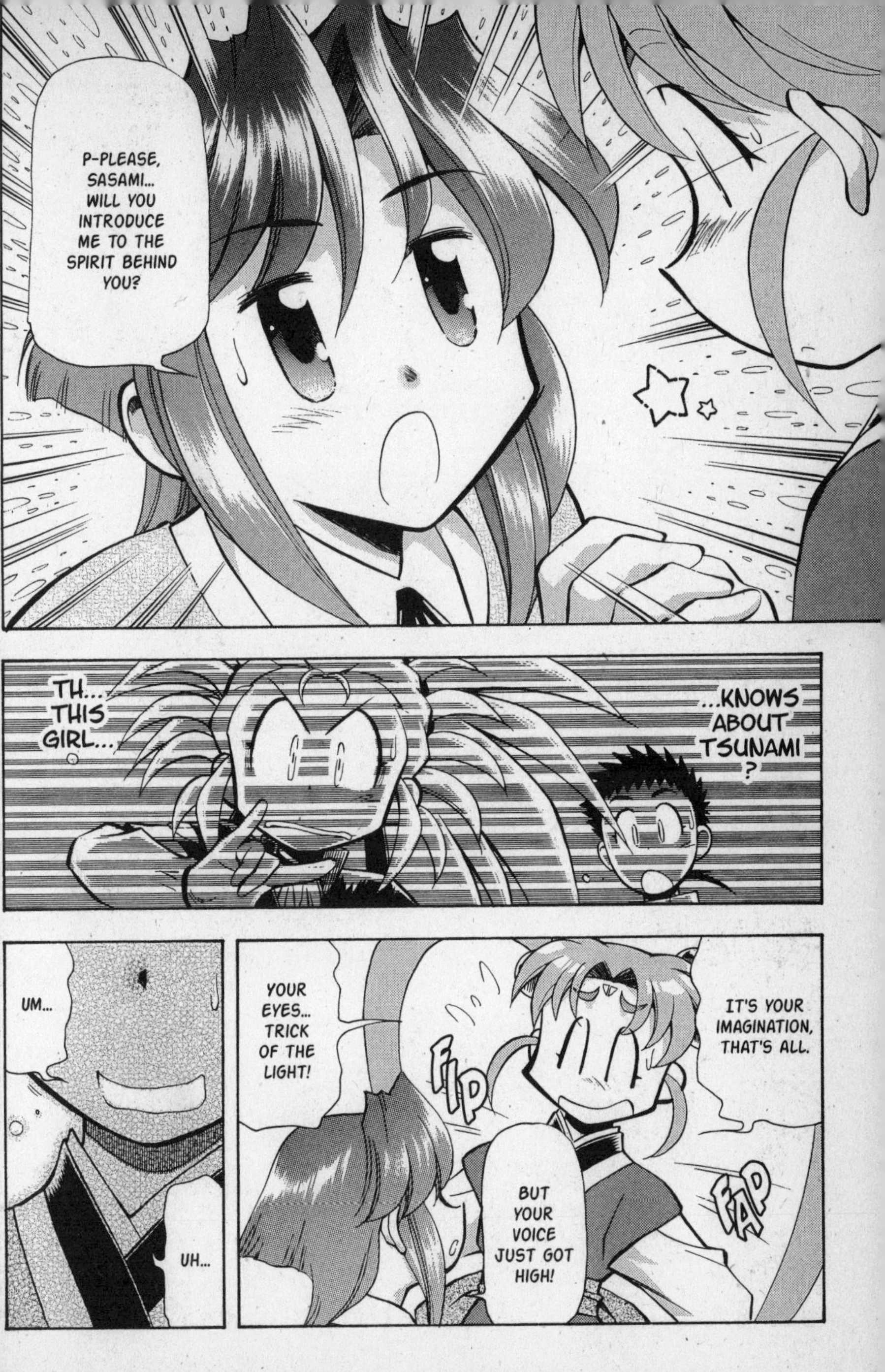
P-PLEASE, SASAMI... WILL YOU INTRODUCE ME TO THE SPIRIT BEHIND YOU?
TH... THIS GIRL...
...KNOWS ABOUT TSUNAMI?
UM...
UH...
YOUR EYES... TRICK OF THE LIGHT!
FIP
IT'S YOUR IMAGINATION, THAT'S ALL.
BUT YOUR VOICE JUST GOT HIGH!
FAP

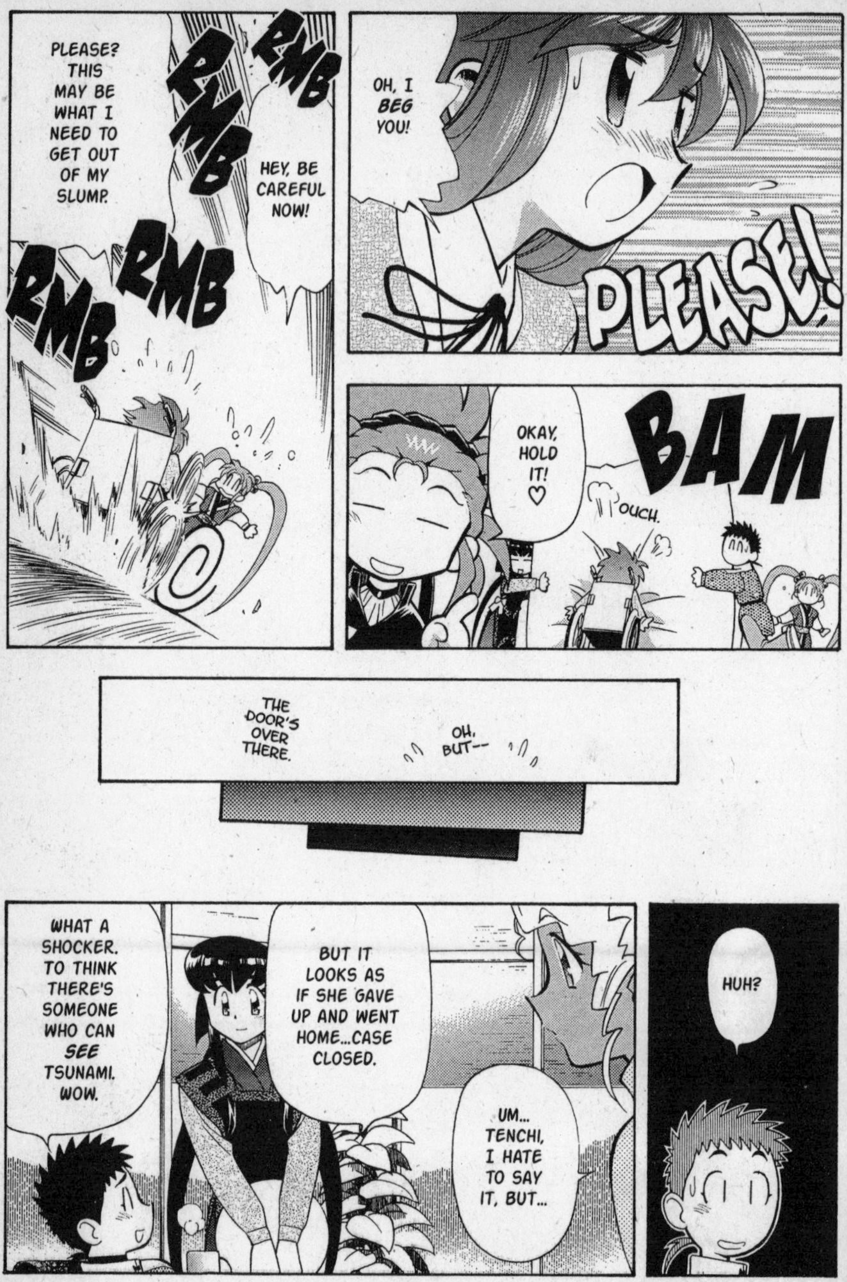

PLEASE? THIS MAY BE WHAT I NEED TO GET OUT OF MY SLUMP.
RMB RMB RMB
HEY, BE CAREFUL NOW!
RMB RMB RMB
OH, I *BEG* YOU!
PLEASE!
OKAY, HOLD IT! ♡
BAM
OUCH.
THE DOOR'S OVER THERE.
OH, BUT--
WHAT A SHOCKER. TO THINK THERE'S SOMEONE WHO CAN *SEE* TSUNAMI. WOW.
BUT IT LOOKS AS IF SHE GAVE UP AND WENT HOME...CASE CLOSED.
UM... TENCHI, I HATE TO SAY IT, BUT...
HUH?

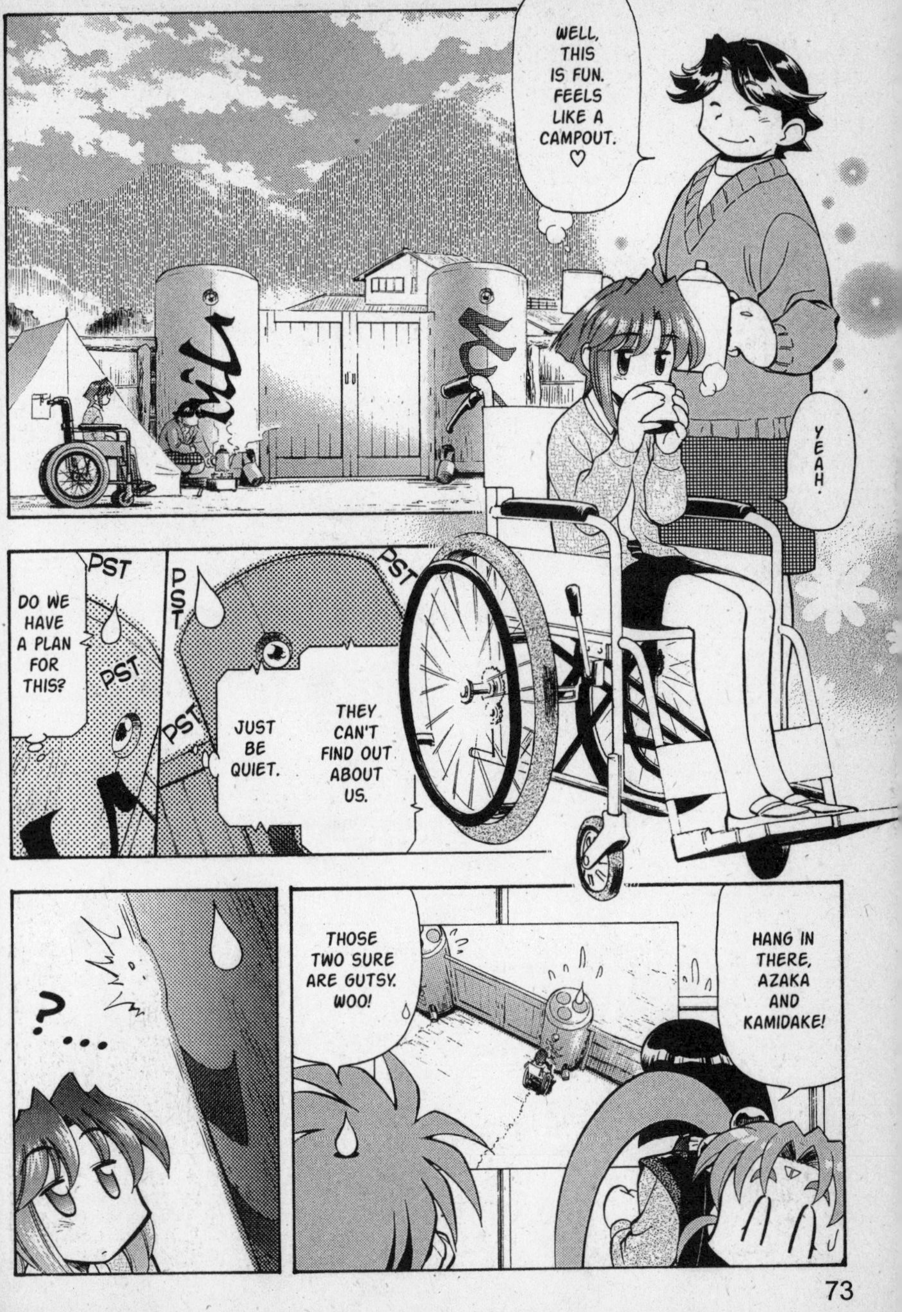
WELL, THIS IS FUN. FEELS LIKE A CAMPOUT. ♡
YEAH.
PST
PST
PST
PST
THEY CAN'T FIND OUT ABOUT US.
JUST BE QUIET.
DO WE HAVE A PLAN FOR THIS?
HANG IN THERE, AZAKA AND KAMIDAKE!
THOSE TWO SURE ARE GUTSY. WOO!
?...

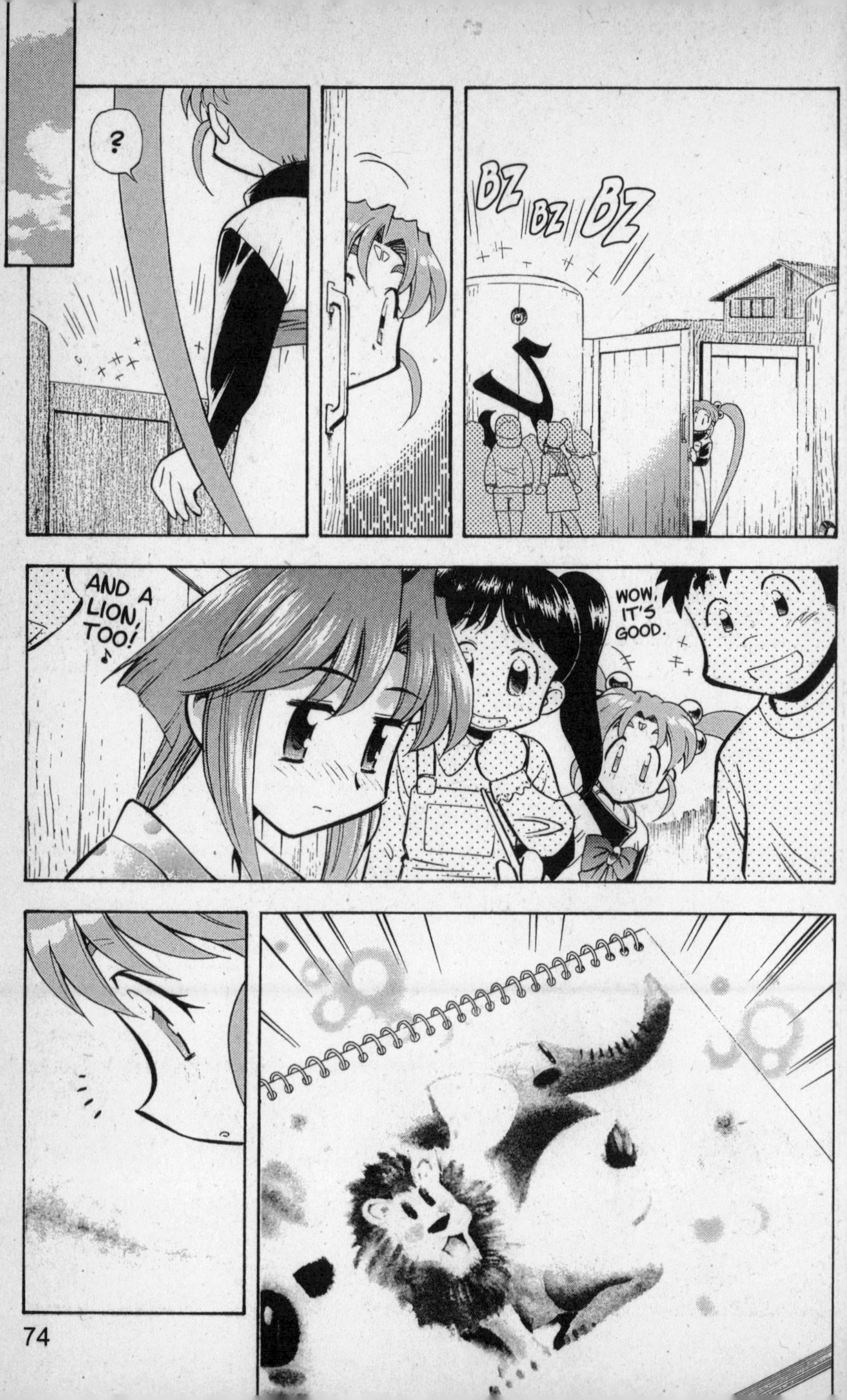
?
BZ BZ BZ
AND A LION, TOO! ♪
WOW, IT'S GOOD.

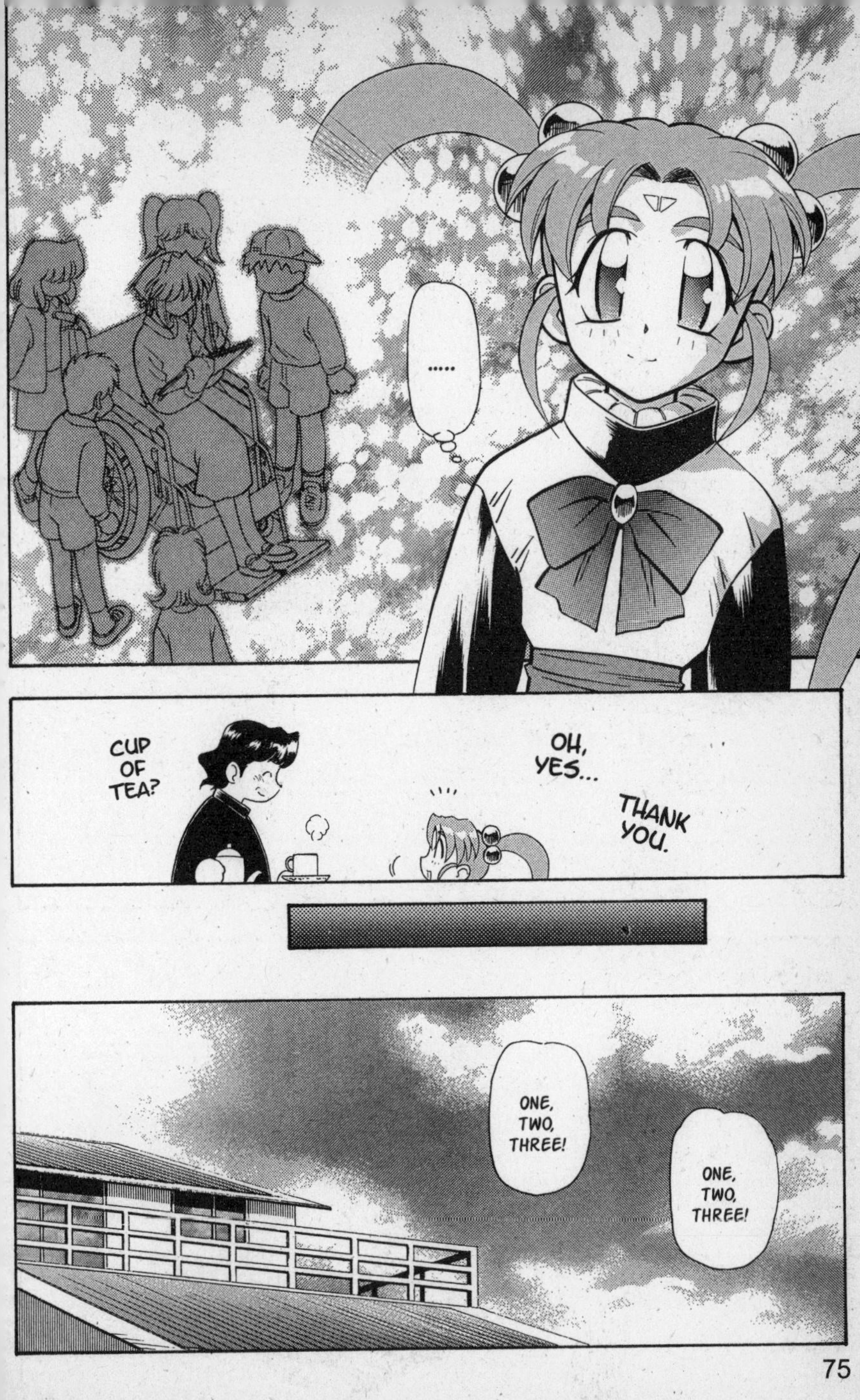
......
CUP OF TEA?
OH, YES...
THANK YOU.
ONE, TWO, THREE!
ONE, TWO, THREE!

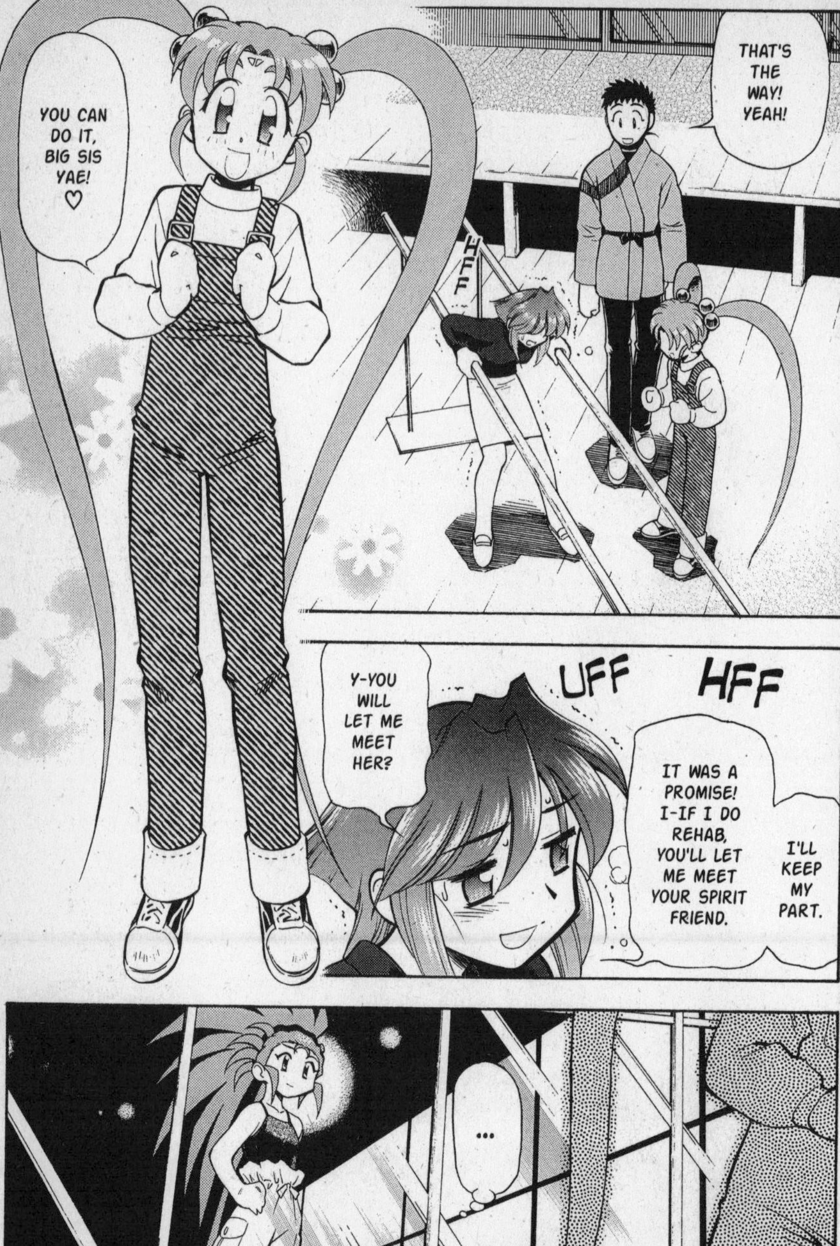
YOU CAN DO IT, BIG SIS YAE! ♡
THAT'S THE WAY! YEAH!
HFF
Y-YOU WILL LET ME MEET HER?
UFF
HFF
IT WAS A PROMISE! I-IF I DO REHAB, YOU'LL LET ME MEET YOUR SPIRIT FRIEND.
I'LL KEEP MY PART.
...

SHE WAS A WITHDRAWN CHILD TO BEGIN WITH. BETWEEN THAT AND HER SPIRITUAL BENT, SHE WAS PICKED ON FROM A TENDER AGE.

THEN THE ACCIDENT WITH HER FATHER LEFT HER PARALYZED FROM THE WAIST DOWN.

SHE HID HERSELF AWAY FOR A GOOD TWO YEARS, REFUSING TO GO TO SCHOOL.

BUT SINCE WINNING THE PRIZE IN THAT CONTEST I MADE HER ENTER, HER ATTITUDE SEEMS TO BE IMPROVING. IN BITS AND PIECES.

WHAT? OH, YES... I HAVE FAITH IN WHAT SHE SAYS.

I CAN'T SEE THIS SPIRIT, BUT YAE CAN. NO QUESTION.

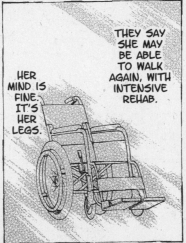

HER MIND IS FINE. IT'S HER LEGS.

THEY SAY SHE MAY BE ABLE TO WALK AGAIN, WITH INTENSIVE REHAB.

THAT'S WHY I'D LIKE TO ASK YOU A FAVOR...

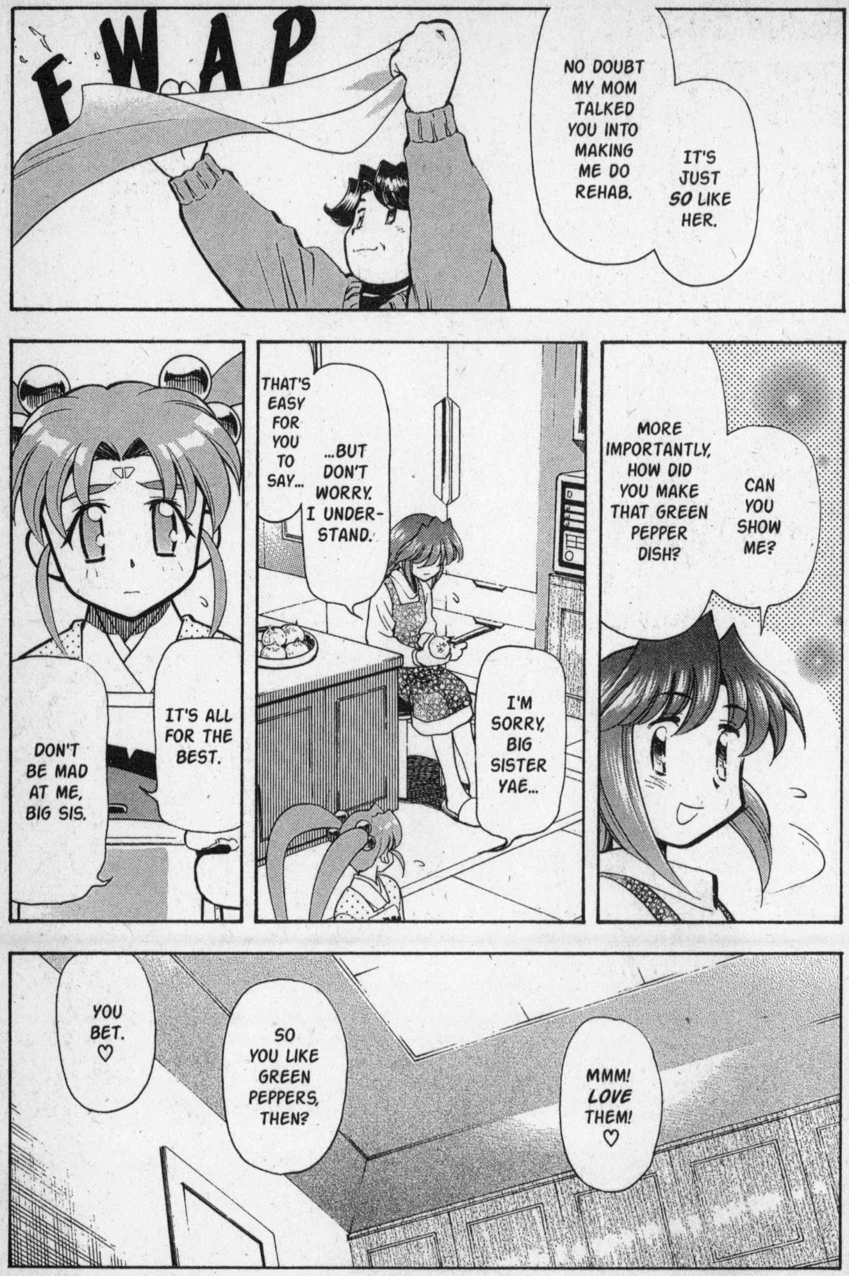
FWAP
NO DOUBT MY MOM TALKED YOU INTO MAKING ME DO REHAB.
IT'S JUST *SO* LIKE HER.
DON'T BE MAD AT ME, BIG SIS.
IT'S ALL FOR THE BEST.
THAT'S EASY FOR YOU TO SAY...
...BUT DON'T WORRY. I UNDERSTAND.
I'M SORRY, BIG SISTER YAE...
MORE IMPORTANTLY, HOW DID YOU MAKE THAT GREEN PEPPER DISH?
CAN YOU SHOW ME?
YOU BET. ♡
SO YOU LIKE GREEN PEPPERS, THEN?
MMM! *LOVE* THEM! ♡

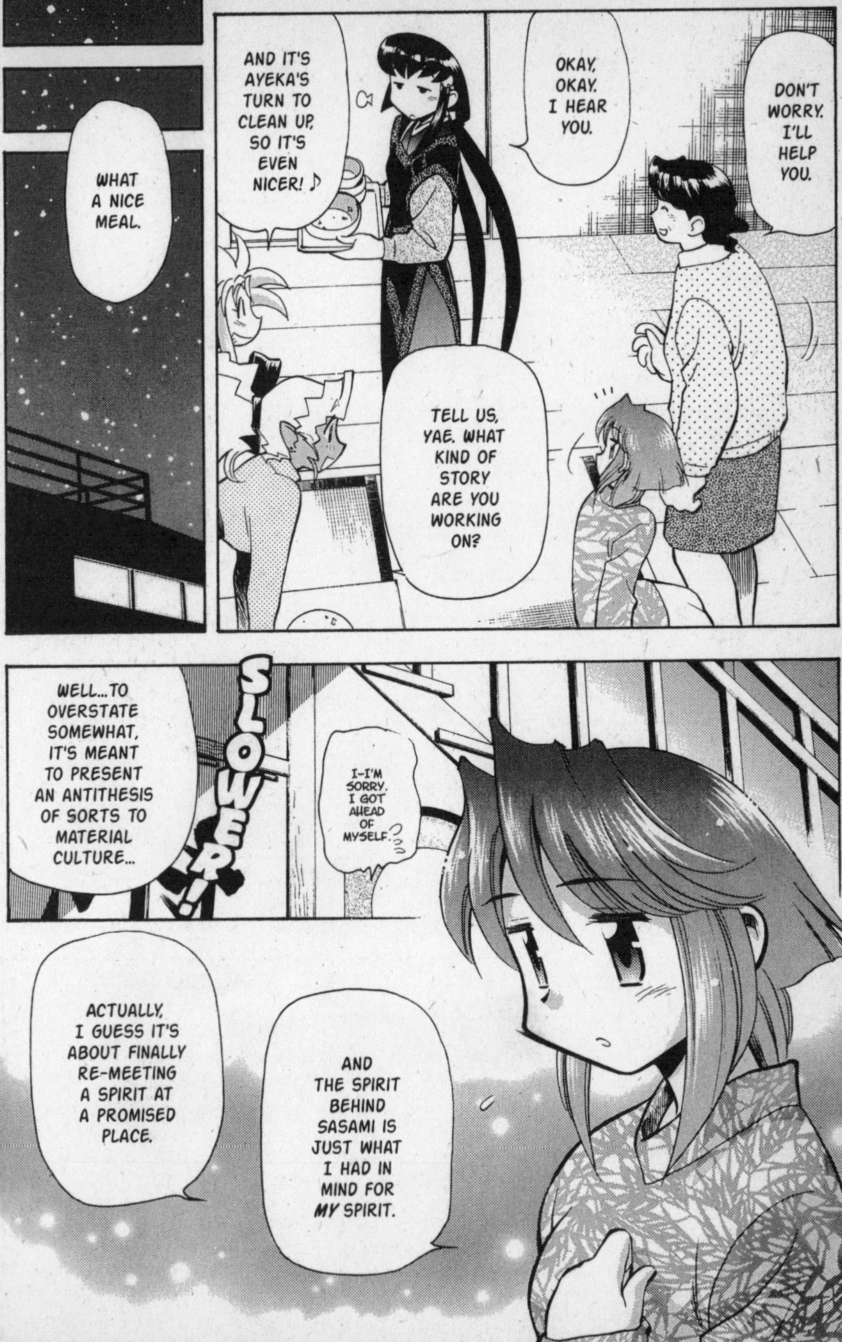
WHAT A NICE MEAL.
AND IT'S AYEKA'S TURN TO CLEAN UP, SO IT'S EVEN NICER! ♪
OKAY, OKAY. I HEAR YOU.
DON'T WORRY. I'LL HELP YOU.
TELL US, YAE. WHAT KIND OF STORY ARE YOU WORKING ON?
WELL...TO OVERSTATE SOMEWHAT, IT'S MEANT TO PRESENT AN ANTITHESIS OF SORTS TO MATERIAL CULTURE...
SLOWER!
I-I'M SORRY. I GOT AHEAD OF MYSELF.
ACTUALLY, I GUESS IT'S ABOUT FINALLY RE-MEETING A SPIRIT AT A PROMISED PLACE.
AND THE SPIRIT BEHIND SASAMI IS JUST WHAT I HAD IN MIND FOR *MY* SPIRIT.

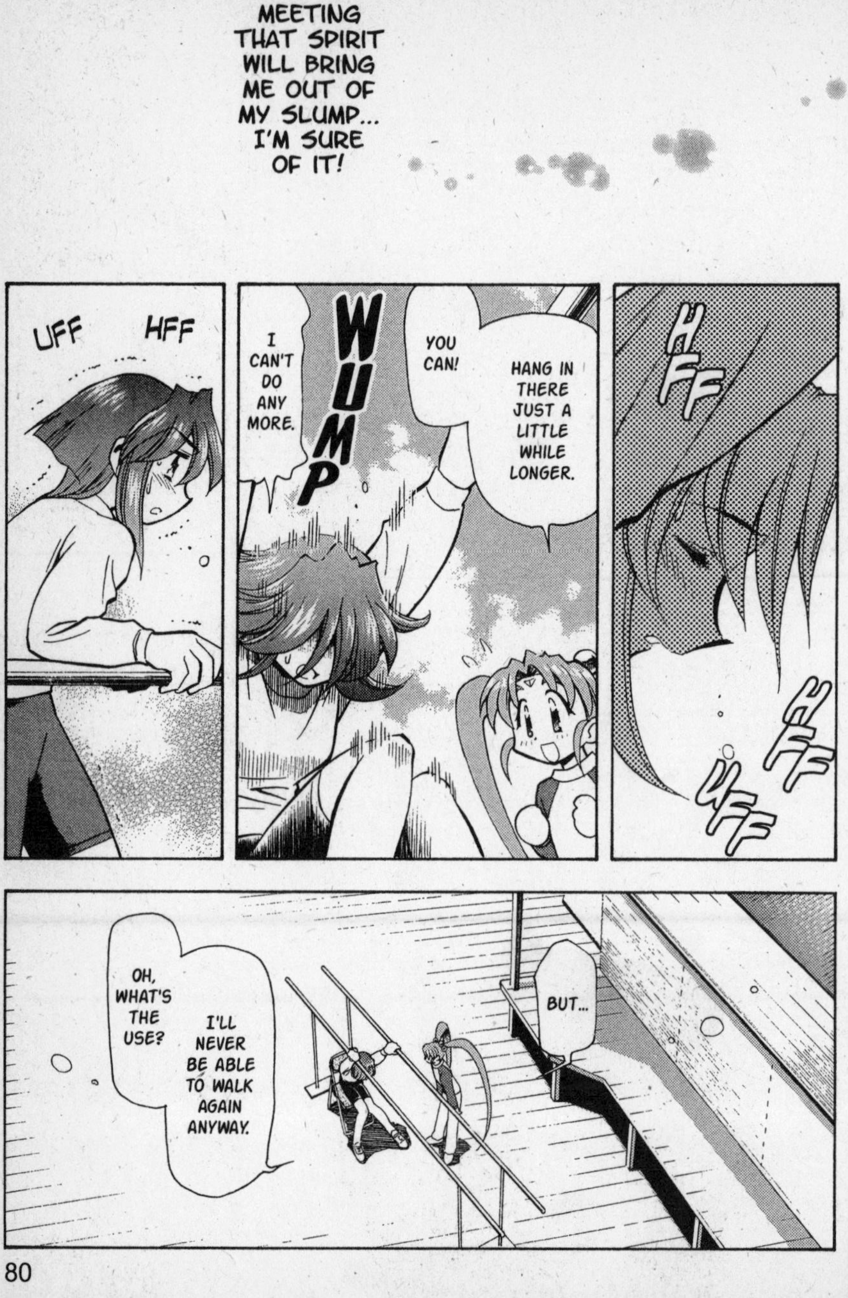
MEETING THAT SPIRIT WILL BRING ME OUT OF MY SLUMP... I'M SURE OF IT!
UFF
HFF
I CAN'T DO ANY MORE.
WUMP
YOU CAN!
HANG IN THERE JUST A LITTLE WHILE LONGER.
HFF
HFF
UFF
OH, WHAT'S THE USE?
I'LL NEVER BE ABLE TO WALK AGAIN ANYWAY.
BUT...

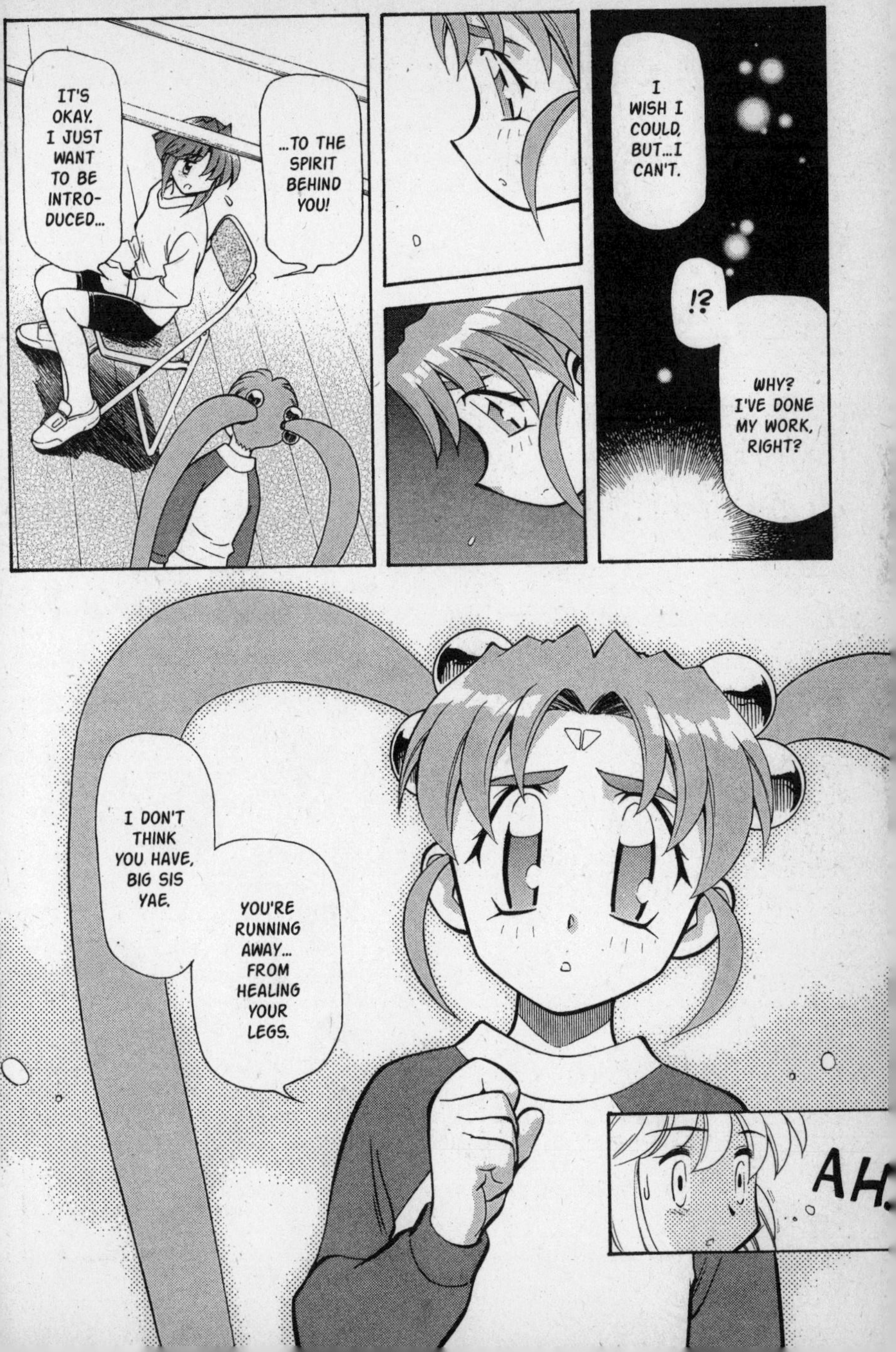
IT'S OKAY. I JUST WANT TO BE INTRO-DUCED...
...TO THE SPIRIT BEHIND YOU!
I WISH I COULD, BUT...I CAN'T.
!?
WHY? I'VE DONE MY WORK, RIGHT?
I DON'T THINK YOU HAVE, BIG SIS YAE.
YOU'RE RUNNING AWAY... FROM HEALING YOUR LEGS.
AH.

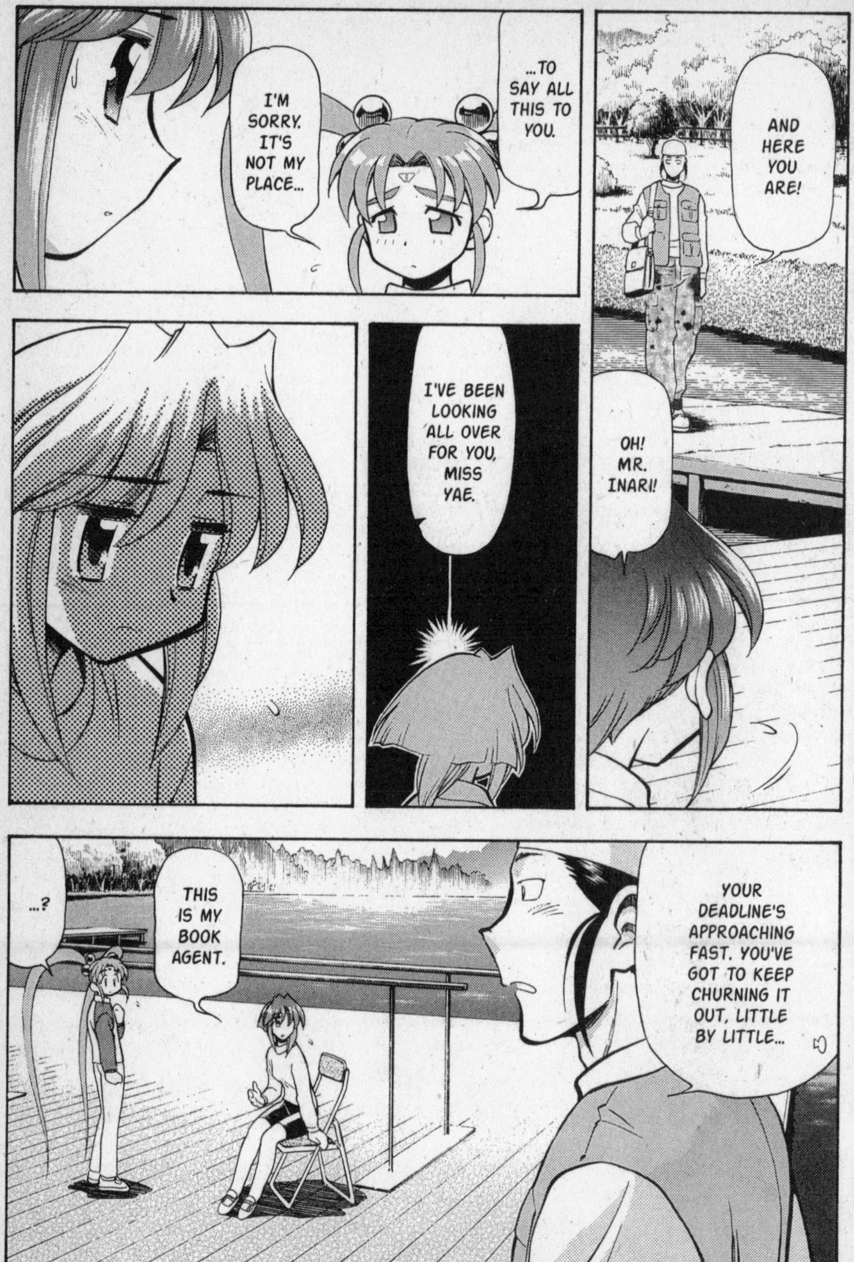
I'M SORRY. IT'S NOT MY PLACE...
...TO SAY ALL THIS TO YOU.
I'VE BEEN LOOKING ALL OVER FOR YOU, MISS YAE.
AND HERE YOU ARE!
OH! MR. INARI!
...?
THIS IS MY BOOK AGENT.
YOUR DEADLINE'S APPROACHING FAST. YOU'VE GOT TO KEEP CHURNING IT OUT, LITTLE BY LITTLE...

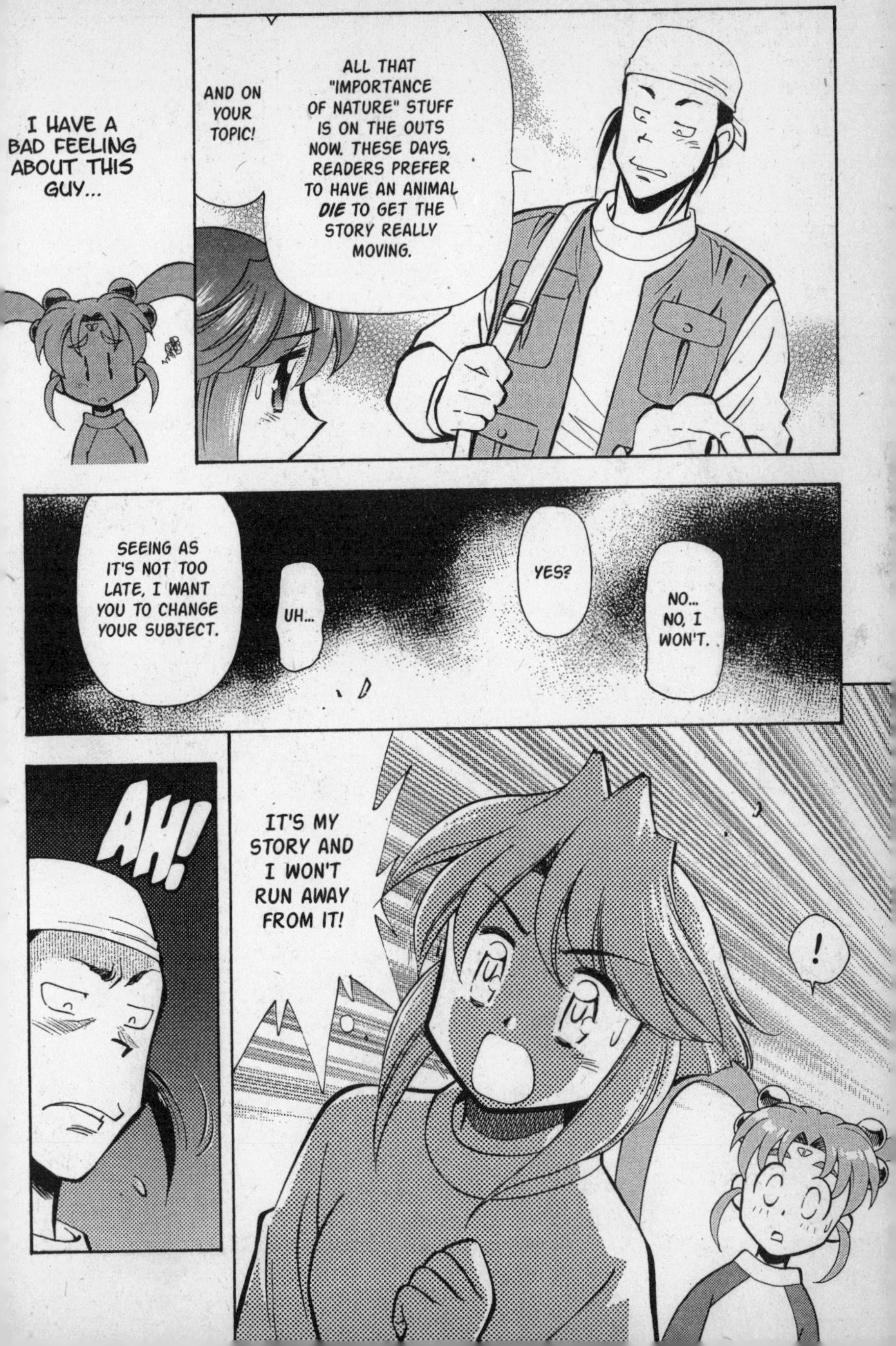
I HAVE A BAD FEELING ABOUT THIS GUY...
AND ON YOUR TOPIC!
ALL THAT "IMPORTANCE OF NATURE" STUFF IS ON THE OUTS NOW. THESE DAYS, READERS PREFER TO HAVE AN ANIMAL DIE TO GET THE STORY REALLY MOVING.
SEEING AS IT'S NOT TOO LATE, I WANT YOU TO CHANGE YOUR SUBJECT.
UH...
YES?
NO... NO, I WON'T.
AH!
IT'S MY STORY AND I WON'T RUN AWAY FROM IT!
!

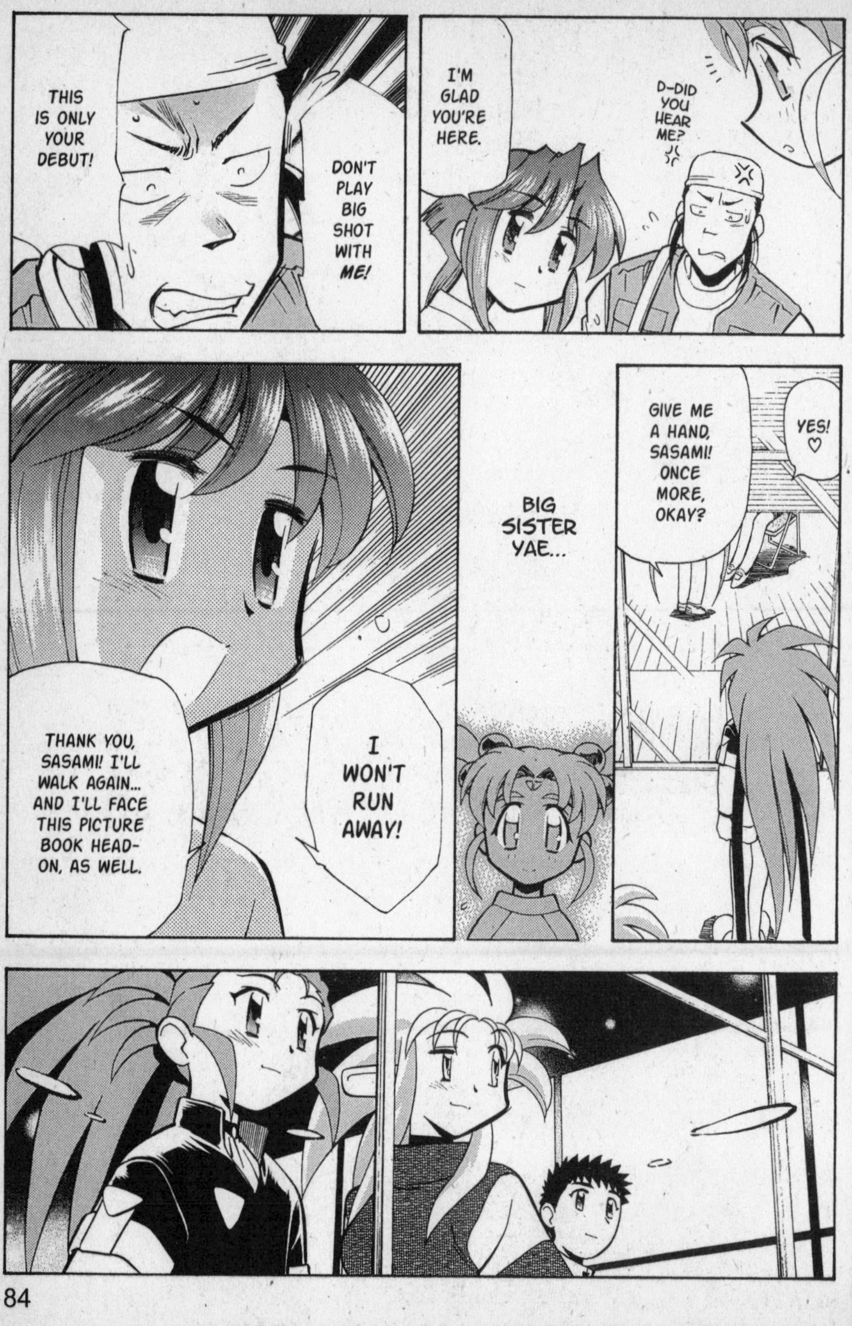
THIS IS ONLY YOUR DEBUT!
DON'T PLAY BIG SHOT WITH *ME!*
I'M GLAD YOU'RE HERE.
D-DID YOU HEAR ME?
THANK YOU, SASAMI! I'LL WALK AGAIN... AND I'LL FACE THIS PICTURE BOOK HEAD-ON, AS WELL.
I WON'T RUN AWAY!
BIG SISTER YAE...
GIVE ME A HAND, SASAMI! ONCE MORE, OKAY?
YES! ♡

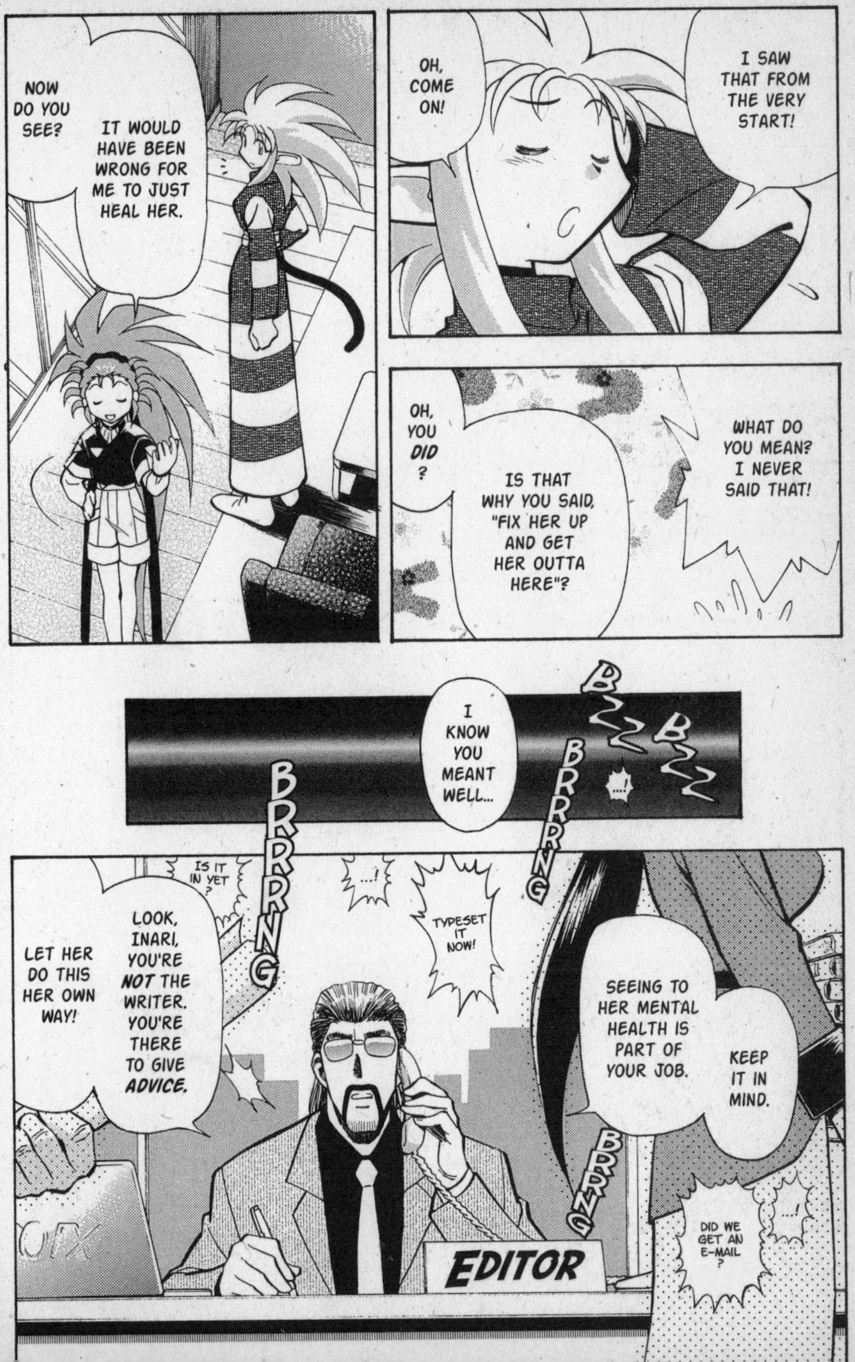
NOW DO YOU SEE?
IT WOULD HAVE BEEN WRONG FOR ME TO JUST HEAL HER.
OH, COME ON!
I SAW THAT FROM THE VERY START!
OH, YOU *DID* ?
IS THAT WHY YOU SAID, "FIX HER UP AND GET HER OUTTA HERE"?
WHAT DO YOU MEAN? I NEVER SAID THAT!
I KNOW YOU MEANT WELL...
BRRRRNG
BZZ
BRRRNG
...!
BZZ
IS IT IN YET ?
...!
TYPESET IT NOW!
LET HER DO THIS HER OWN WAY!
LOOK, INARI, YOU'RE *NOT* THE WRITER. YOU'RE THERE TO GIVE *ADVICE.*
SEEING TO HER MENTAL HEALTH IS PART OF YOUR JOB.
KEEP IT IN MIND.
BRRRNG
EDITOR
DID WE GET AN E-MAIL ?
...!

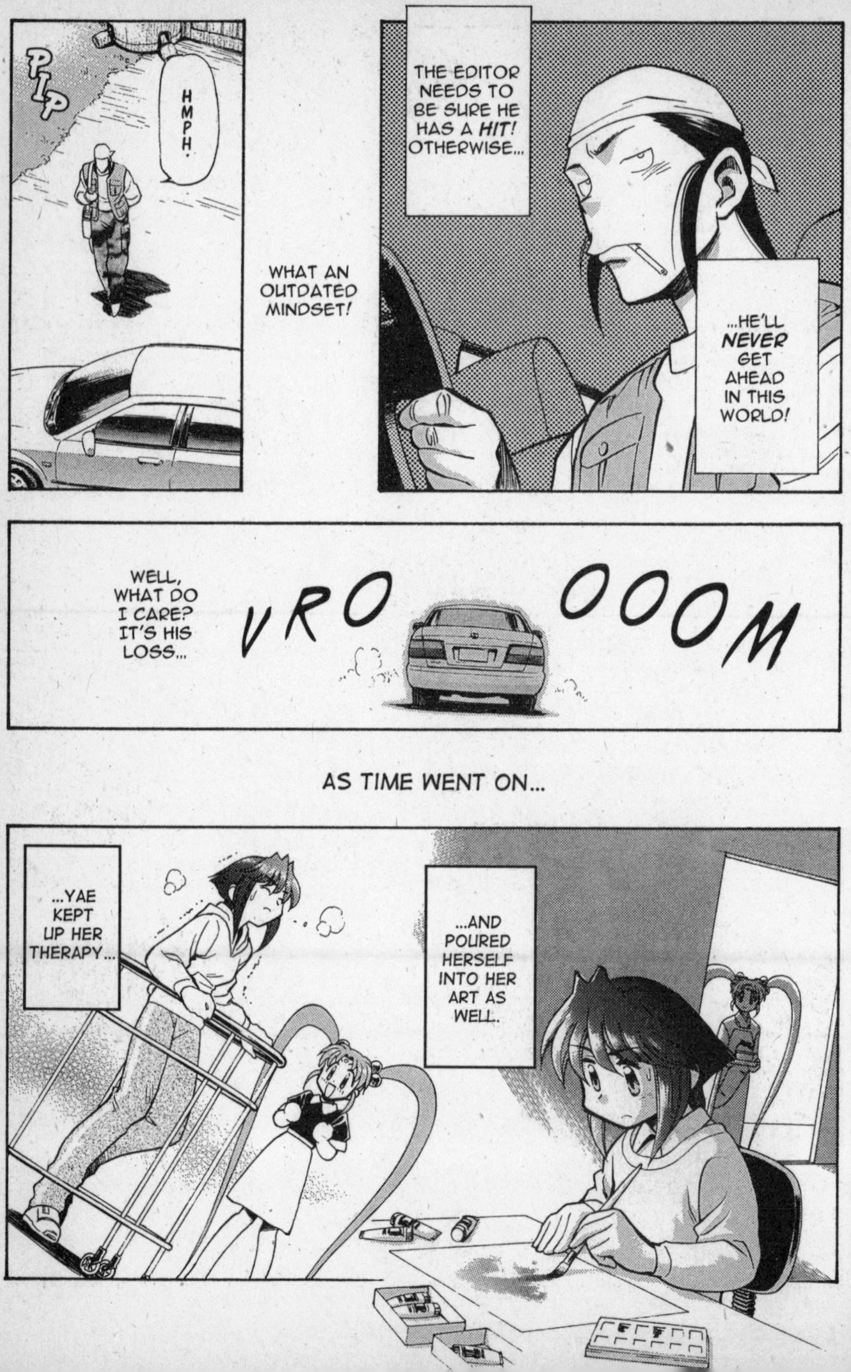
PIP
HMPH.
WHAT AN OUTDATED MINDSET!
THE EDITOR NEEDS TO BE SURE HE HAS A HIT! OTHERWISE...
...HE'LL NEVER GET AHEAD IN THIS WORLD!
WELL, WHAT DO I CARE? IT'S HIS LOSS...
VROOOOM
AS TIME WENT ON...
...YAE KEPT UP HER THERAPY...
...AND POURED HERSELF INTO HER ART AS WELL.

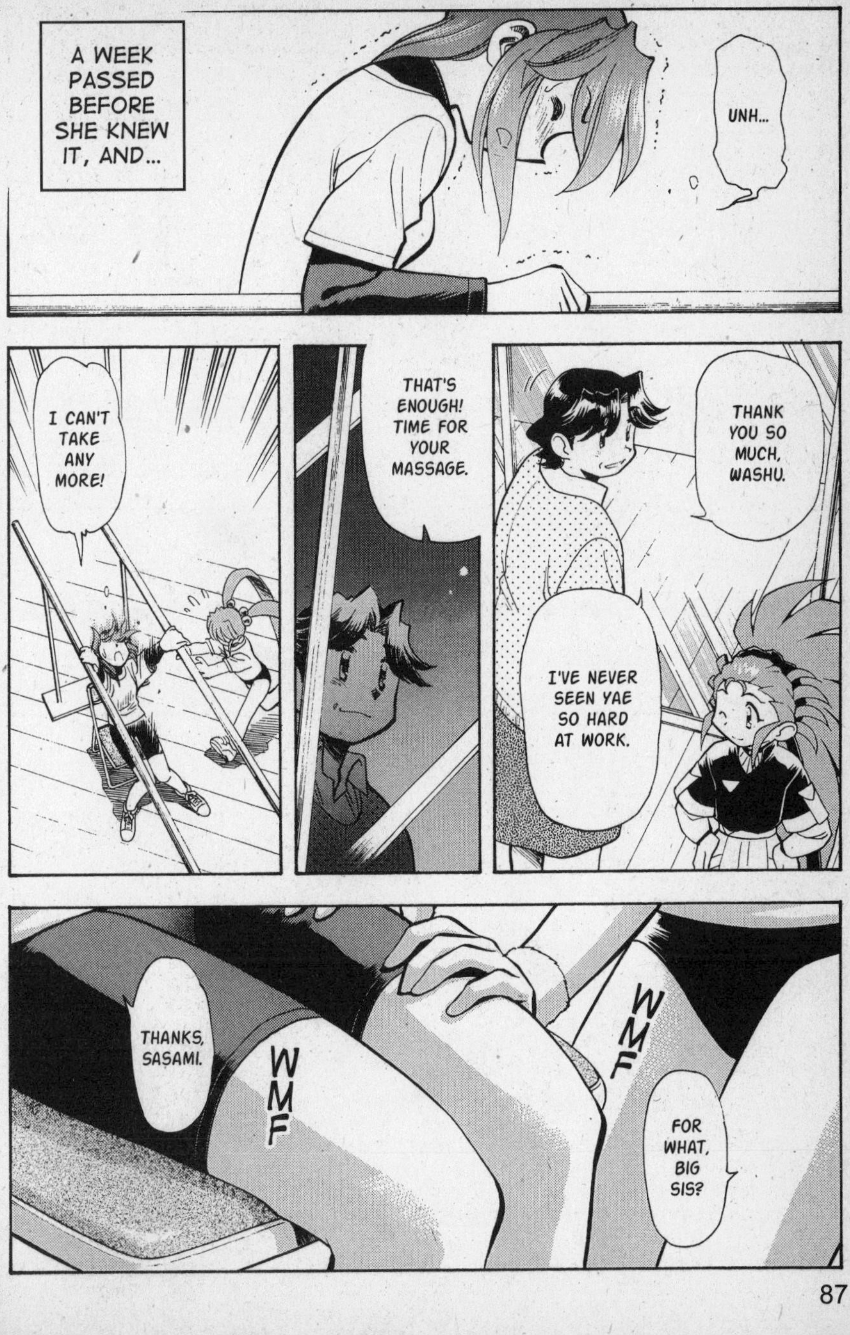
A WEEK PASSED BEFORE SHE KNEW IT, AND...
UNH...
I CAN'T TAKE ANY MORE!
THAT'S ENOUGH! TIME FOR YOUR MASSAGE.
THANK YOU SO MUCH, WASHU.
I'VE NEVER SEEN YAE SO HARD AT WORK.
THANKS, SASAMI.
WMF
WMF
FOR WHAT, BIG SIS?

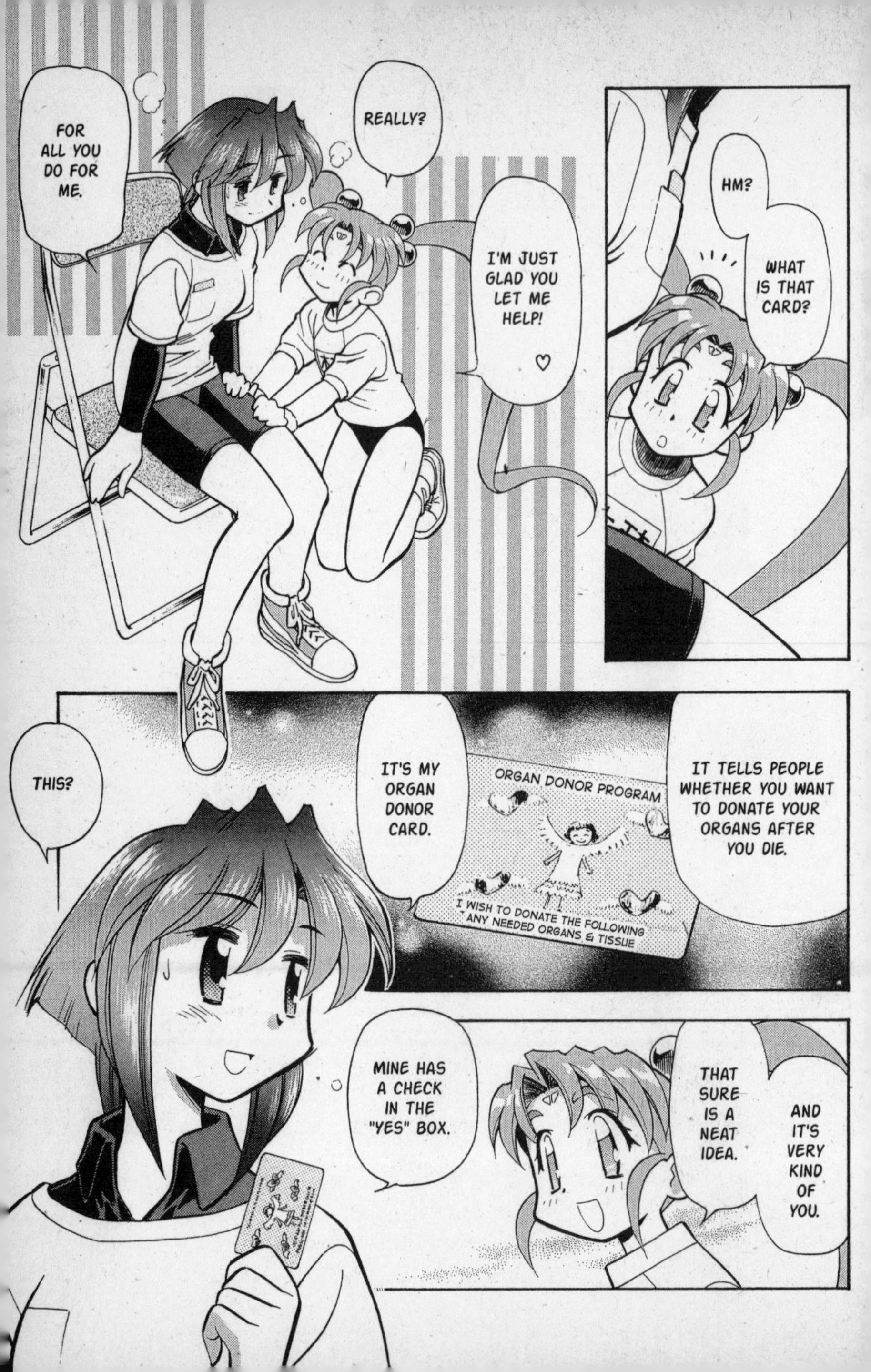
FOR ALL YOU DO FOR ME.
REALLY?
I'M JUST GLAD YOU LET ME HELP! ♡
HM?
WHAT IS THAT CARD?
THIS?
IT'S MY ORGAN DONOR CARD.
ORGAN DONOR PROGRAM
I WISH TO DONATE THE FOLLOWING
ANY NEEDED ORGANS & TISSUE
IT TELLS PEOPLE WHETHER YOU WANT TO DONATE YOUR ORGANS AFTER YOU DIE.
MINE HAS A CHECK IN THE "YES" BOX.
THAT SURE IS A NEAT IDEA.
AND IT'S VERY KIND OF YOU.

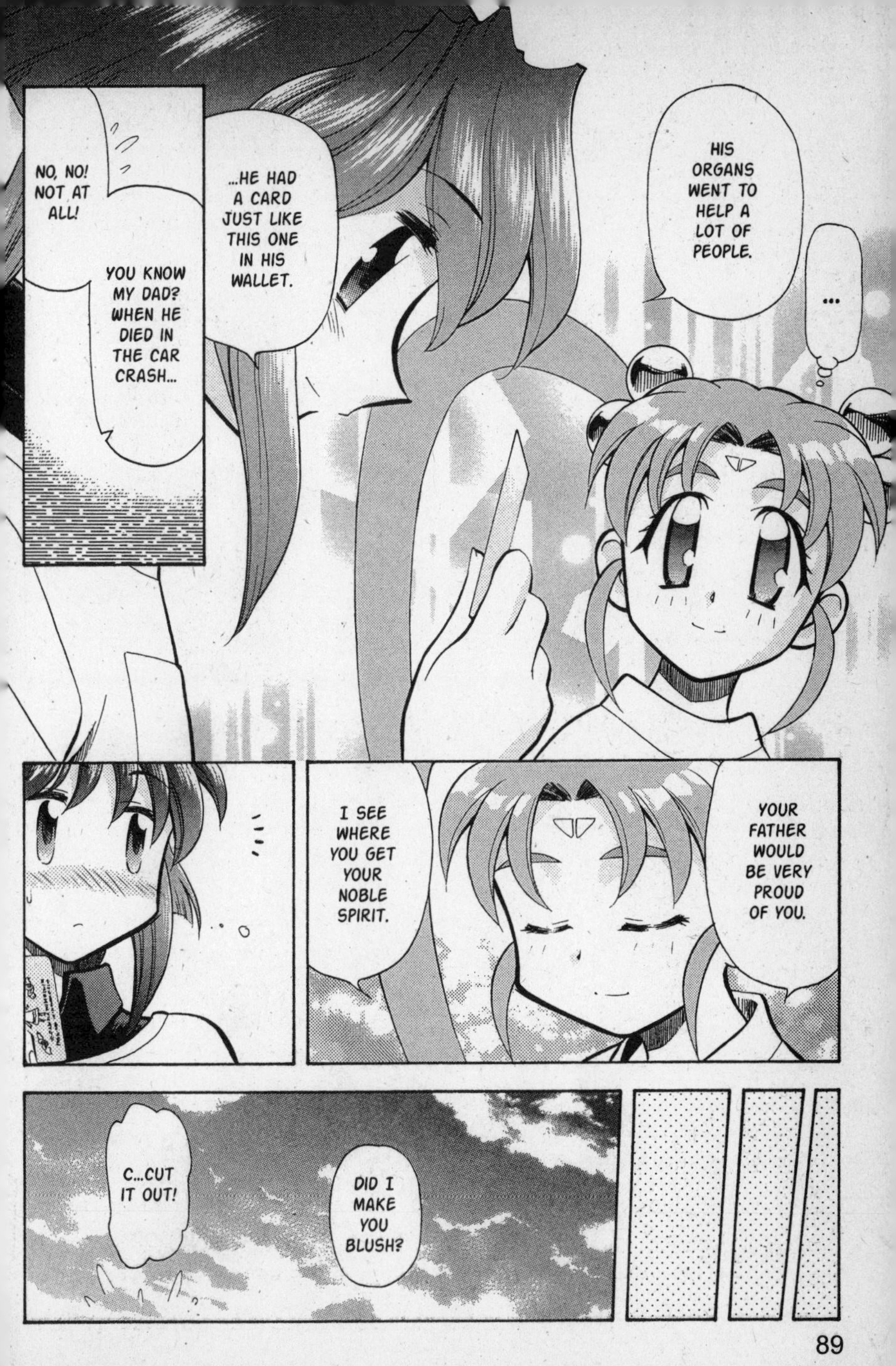

NO, NO! NOT AT ALL!
YOU KNOW MY DAD? WHEN HE DIED IN THE CAR CRASH...
...HE HAD A CARD JUST LIKE THIS ONE IN HIS WALLET.
HIS ORGANS WENT TO HELP A LOT OF PEOPLE.
...
I SEE WHERE YOU GET YOUR NOBLE SPIRIT.
YOUR FATHER WOULD BE VERY PROUD OF YOU.
C...CUT IT OUT!
DID I MAKE YOU BLUSH?

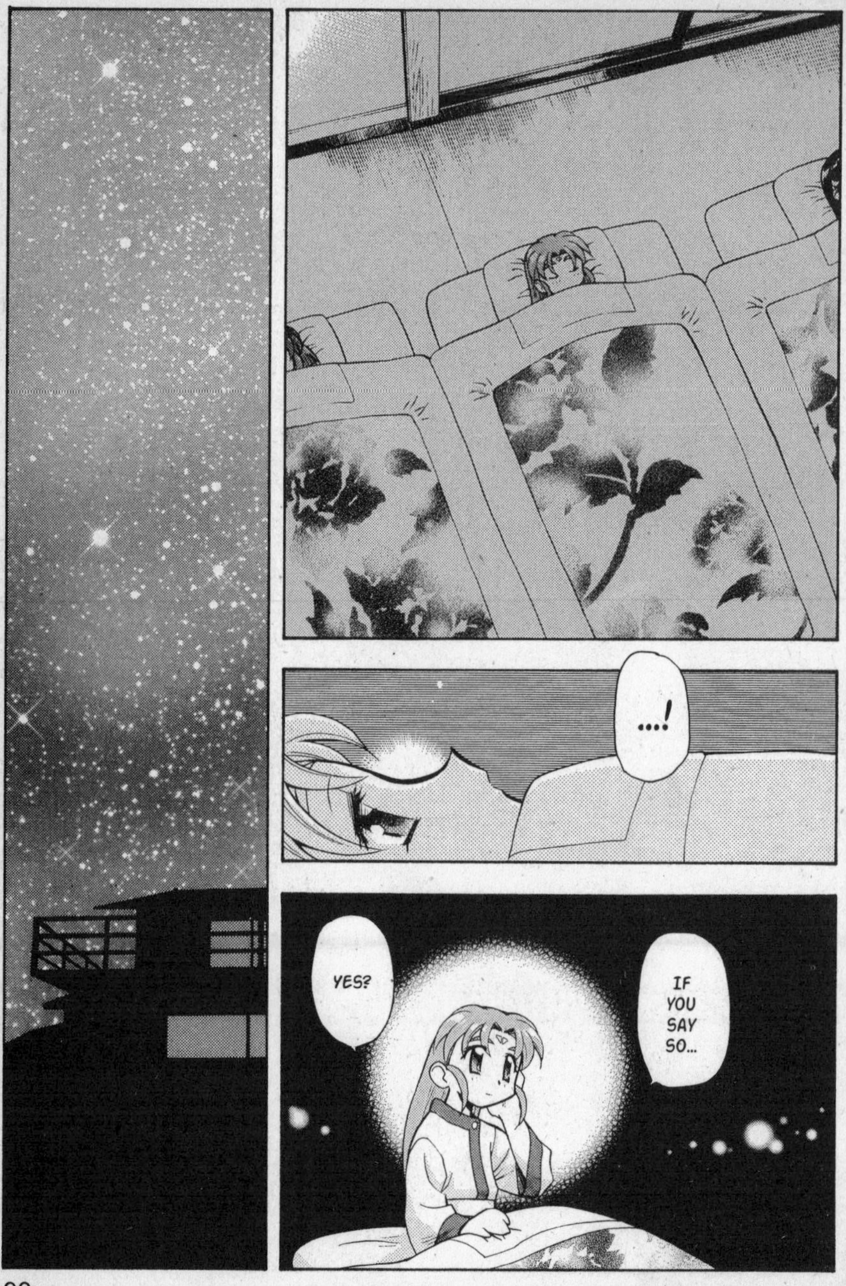
...!
YES?
IF YOU SAY SO...

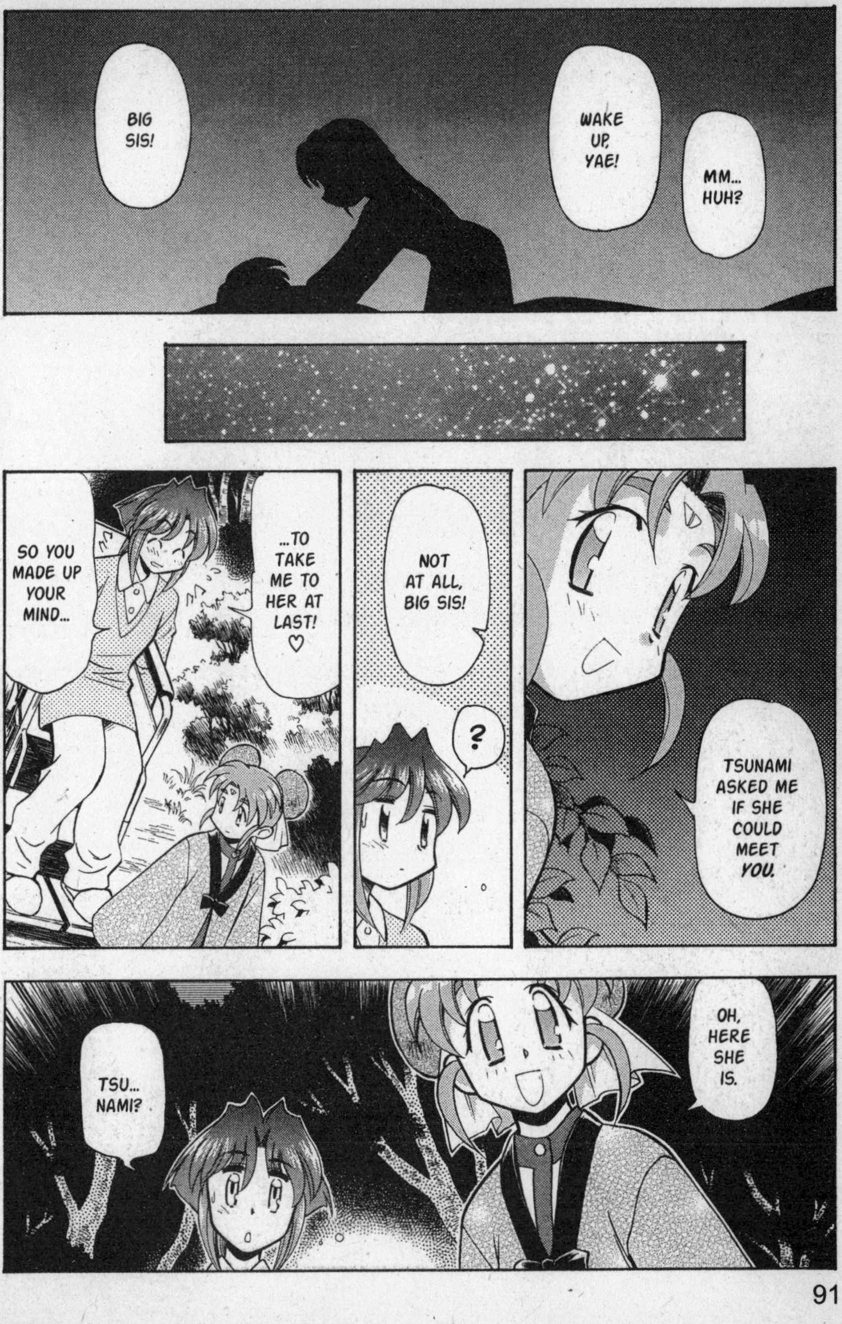
BIG SIS!
WAKE UP, YAE!
MM... HUH?
SO YOU MADE UP YOUR MIND...
...TO TAKE ME TO HER AT LAST! ♡
NOT AT ALL, BIG SIS!
?
TSUNAMI ASKED ME IF SHE COULD MEET YOU.
TSU... NAMI?
OH, HERE SHE IS.

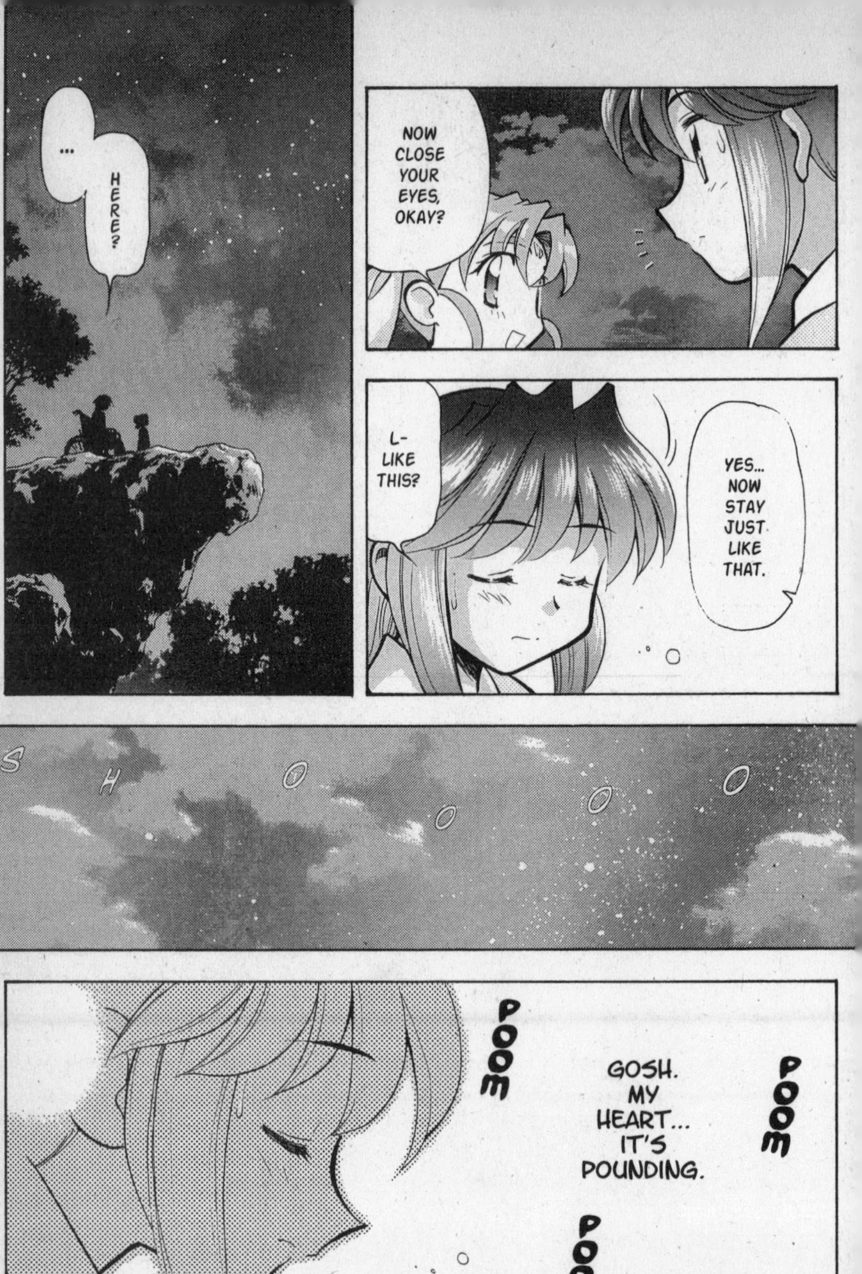
...
HERE?
NOW CLOSE YOUR EYES, OKAY?
L-LIKE THIS?
YES... NOW STAY JUST LIKE THAT.
SHOOOOO
POOM
GOSH. MY HEART... IT'S POUNDING.
POOM
POOM

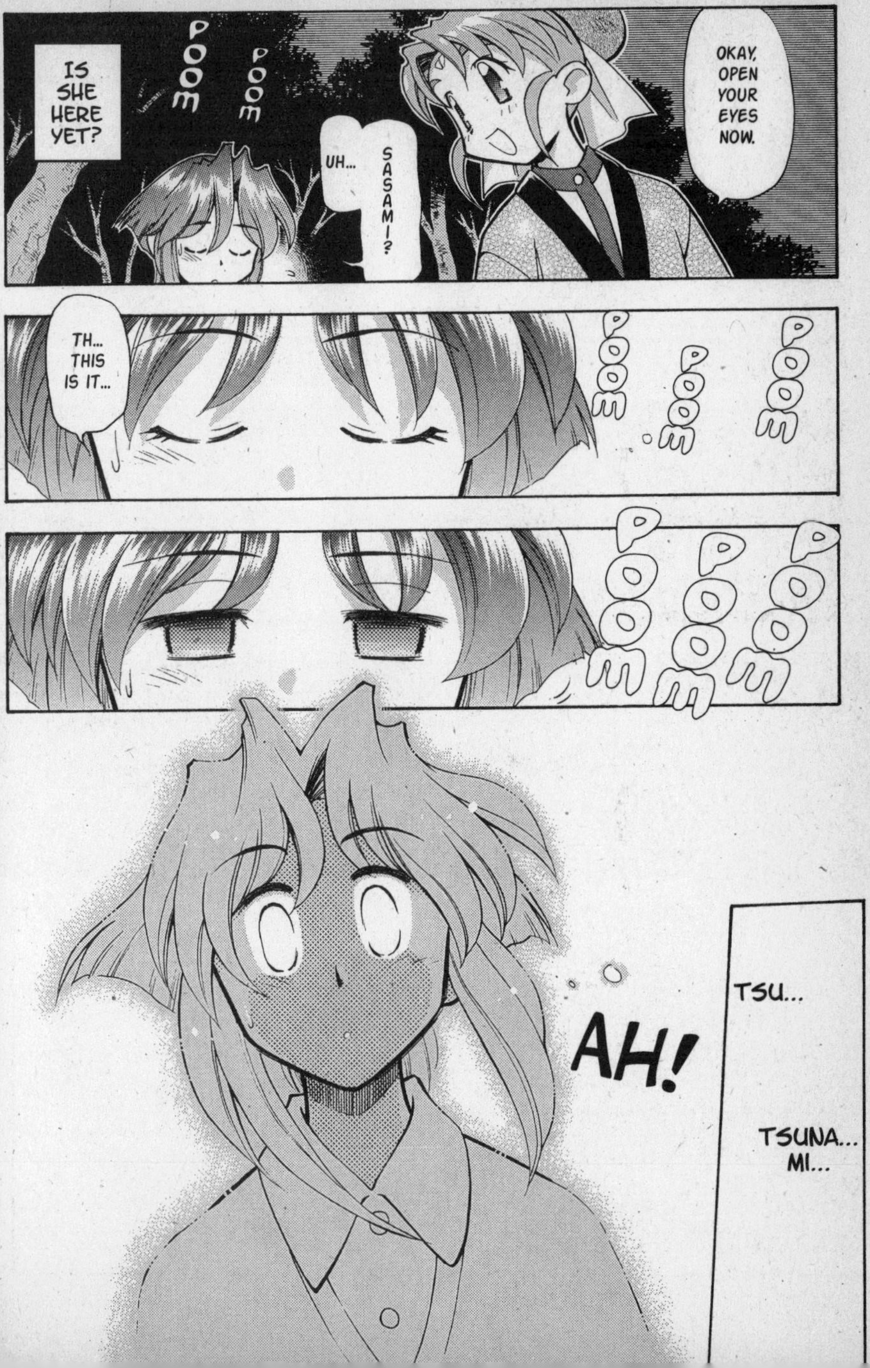
IS SHE HERE YET?
POOM
POOM
UH... SASAMI?
OKAY, OPEN YOUR EYES NOW.
TH... THIS IS IT...
POOM
POOM
POOM
POOM
POOM
POOM
AH!
TSU...
TSUNA... MI...

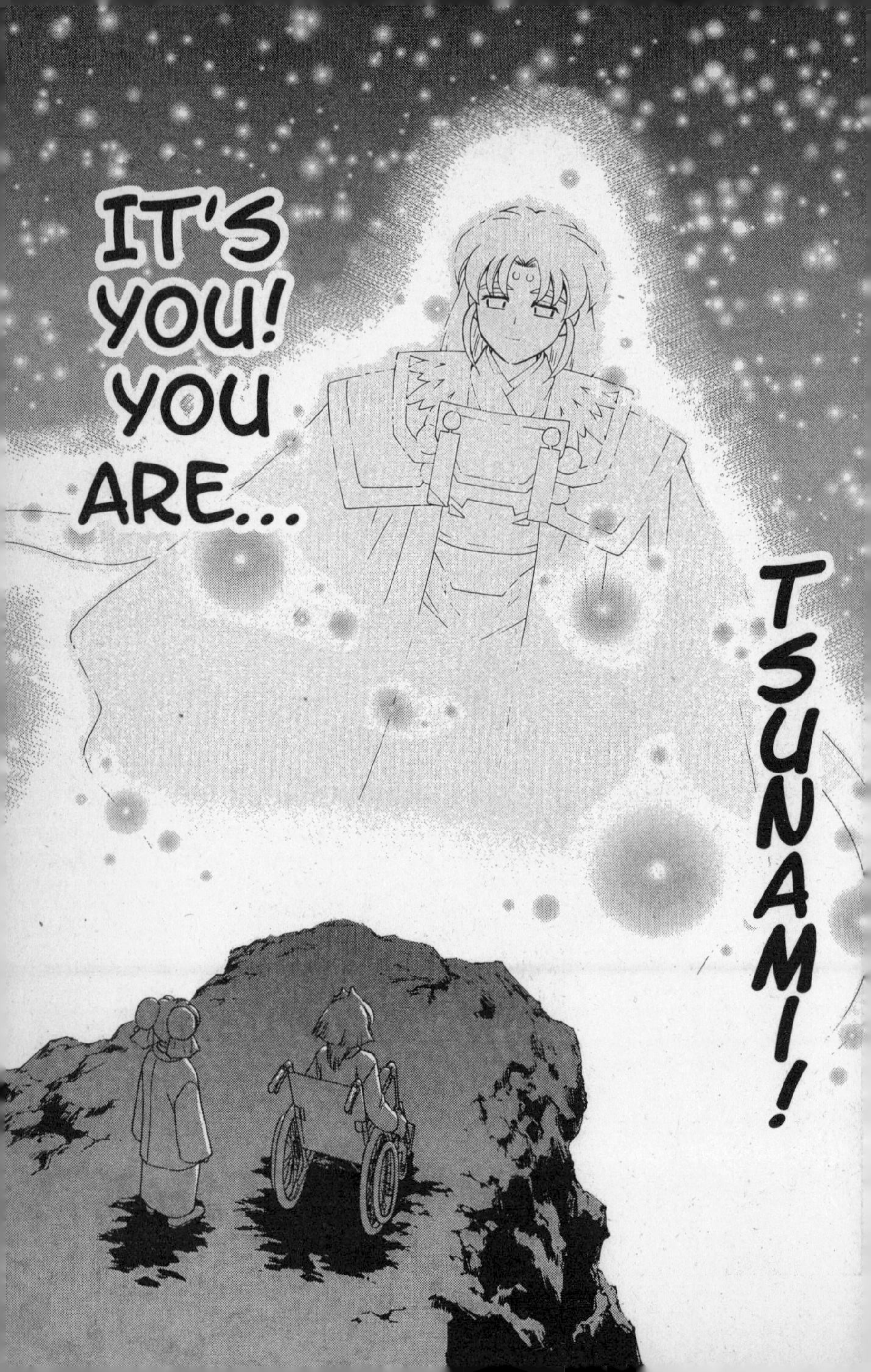
IT'S YOU! YOU ARE...
TSUNAMI!

Chapter 4: Empathy

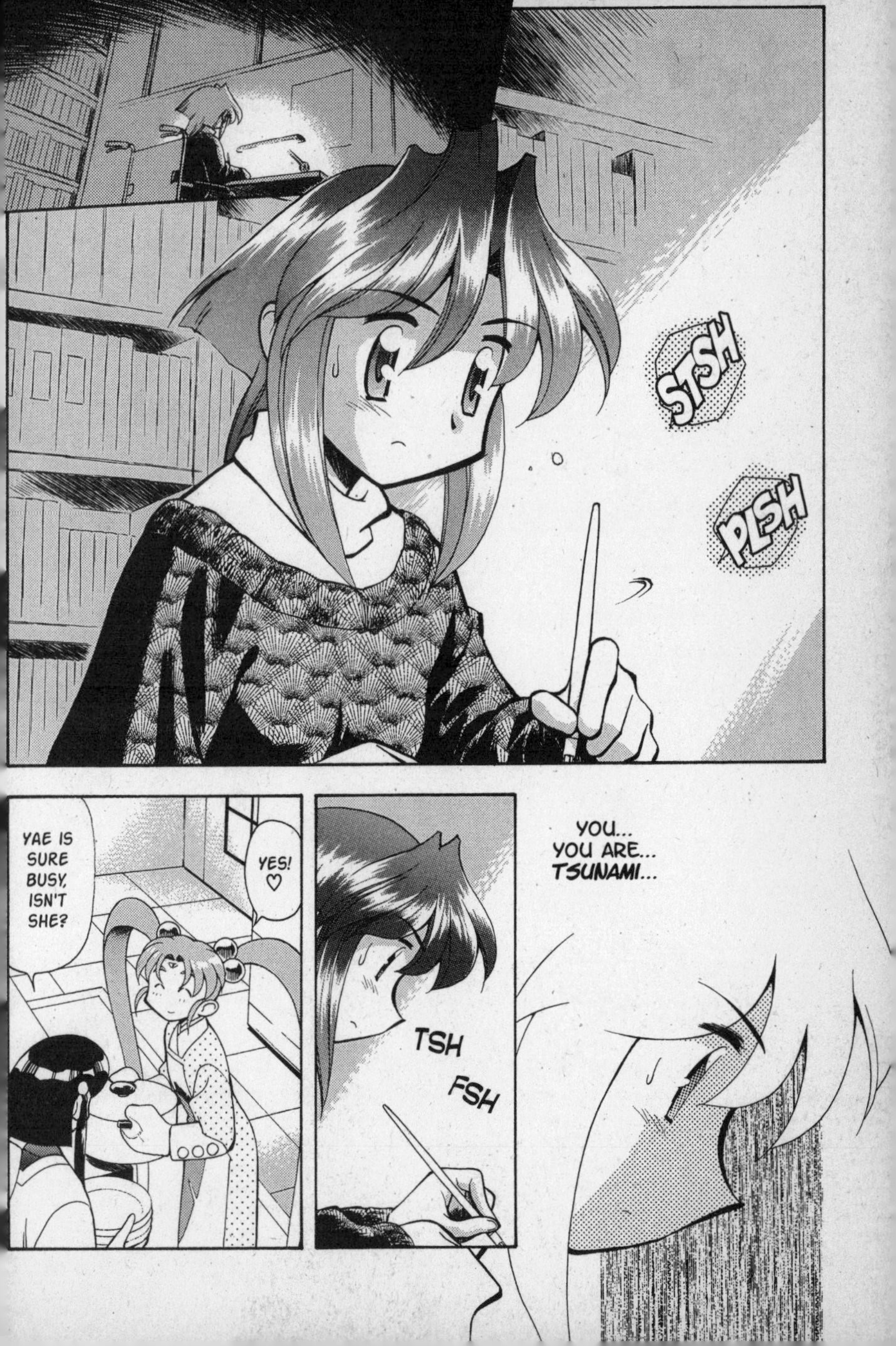
STSH
PLSH
YAE IS SURE BUSY, ISN'T SHE?
YES! ♥
TSH
FSH
YOU... YOU ARE... TSUNAMI...

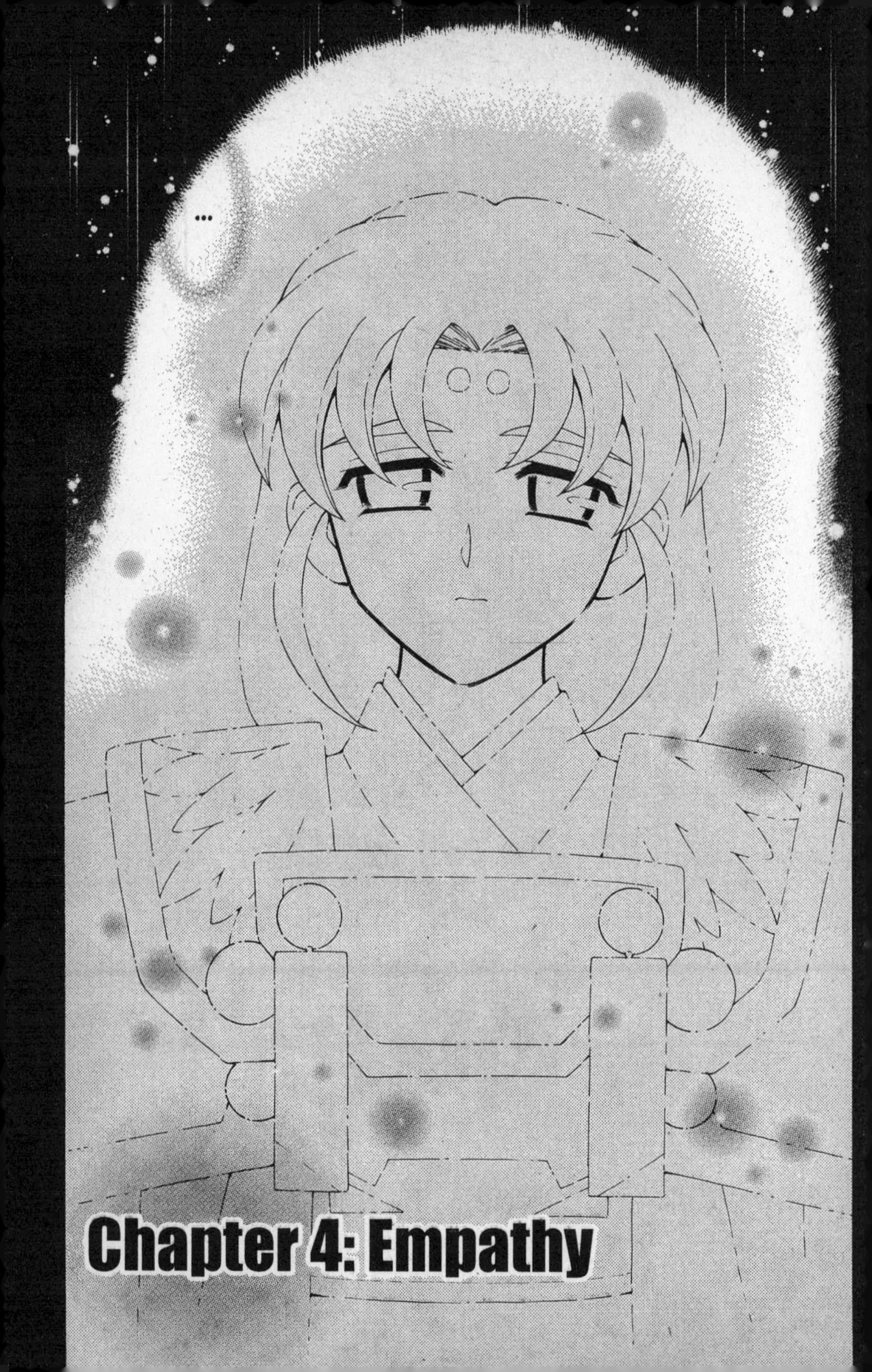
...
Chapter 4: Empathy

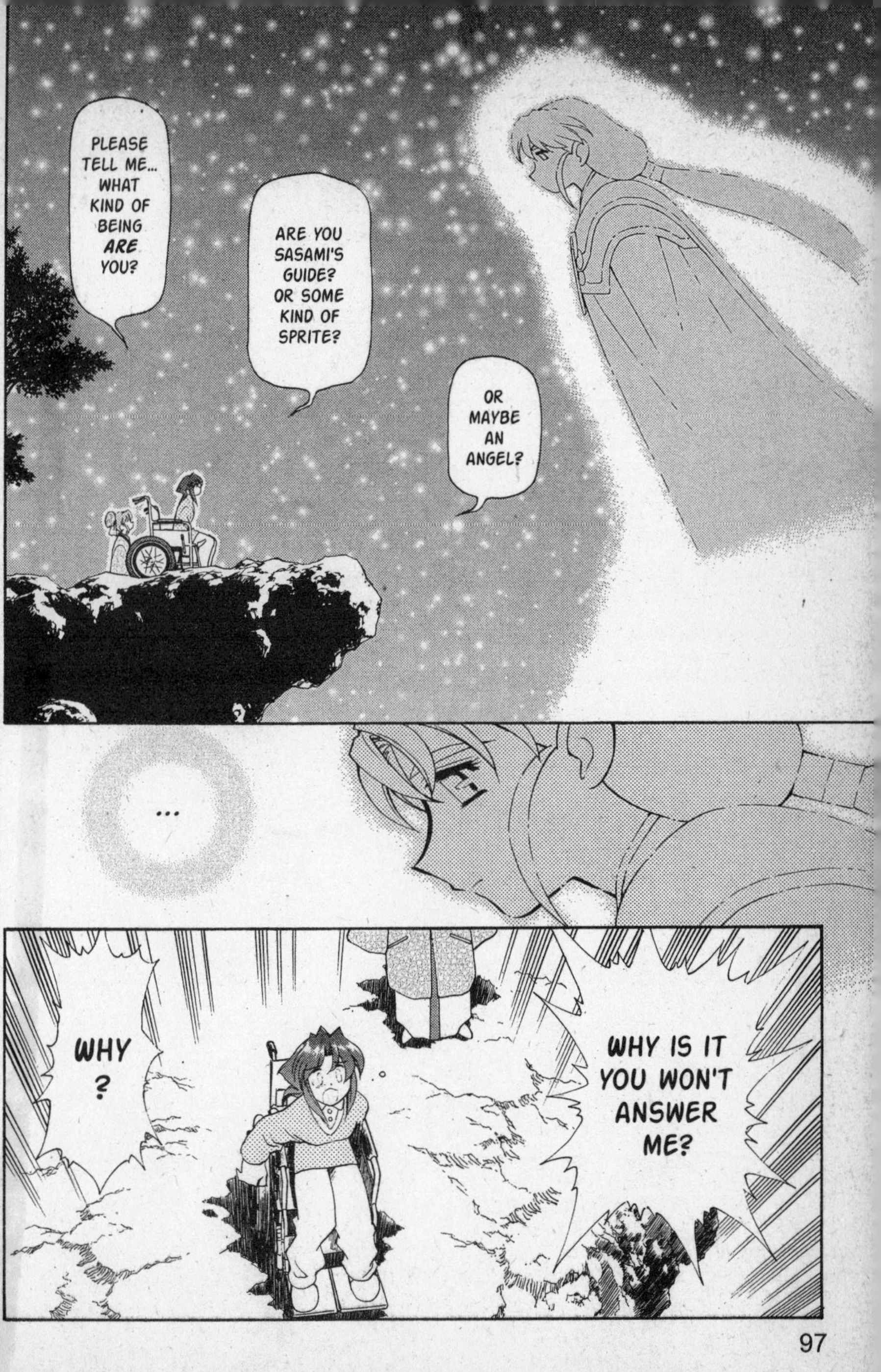
PLEASE TELL ME... WHAT KIND OF BEING *ARE* YOU?
ARE YOU SASAMI'S GUIDE? OR SOME KIND OF SPRITE?
OR MAYBE AN ANGEL?
...
WHY?
WHY IS IT YOU WON'T ANSWER ME?

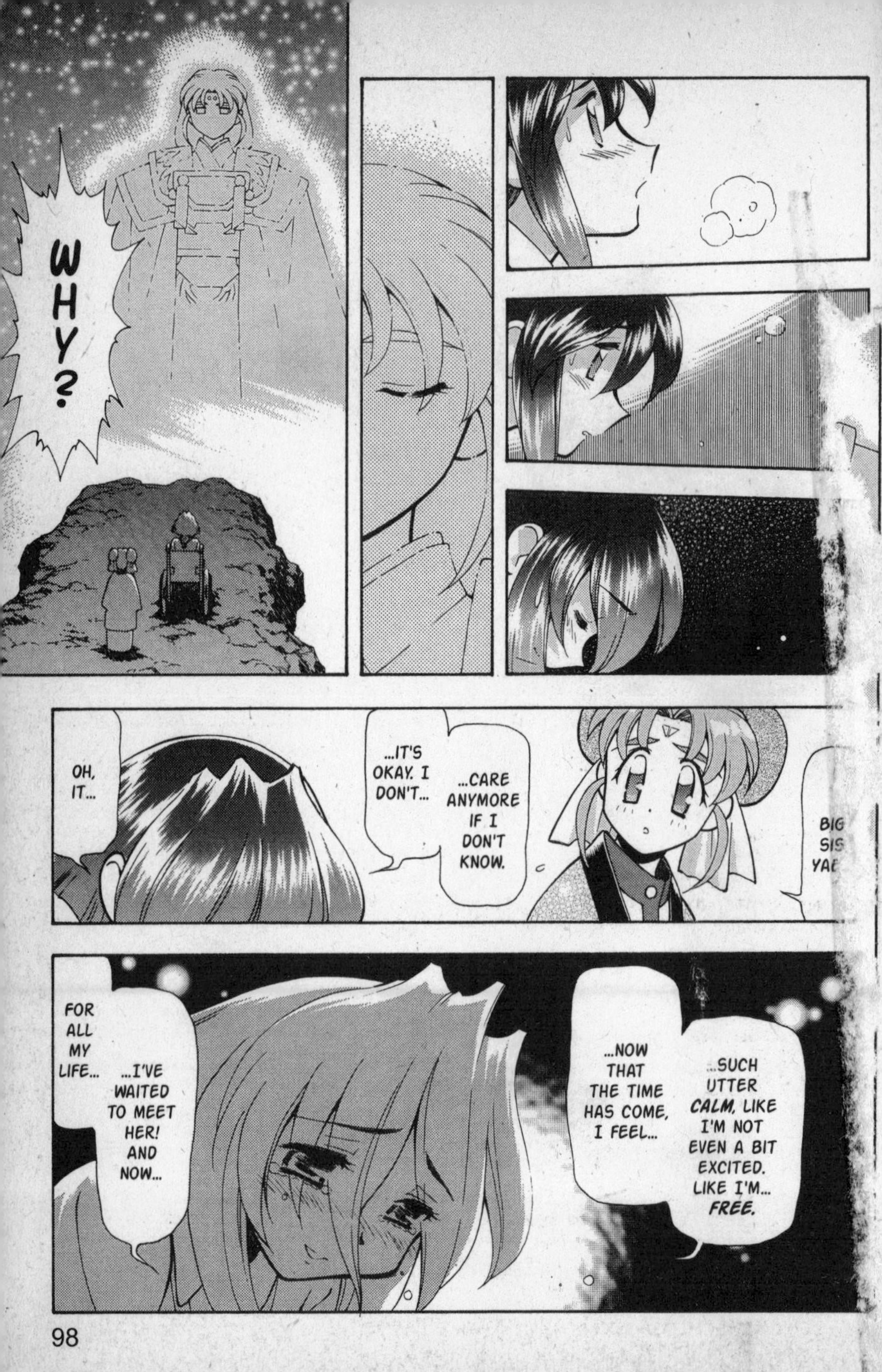
WHY?
OH, IT...
...IT'S OKAY. I DON'T...
...CARE ANYMORE IF I DON'T KNOW.
BIG SIS
FOR ALL MY LIFE...
...I'VE WAITED TO MEET HER! AND NOW...
...NOW THAT THE TIME HAS COME, I FEEL...
...SUCH UTTER CALM, LIKE I'M NOT EVEN A BIT EXCITED. LIKE I'M... FREE.

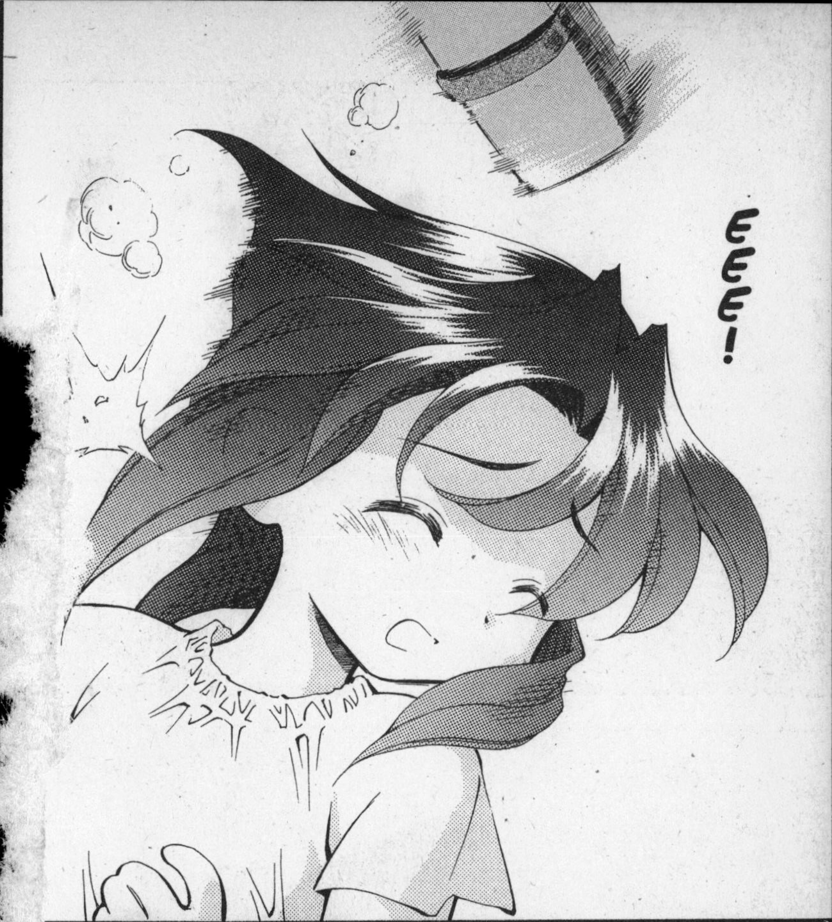
EEEE!

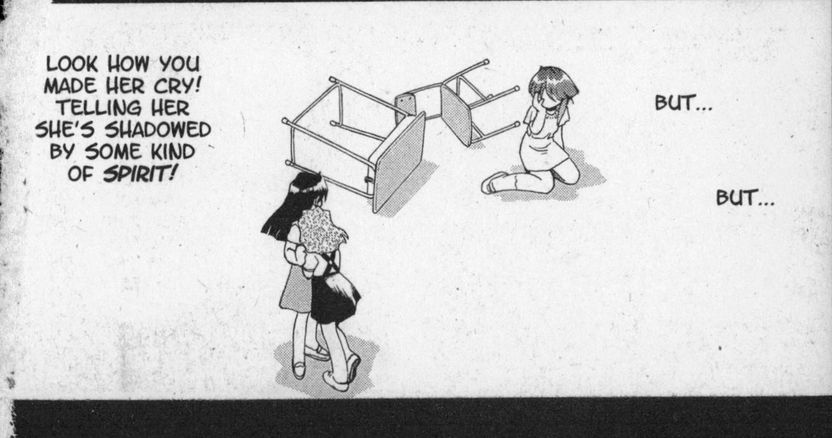
LOOK HOW YOU MADE HER CRY! TELLING HER SHE'S SHADOWED BY SOME KIND OF SPIRIT!
BUT...
BUT...

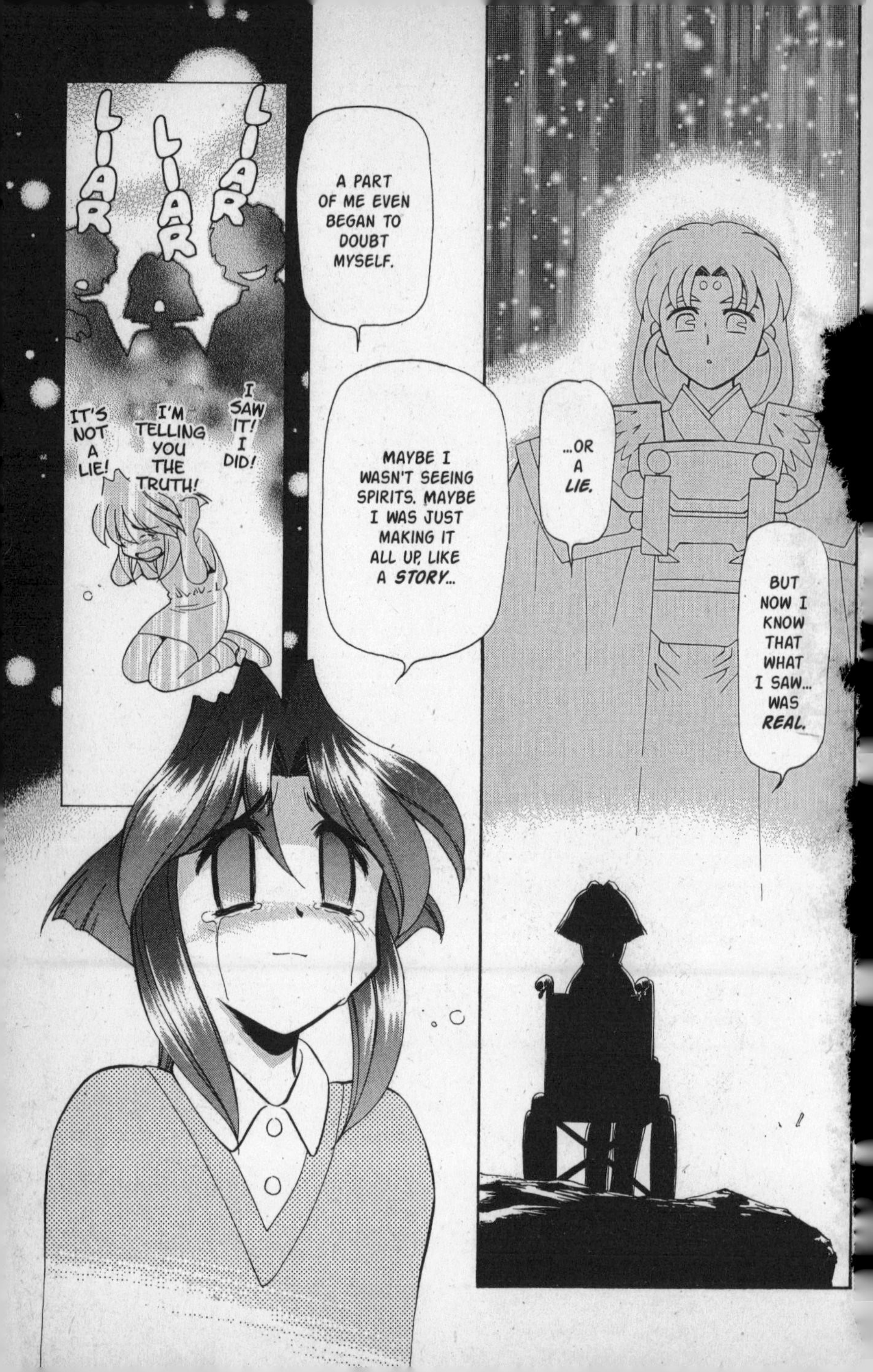
LIAR
LIAR
LIAR
IT'S NOT A LIE!
I'M TELLING YOU THE TRUTH!
I SAW IT! I DID!
A PART OF ME EVEN BEGAN TO DOUBT MYSELF.
MAYBE I WASN'T SEEING SPIRITS. MAYBE I WAS JUST MAKING IT ALL UP, LIKE A *STORY*...
...OR A *LIE.*
BUT NOW I KNOW THAT WHAT I SAW... WAS *REAL.*

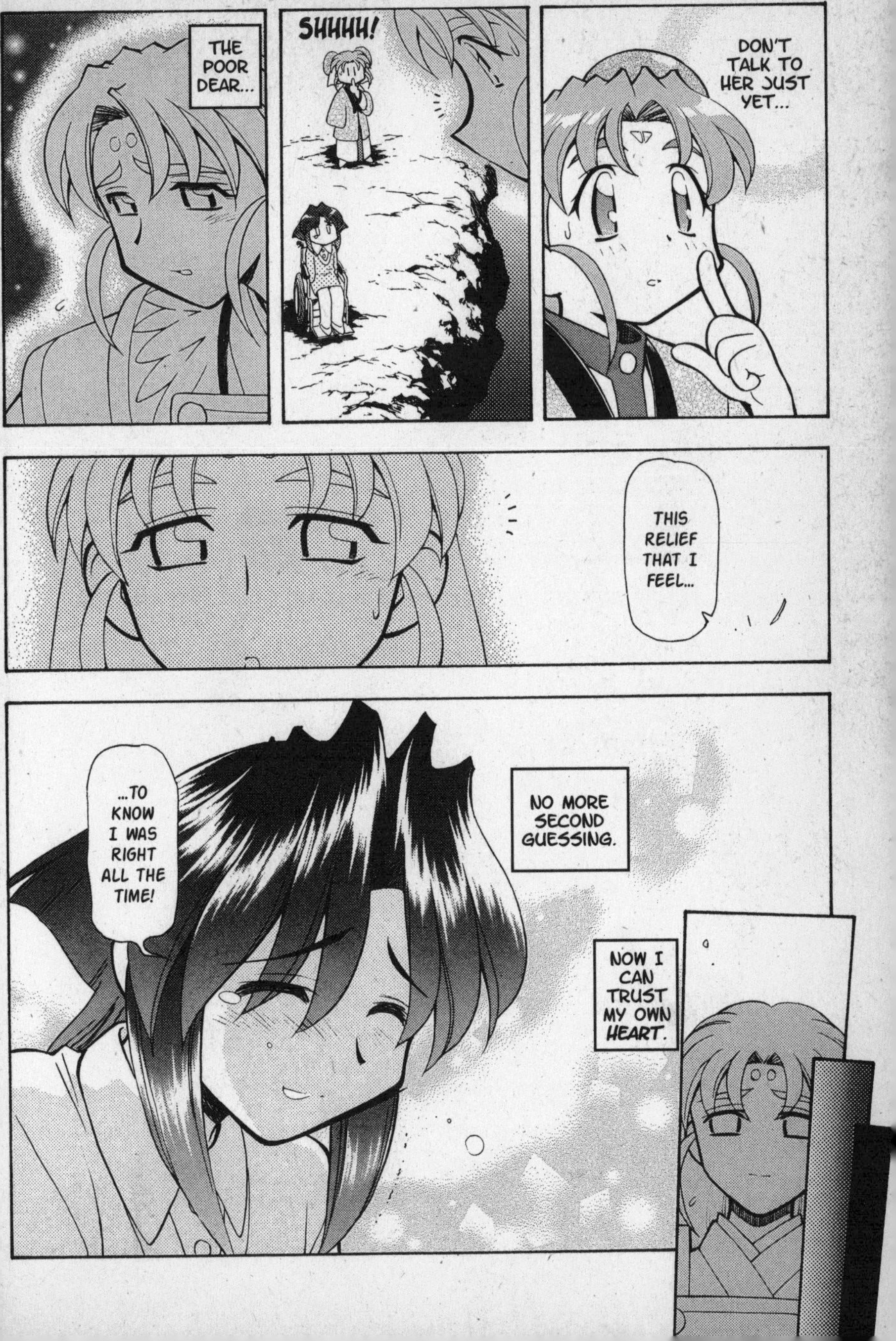
THE POOR DEAR...
SHHHH!
DON'T TALK TO HER JUST YET...
THIS RELIEF THAT I FEEL...
...TO KNOW I WAS RIGHT ALL THE TIME!
NO MORE SECOND GUESSING.
NOW I CAN TRUST MY OWN HEART.

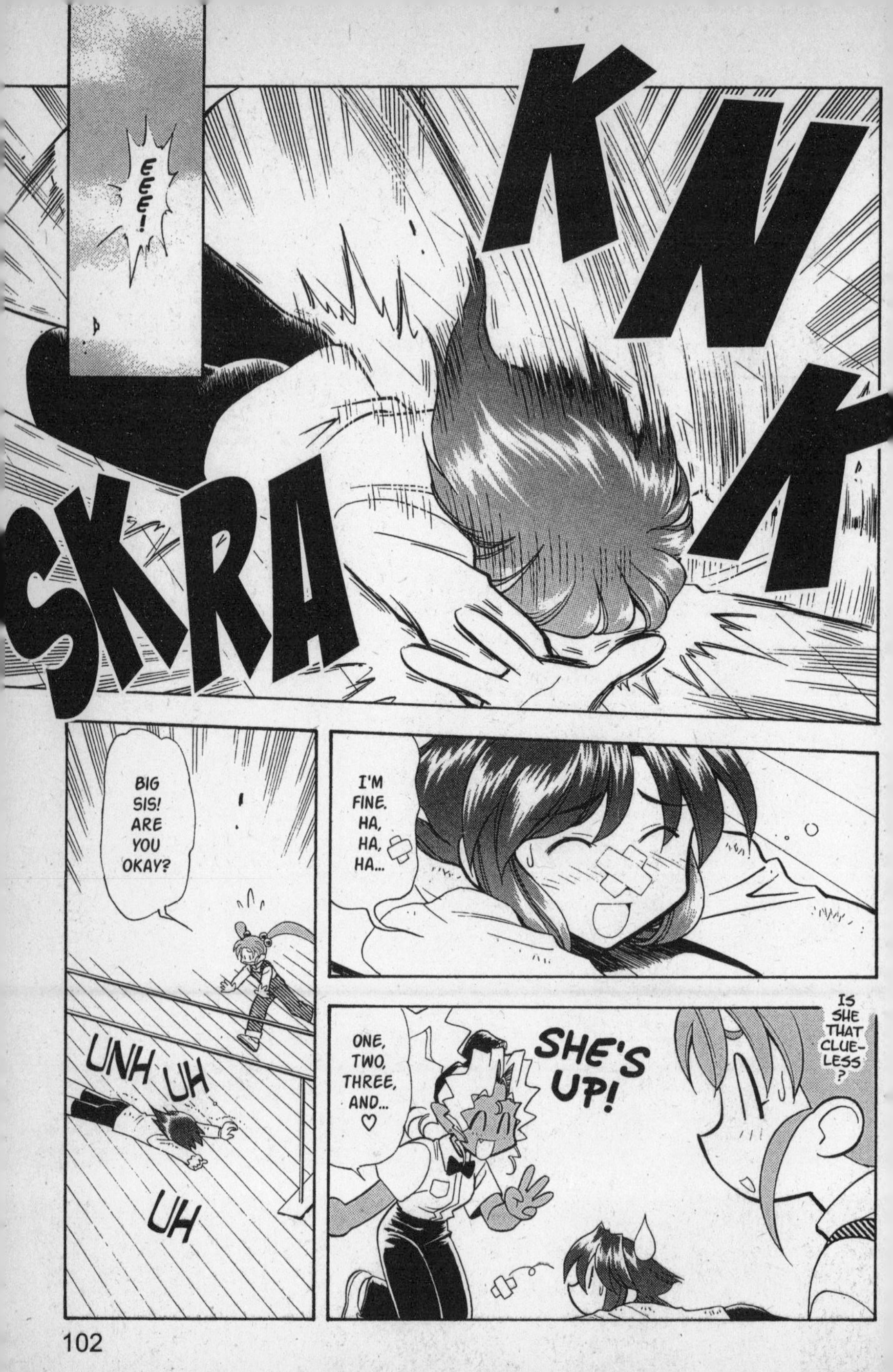
EEE!
SKRA
KNK
BIG SIS! ARE YOU OKAY?
UNH UH
UH
I'M FINE. HA, HA, HA...
ONE, TWO, THREE, AND... ♡
SHE'S UP!
IS SHE THAT CLUELESS?

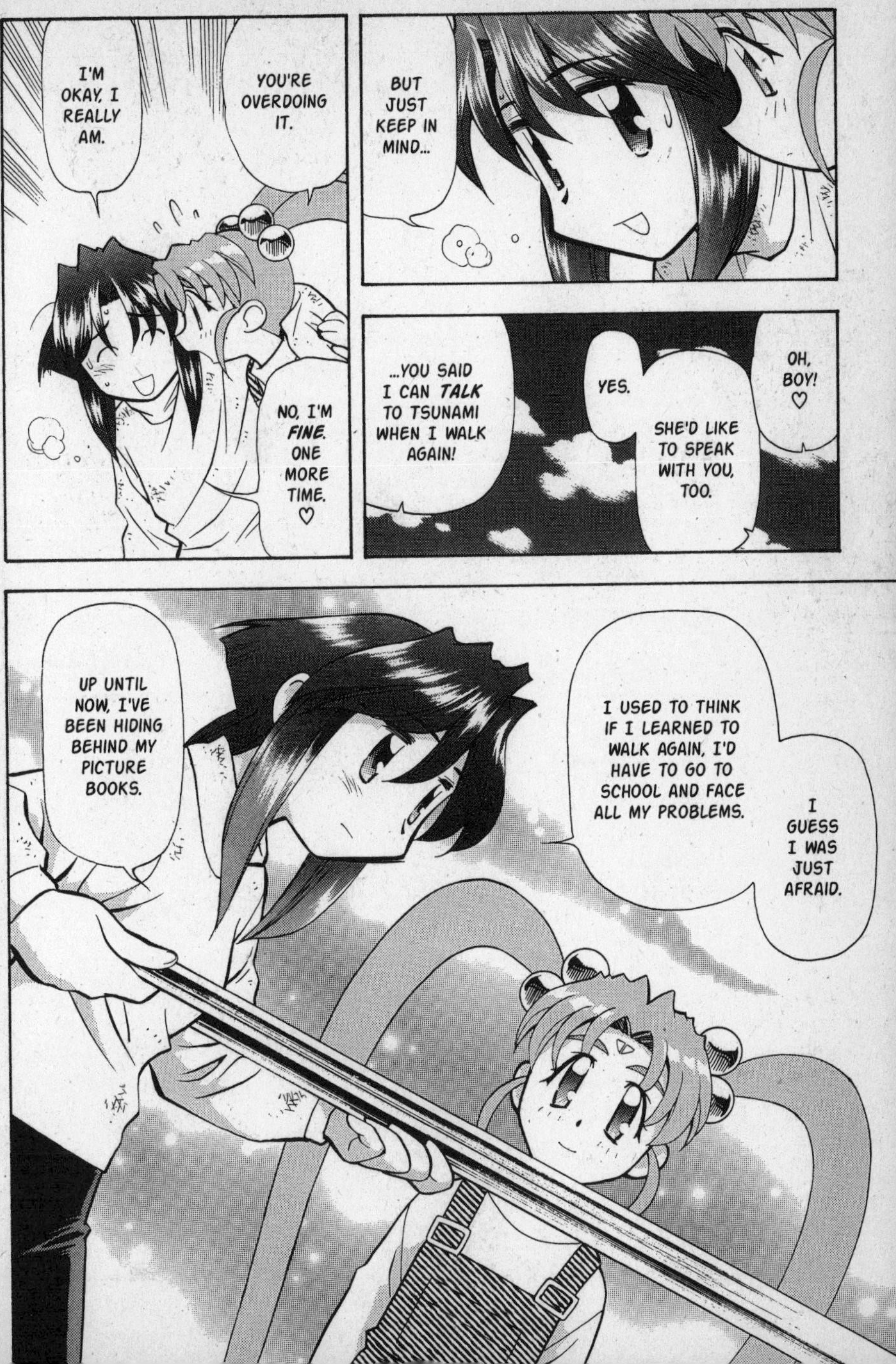
I'M OKAY, I REALLY AM.
YOU'RE OVERDOING IT.
NO, I'M *FINE*. ONE MORE TIME. ♡
BUT JUST KEEP IN MIND...
...YOU SAID I CAN *TALK* TO TSUNAMI WHEN I WALK AGAIN!
YES.
SHE'D LIKE TO SPEAK WITH YOU, TOO.
OH, BOY! ♡
UP UNTIL NOW, I'VE BEEN HIDING BEHIND MY PICTURE BOOKS.
I USED TO THINK IF I LEARNED TO WALK AGAIN, I'D HAVE TO GO TO SCHOOL AND FACE ALL MY PROBLEMS.
I GUESS I WAS JUST AFRAID.

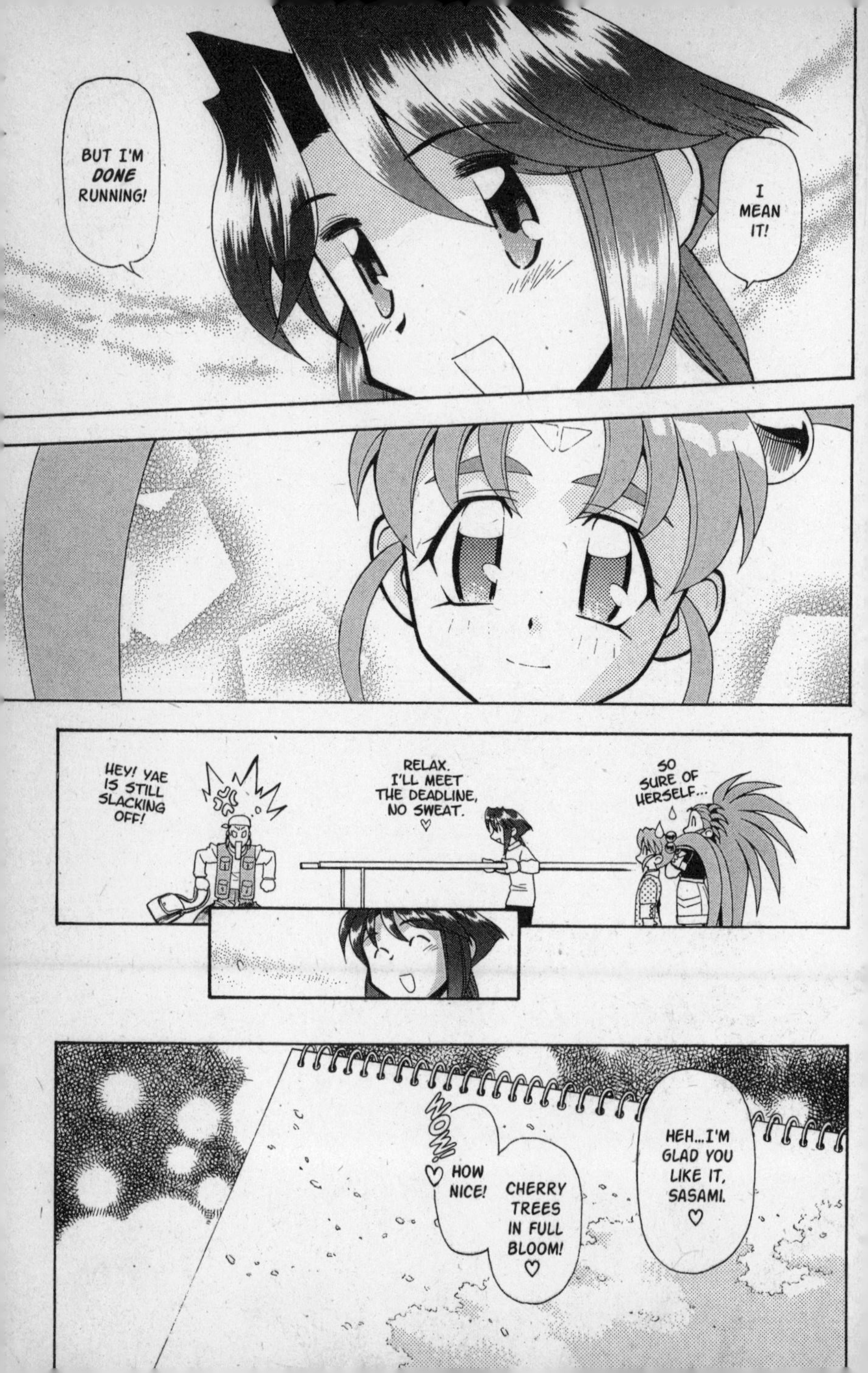
BUT I'M *DONE* RUNNING!
I MEAN IT!
HEY! YAE IS STILL SLACKING OFF!
RELAX. I'LL MEET THE DEADLINE, NO SWEAT. ♡
SO SURE OF HERSELF...
WOW!
♡ HOW NICE!
CHERRY TREES IN FULL BLOOM! ♡
HEH...I'M GLAD YOU LIKE IT, SASAMI. ♡

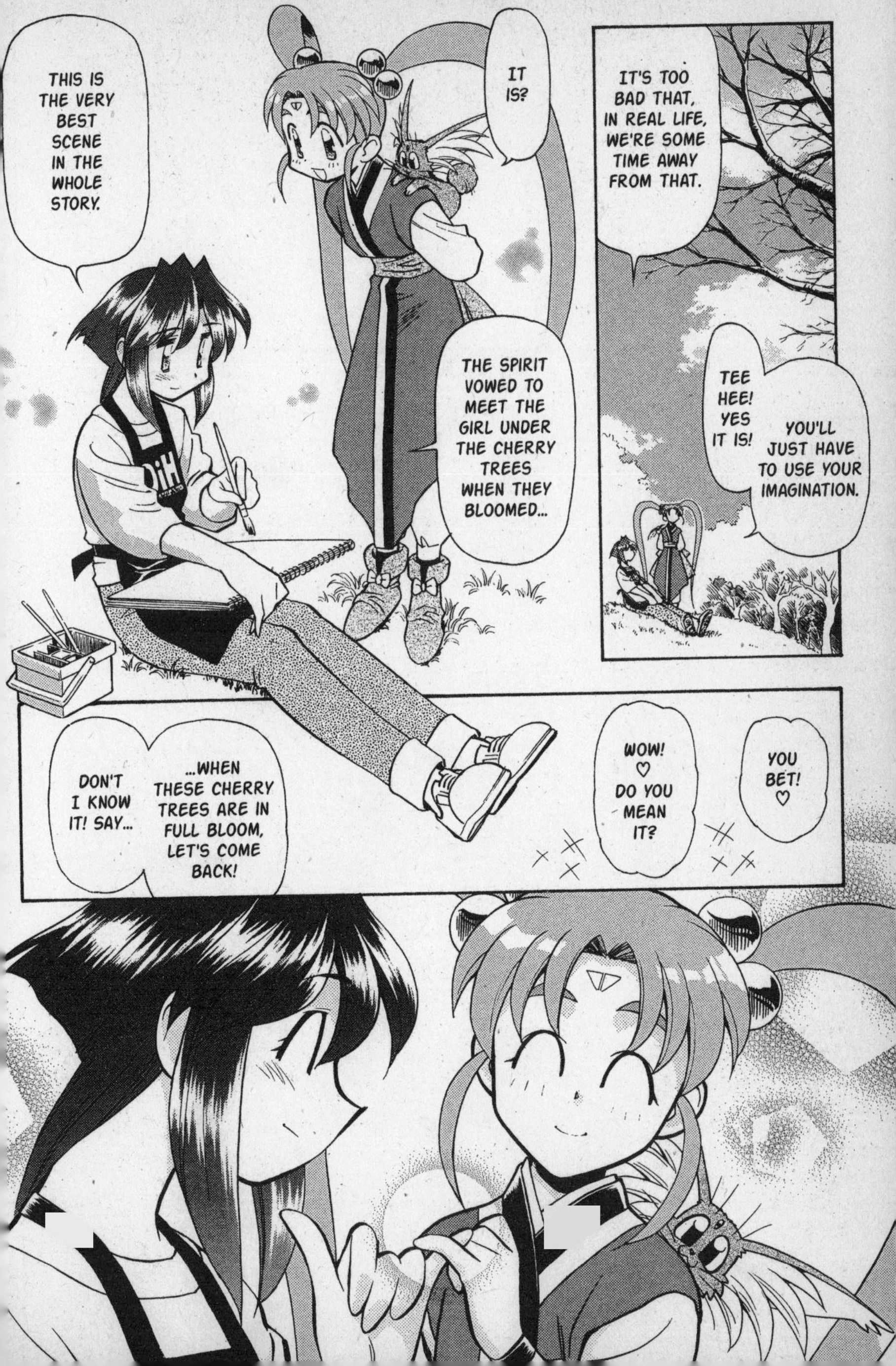
THIS IS THE VERY BEST SCENE IN THE WHOLE STORY.
IT IS?
THE SPIRIT VOWED TO MEET THE GIRL UNDER THE CHERRY TREES WHEN THEY BLOOMED...
IT'S TOO BAD THAT, IN REAL LIFE, WE'RE SOME TIME AWAY FROM THAT.
TEE HEE! YES IT IS!
YOU'LL JUST HAVE TO USE YOUR IMAGINATION.
DON'T I KNOW IT! SAY...
...WHEN THESE CHERRY TREES ARE IN FULL BLOOM, LET'S COME BACK!
WOW! ♡ DO YOU MEAN IT?
YOU BET! ♡

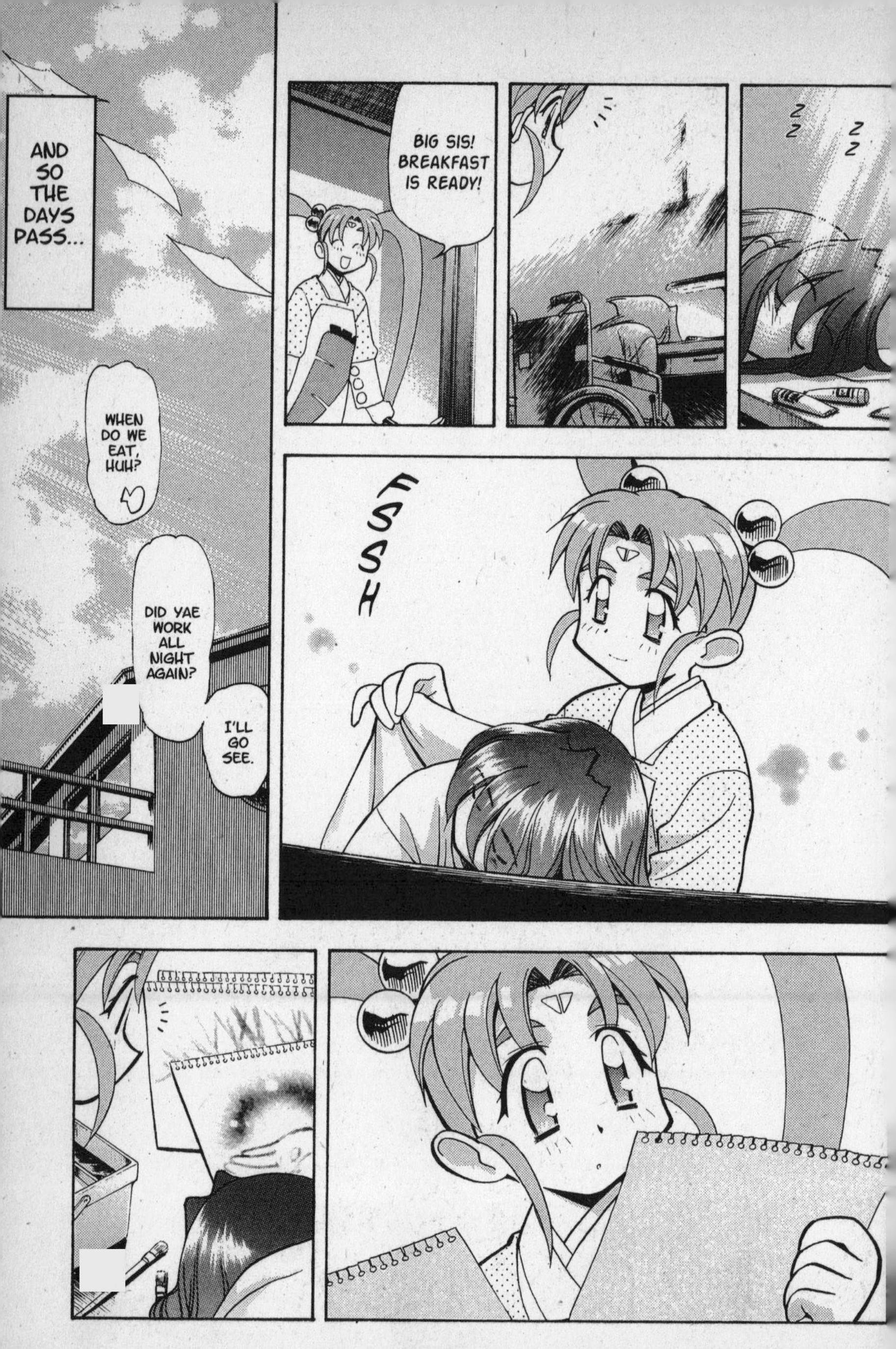
AND SO THE DAYS PASS...
WHEN DO WE EAT, HUH?
DID YAE WORK ALL NIGHT AGAIN?
I'LL GO SEE.
BIG SIS! BREAKFAST IS READY!
Z Z
Z Z
FSSH

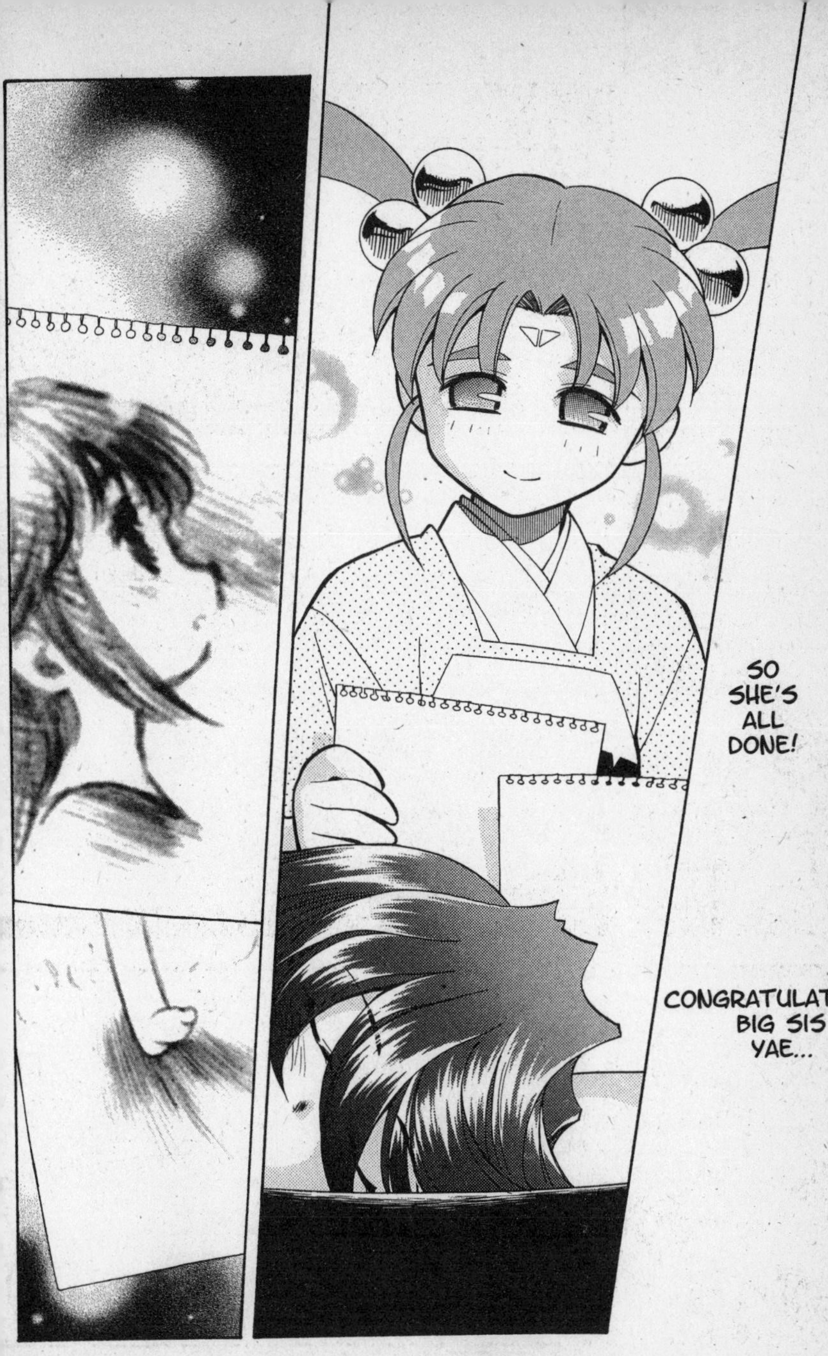
SO SHE'S ALL DONE!
CONGRATULATIONS, BIG SIS YAE...

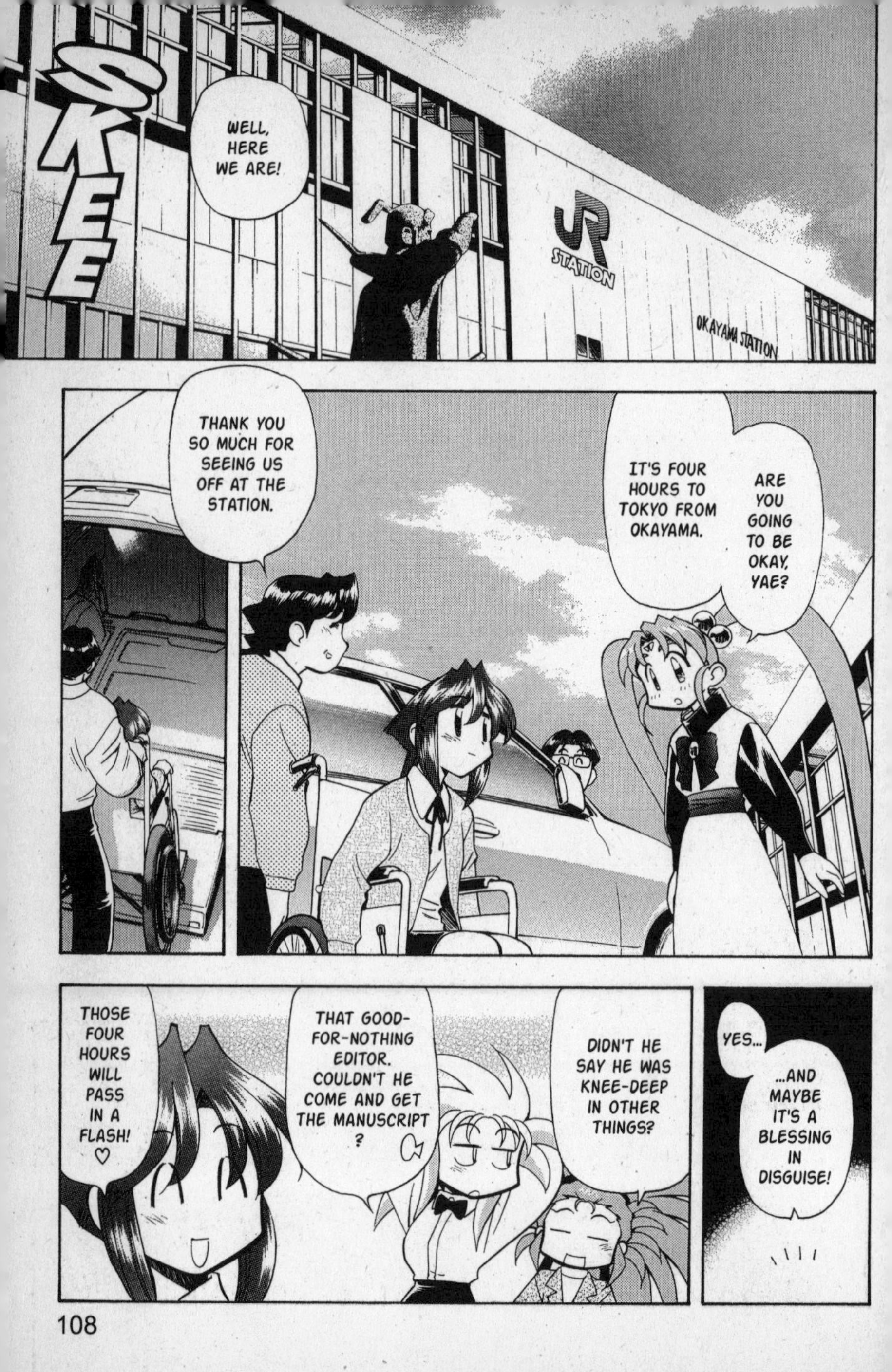
SKEE
WELL, HERE WE ARE!
JR STATION
OKAYAMA STATION
THANK YOU SO MUCH FOR SEEING US OFF AT THE STATION.
IT'S FOUR HOURS TO TOKYO FROM OKAYAMA.
ARE YOU GOING TO BE OKAY, YAE?
THOSE FOUR HOURS WILL PASS IN A FLASH! ♡
THAT GOOD-FOR-NOTHING EDITOR. COULDN'T HE COME AND GET THE MANUSCRIPT?
DIDN'T HE SAY HE WAS KNEE-DEEP IN OTHER THINGS?
YES...
...AND MAYBE IT'S A BLESSING IN DISGUISE!

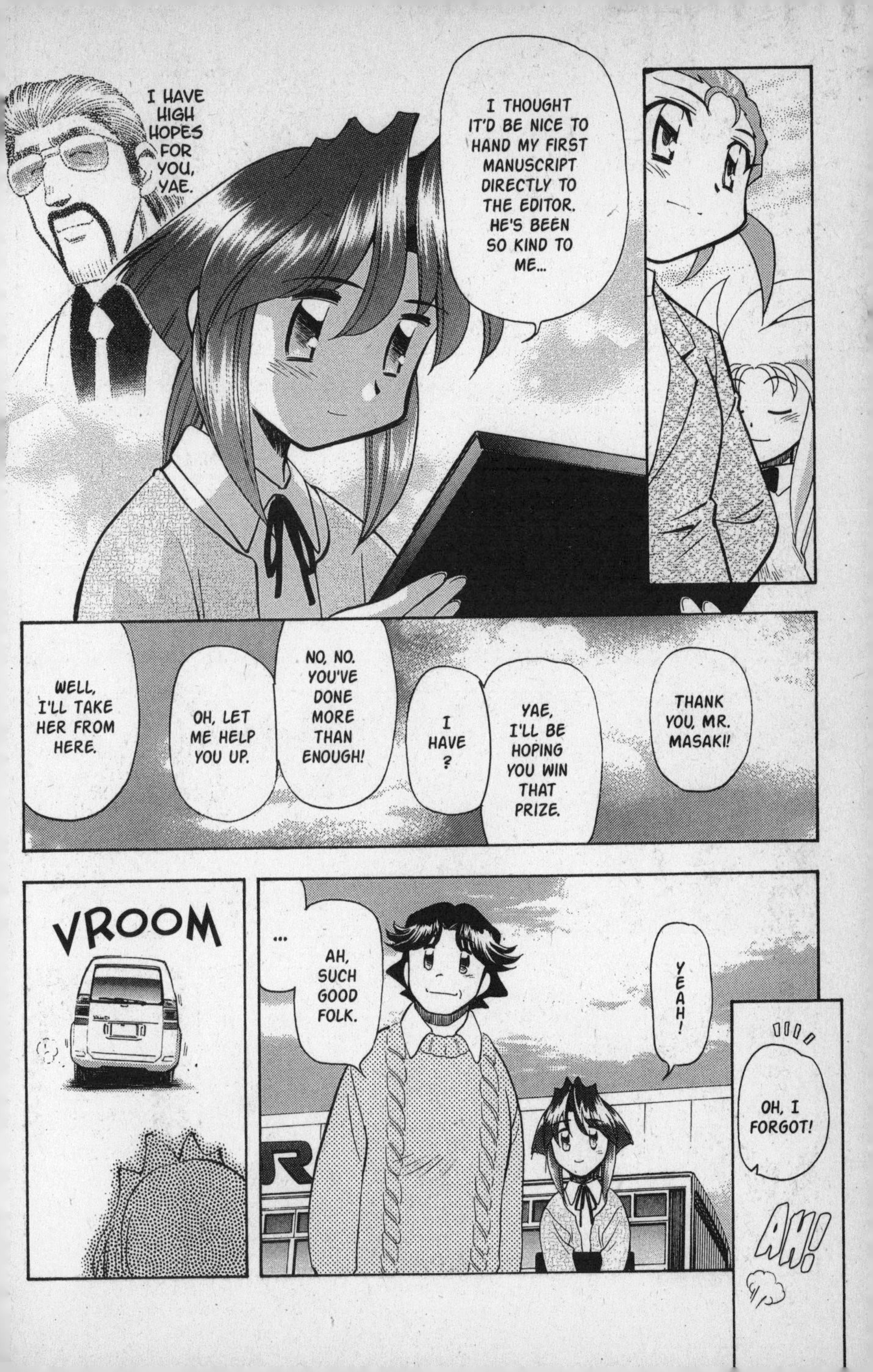
I HAVE HIGH HOPES FOR YOU, YAE.
I THOUGHT IT'D BE NICE TO HAND MY FIRST MANUSCRIPT DIRECTLY TO THE EDITOR. HE'S BEEN SO KIND TO ME...
WELL, I'LL TAKE HER FROM HERE.
OH, LET ME HELP YOU UP.
NO, NO. YOU'VE DONE MORE THAN ENOUGH!
I HAVE?
YAE, I'LL BE HOPING YOU WIN THAT PRIZE.
THANK YOU, MR. MASAKI!
VROOM
...
AH, SUCH GOOD FOLK.
YEAH!
OH, I FORGOT!
AH!

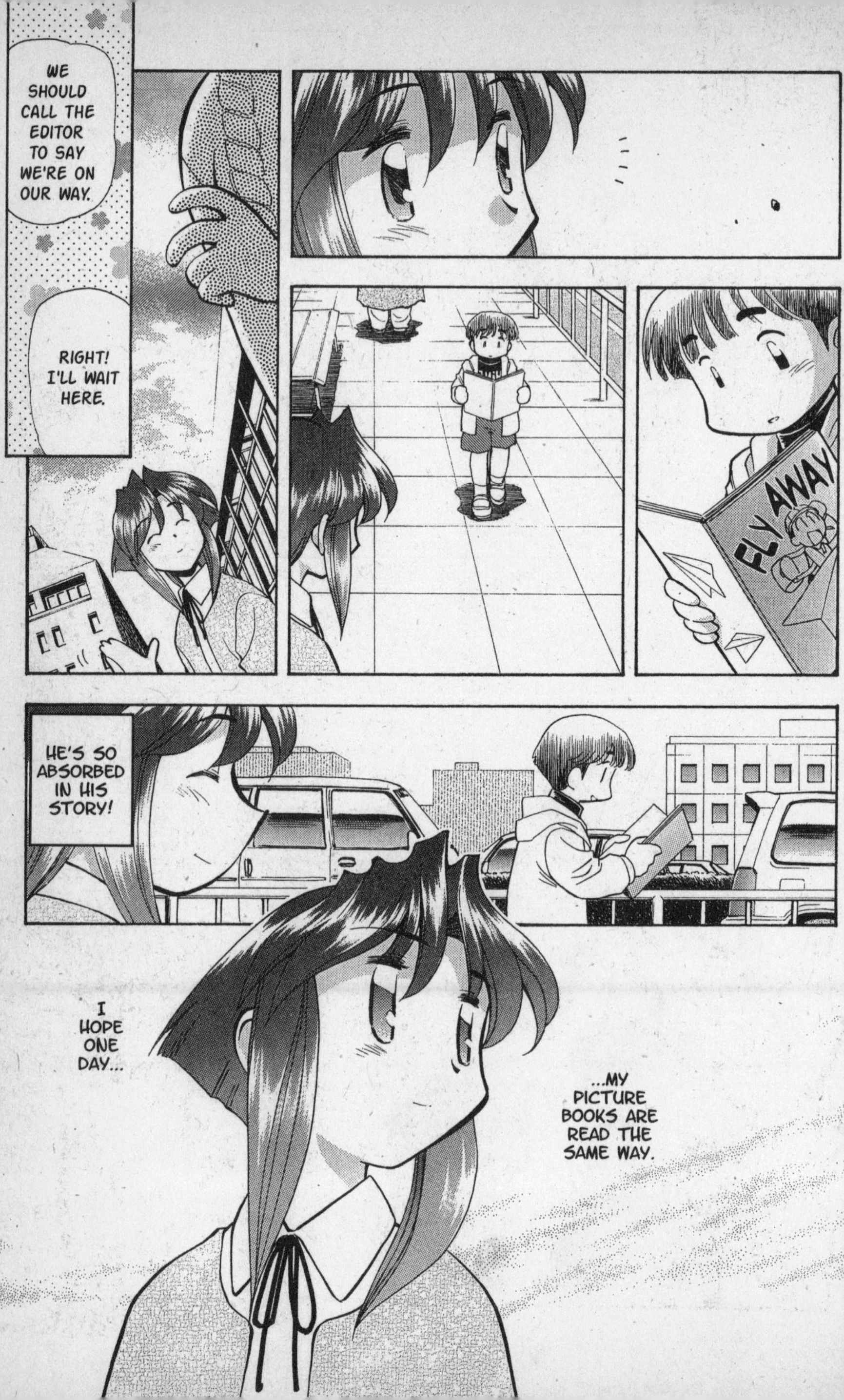
WE SHOULD CALL THE EDITOR TO SAY WE'RE ON OUR WAY.
RIGHT! I'LL WAIT HERE.
FLY AWAY
HE'S SO ABSORBED IN HIS STORY!
I HOPE ONE DAY...
...MY PICTURE BOOKS ARE READ THE SAME WAY.

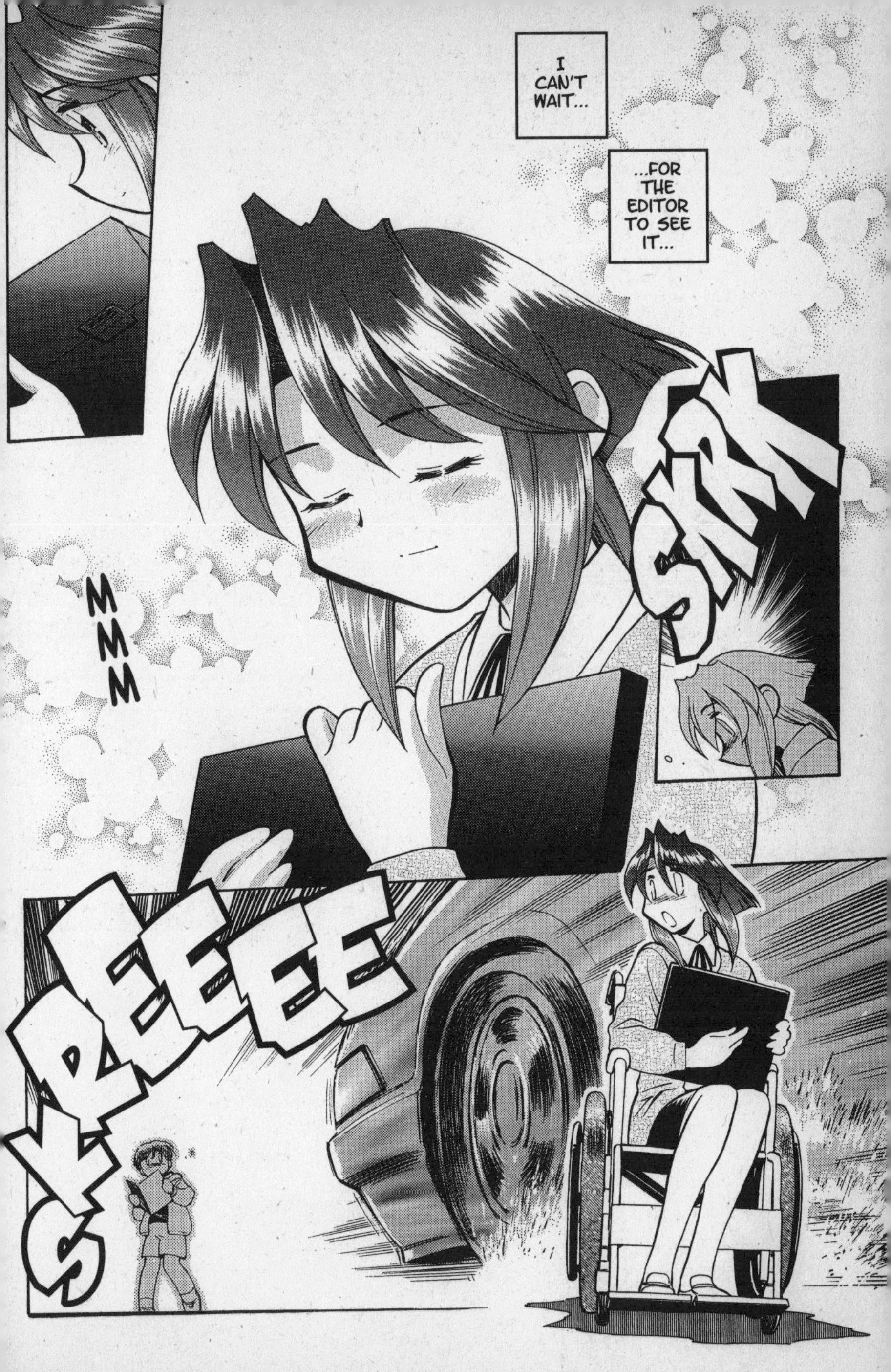
I CAN'T WAIT...
...FOR THE EDITOR TO SEE IT...
MMM
SKRK
SKREEEE

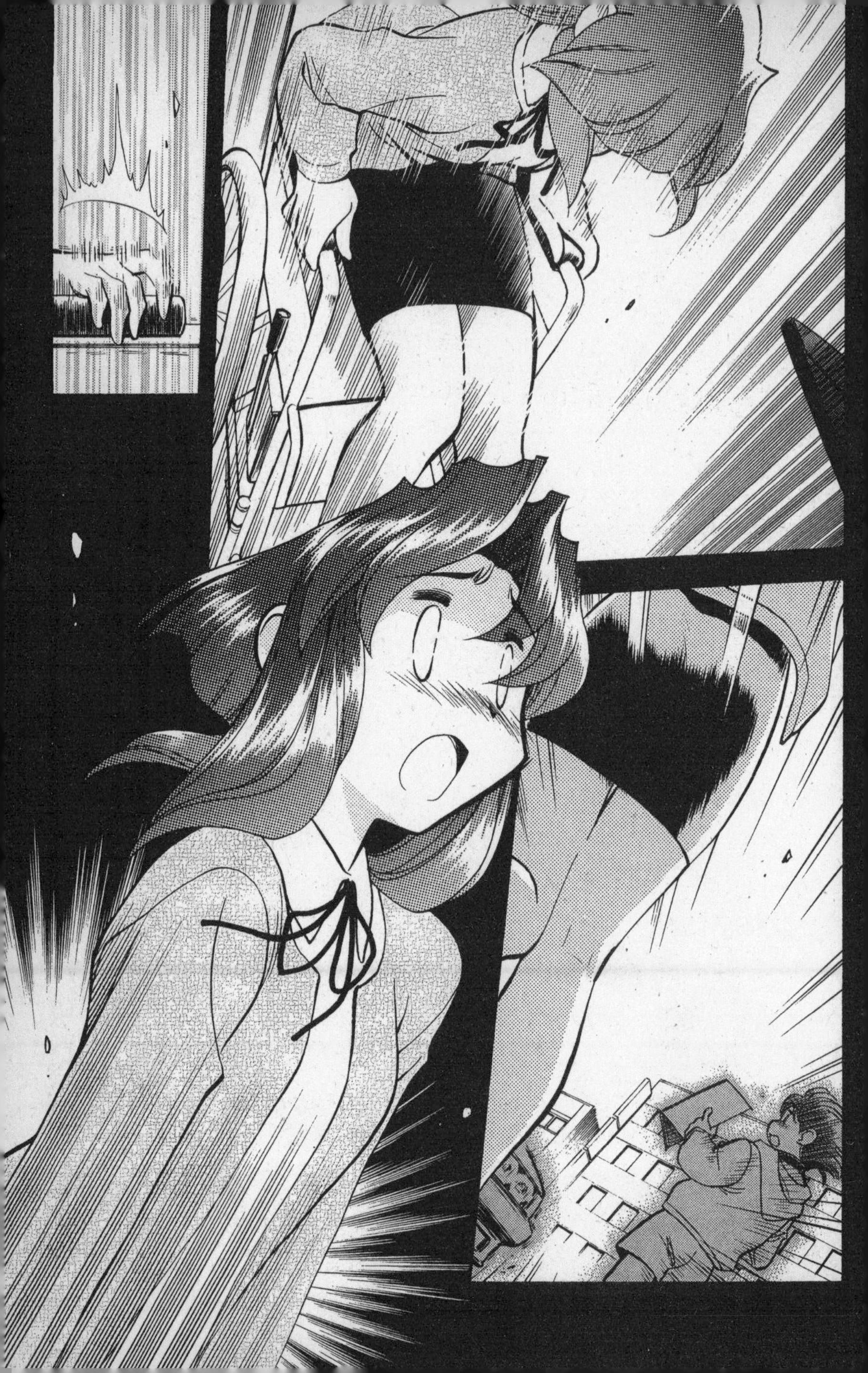

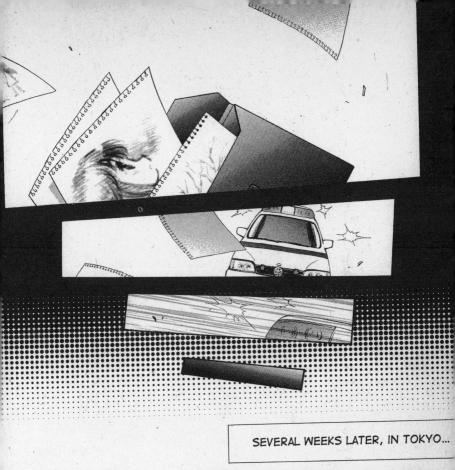

SEVERAL WEEKS LATER, IN TOKYO...

AND NOW, AT LONG LAST, THE GRAND PRIZE...

...BUT FIRST, WE HAVE SOME VERY SAD NEWS TO SHARE WITH YOU.

KAKUBUN PUBLISHING

Picture Book Grand Prize Award

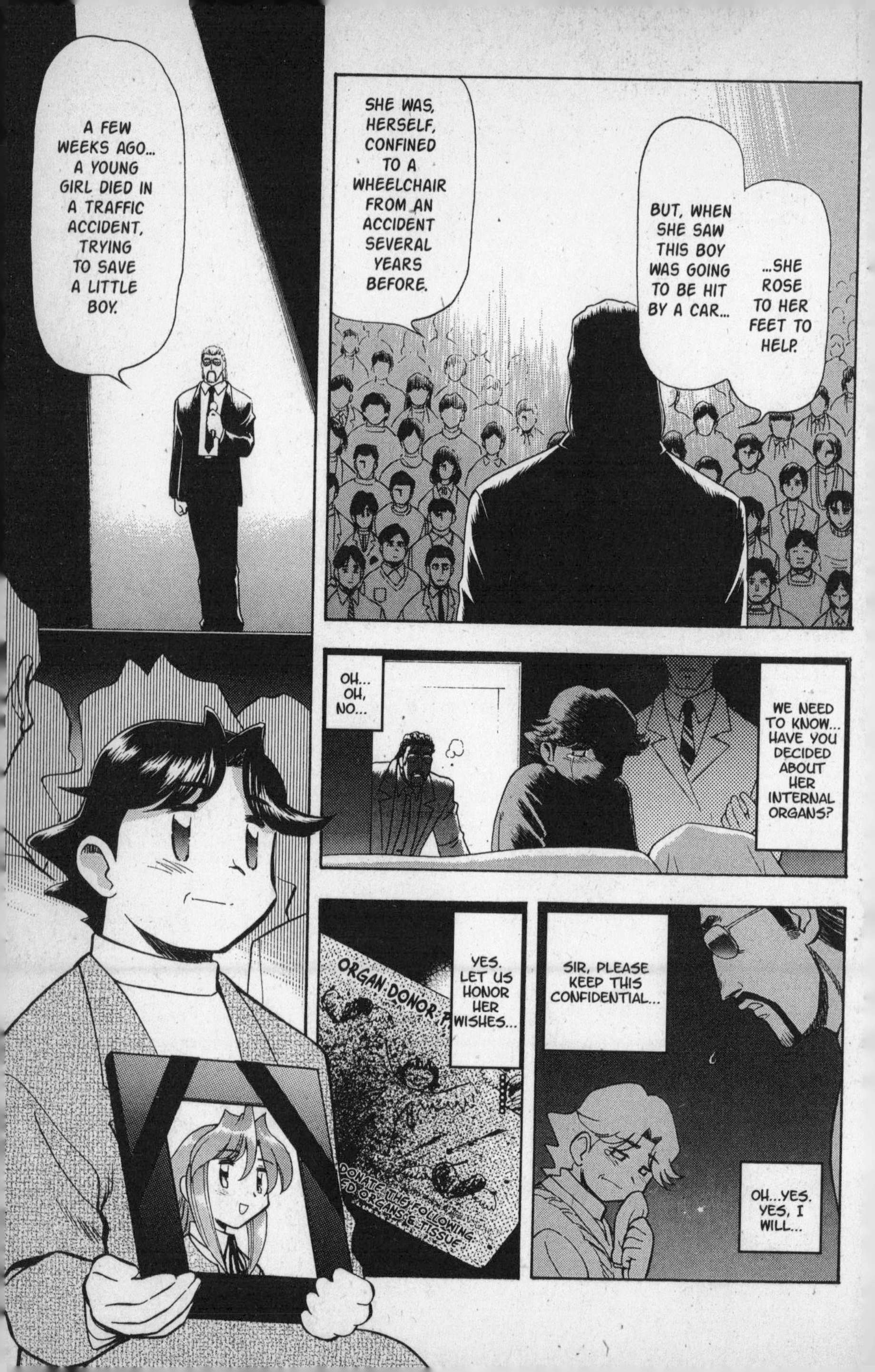
A FEW WEEKS AGO... A YOUNG GIRL DIED IN A TRAFFIC ACCIDENT, TRYING TO SAVE A LITTLE BOY.
SHE WAS, HERSELF, CONFINED TO A WHEELCHAIR FROM AN ACCIDENT SEVERAL YEARS BEFORE.
BUT, WHEN SHE SAW THIS BOY WAS GOING TO BE HIT BY A CAR...
...SHE ROSE TO HER FEET TO HELP.
OH... OH, NO...
WE NEED TO KNOW... HAVE YOU DECIDED ABOUT HER INTERNAL ORGANS?
YES. LET US HONOR HER WISHES...
ORGAN DONOR
DONATE THE FOLLOWING
ORGANS & TISSUE
SIR, PLEASE KEEP THIS CONFIDENTIAL...
OH...YES. YES, I WILL...

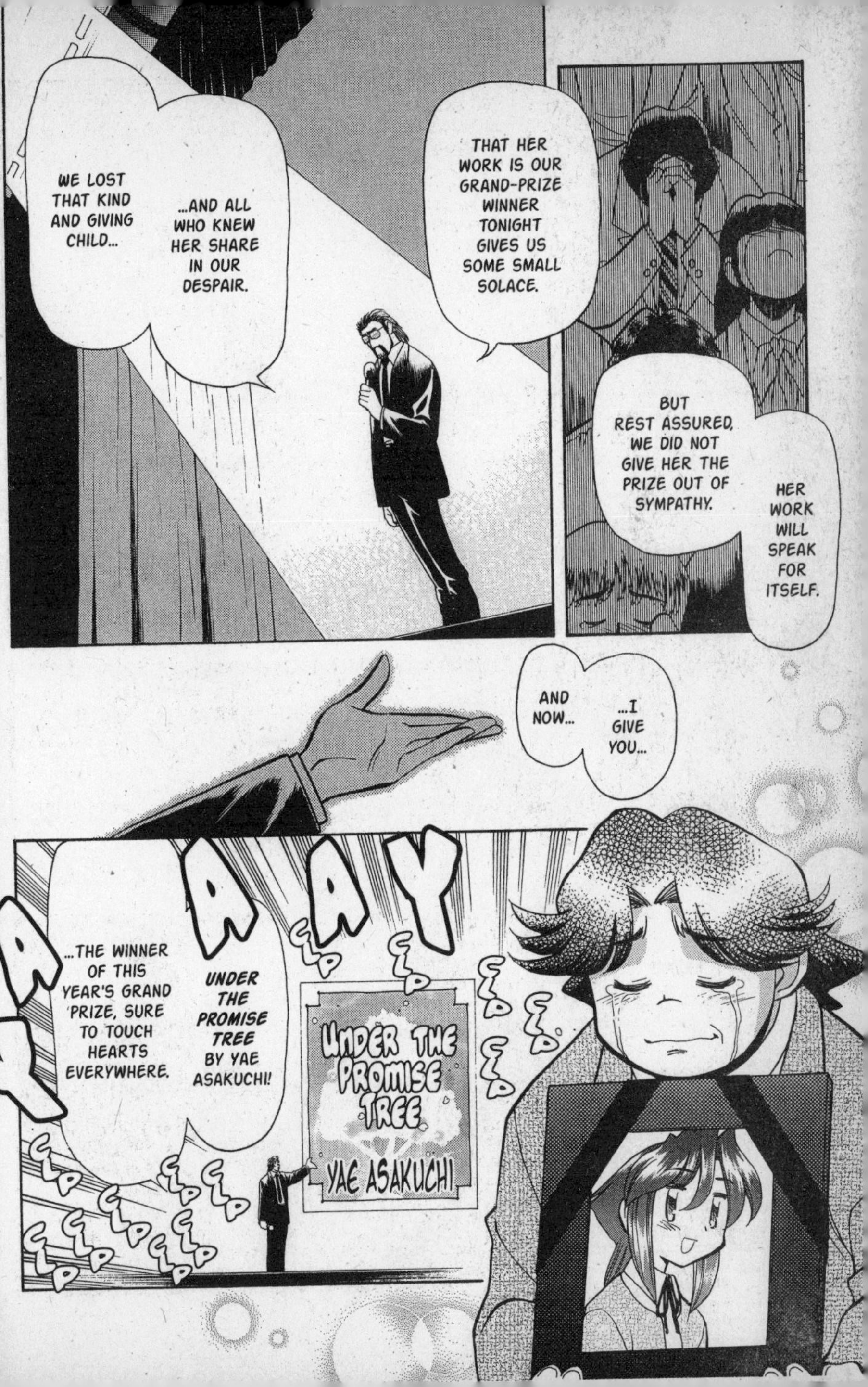
WE LOST THAT KIND AND GIVING CHILD...
...AND ALL WHO KNEW HER SHARE IN OUR DESPAIR.
THAT HER WORK IS OUR GRAND-PRIZE WINNER TONIGHT GIVES US SOME SMALL SOLACE.
BUT REST ASSURED, WE DID NOT GIVE HER THE PRIZE OUT OF SYMPATHY.
HER WORK WILL SPEAK FOR ITSELF.
AND NOW...
...I GIVE YOU...
...THE WINNER OF THIS YEAR'S GRAND PRIZE, SURE TO TOUCH HEARTS EVERYWHERE.
UNDER THE PROMISE TREE BY YAE ASAKUCHI!
UNDER THE PROMISE TREE
YAE ASAKUCHI
CLP CLP CLP

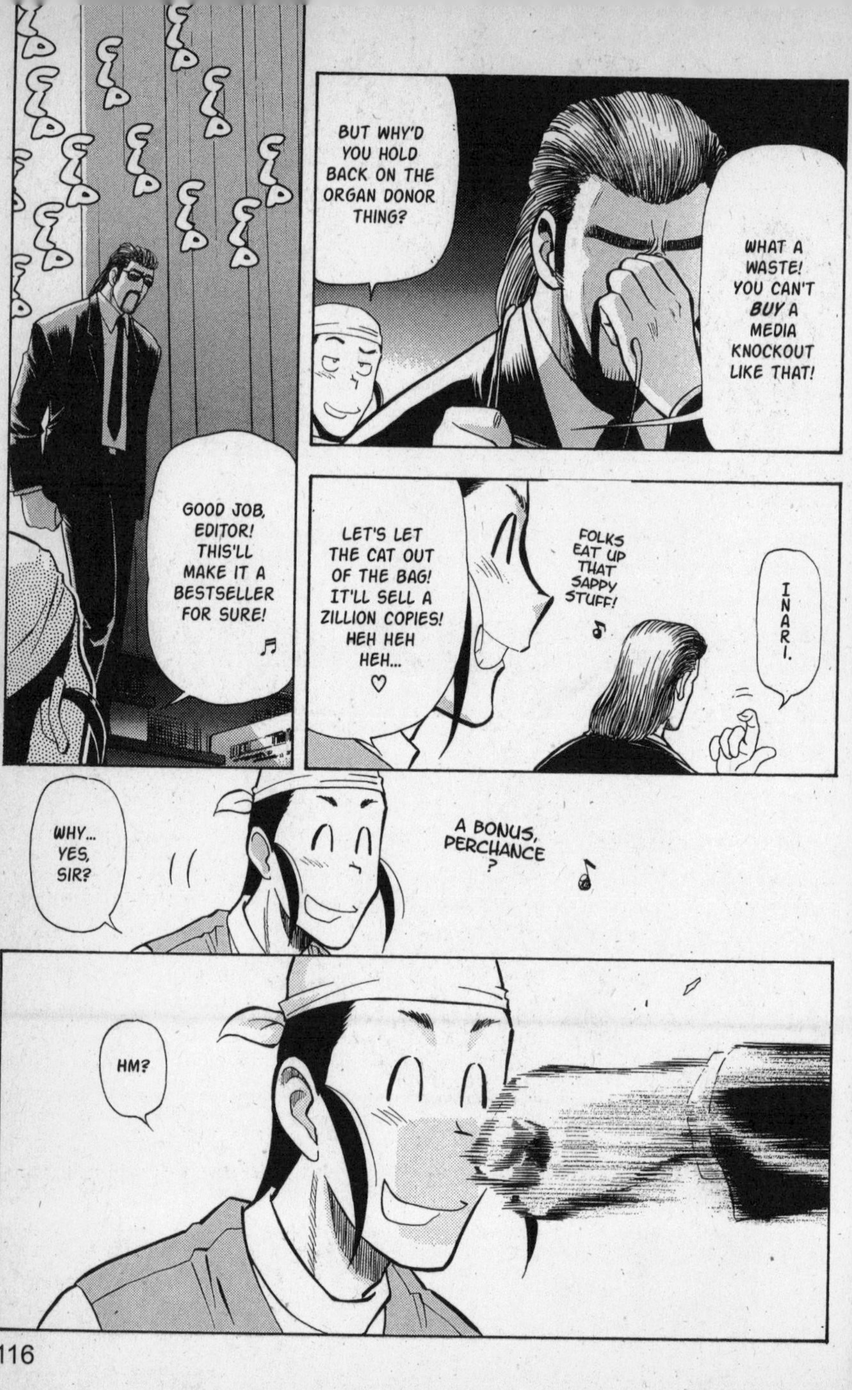
CLP CLP CLP CLP CLP CLP CLP CLP CLP CLP
GOOD JOB, EDITOR! THIS'LL MAKE IT A BESTSELLER FOR SURE! ♬
BUT WHY'D YOU HOLD BACK ON THE ORGAN DONOR THING?
WHAT A WASTE! YOU CAN'T *BUY* A MEDIA KNOCKOUT LIKE THAT!
LET'S LET THE CAT OUT OF THE BAG! IT'LL SELL A ZILLION COPIES! HEH HEH HEH... ♡
FOLKS EAT UP THAT SAPPY STUFF! ♪
INARI.
WHY... YES, SIR?
A BONUS, PERCHANCE? ♪
HM?

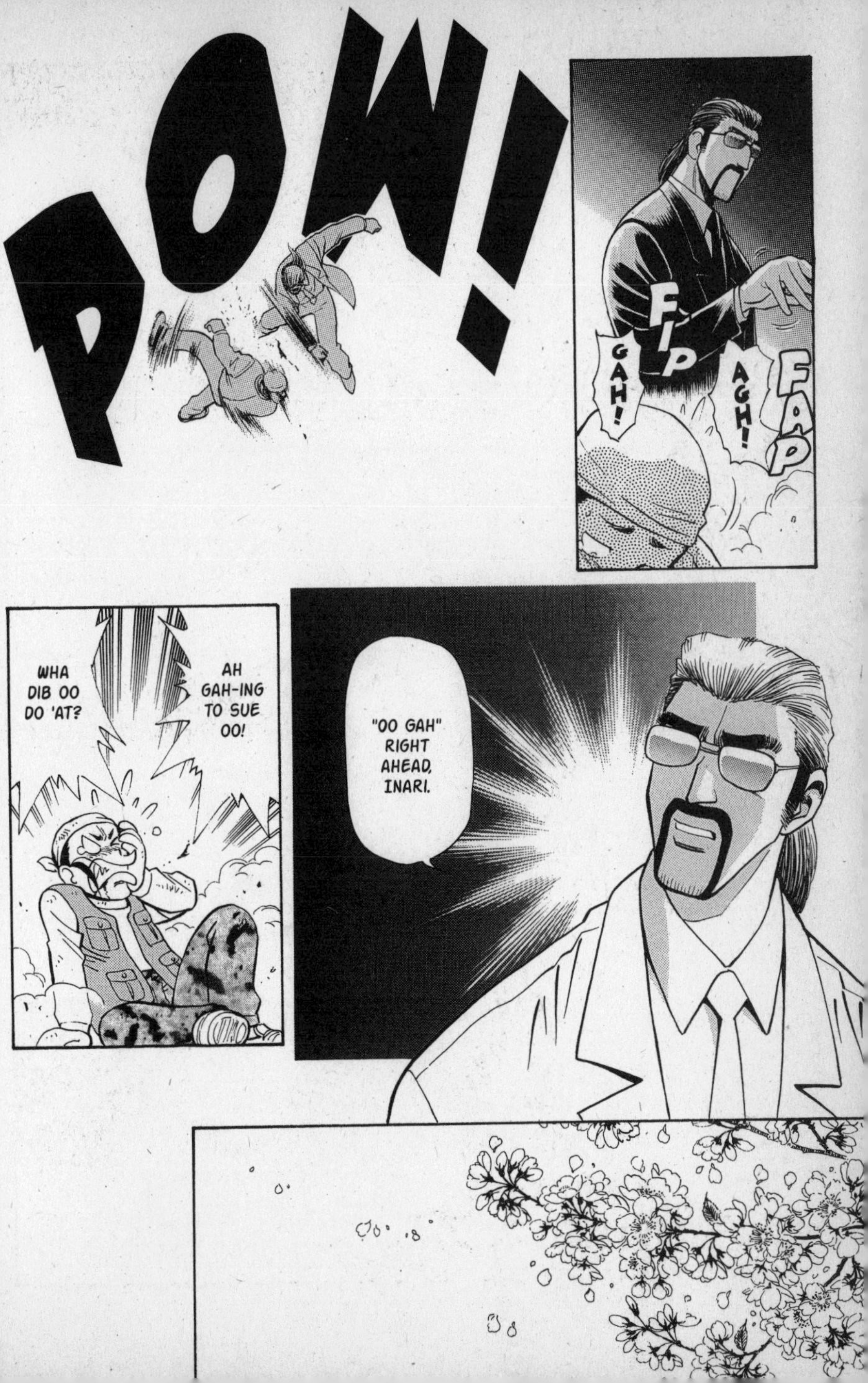
POW!!
FIP
GAH!
AGH!
FAP
WHA DIB OO DO 'AT?
AH GAH-ING TO SUE OO!
"OO GAH" RIGHT AHEAD, INARI.

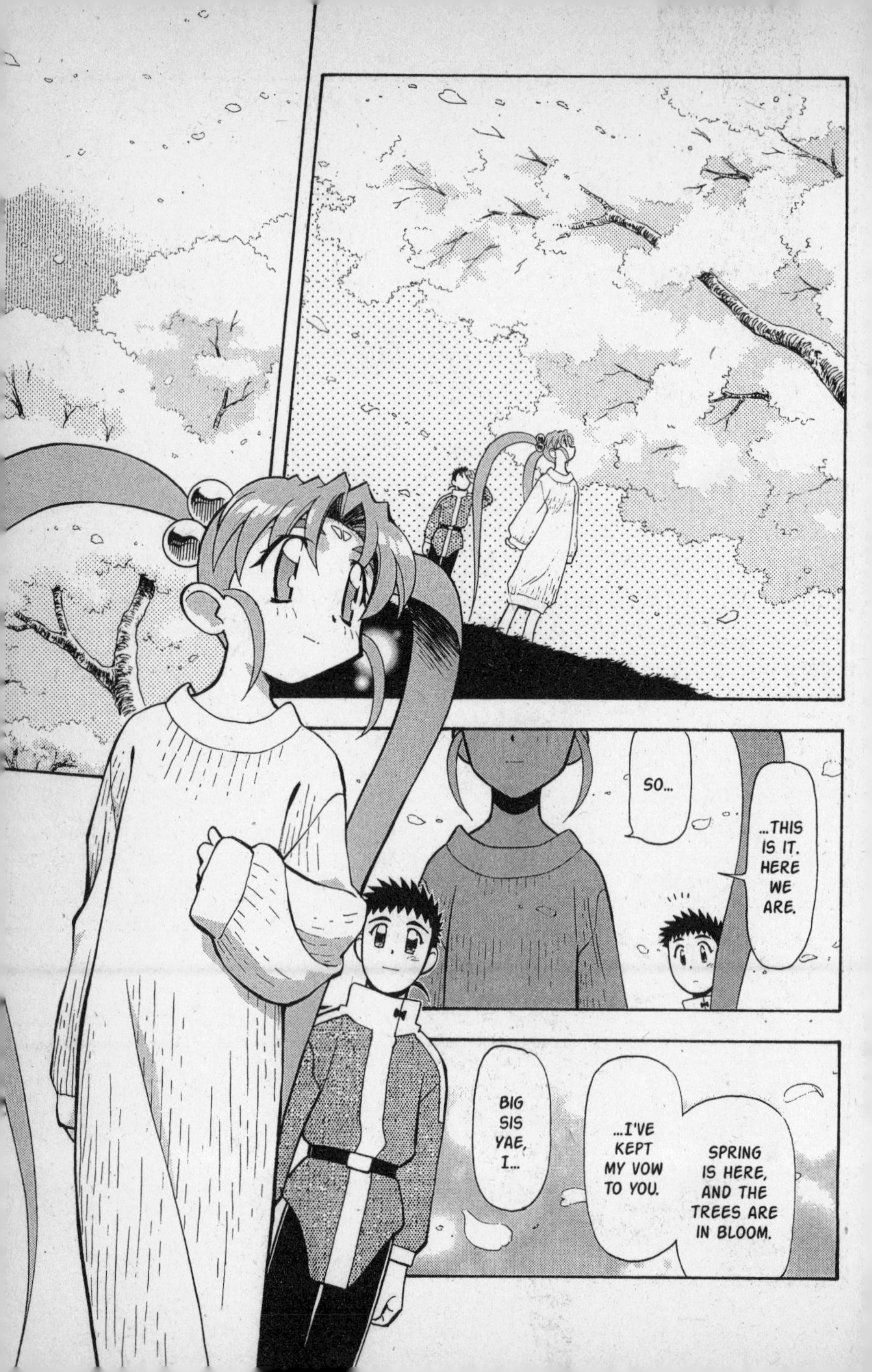
SO...
...THIS IS IT. HERE WE ARE.
BIG SIS YAE, I...
...I'VE KEPT MY VOW TO YOU.
SPRING IS HERE, AND THE TREES ARE IN BLOOM.

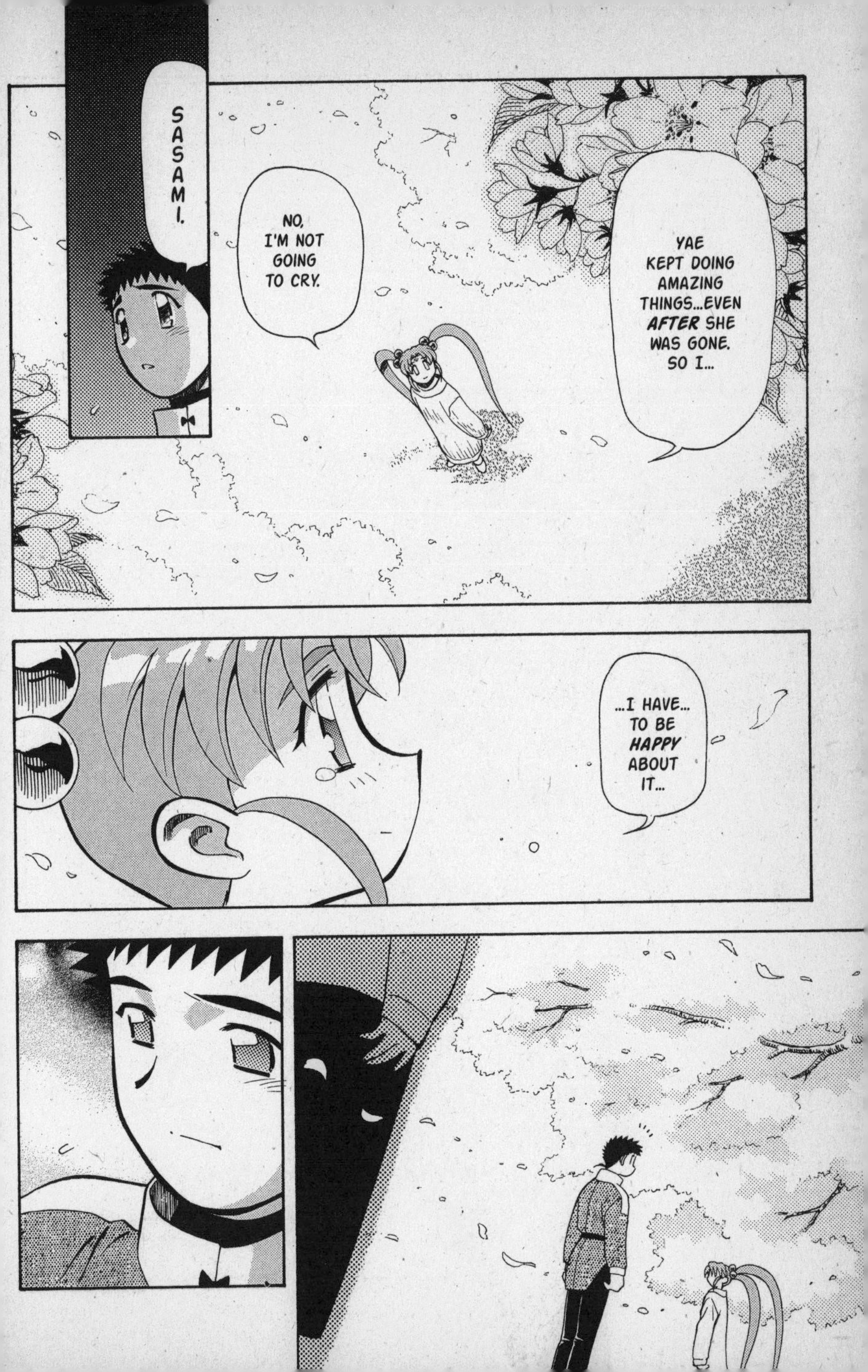
SASAMI.
NO, I'M NOT GOING TO CRY.
YAE KEPT DOING AMAZING THINGS...EVEN AFTER SHE WAS GONE. SO I...
...I HAVE... TO BE HAPPY ABOUT IT...

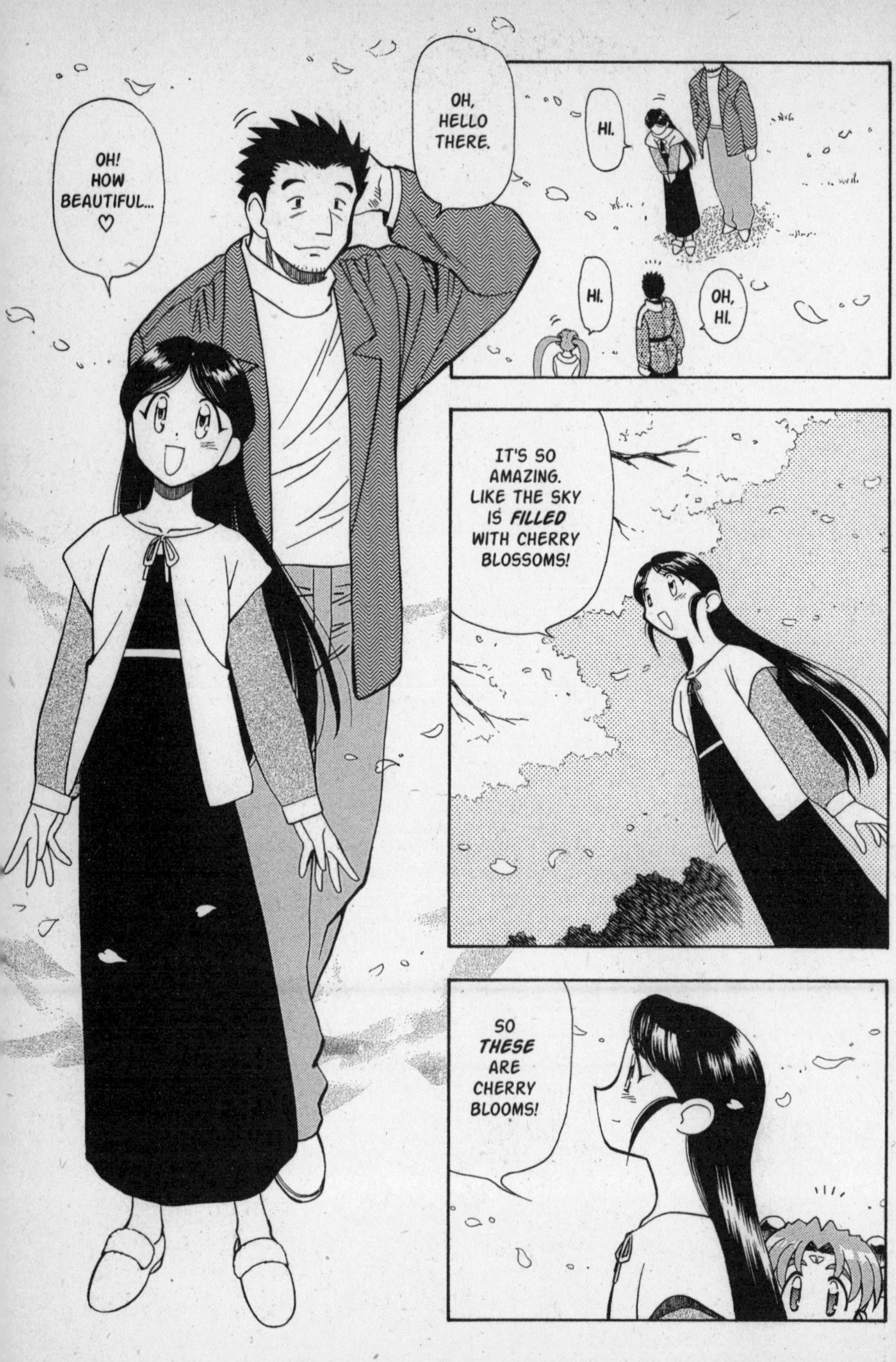
OH! HOW BEAUTIFUL... ♡
OH, HELLO THERE.
HI.
HI.
OH, HI.
IT'S SO AMAZING. LIKE THE SKY IS *FILLED* WITH CHERRY BLOSSOMS!
SO *THESE* ARE CHERRY BLOOMS!

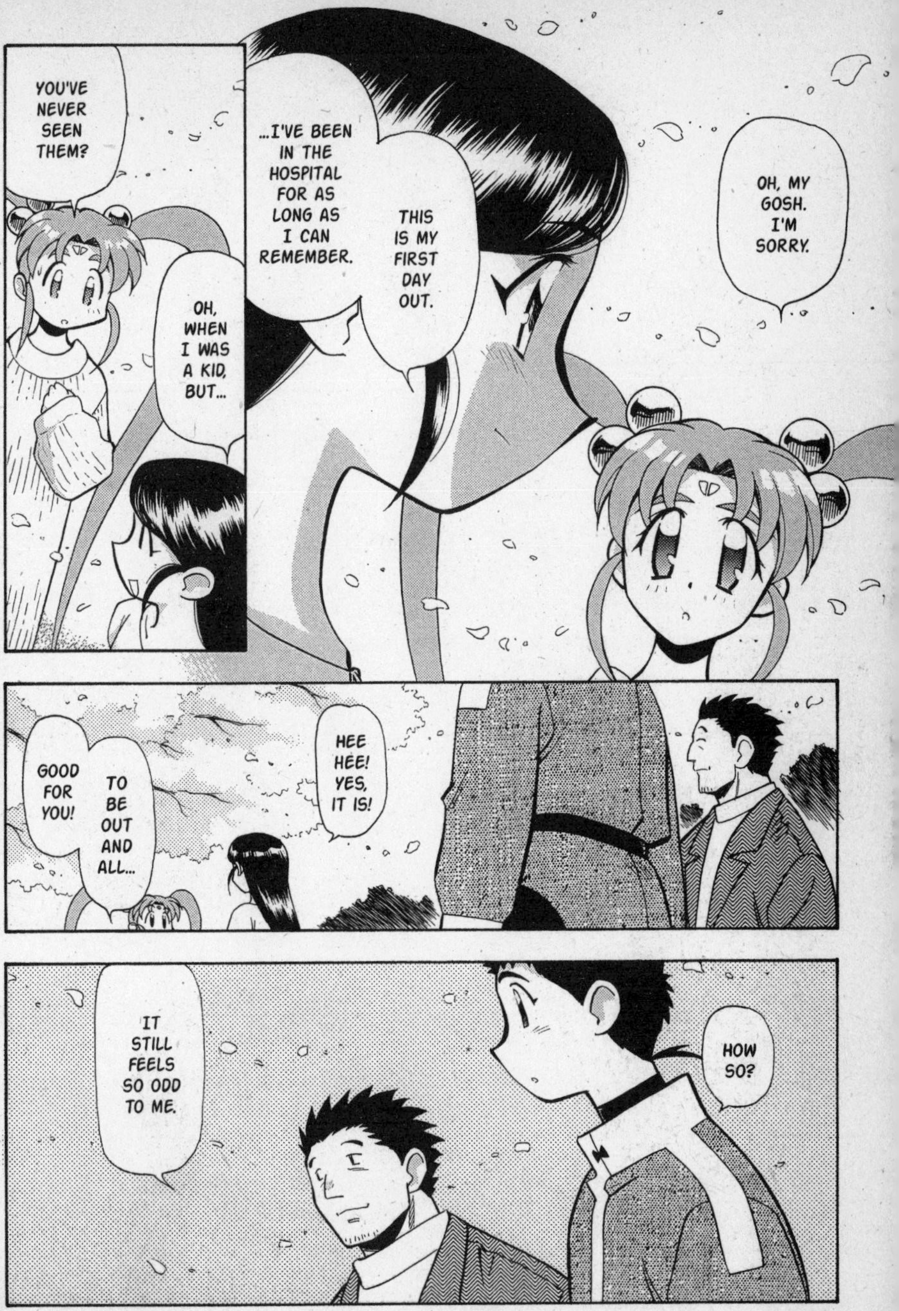
YOU'VE NEVER SEEN THEM?
OH, WHEN I WAS A KID, BUT...
...I'VE BEEN IN THE HOSPITAL FOR AS LONG AS I CAN REMEMBER.
THIS IS MY FIRST DAY OUT.
OH, MY GOSH. I'M SORRY.
GOOD FOR YOU!
TO BE OUT AND ALL...
HEE HEE! YES, IT IS!
IT STILL FEELS SO ODD TO ME.
HOW SO?

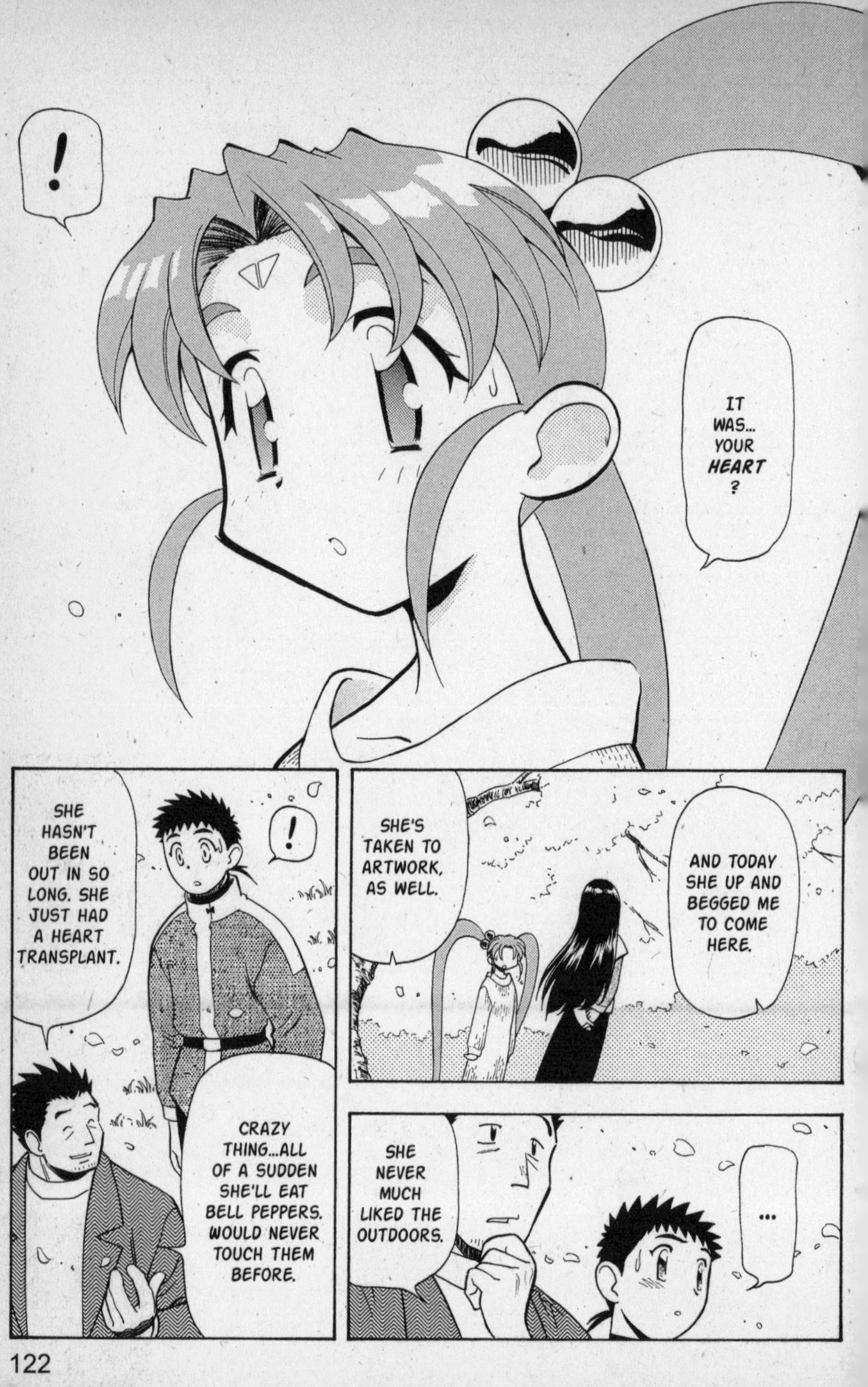
!
IT WAS... YOUR HEART?
SHE HASN'T BEEN OUT IN SO LONG. SHE JUST HAD A HEART TRANSPLANT.
!
CRAZY THING...ALL OF A SUDDEN SHE'LL EAT BELL PEPPERS. WOULD NEVER TOUCH THEM BEFORE.
SHE'S TAKEN TO ARTWORK, AS WELL.
AND TODAY SHE UP AND BEGGED ME TO COME HERE.
SHE NEVER MUCH LIKED THE OUTDOORS.
...

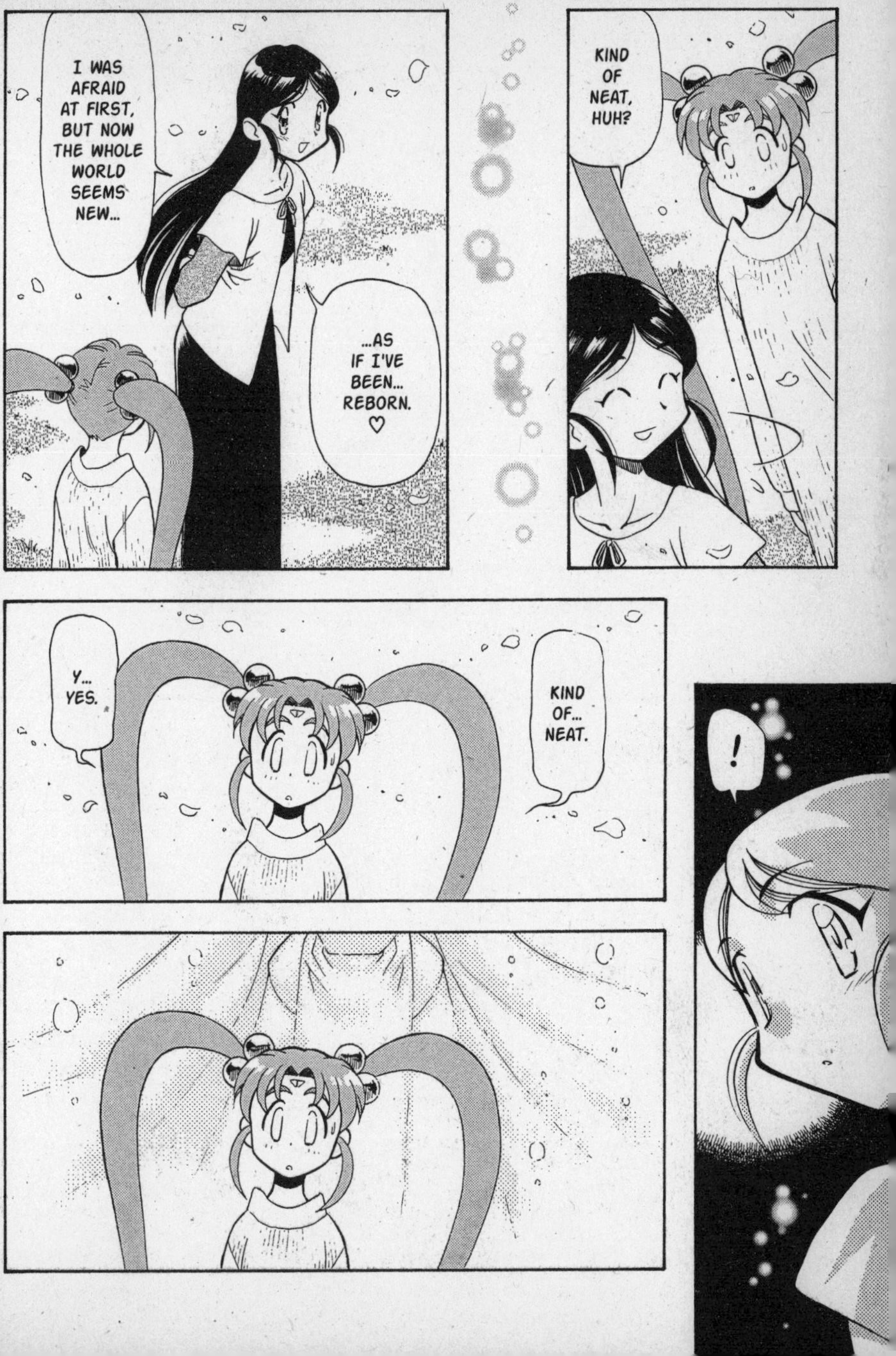
I WAS AFRAID AT FIRST, BUT NOW THE WHOLE WORLD SEEMS NEW...
...AS IF I'VE BEEN... REBORN. ♡
KIND OF NEAT, HUH?
Y... YES.
KIND OF... NEAT.
!

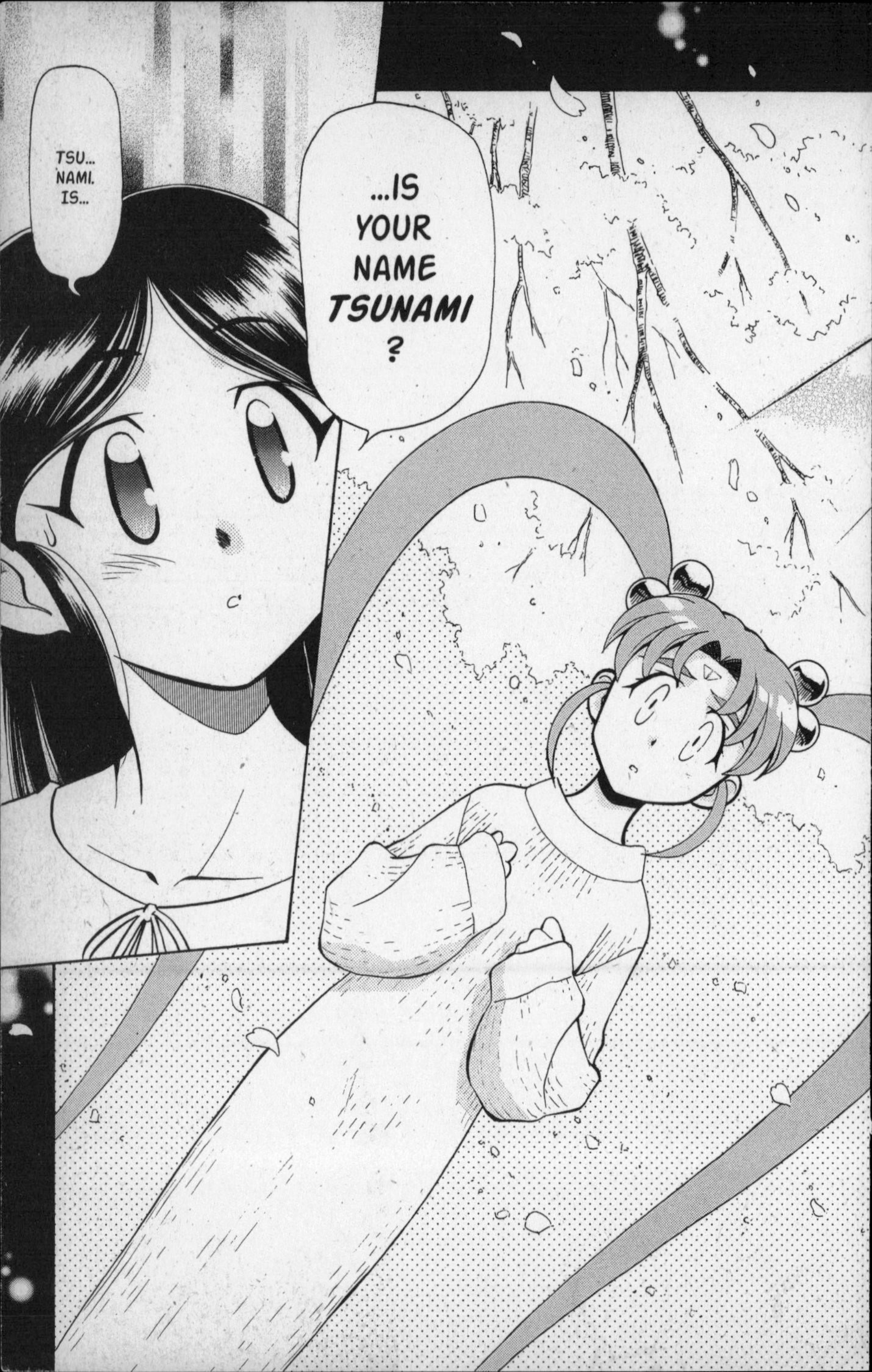
TSU... NAMI. IS...
...IS YOUR NAME TSUNAMI ?

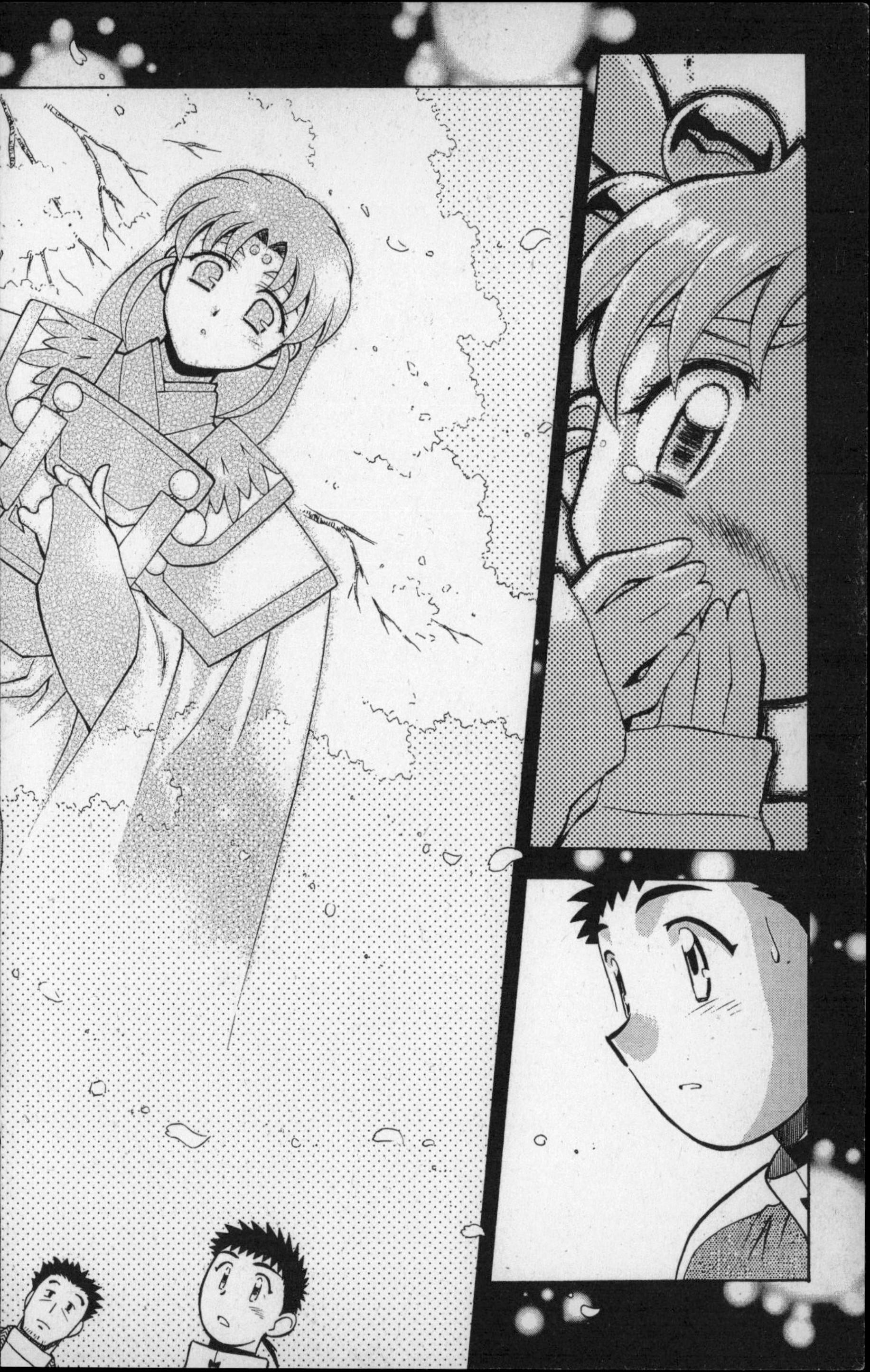

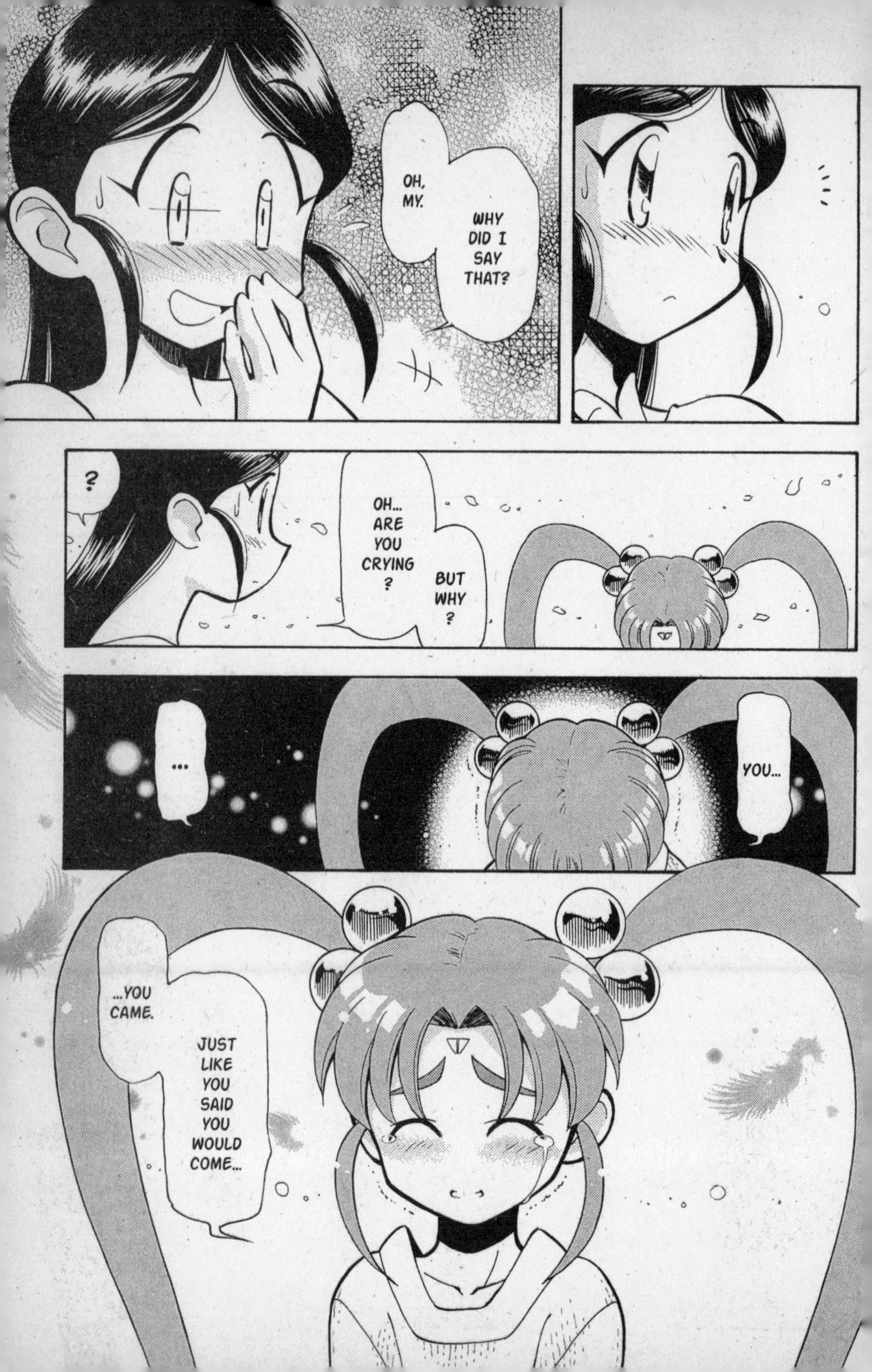
OH, MY.
WHY DID I SAY THAT?
?
OH... ARE YOU CRYING?
BUT WHY?
...
YOU...
...YOU CAME.
JUST LIKE YOU SAID YOU WOULD COME...

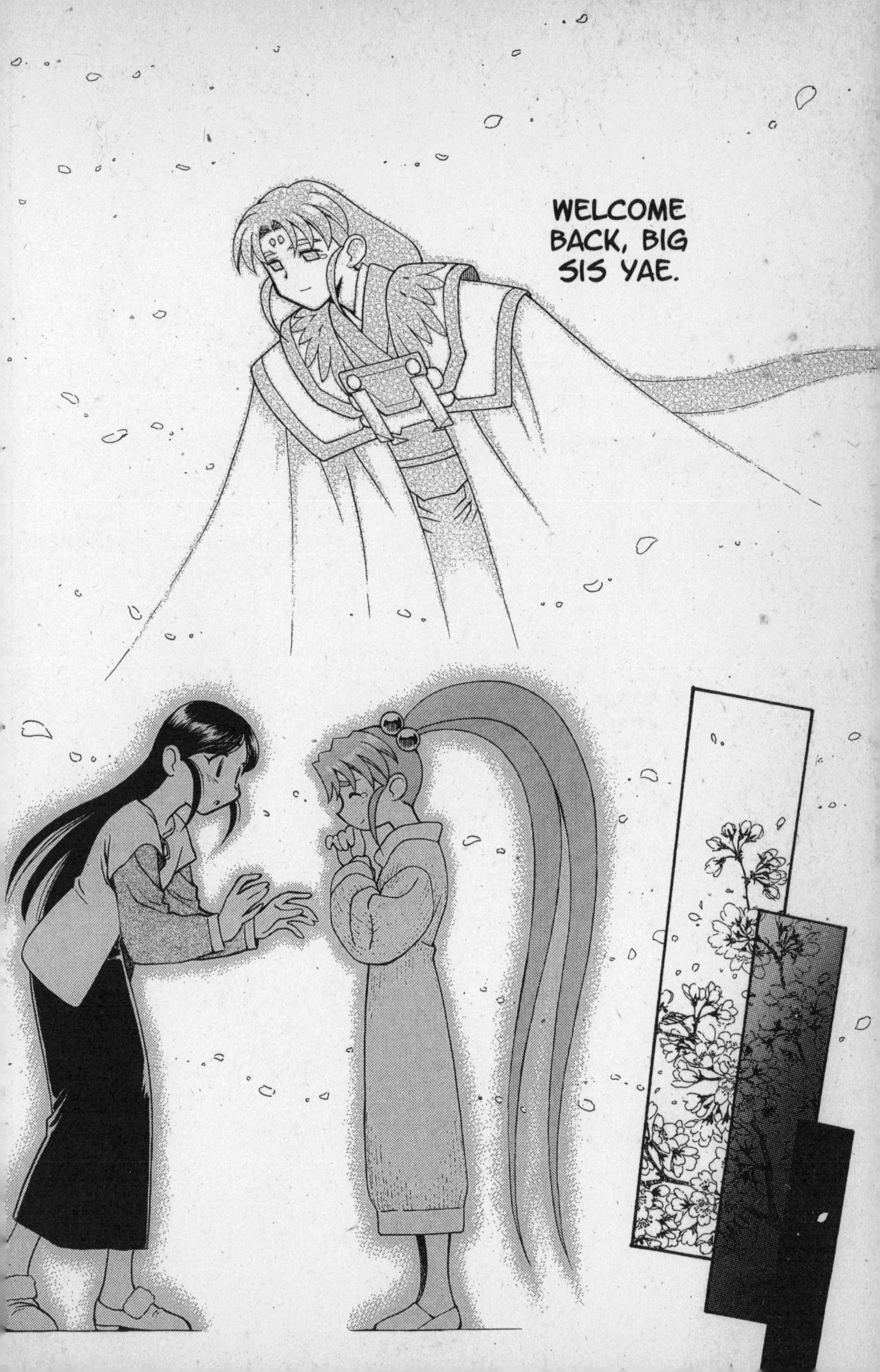
WELCOME BACK, BIG SIS YAE.

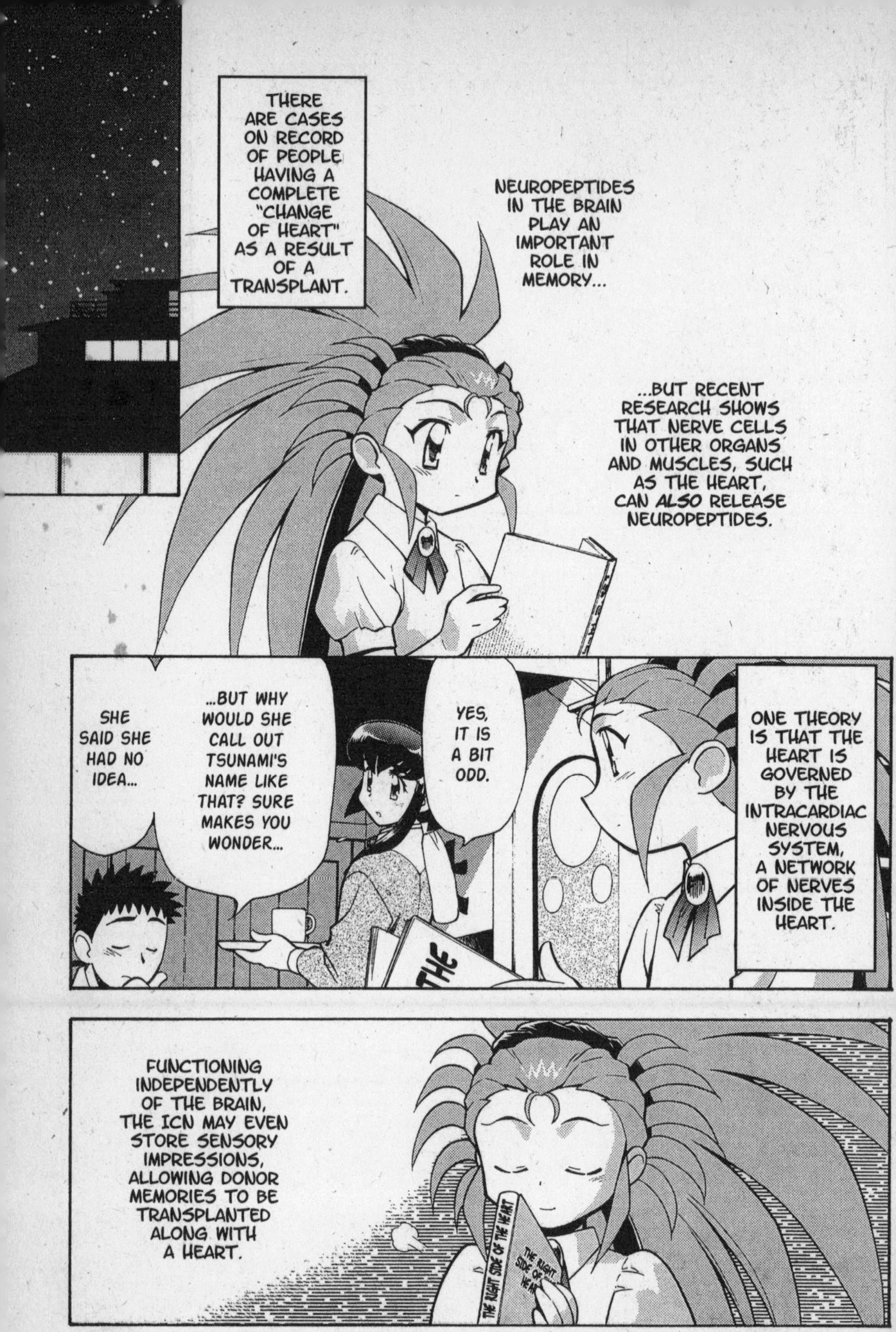
THERE ARE CASES ON RECORD OF PEOPLE HAVING A COMPLETE "CHANGE OF HEART" AS A RESULT OF A TRANSPLANT.
NEUROPEPTIDES IN THE BRAIN PLAY AN IMPORTANT ROLE IN MEMORY...
...BUT RECENT RESEARCH SHOWS THAT NERVE CELLS IN OTHER ORGANS AND MUSCLES, SUCH AS THE HEART, CAN *ALSO* RELEASE NEUROPEPTIDES.
SHE SAID SHE HAD NO IDEA...
...BUT WHY WOULD SHE CALL OUT TSUNAMI'S NAME LIKE THAT? SURE MAKES YOU WONDER...
YES, IT IS A BIT ODD.
ONE THEORY IS THAT THE HEART IS GOVERNED BY THE INTRACARDIAC NERVOUS SYSTEM, A NETWORK OF NERVES INSIDE THE HEART.
THE
FUNCTIONING INDEPENDENTLY OF THE BRAIN, THE ICN MAY EVEN STORE SENSORY IMPRESSIONS, ALLOWING DONOR MEMORIES TO BE TRANSPLANTED ALONG WITH A HEART.
THE RIGHT SIDE OF THE HEART

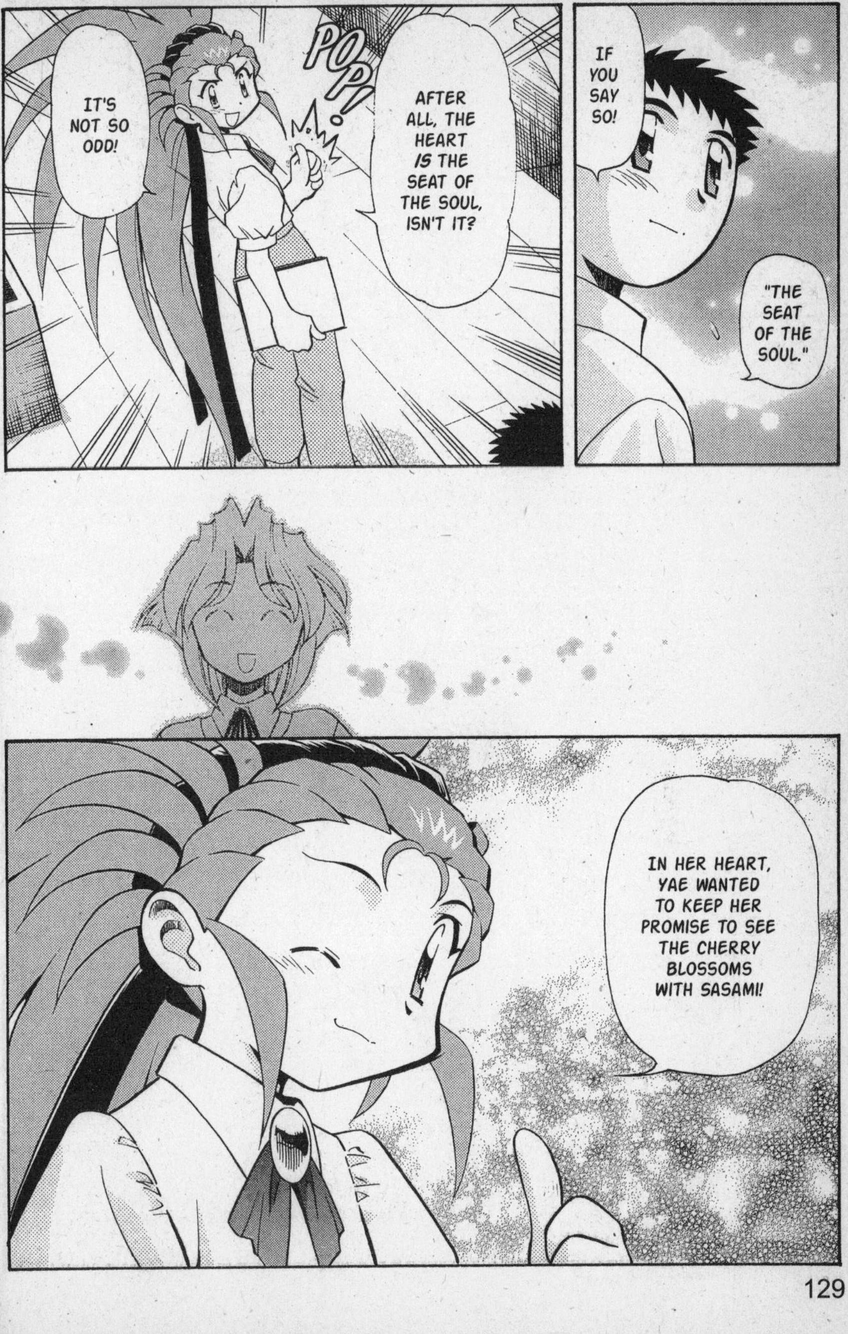
IT'S NOT SO ODD!
POP!
AFTER ALL, THE HEART *IS* THE SEAT OF THE SOUL, ISN'T IT?
IF YOU SAY SO!
"THE SEAT OF THE SOUL."
IN HER HEART, YAE WANTED TO KEEP HER PROMISE TO SEE THE CHERRY BLOSSOMS WITH SASAMI!

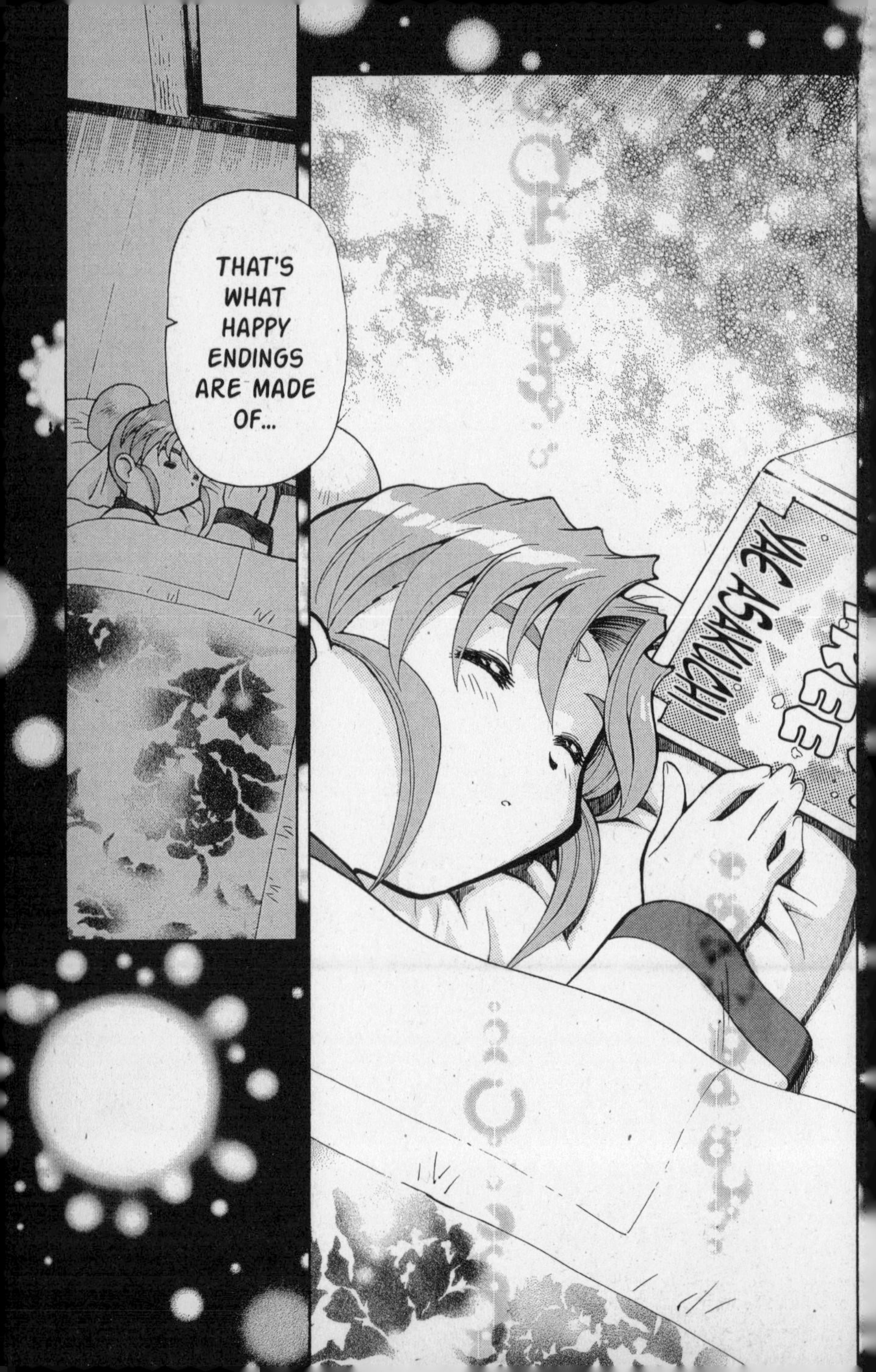
THAT'S WHAT HAPPY ENDINGS ARE MADE OF...
YAE ASAKUCHI

Chapter 5: Games

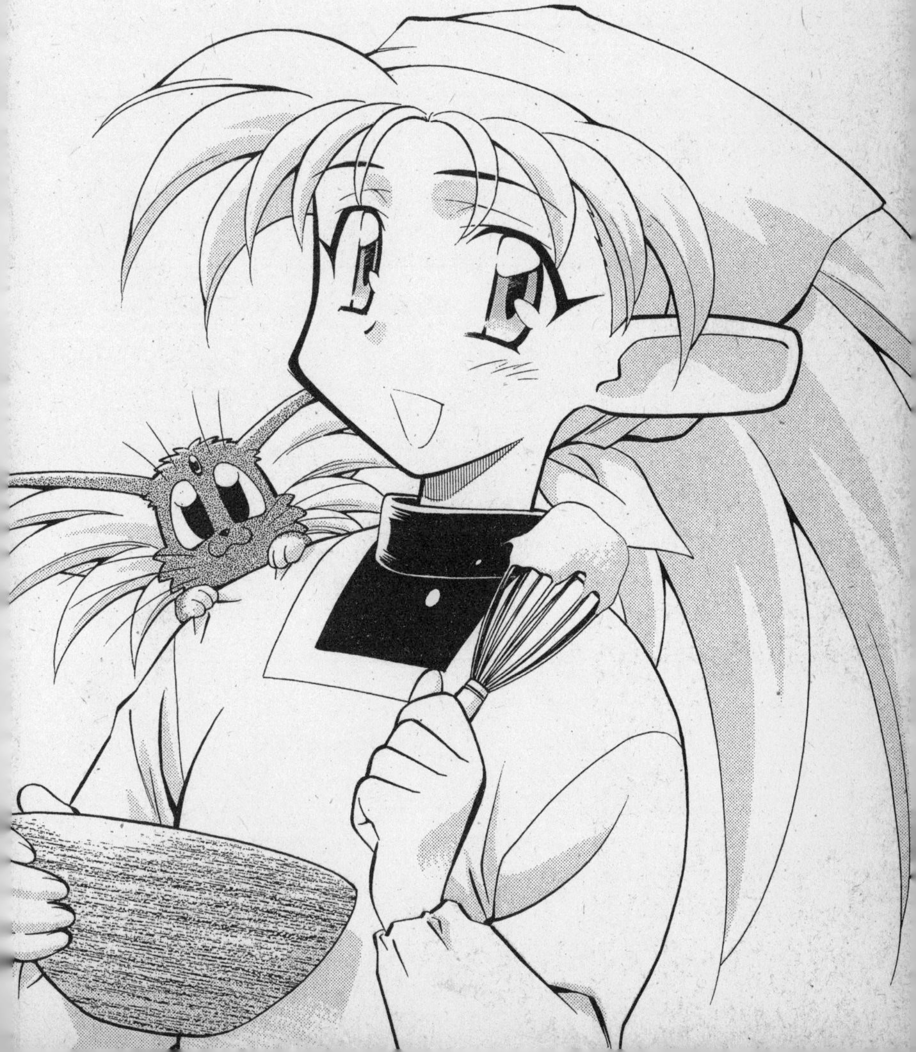

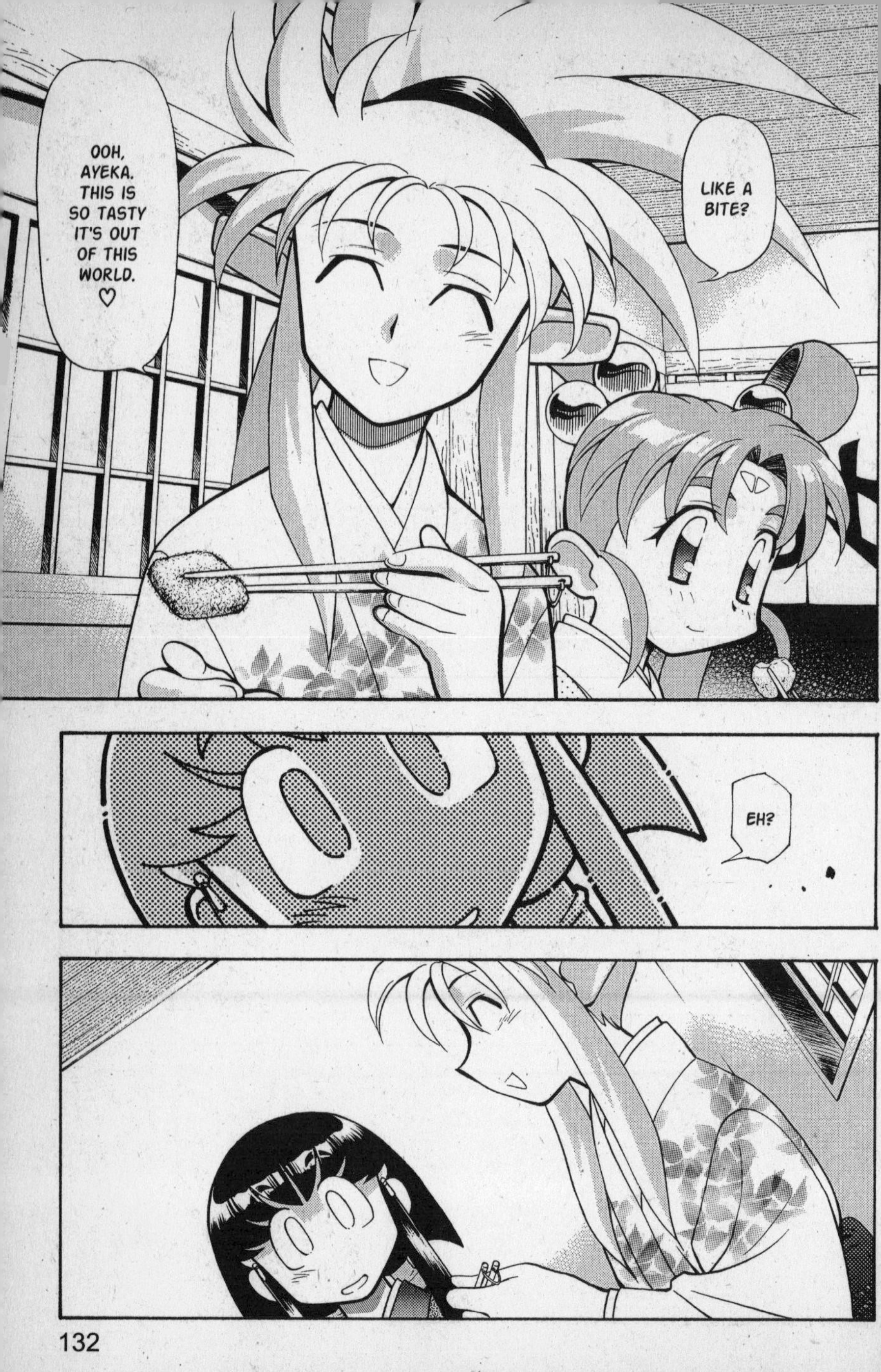
OOH, AYEKA. THIS IS SO TASTY IT'S OUT OF THIS WORLD. ♡
LIKE A BITE?
EH?

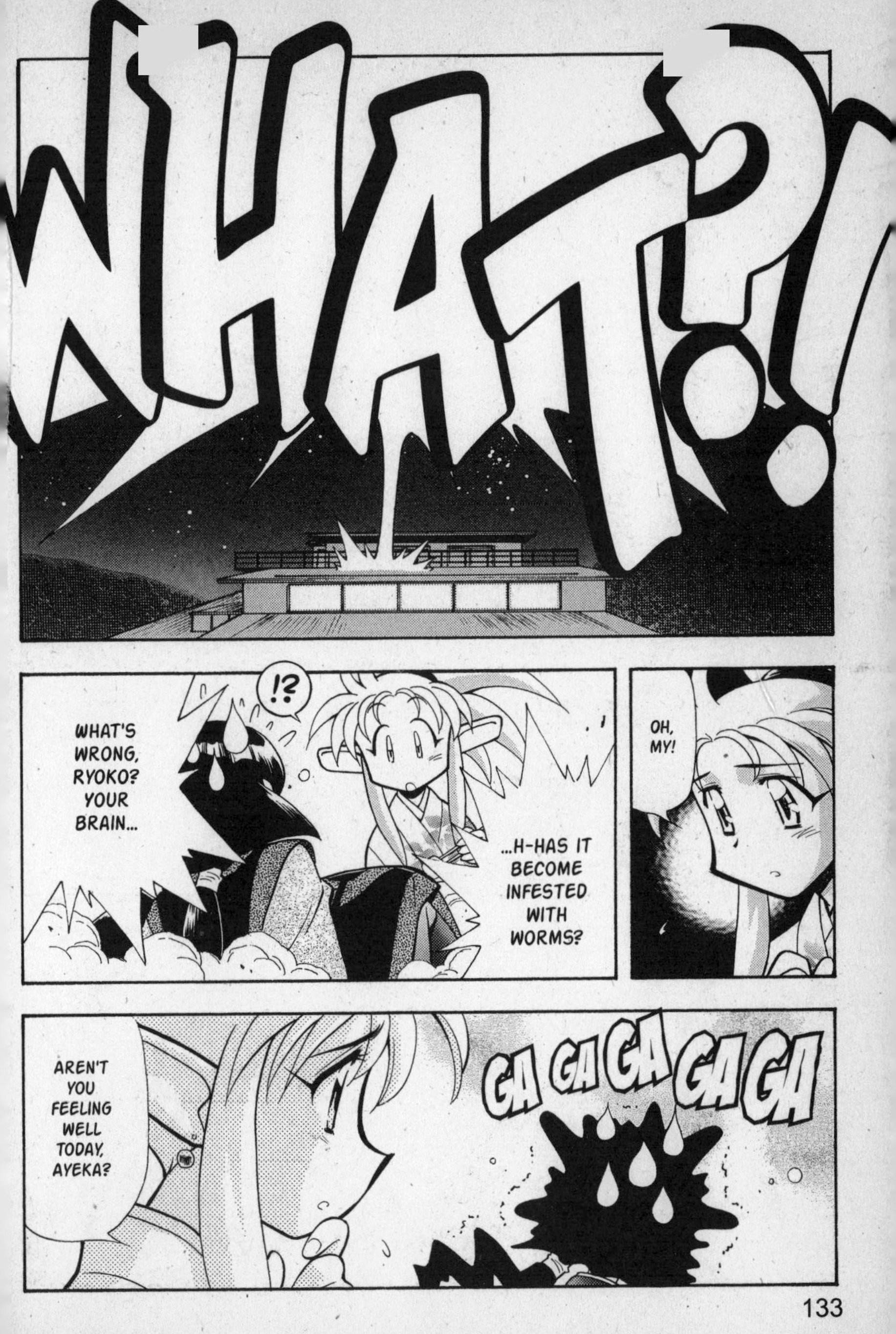
WHAT?!
!?
WHAT'S WRONG, RYOKO? YOUR BRAIN...
...H-HAS IT BECOME INFESTED WITH WORMS?
OH, MY!
AREN'T YOU FEELING WELL TODAY, AYEKA?
GA GA GA GA GA GA

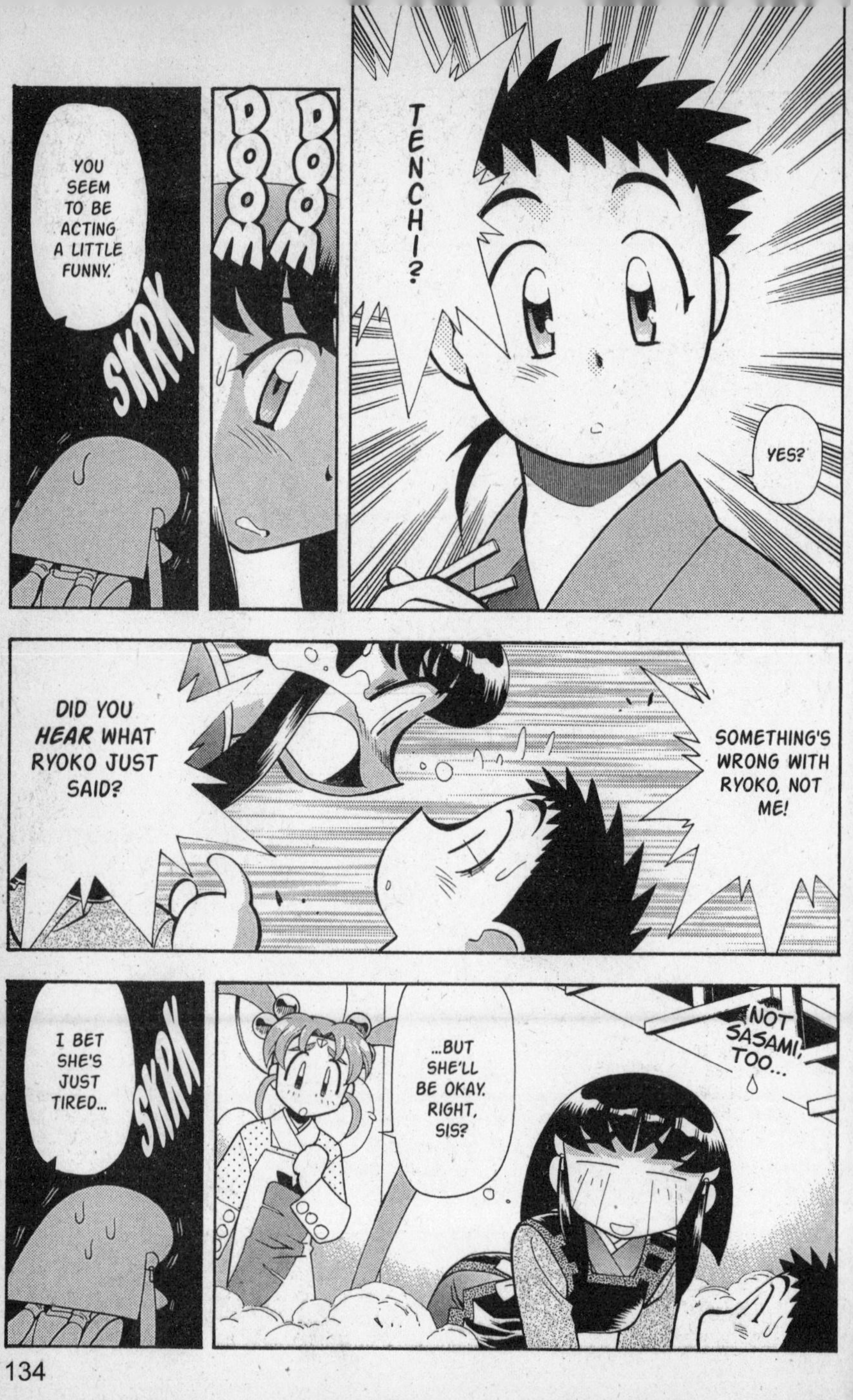
YOU SEEM TO BE ACTING A LITTLE FUNNY.
SKRK
DOOM DOOM
TENCHI?
YES?
DID YOU HEAR WHAT RYOKO JUST SAID?
SOMETHING'S WRONG WITH RYOKO, NOT ME!
I BET SHE'S JUST TIRED...
SKRK
...BUT SHE'LL BE OKAY. RIGHT, SIS?
NOT SASAMI, TOO...

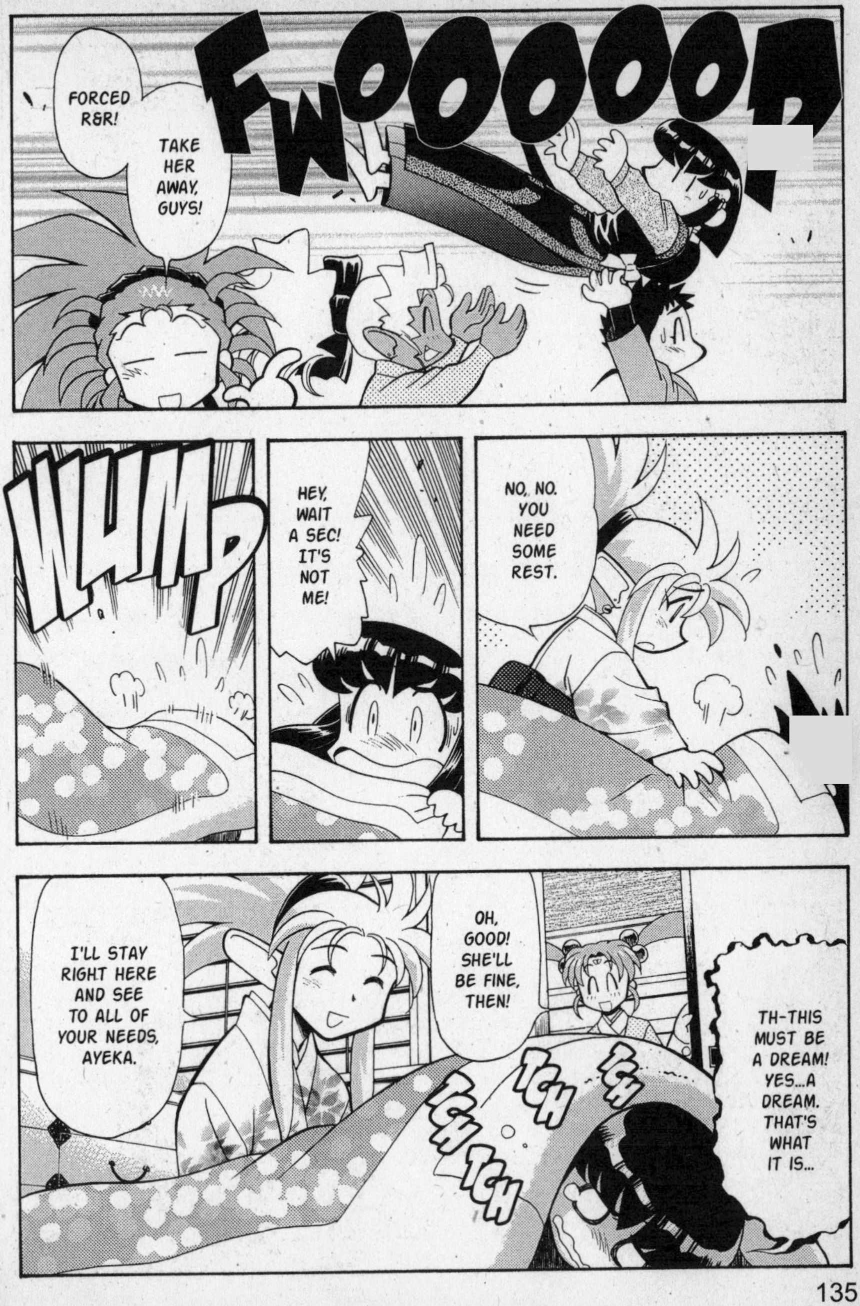
FORCED R&R!
TAKE HER AWAY, GUYS!
FWOOOOOP
WHUMP
HEY, WAIT A SEC! IT'S NOT ME!
NO, NO. YOU NEED SOME REST.
I'LL STAY RIGHT HERE AND SEE TO ALL OF YOUR NEEDS, AYEKA.
OH, GOOD! SHE'LL BE FINE, THEN!
TCH TCH TCH TCH
TH-THIS MUST BE A DREAM! YES...A DREAM. THAT'S WHAT IT IS...

PLEASE LET ME WAKE UP!

OH OH OH OH OH

PLEASE!

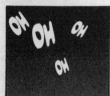

OH OH OH OH

TWEE TWEE

...MM.

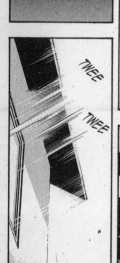

TWEE

TWEE

...

...

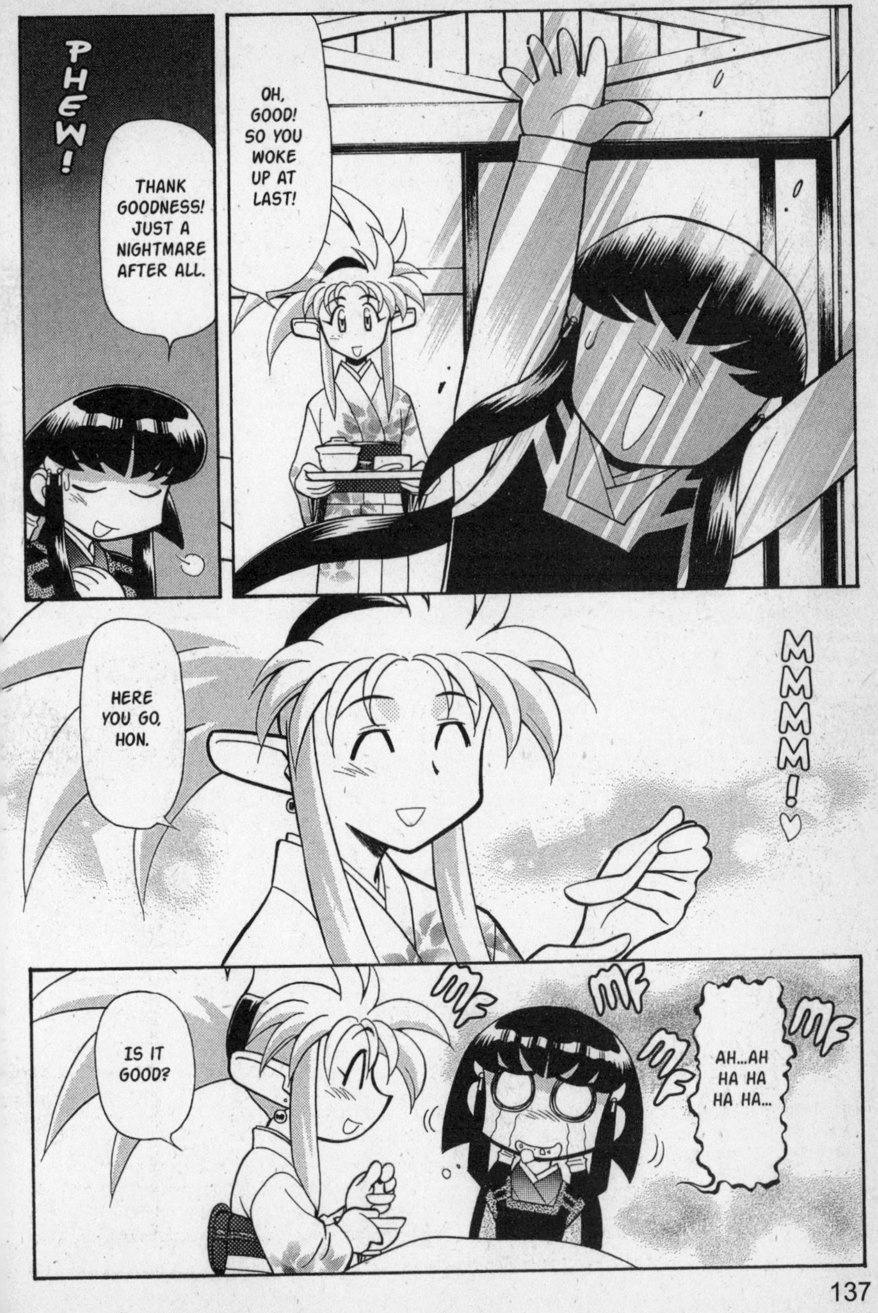
PHEW!
THANK GOODNESS! JUST A NIGHTMARE AFTER ALL.
OH, GOOD! SO YOU WOKE UP AT LAST!
HERE YOU GO, HON.
MMMMM!♥
IS IT GOOD?
MF
MF
MF
MF
AH...AH HA HA HA HA...

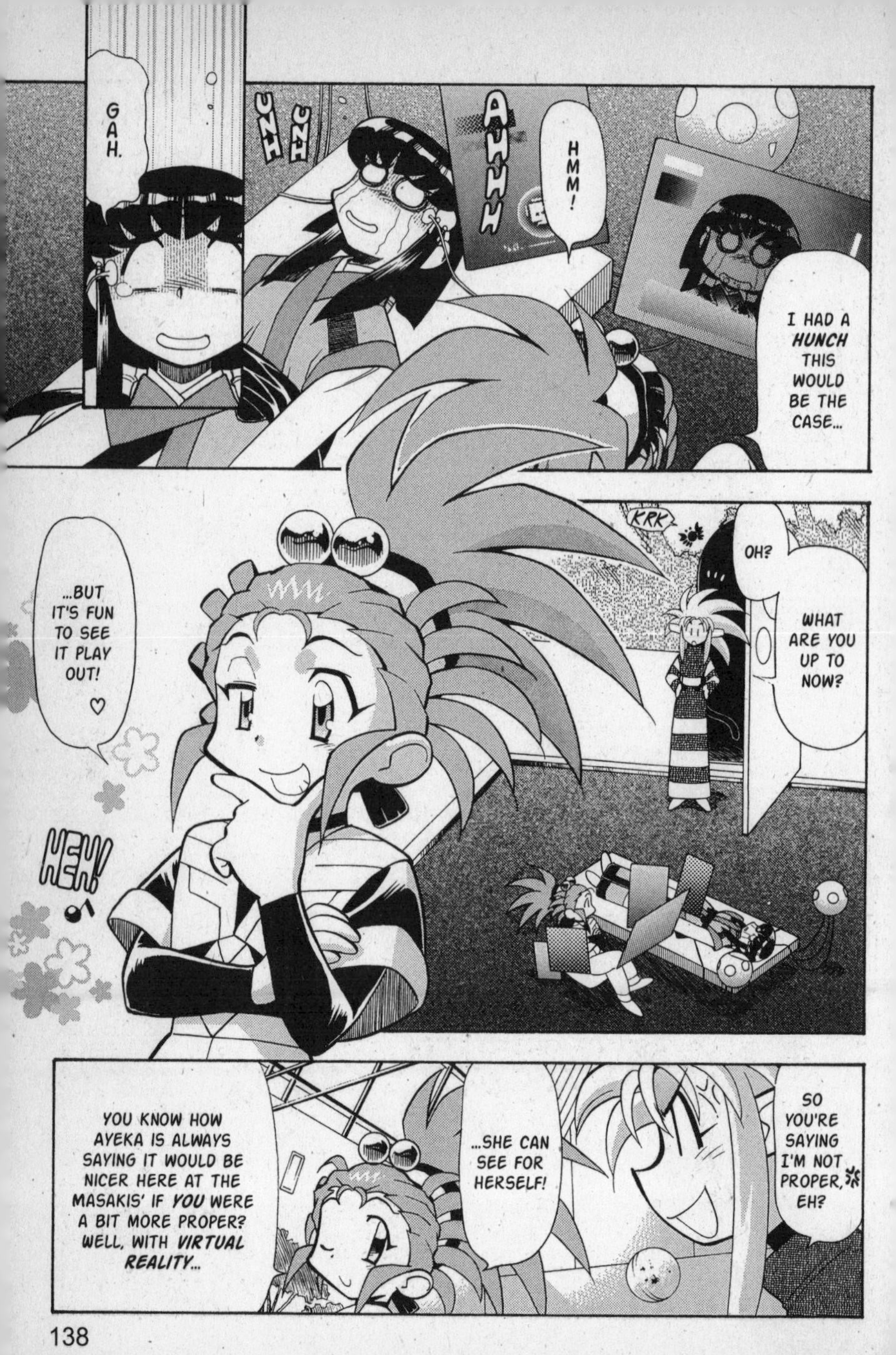
GAH.
UNH
UNH
AHHHH
HMM!
I HAD A HUNCH THIS WOULD BE THE CASE...
...BUT IT'S FUN TO SEE IT PLAY OUT! ♡
HEH!
KRK
OH?
WHAT ARE YOU UP TO NOW?
YOU KNOW HOW AYEKA IS ALWAYS SAYING IT WOULD BE NICER HERE AT THE MASAKIS' IF YOU WERE A BIT MORE PROPER? WELL, WITH VIRTUAL REALITY...
...SHE CAN SEE FOR HERSELF!
SO YOU'RE SAYING I'M NOT PROPER, EH?

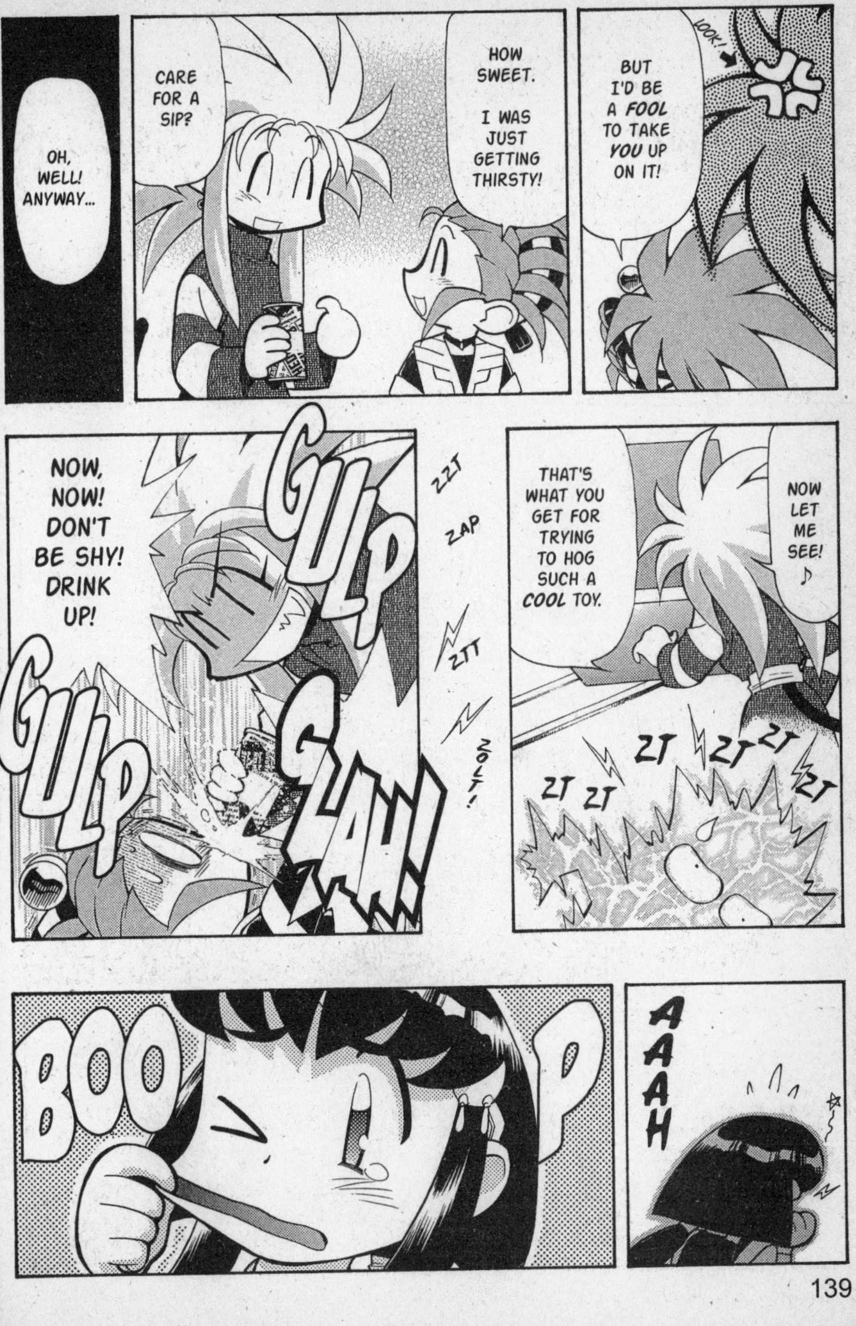

OH, WELL! ANYWAY...
CARE FOR A SIP?
HOW SWEET.
I WAS JUST GETTING THIRSTY!
LOOK!
BUT I'D BE A FOOL TO TAKE YOU UP ON IT!
NOW, NOW! DON'T BE SHY! DRINK UP!
GULP
GULP
GLAH!
ZZT
ZAP
ZTT
ZOLT!
THAT'S WHAT YOU GET FOR TRYING TO HOG SUCH A COOL TOY.
NOW LET ME SEE! ♪
ZT ZT ZT ZT ZT ZT
BOOP
AAAH

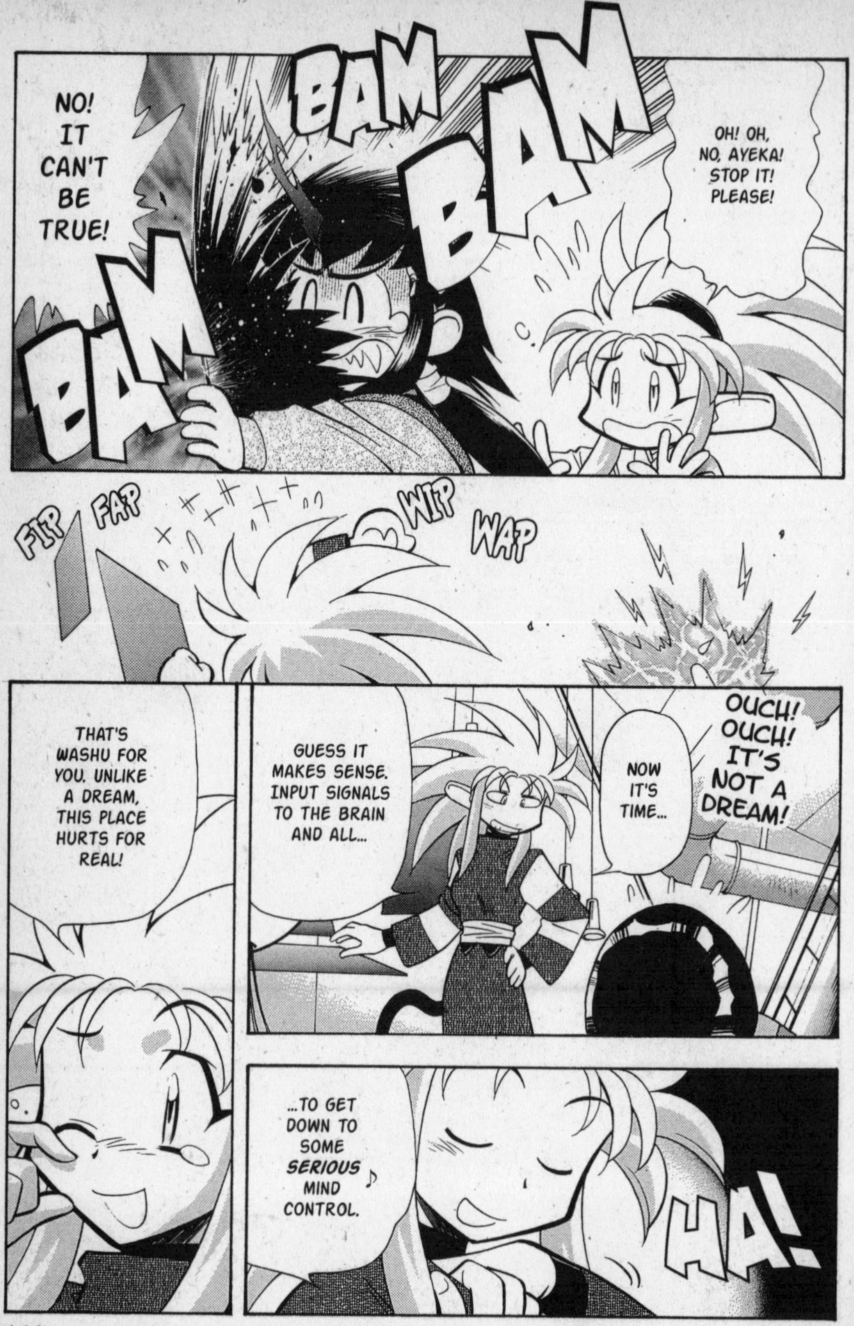
NO! IT CAN'T BE TRUE!
BAM BAM
BAM BAM
OH! OH, NO, AYEKA! STOP IT! PLEASE!
FIP FAP
WIP WAP
THAT'S WASHU FOR YOU. UNLIKE A DREAM, THIS PLACE HURTS FOR REAL!
GUESS IT MAKES SENSE. INPUT SIGNALS TO THE BRAIN AND ALL...
NOW IT'S TIME...
OUCH! OUCH! IT'S NOT A DREAM!
...TO GET DOWN TO SOME *SERIOUS* MIND CONTROL. ♪
HA!

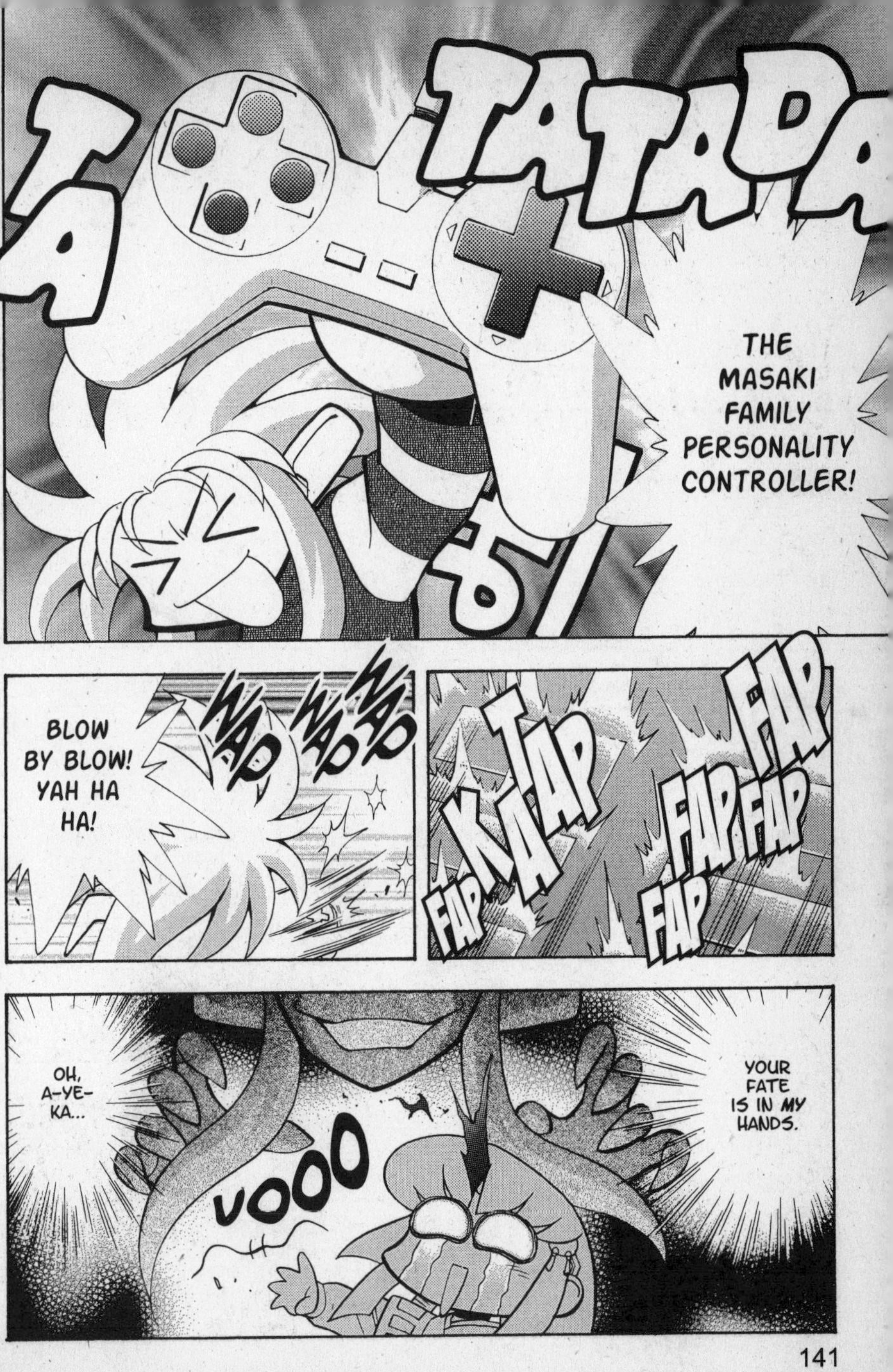
TA
TATADA
THE MASAKI FAMILY PERSONALITY CONTROLLER!
BLOW BY BLOW! YAH HA HA!
WAP
WAP
WAP
FAP
KATAP
FAP
FAP
FAP
FAP
OH, A-YE-KA...
VOOO
YOUR FATE IS IN MY HANDS.

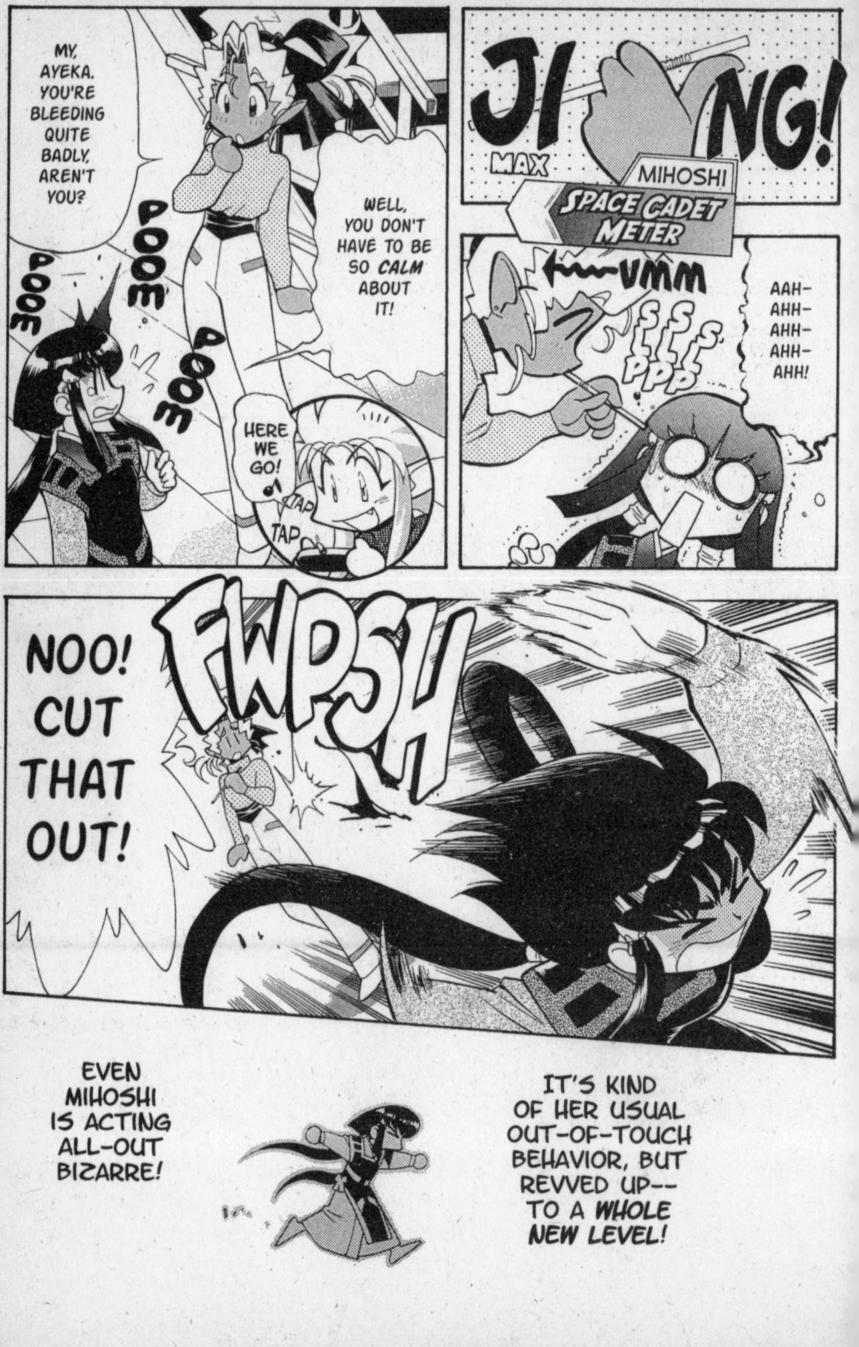
MY, AYEKA. YOU'RE BLEEDING QUITE BADLY, AREN'T YOU?
POOM POOM POOM POOM
WELL, YOU DON'T HAVE TO BE SO CALM ABOUT IT!
HERE WE GO!
TAP TAP
JI NG!
MAX
MIHOSHI
SPACE CADET METER
VMM
AAH-AHH-AHH-AHH-AHH!
FWPSH
NOO! CUT THAT OUT!
EVEN MIHOSHI IS ACTING ALL-OUT BIZARRE!
IT'S KIND OF HER USUAL OUT-OF-TOUCH BEHAVIOR, BUT REVVED UP-- TO A WHOLE NEW LEVEL!

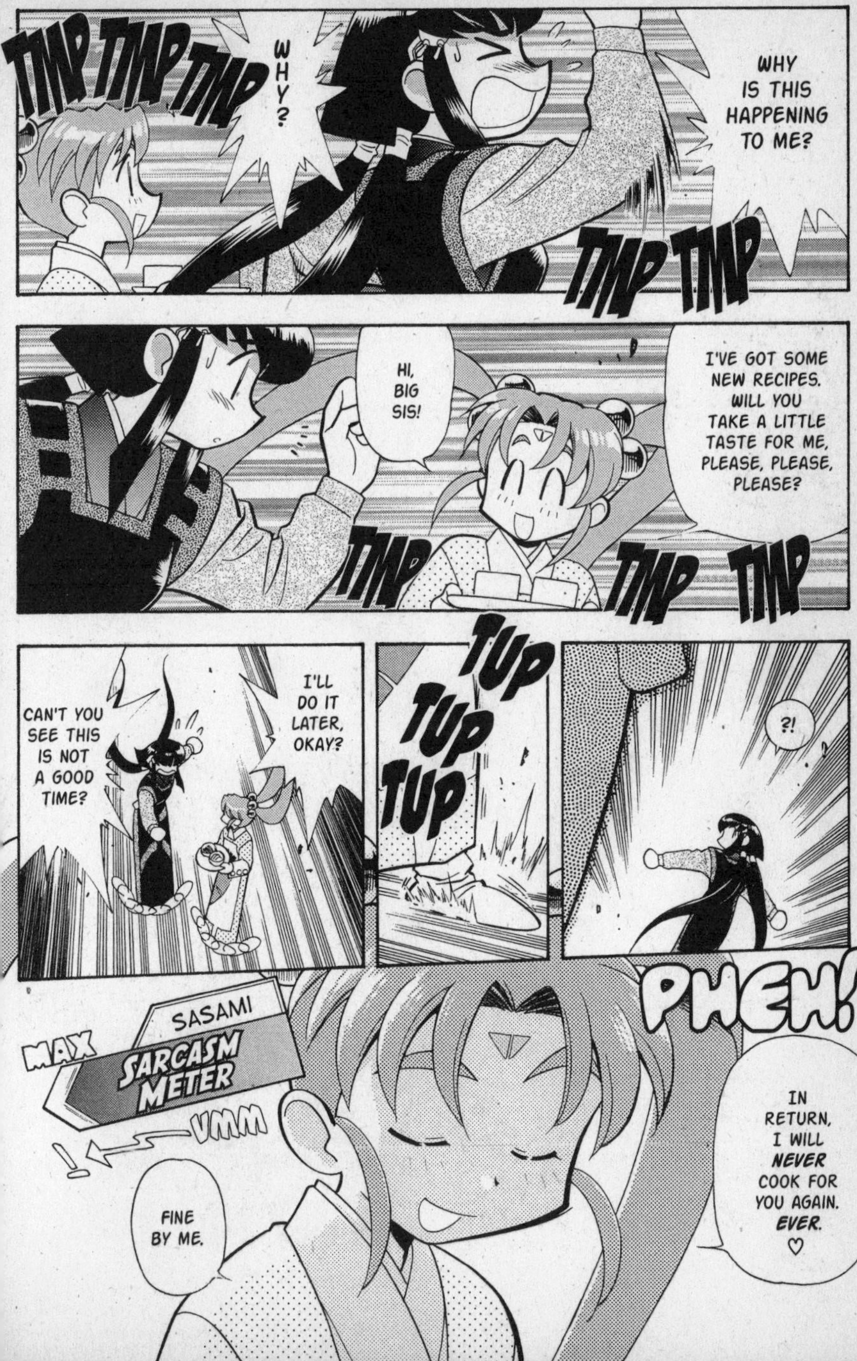
TMP TMP TMP
WHY?
WHY IS THIS HAPPENING TO ME?
TMP TMP
HI, BIG SIS!
I'VE GOT SOME NEW RECIPES. WILL YOU TAKE A LITTLE TASTE FOR ME, PLEASE, PLEASE, PLEASE?
TMP
TMP TMP
CAN'T YOU SEE THIS IS NOT A GOOD TIME?
I'LL DO IT LATER, OKAY?
TUP TUP TUP
?!
SASAMI
MAX
SARCASM METER
PHEH!
UMM
IN RETURN, I WILL *NEVER* COOK FOR YOU AGAIN. *EVER.* ♡
FINE BY ME.

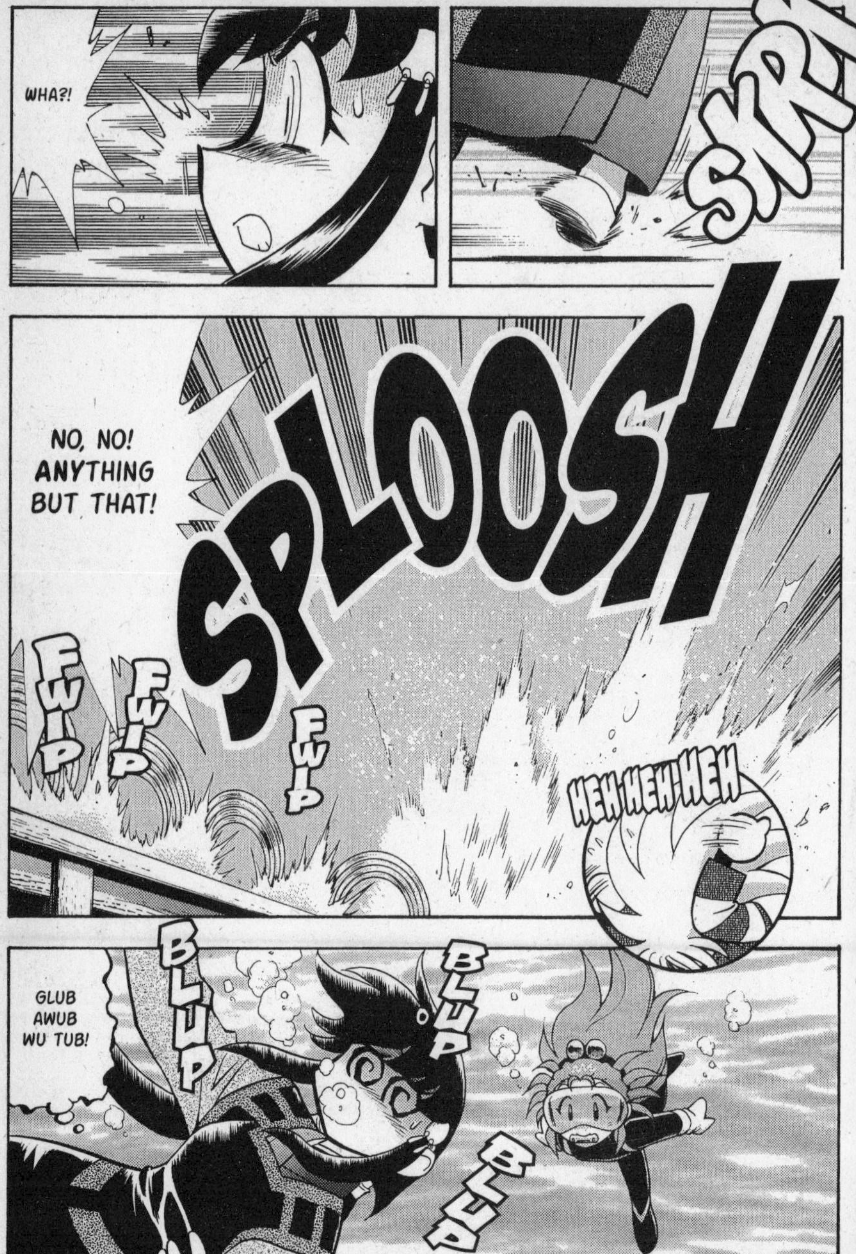
WHA?!
SKRK
NO, NO! ANYTHING BUT THAT!
SPLOOSH
FWIP
FWIP
FWIP
HEH HEH HEH
GLUB AWUB WU TUB!
BLUP
BLUP
BLUP

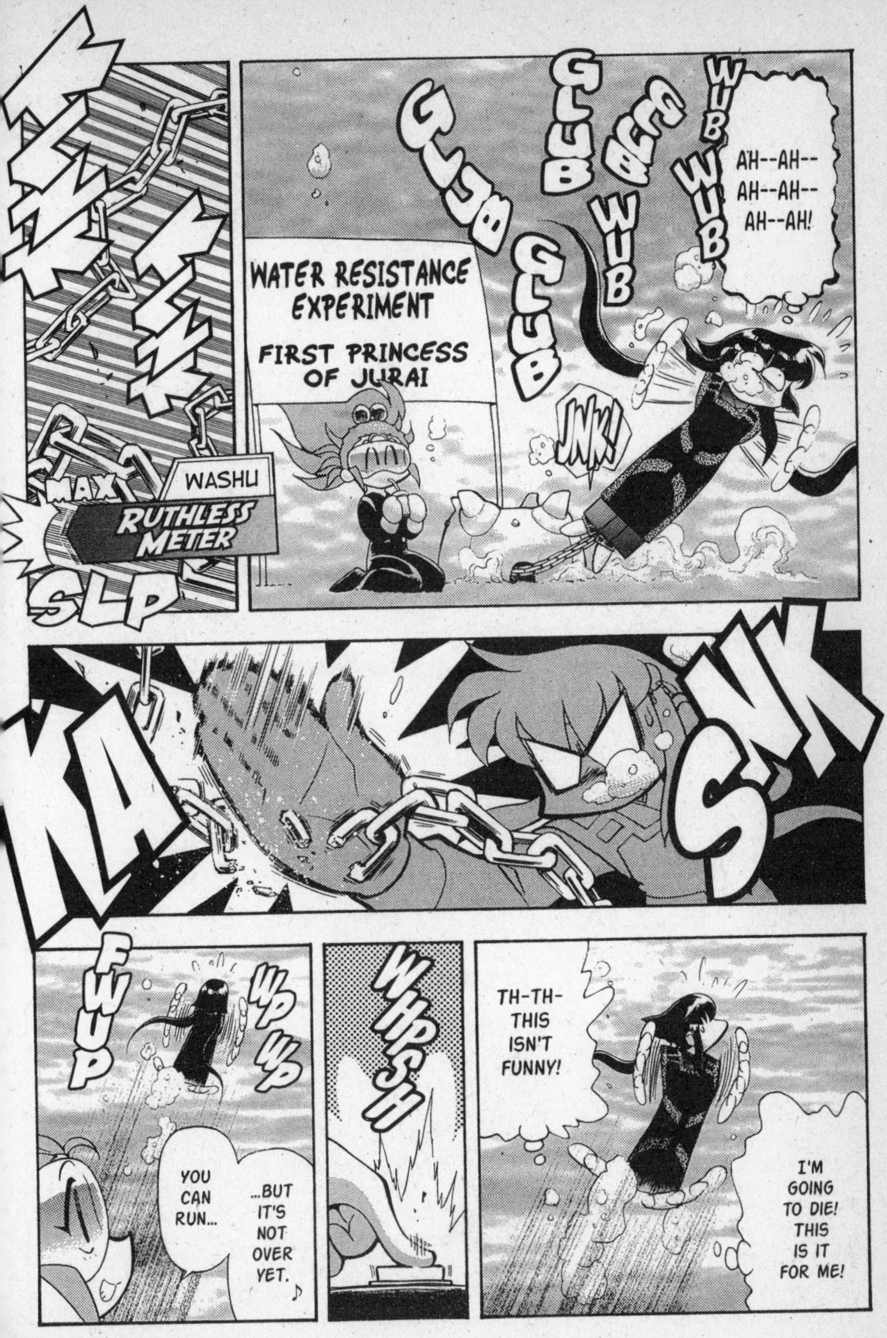

MAX
WASHU
RUTHLESS METER
SLP
GLUB
GLUB
GLUB
GLUB
WUB
WUB
WUB
WUB
WUB
AH--AH--
AH--AH--
AH--AH!
WATER RESISTANCE EXPERIMENT
FIRST PRINCESS OF JURAI
JNK!
KA
SNK
FWUP
WP WP
YOU CAN RUN...
...BUT IT'S NOT OVER YET. ♪
WHRSH
TH-TH-THIS ISN'T FUNNY!
I'M GOING TO DIE! THIS IS IT FOR ME!

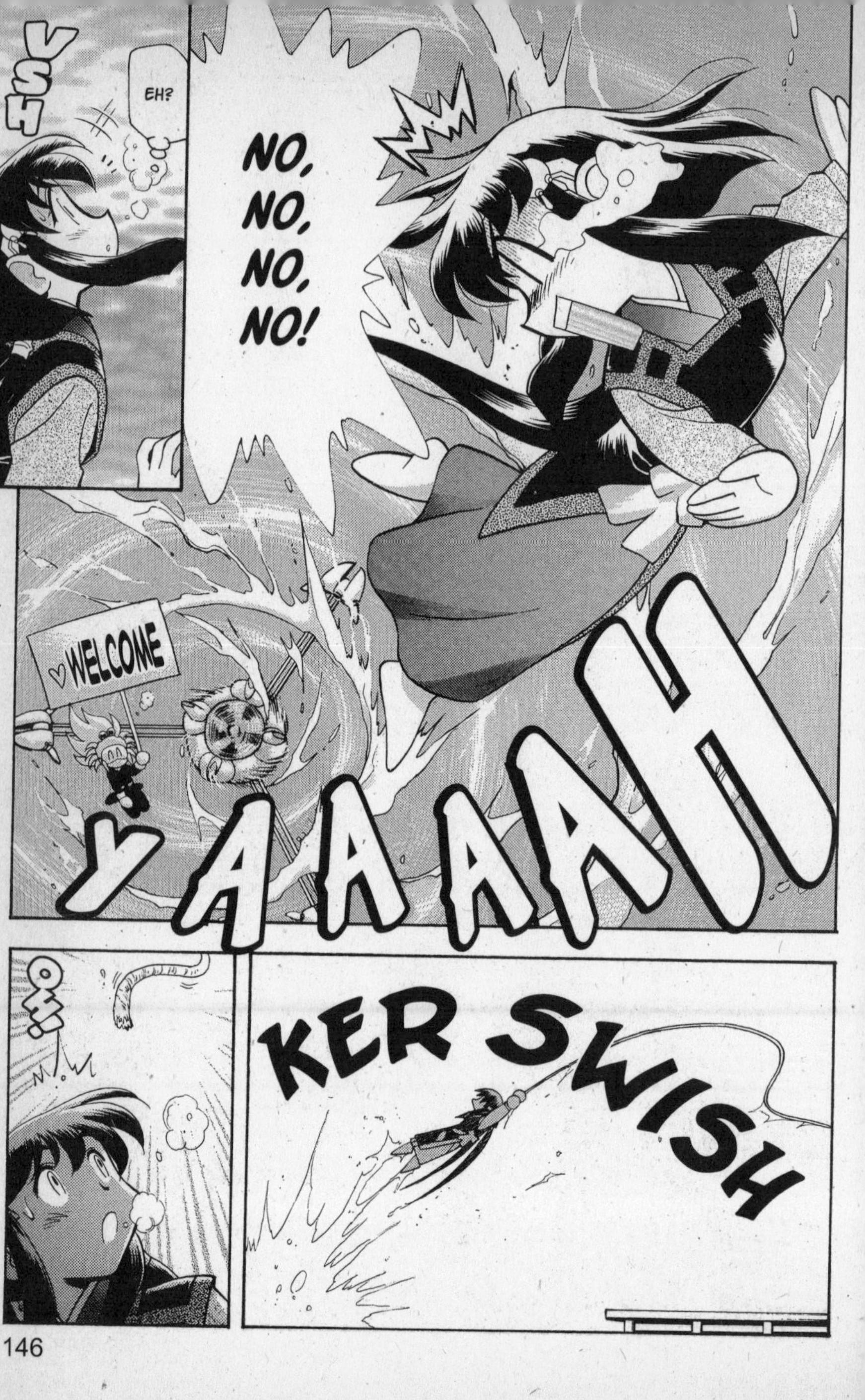
VSH
EH?
NO, NO, NO, NO!
WELCOME
YAAAH
OW!
KER SWISH

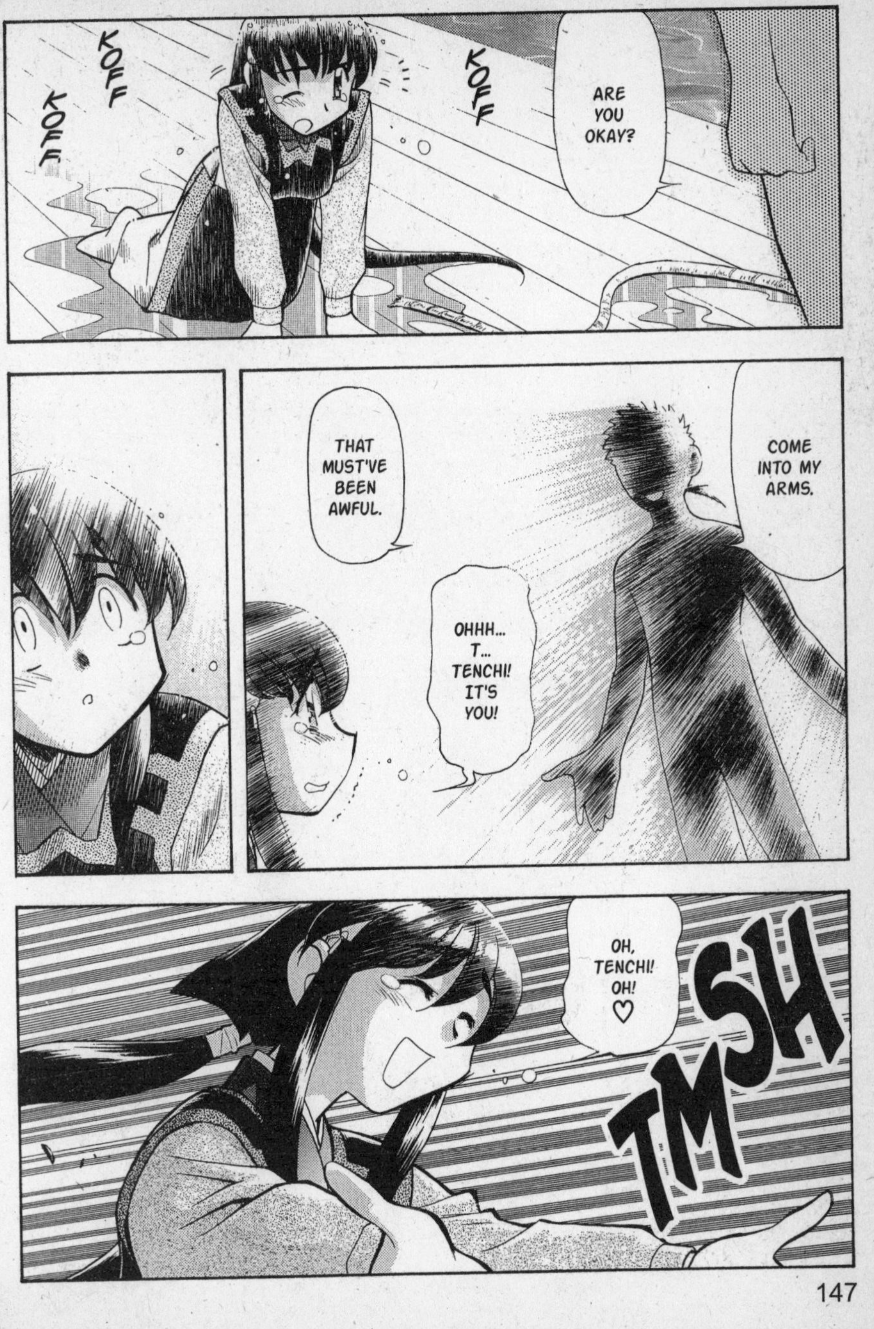
KOFF
KOFF
KOFF
ARE YOU OKAY?
THAT MUST'VE BEEN AWFUL.
OHHH... T... TENCHI! IT'S YOU!
COME INTO MY ARMS.
OH, TENCHI! OH! ♡
TMSH

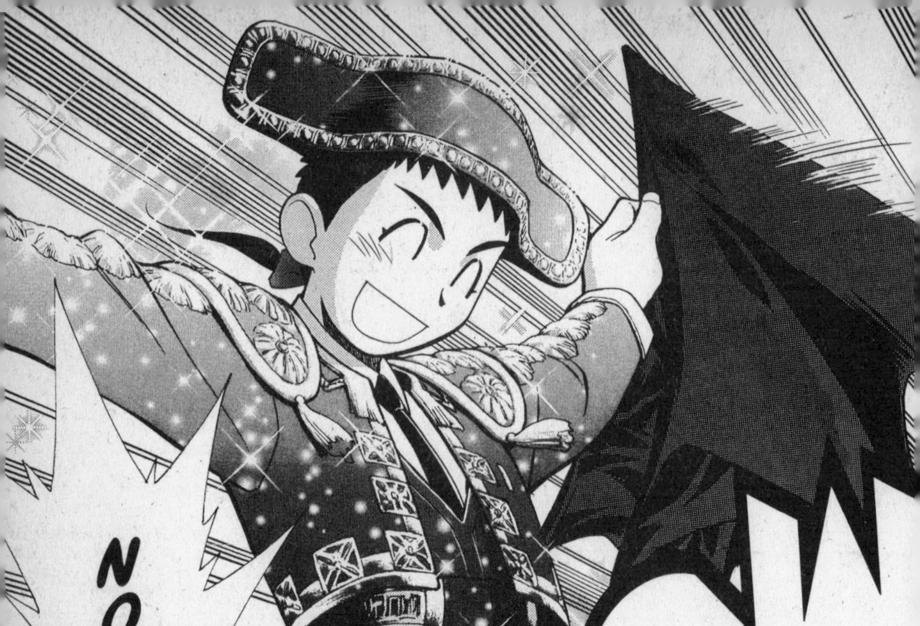
NOOOOO!
MAX
TENCHI
OUT THERE METER
UMKRAK
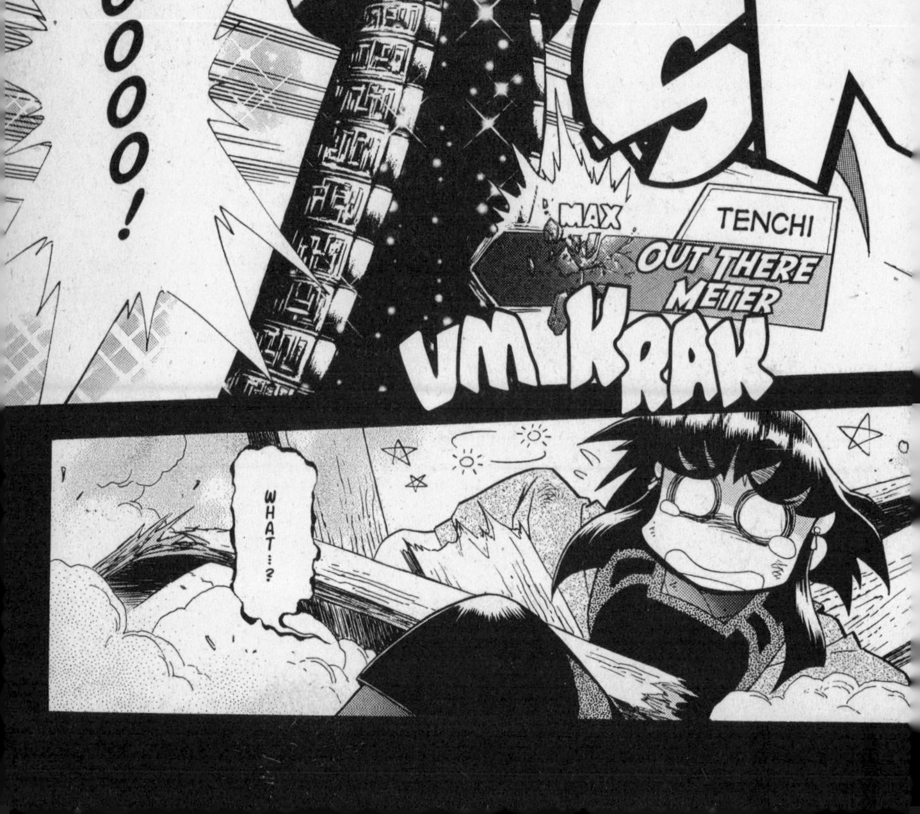
WHAT...?

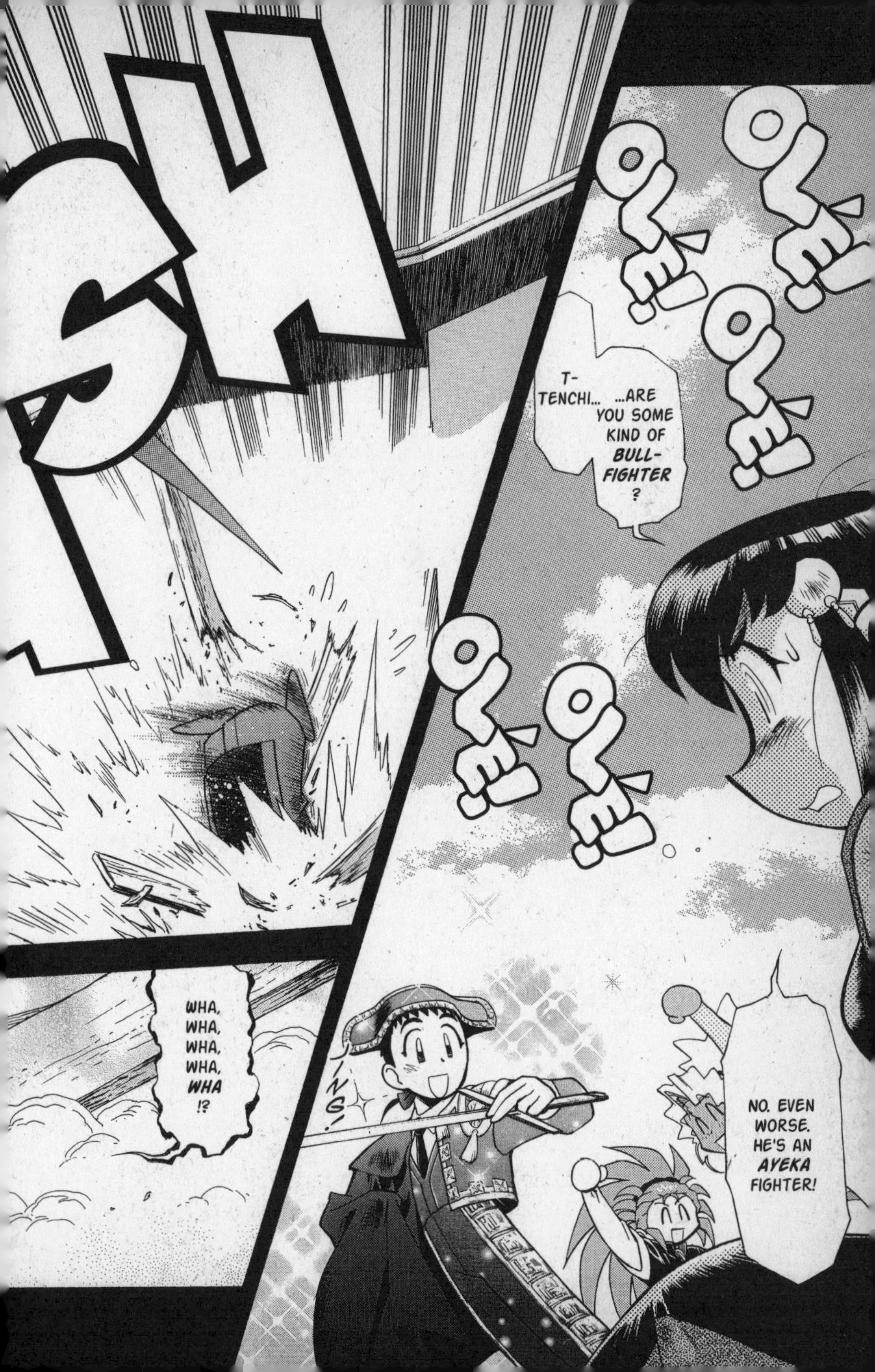
WHA, WHA, WHA, WHA, WHA!?
OLÉ! OLÉ! OLÉ! OLÉ!
T-TENCHI... ...ARE YOU SOME KIND OF BULL-FIGHTER?
OLÉ! OLÉ!
NO. EVEN WORSE. HE'S AN AYEKA FIGHTER!

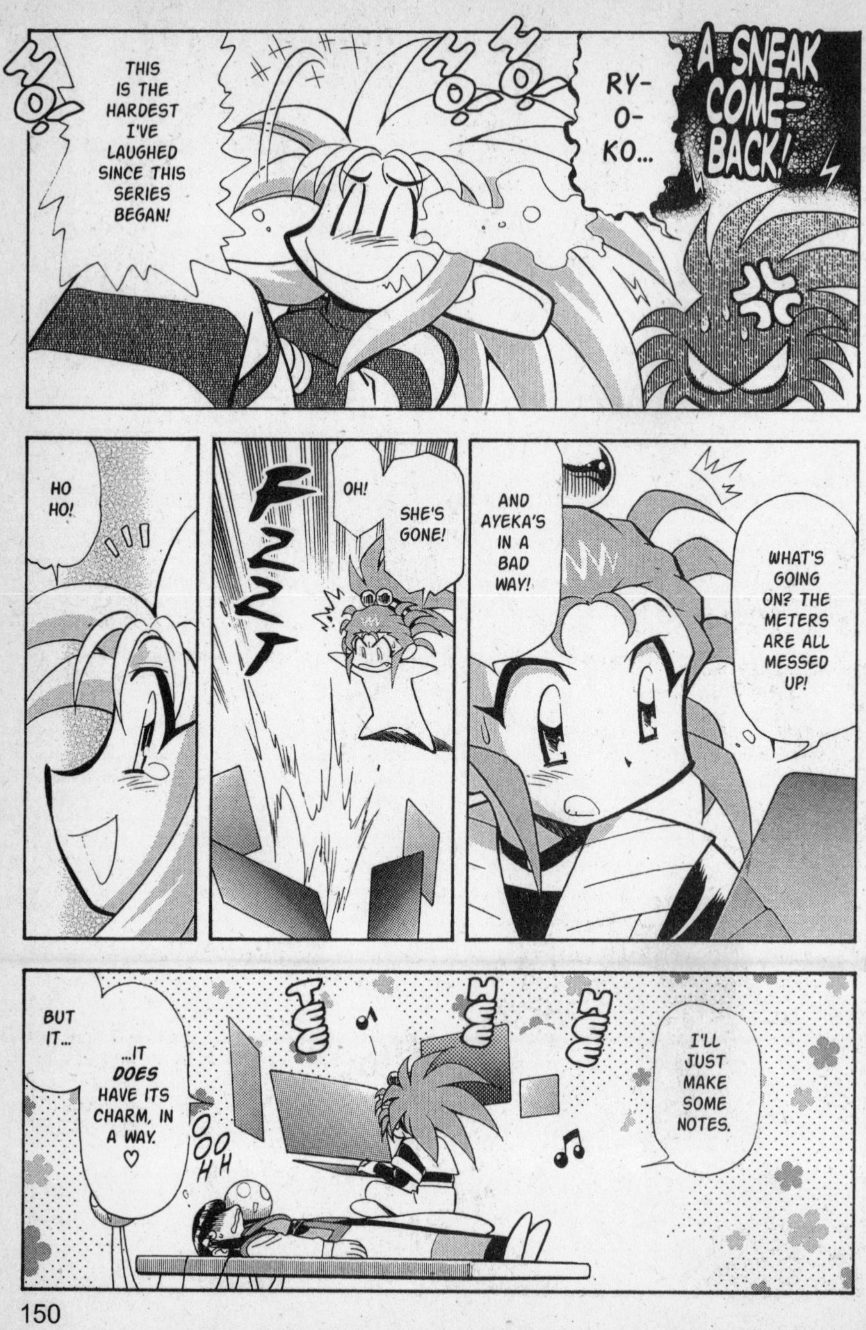
HO HO!
THIS IS THE HARDEST I'VE LAUGHED SINCE THIS SERIES BEGAN!
HO! HO!
RY-O-KO...
A SNEAK COME-BACK!
HO HO!
FZZT
OH!
SHE'S GONE!
AND AYEKA'S IN A BAD WAY!
WHAT'S GOING ON? THE METERS ARE ALL MESSED UP!
BUT IT...
...IT DOES HAVE ITS CHARM, IN A WAY. ♡
OOOHH
TEE HEE HEE
I'LL JUST MAKE SOME NOTES.

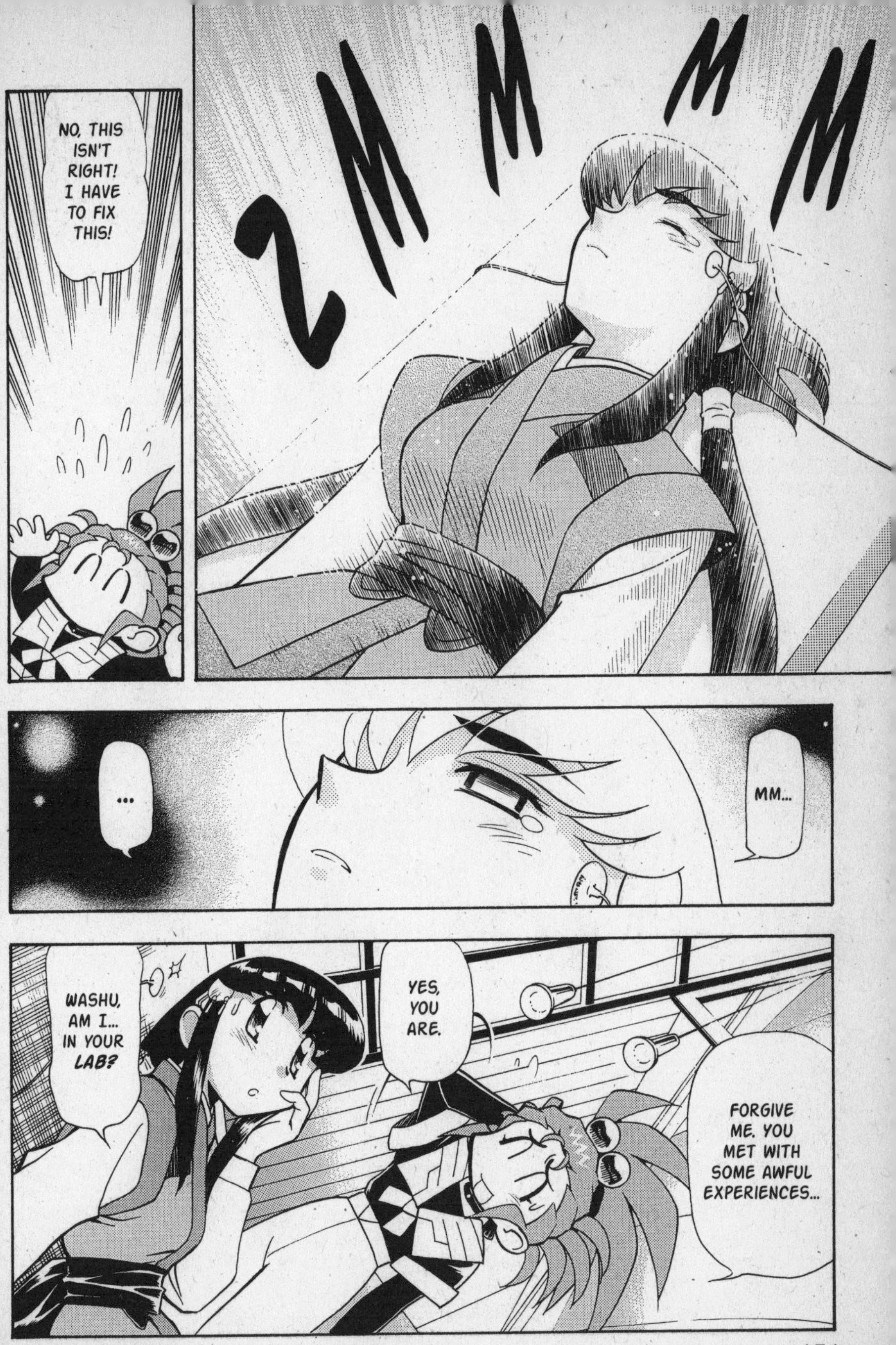
NO, THIS ISN'T RIGHT! I HAVE TO FIX THIS!
ZMMMMM
...
MM...
WASHU, AM I... IN YOUR LAB?
YES, YOU ARE.
FORGIVE ME. YOU MET WITH SOME AWFUL EXPERIENCES...

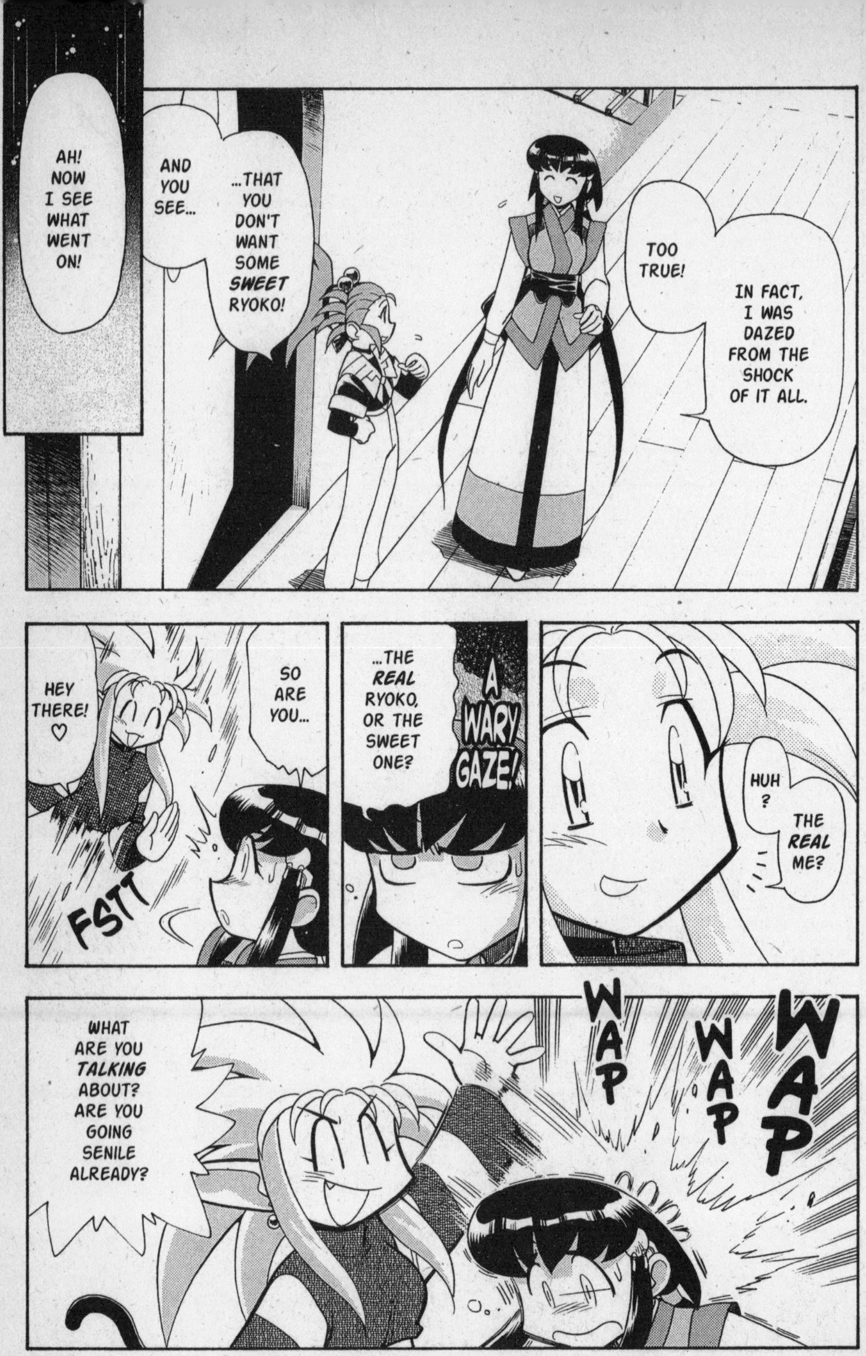
AH! NOW I SEE WHAT WENT ON!
AND YOU SEE...
...THAT YOU DON'T WANT SOME SWEET RYOKO!
TOO TRUE!
IN FACT, I WAS DAZED FROM THE SHOCK OF IT ALL.
HEY THERE! ♡
SO ARE YOU...
FSTT
...THE REAL RYOKO, OR THE SWEET ONE?
A WARY GAZE!
HUH?
THE REAL ME?
WHAT ARE YOU TALKING ABOUT? ARE YOU GOING SENILE ALREADY?
WAP
WAP
WAP

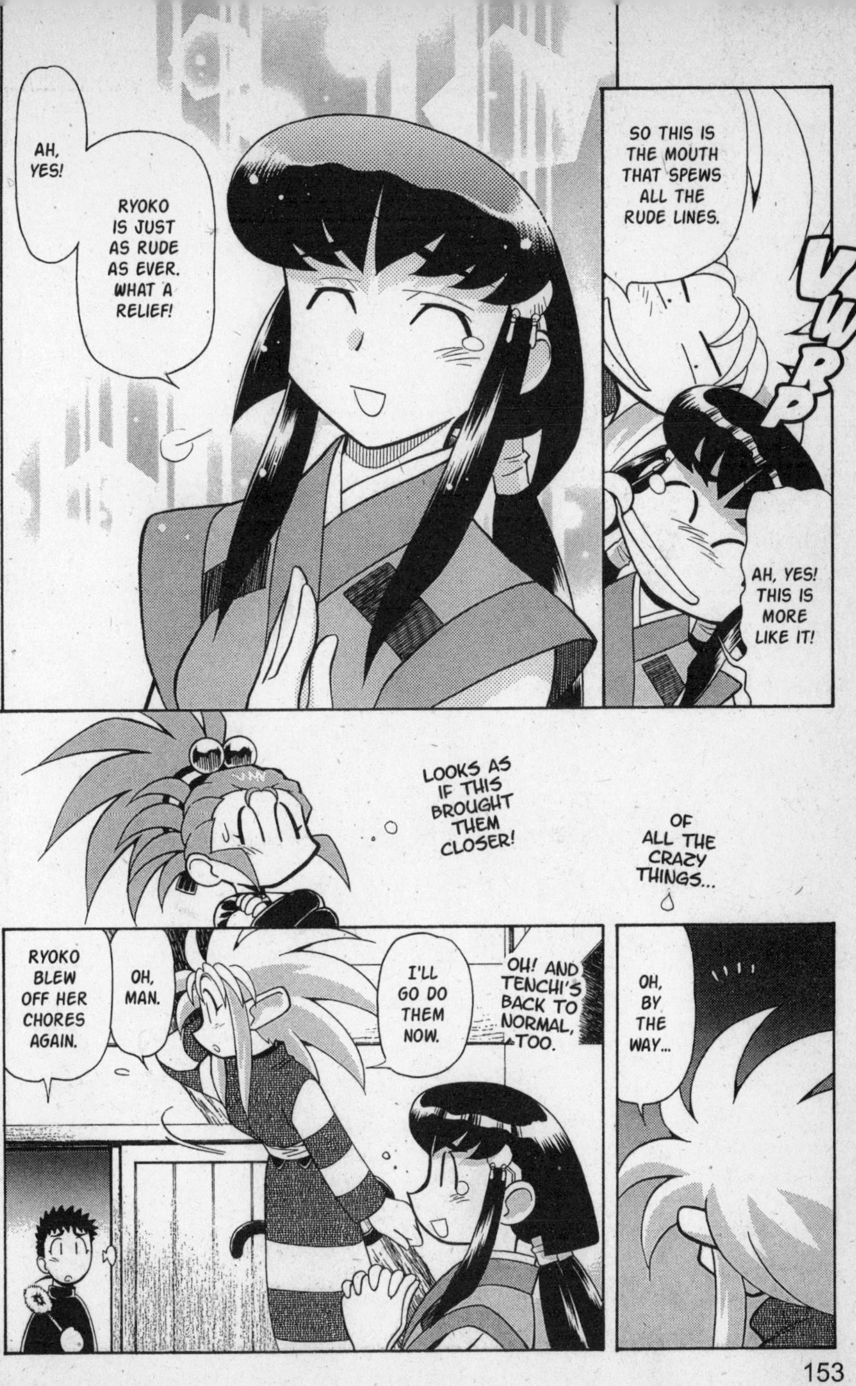
AH, YES!
RYOKO IS JUST AS RUDE AS EVER. WHAT A RELIEF!
SO THIS IS THE MOUTH THAT SPEWS ALL THE RUDE LINES.
VWRP
AH, YES! THIS IS MORE LIKE IT!
LOOKS AS IF THIS BROUGHT THEM CLOSER!
OF ALL THE CRAZY THINGS...
RYOKO BLEW OFF HER CHORES AGAIN.
OH, MAN.
I'LL GO DO THEM NOW.
OH! AND TENCHI'S BACK TO NORMAL, TOO.
OH, BY THE WAY...

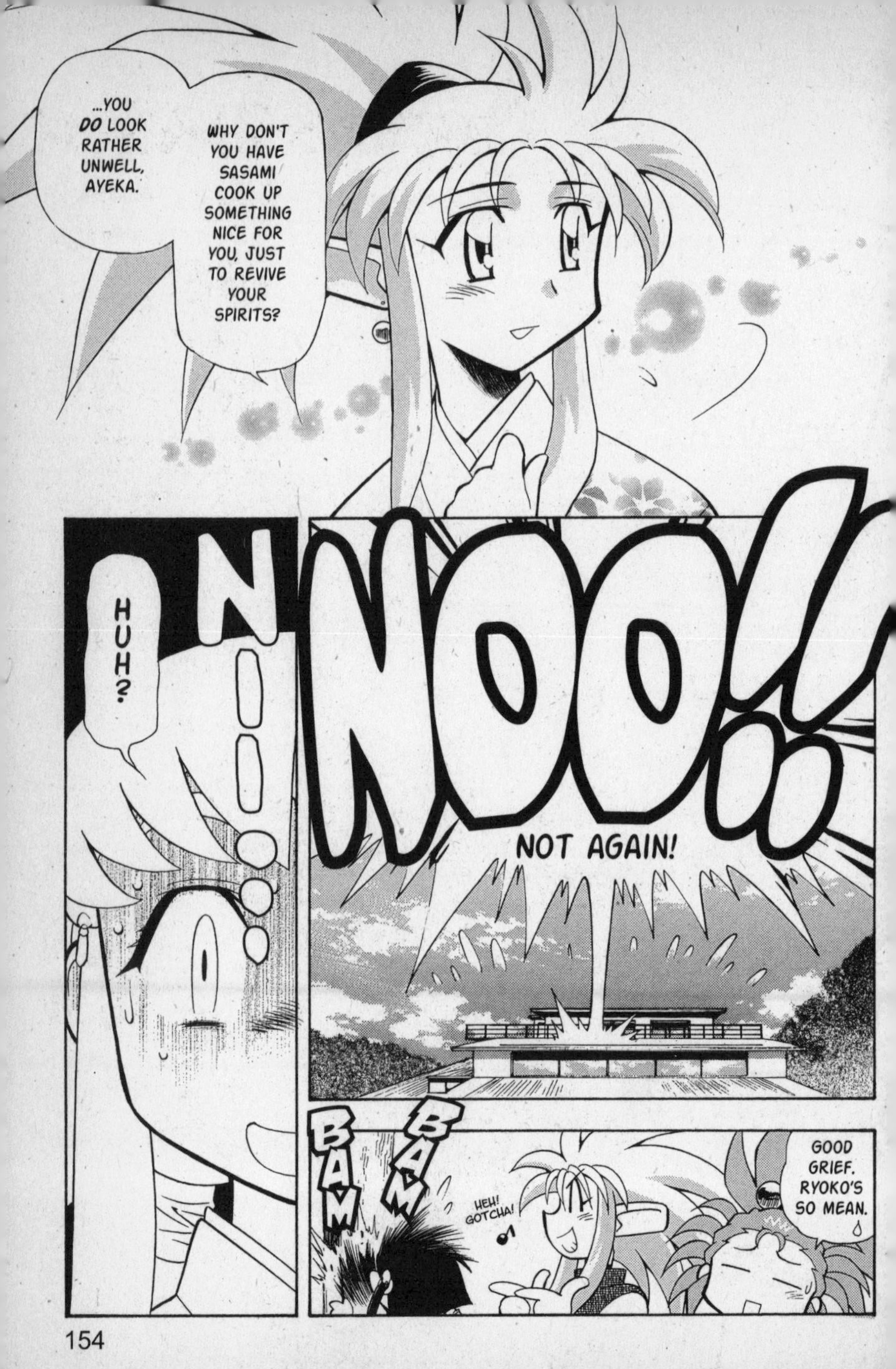
...YOU DO LOOK RATHER UNWELL, AYEKA.
WHY DON'T YOU HAVE SASAMI COOK UP SOMETHING NICE FOR YOU, JUST TO REVIVE YOUR SPIRITS?
HUH?
N
NOO!!
NOT AGAIN!
BAM
BAM
HEH! GOTCHA!
GOOD GRIEF. RYOKO'S SO MEAN.

Chapter 6: Deterrent

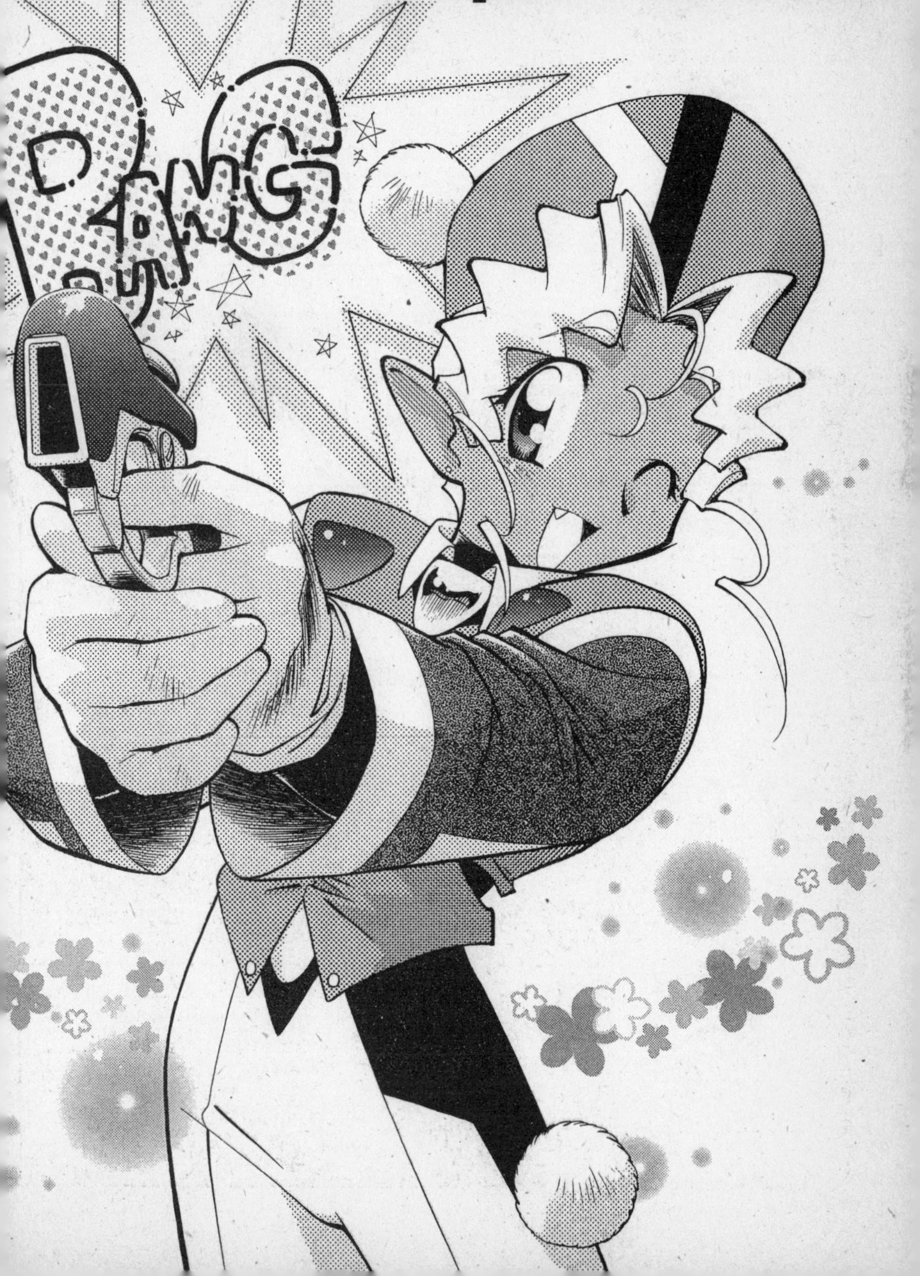
BANG

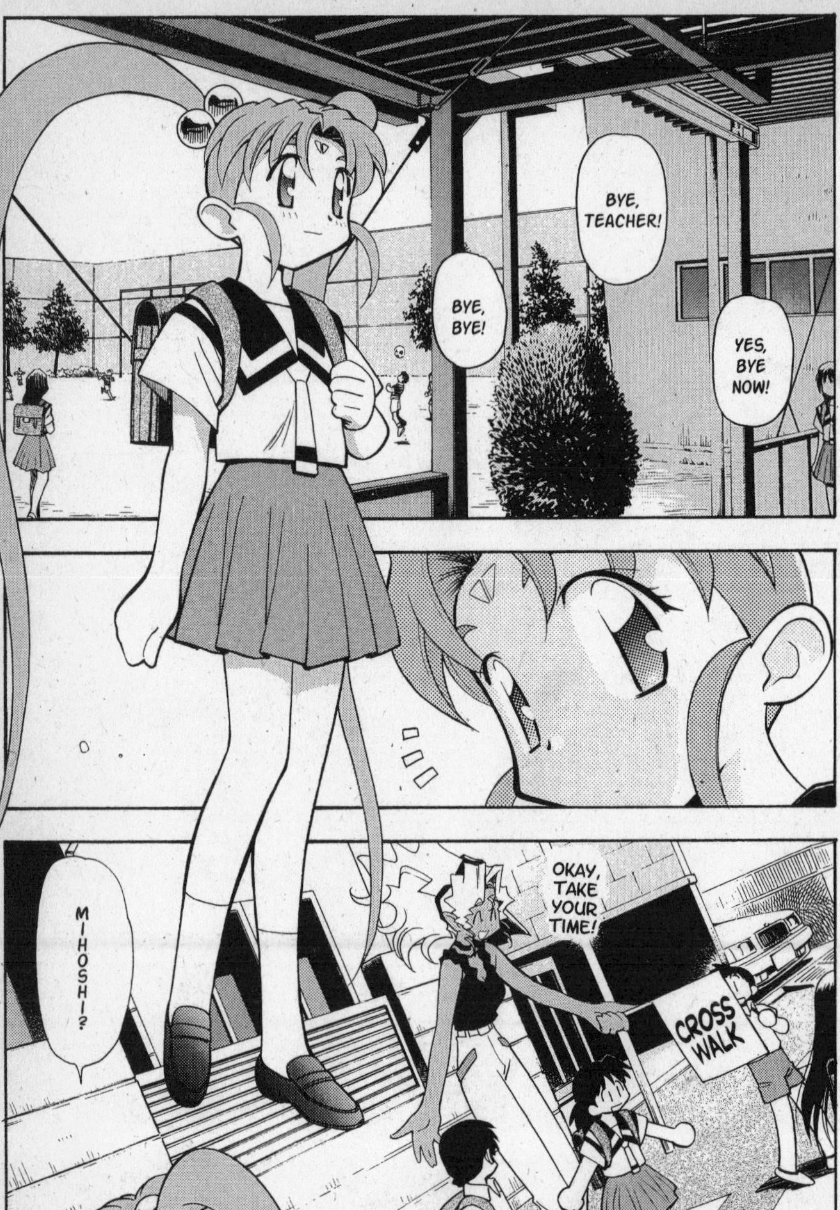
BYE, BYE!
BYE, TEACHER!
YES, BYE NOW!
MIHOSHI!?
...
OKAY, TAKE YOUR TIME!
CROSS WALK

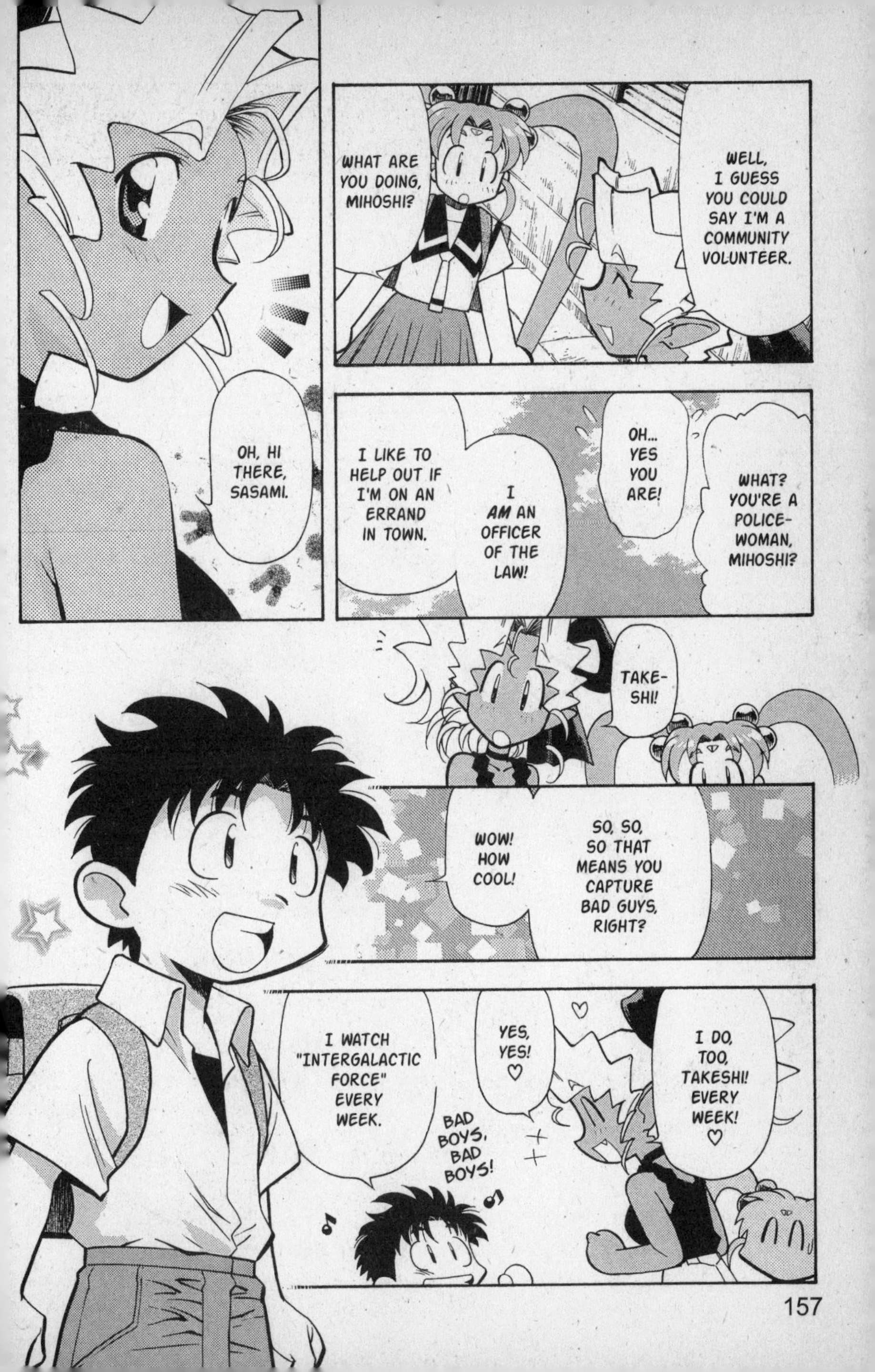
OH, HI THERE, SASAMI.
WHAT ARE YOU DOING, MIHOSHI?
WELL, I GUESS YOU COULD SAY I'M A COMMUNITY VOLUNTEER.
I LIKE TO HELP OUT IF I'M ON AN ERRAND IN TOWN.
I *AM* AN OFFICER OF THE LAW!
OH... YES YOU ARE!
WHAT? YOU'RE A POLICE-WOMAN, MIHOSHI?
TAKE-SHI!
WOW! HOW COOL!
SO, SO, SO THAT MEANS YOU CAPTURE BAD GUYS, RIGHT?
I WATCH "INTERGALACTIC FORCE" EVERY WEEK.
YES, YES! ♡
BAD BOYS, BAD BOYS!
I DO, TOO, TAKESHI! EVERY WEEK! ♡

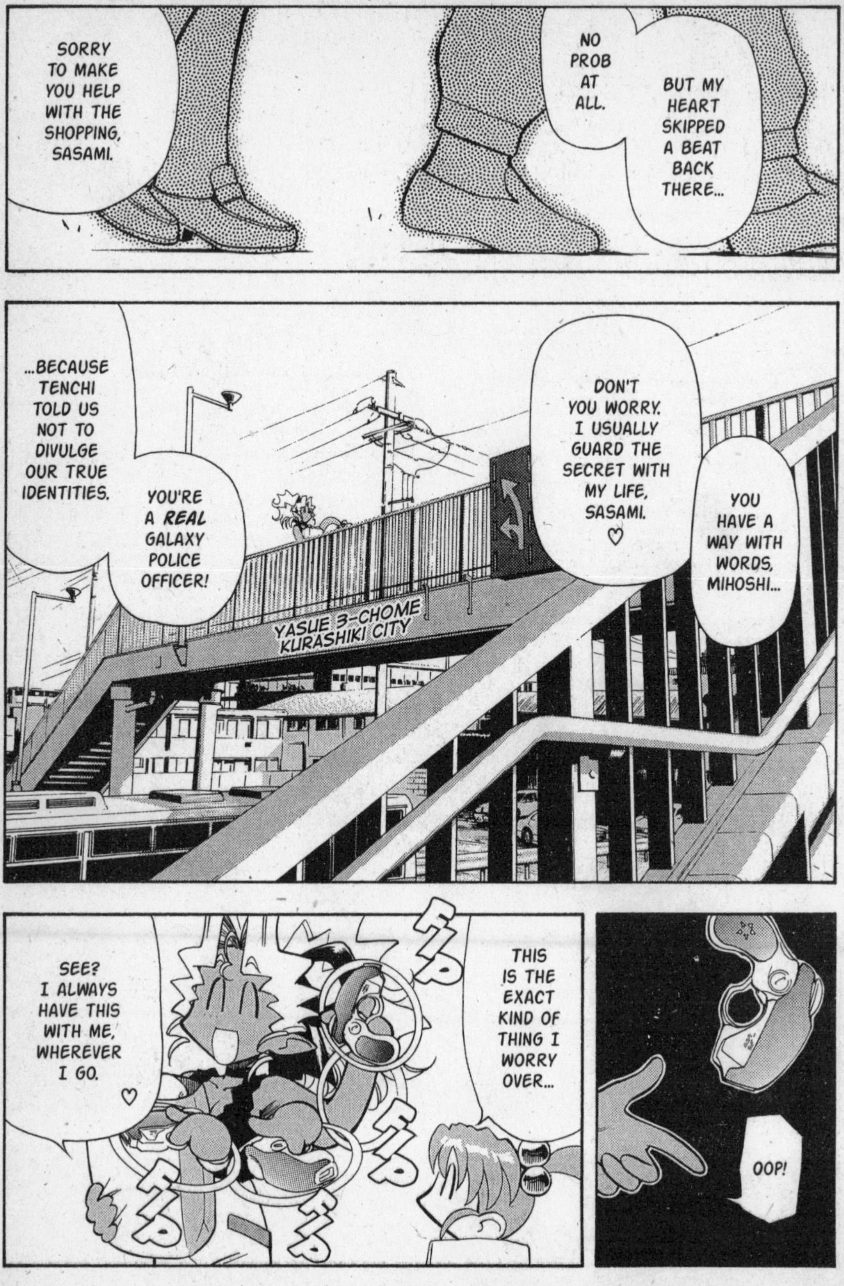
SORRY TO MAKE YOU HELP WITH THE SHOPPING, SASAMI.
NO PROB AT ALL.
BUT MY HEART SKIPPED A BEAT BACK THERE...
...BECAUSE TENCHI TOLD US NOT TO DIVULGE OUR TRUE IDENTITIES.
YOU'RE A *REAL* GALAXY POLICE OFFICER!
YASUE 3-CHOME KURASHIKI CITY
DON'T YOU WORRY. I USUALLY GUARD THE SECRET WITH MY LIFE, SASAMI. ♡
YOU HAVE A WAY WITH WORDS, MIHOSHI...
SEE? I ALWAYS HAVE THIS WITH ME, WHEREVER I GO. ♡
FLIP
FLIP
FLIP
FLIP
THIS IS THE EXACT KIND OF THING I WORRY OVER...
OOP!

UH. SO, UM...

TCH

...

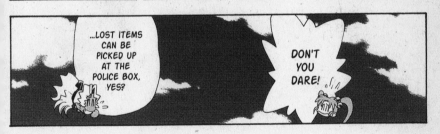

...LOST ITEMS CAN BE PICKED UP AT THE POLICE BOX, YES?

DON'T YOU DARE!

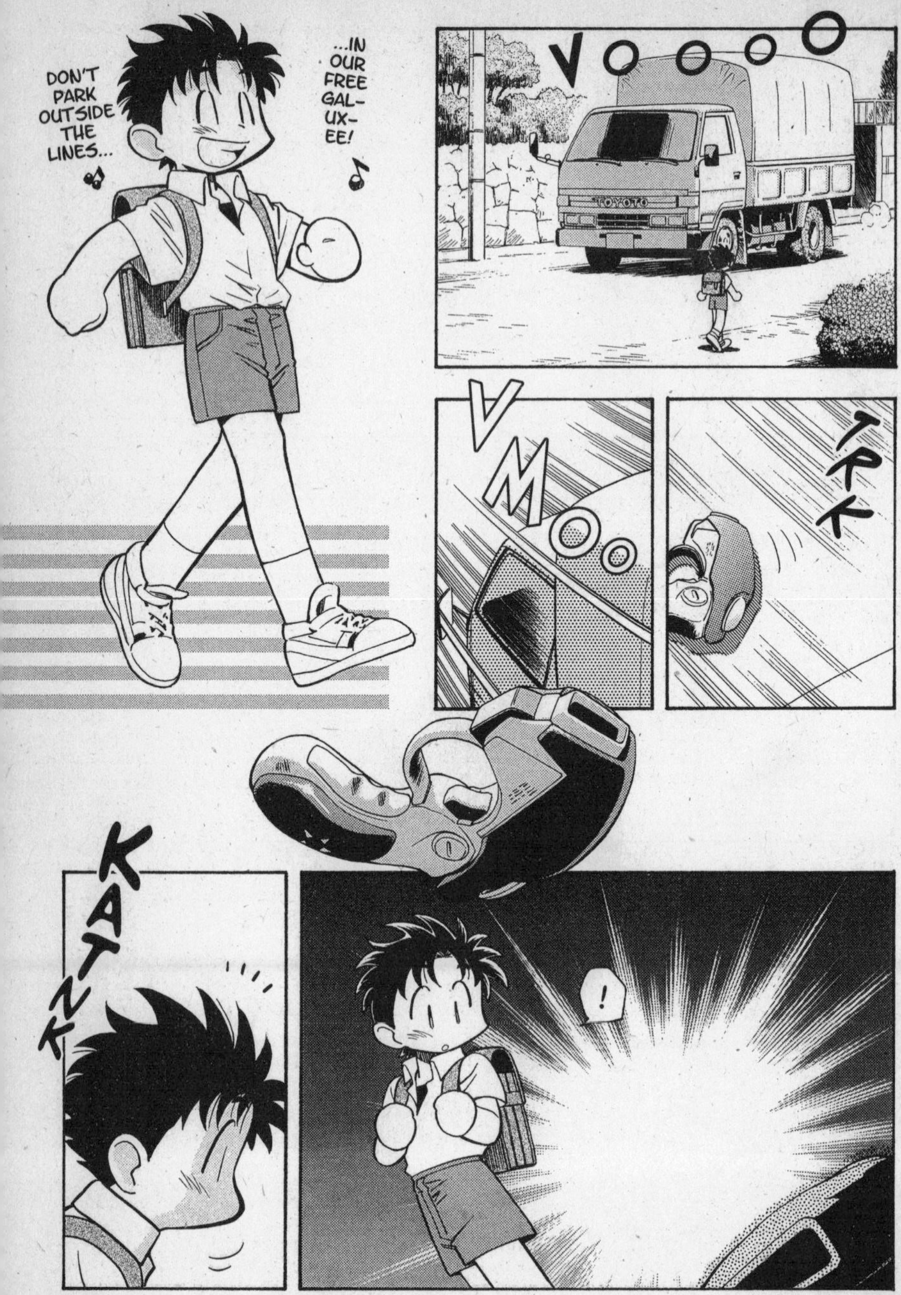
DON'T PARK OUTSIDE THE LINES...
...IN OUR FREE GAL-UX-EE!
VOOOOO
TOYOTO
VMOOO
TRK
KATNK
!

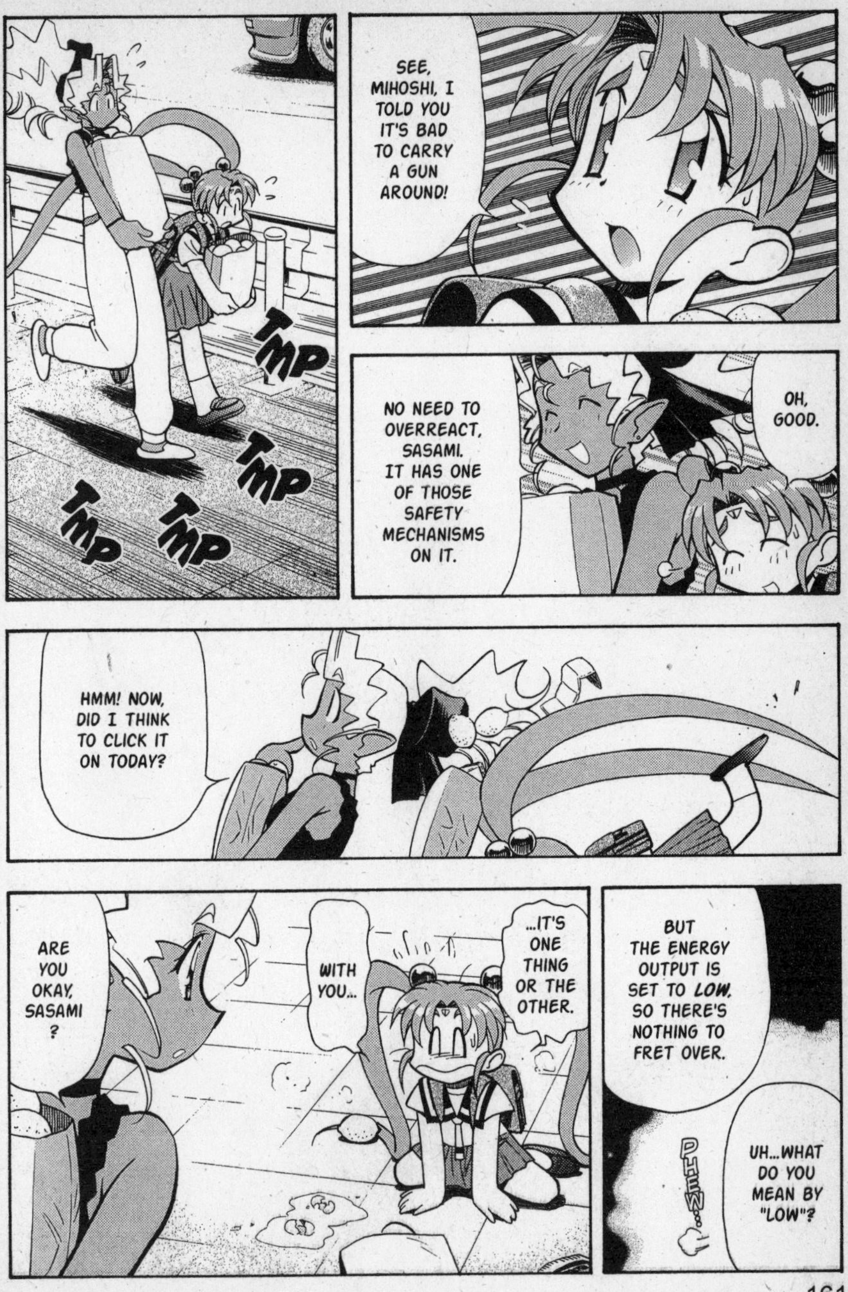

TMP
TMP
TMP
TMP
SEE, MIHOSHI, I TOLD YOU IT'S BAD TO CARRY A GUN AROUND!
NO NEED TO OVERREACT, SASAMI. IT HAS ONE OF THOSE SAFETY MECHANISMS ON IT.
OH, GOOD.
HMM! NOW, DID I THINK TO CLICK IT ON TODAY?
ARE YOU OKAY, SASAMI?
WITH YOU...
...IT'S ONE THING OR THE OTHER.
BUT THE ENERGY OUTPUT IS SET TO *LOW*, SO THERE'S NOTHING TO FRET OVER.
PHEW...
UH...WHAT DO YOU MEAN BY "LOW"?

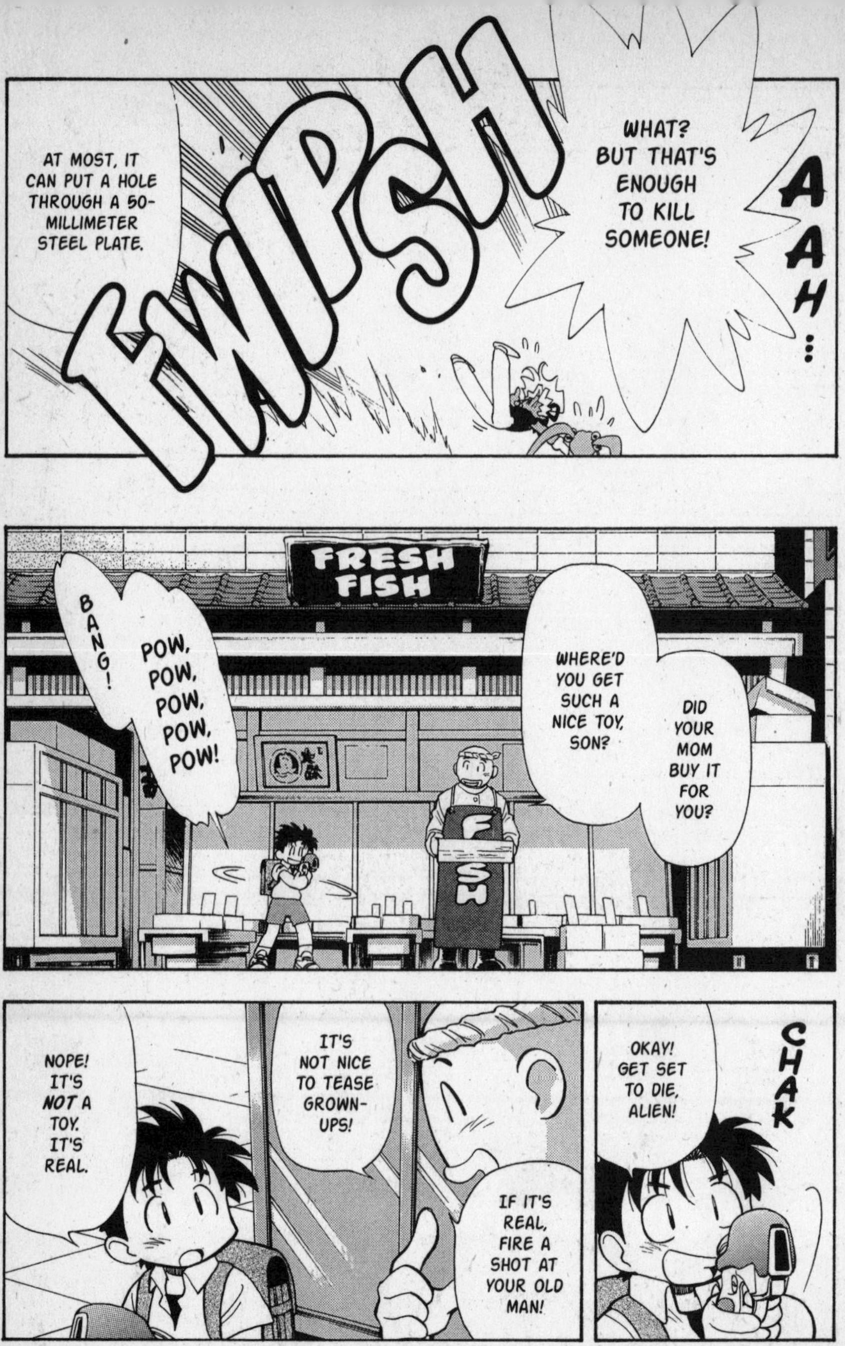
AT MOST, IT CAN PUT A HOLE THROUGH A 50-MILLIMETER STEEL PLATE.
FWIPSH
WHAT? BUT THAT'S ENOUGH TO KILL SOMEONE!
AAH...
FRESH FISH
BANG!
POW, POW, POW, POW, POW!
WHERE'D YOU GET SUCH A NICE TOY, SON?
DID YOUR MOM BUY IT FOR YOU?
FISH
NOPE! IT'S *NOT* A TOY. IT'S REAL.
IT'S NOT NICE TO TEASE GROWN-UPS!
IF IT'S REAL, FIRE A SHOT AT YOUR OLD MAN!
CHAK
OKAY! GET SET TO DIE, ALIEN!

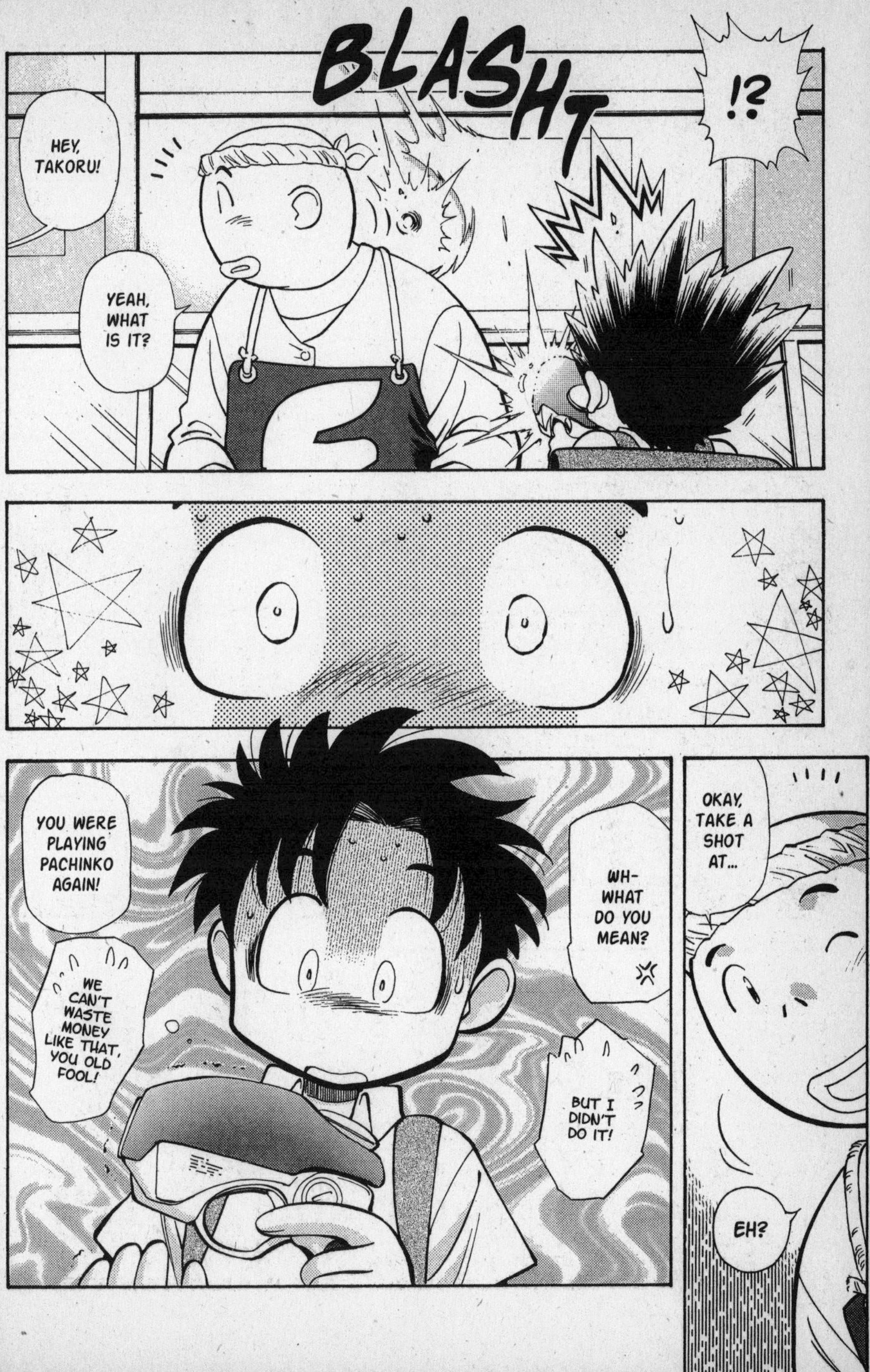
BLASHT
HEY, TAKORU!
!?
YEAH, WHAT IS IT?
YOU WERE PLAYING PACHINKO AGAIN!
WE CAN'T WASTE MONEY LIKE THAT, YOU OLD FOOL!
WH-WHAT DO YOU MEAN?
BUT I DIDN'T DO IT!
OKAY, TAKE A SHOT AT...
EH?

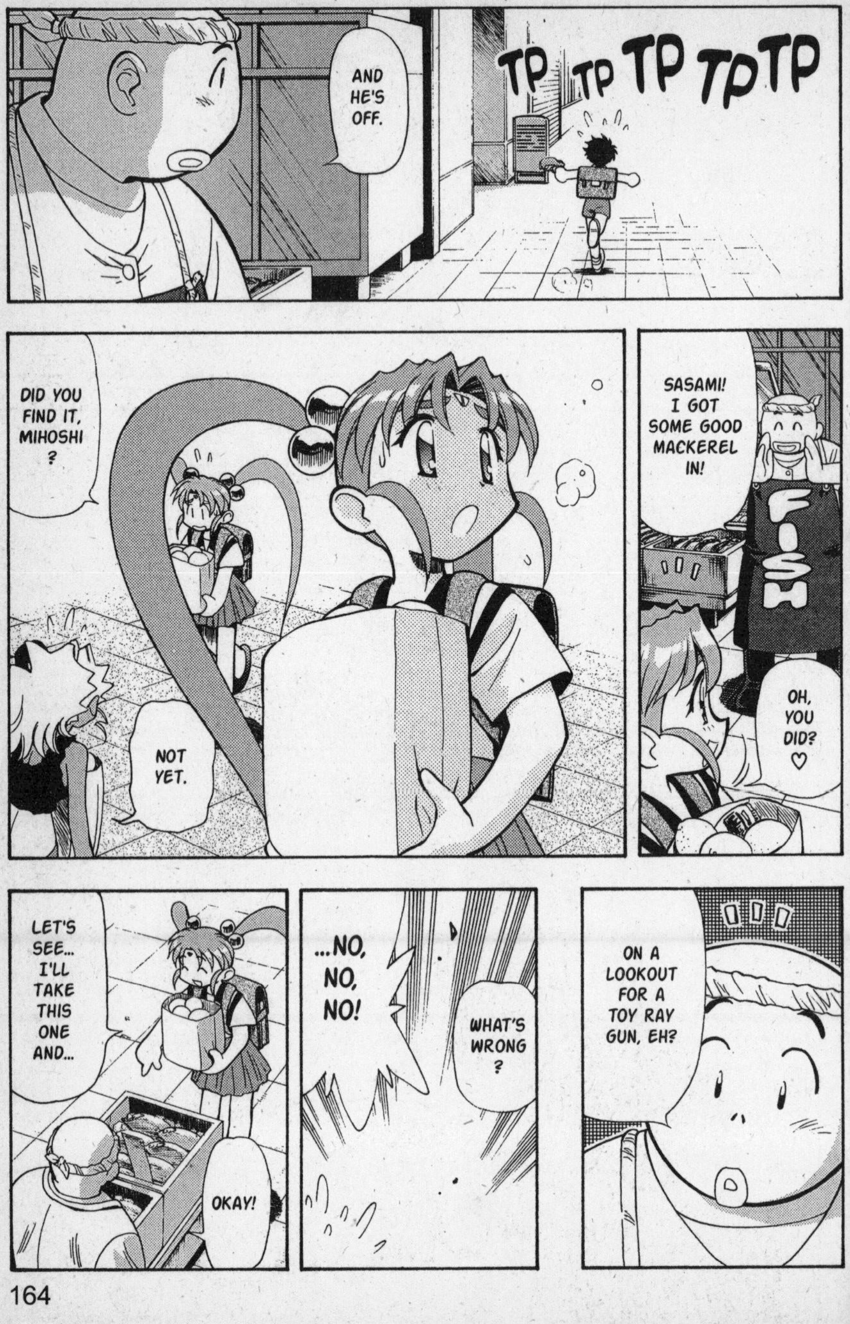
AND HE'S OFF.
TP TP TP TP TP
DID YOU FIND IT, MIHOSHI?
NOT YET.
SASAMI! I GOT SOME GOOD MACKEREL IN!
FISH
OH, YOU DID? ♡
LET'S SEE... I'LL TAKE THIS ONE AND...
OKAY!
...NO, NO, NO!
WHAT'S WRONG?
ON A LOOKOUT FOR A TOY RAY GUN, EH?

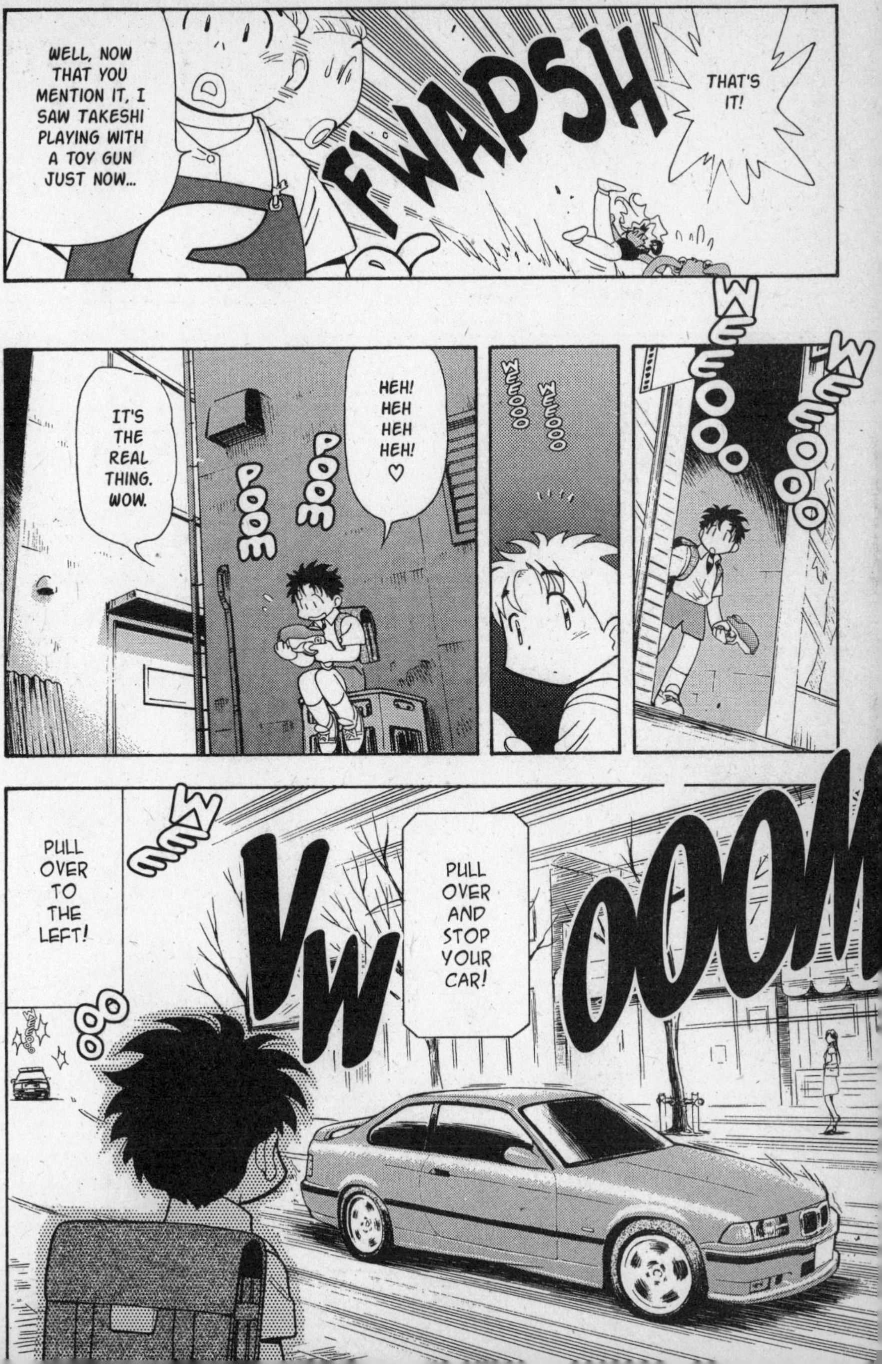
WELL, NOW THAT YOU MENTION IT, I SAW TAKESHI PLAYING WITH A TOY GUN JUST NOW...
FWAPSH
THAT'S IT!
WEEOOO
WEEOOO
IT'S THE REAL THING. WOW.
POOM POOM
HEH! HEH HEH HEH! ♡
WEE
PULL OVER TO THE LEFT!
VWOOOM
PULL OVER AND STOP YOUR CAR!
OOO

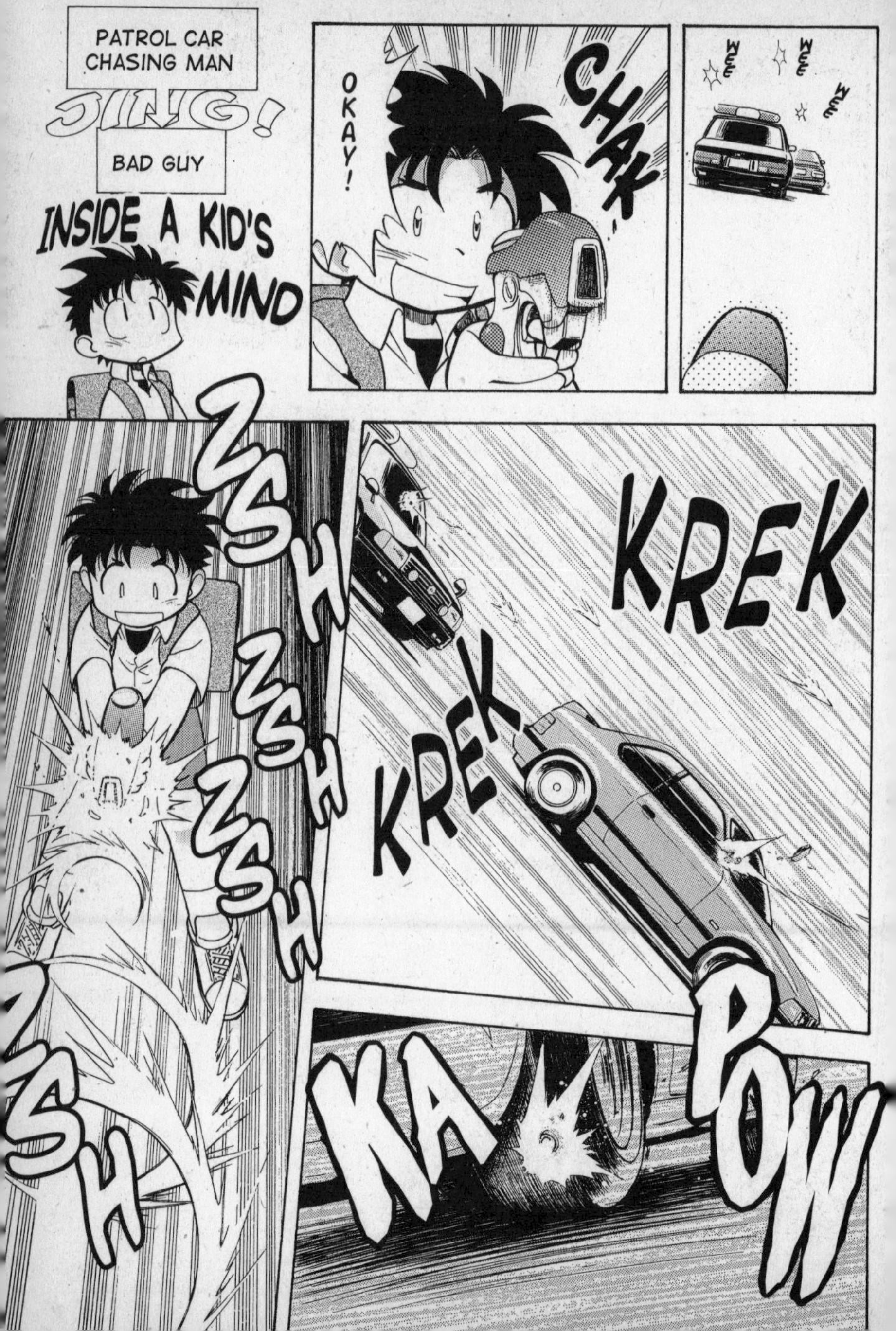
PATROL CAR CHASING MAN
JING!
BAD GUY
INSIDE A KID'S MIND
OKAY!
CHAK
WEE WEE WEE
ZUSH ZUSH ZUSH
KREK
KREK
KA POW

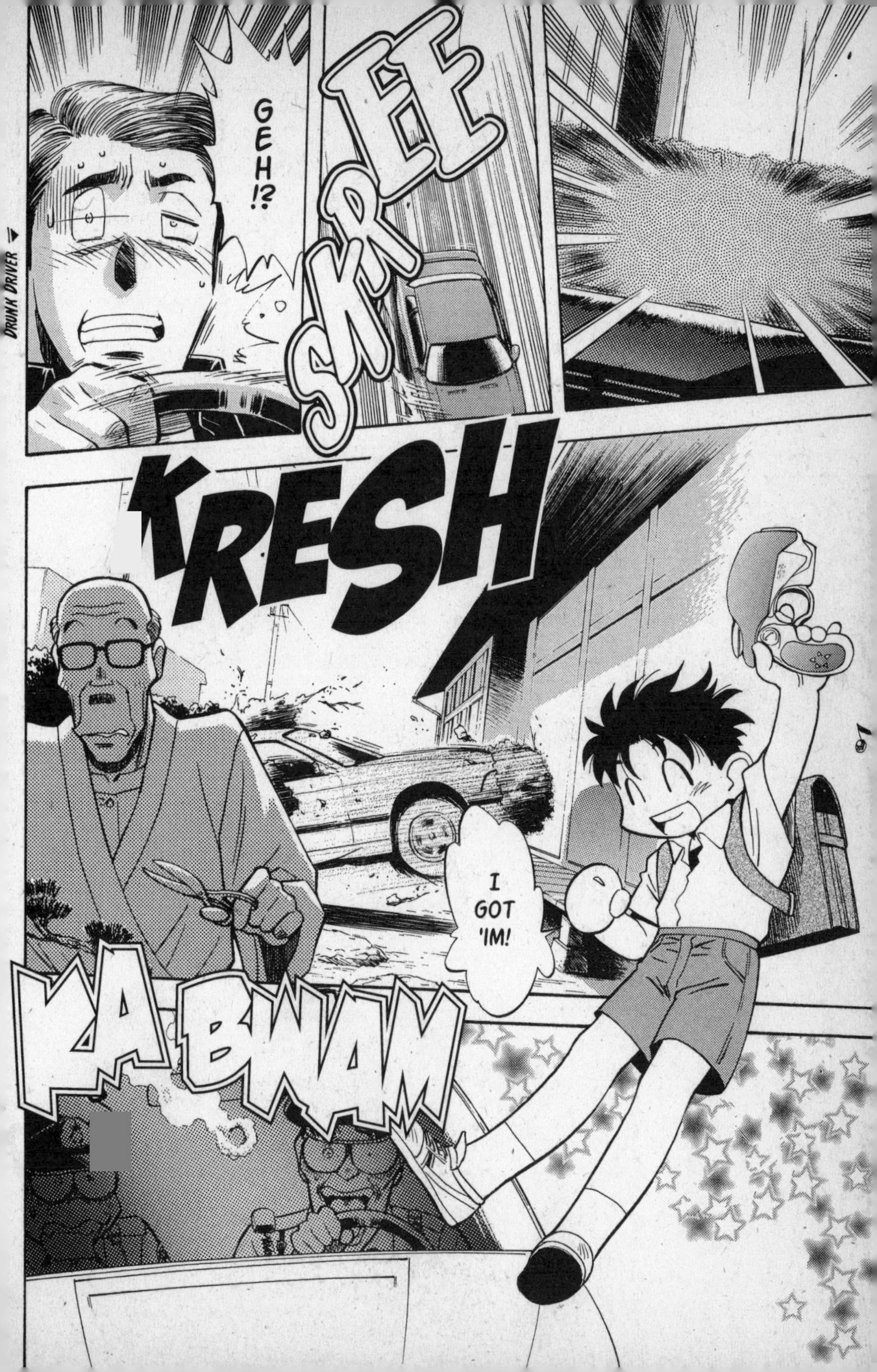
DRUNK DRIVER
GEH!?
SKREE
KRESH
I GOT 'IM!
KA-BWAM

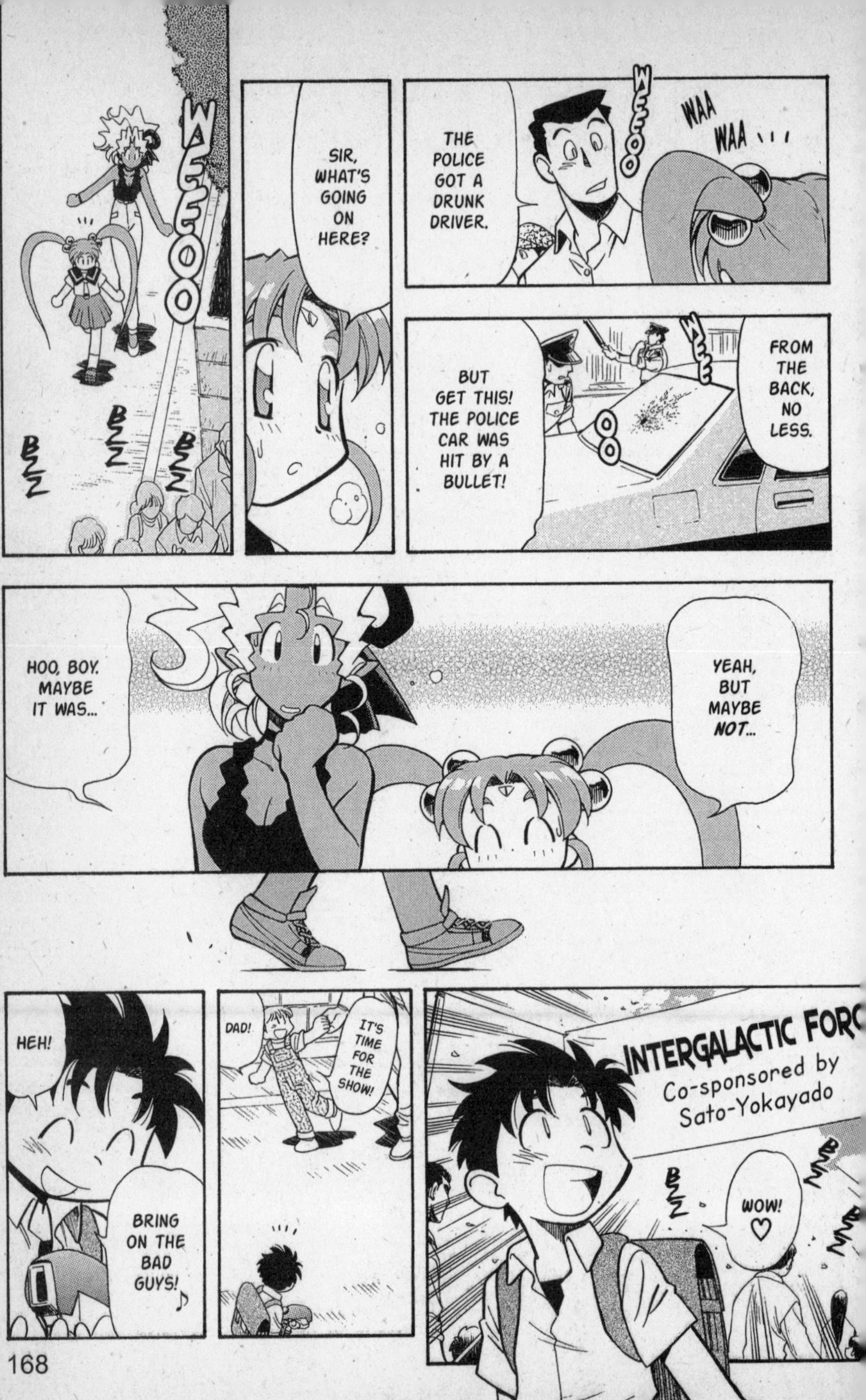

WEEOO
BZZ
BZZ
BZZ
SIR, WHAT'S GOING ON HERE?
THE POLICE GOT A DRUNK DRIVER.
WEEOO
WAA WAA
BUT GET THIS! THE POLICE CAR WAS HIT BY A BULLET!
FROM THE BACK, NO LESS.
HOO, BOY. MAYBE IT WAS...
YEAH, BUT MAYBE *NOT*...
HEH!
BRING ON THE BAD GUYS! ♪
DAD!
IT'S TIME FOR THE SHOW!
INTERGALACTIC FORC
Co-sponsored by Sato-Yokayado
BZZ
WOW! ♡

THEY HAD THEIR GROCERIES DELIVERED. ↓

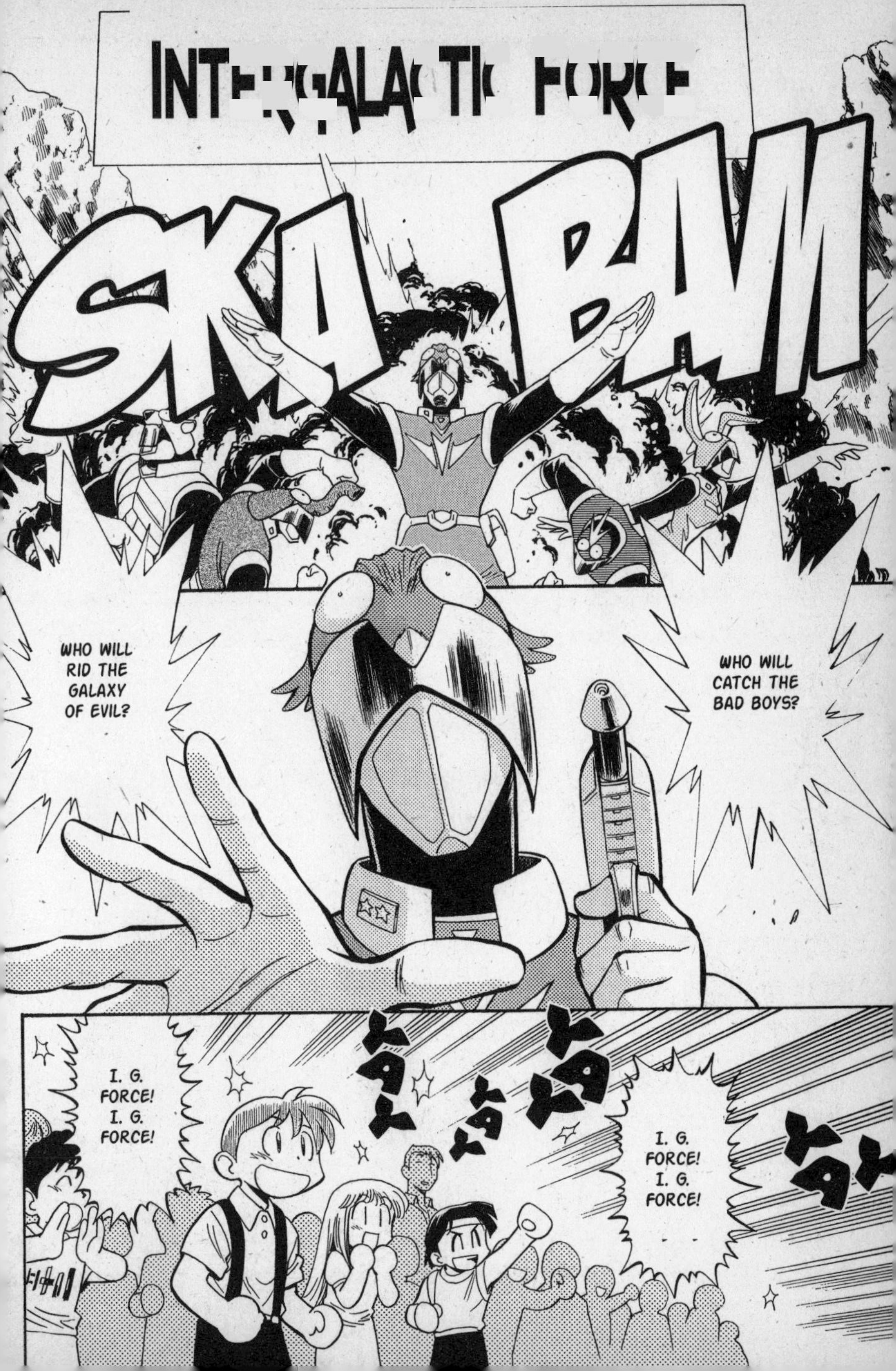
INTERGALACTIC FORCE
SKA-BAM
WHO WILL RID THE GALAXY OF EVIL?
WHO WILL CATCH THE BAD BOYS?
I. G. FORCE! I. G. FORCE!
I. G. FORCE! I. G. FORCE!

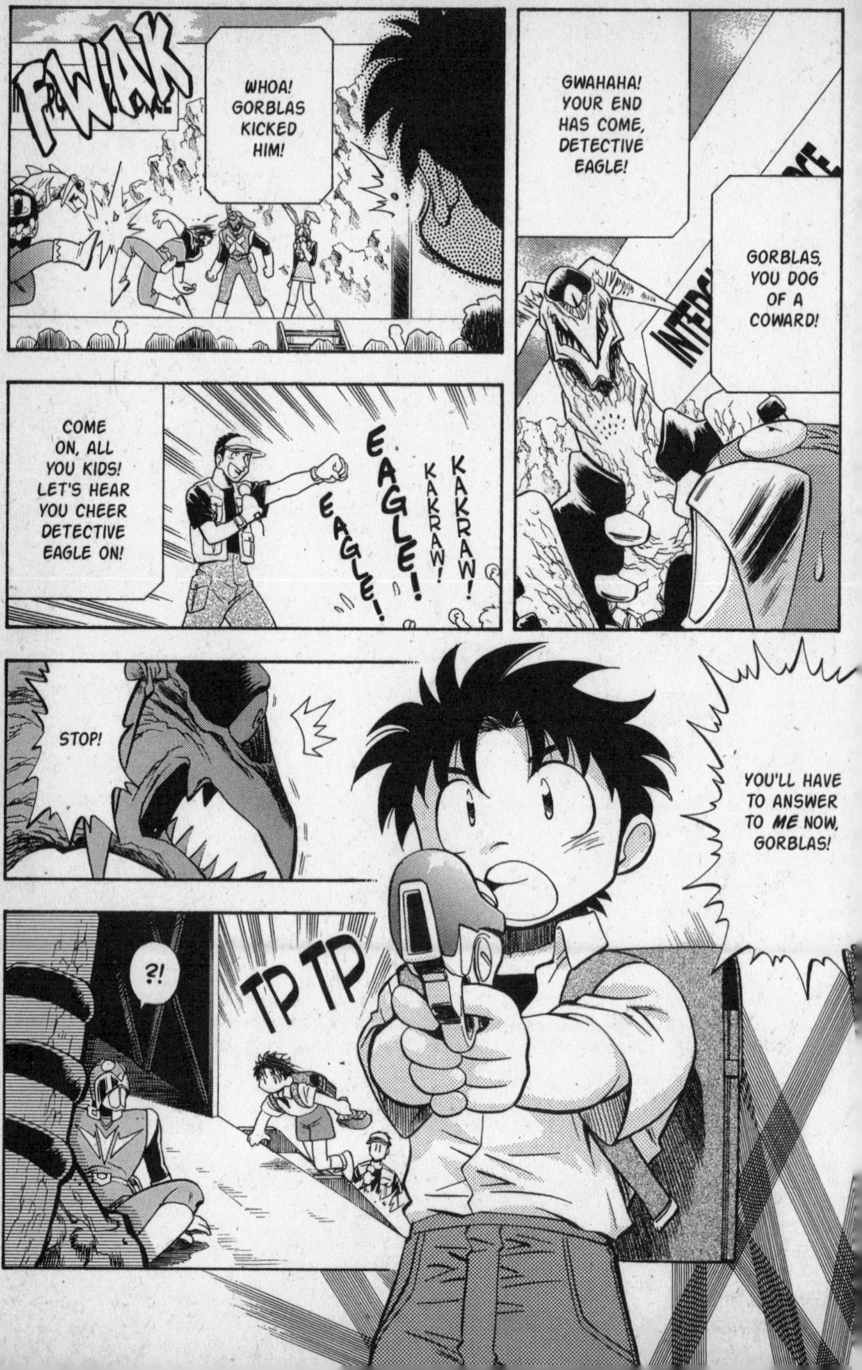
FWAK
WHOA! GORBLAS KICKED HIM!
COME ON, ALL YOU KIDS! LET'S HEAR YOU CHEER DETECTIVE EAGLE ON!
EAGLE!
EAGLE!
KAKRAW!
KAKRAW!
GWAHAHA! YOUR END HAS COME, DETECTIVE EAGLE!
GORBLAS, YOU DOG OF A COWARD!
STOP!
YOU'LL HAVE TO ANSWER TO *ME* NOW, GORBLAS!
?!
TP TP

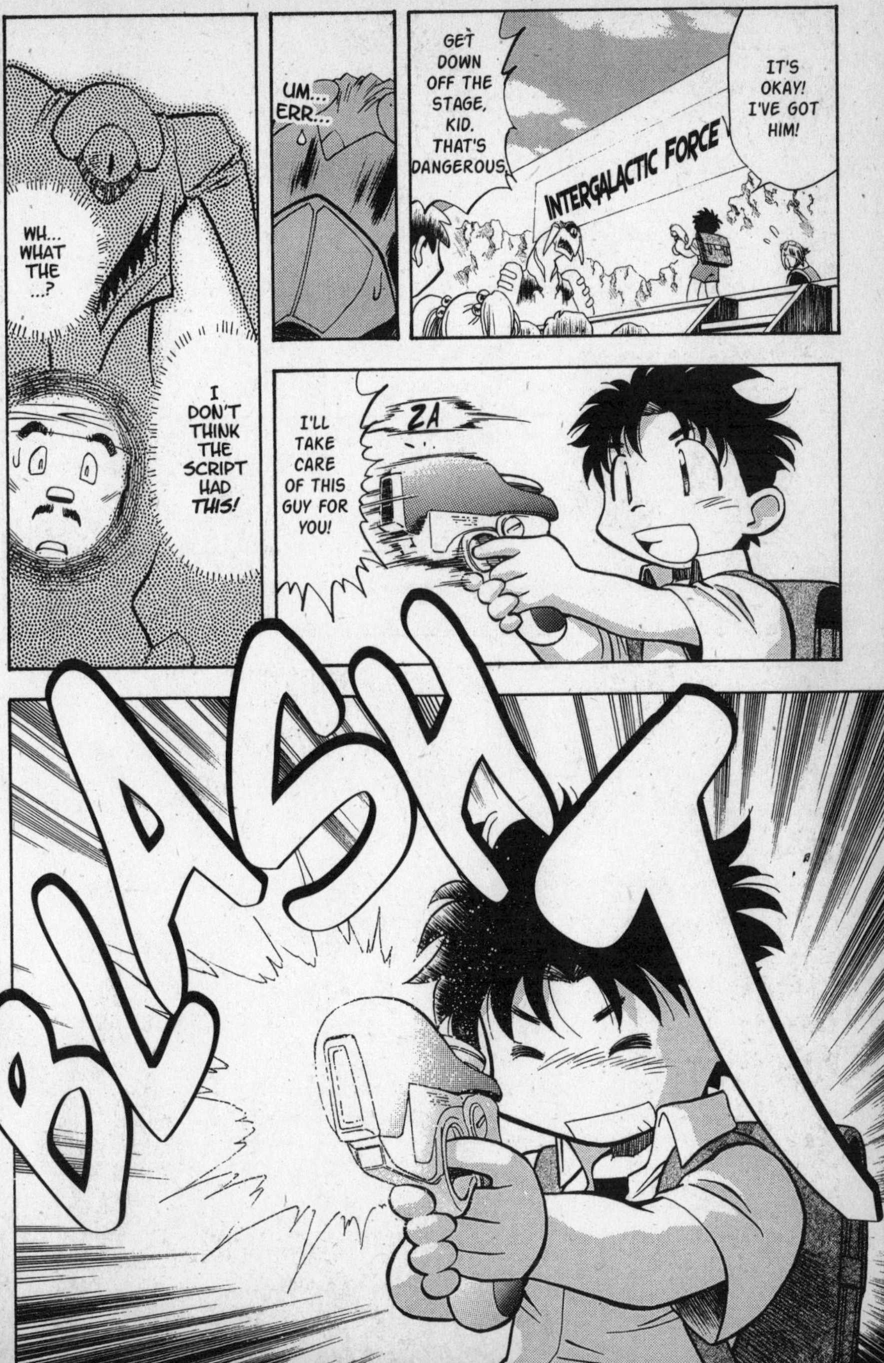

WH... WHAT THE ...?
I DON'T THINK THE SCRIPT HAD THIS!
UM... ERR...
GET DOWN OFF THE STAGE, KID. THAT'S DANGEROUS.
INTERGALACTIC FORCE
IT'S OKAY! I'VE GOT HIM!
I'LL TAKE CARE OF THIS GUY FOR YOU!
ZA
BLASH

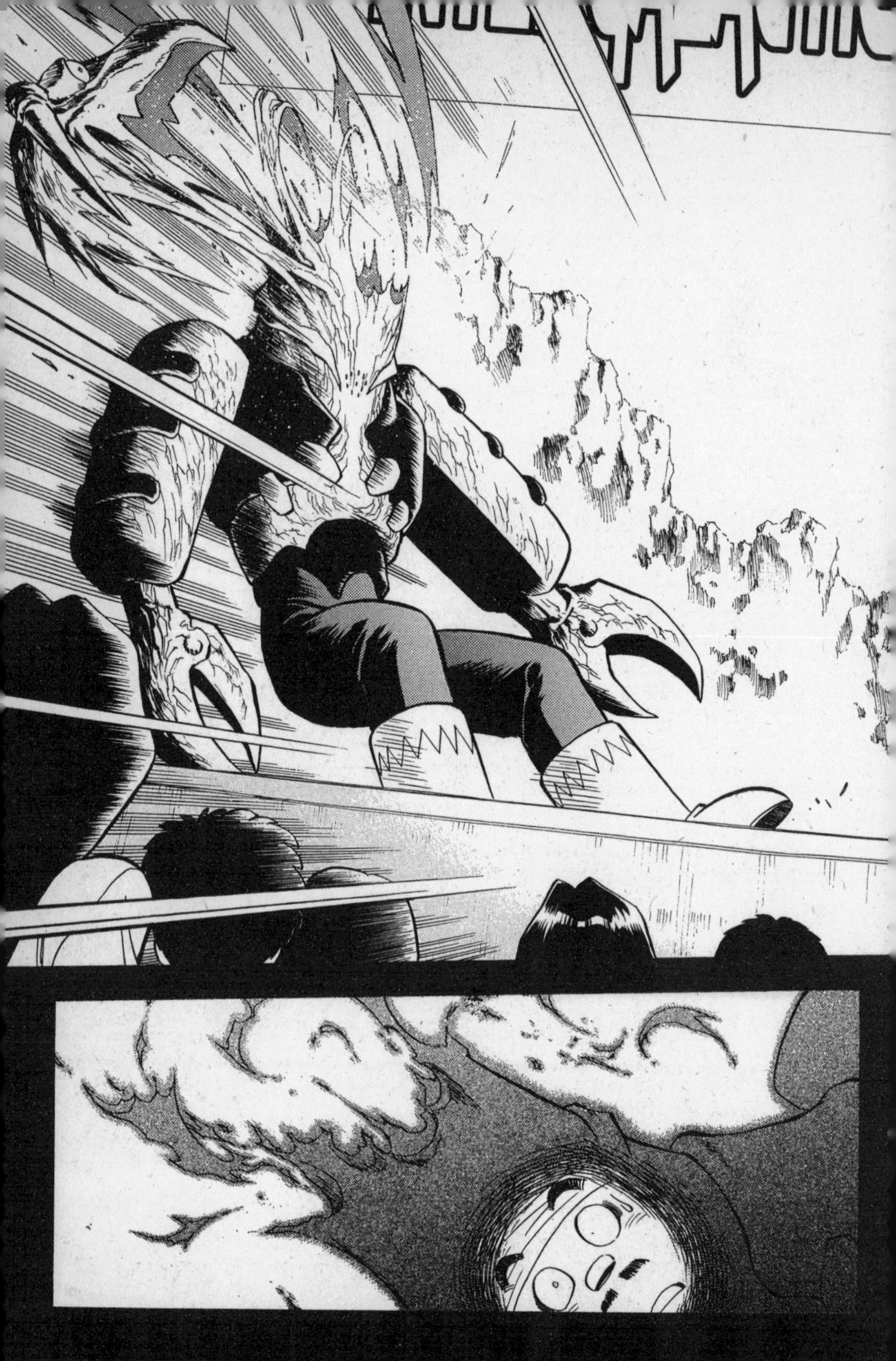

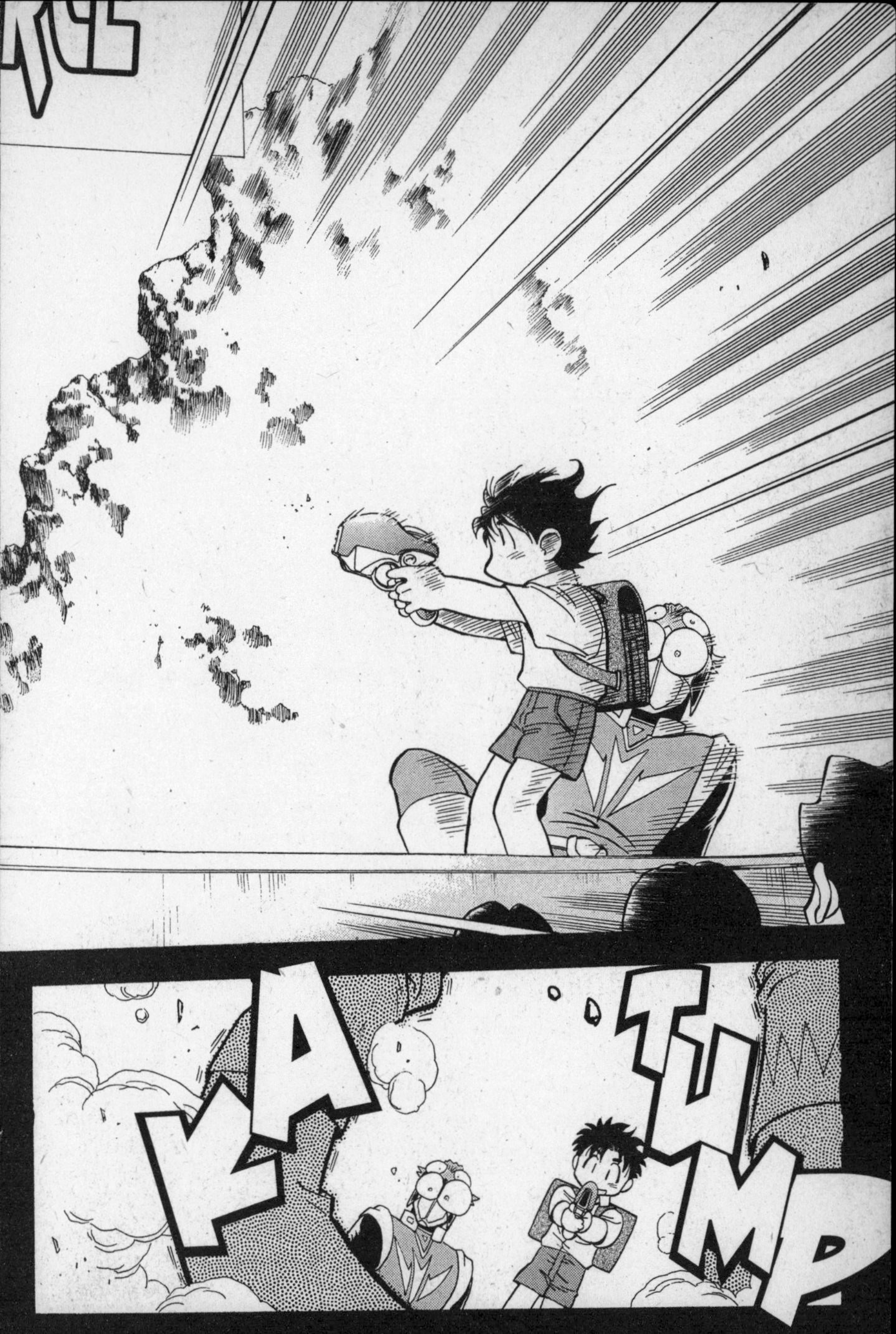
KATUMP

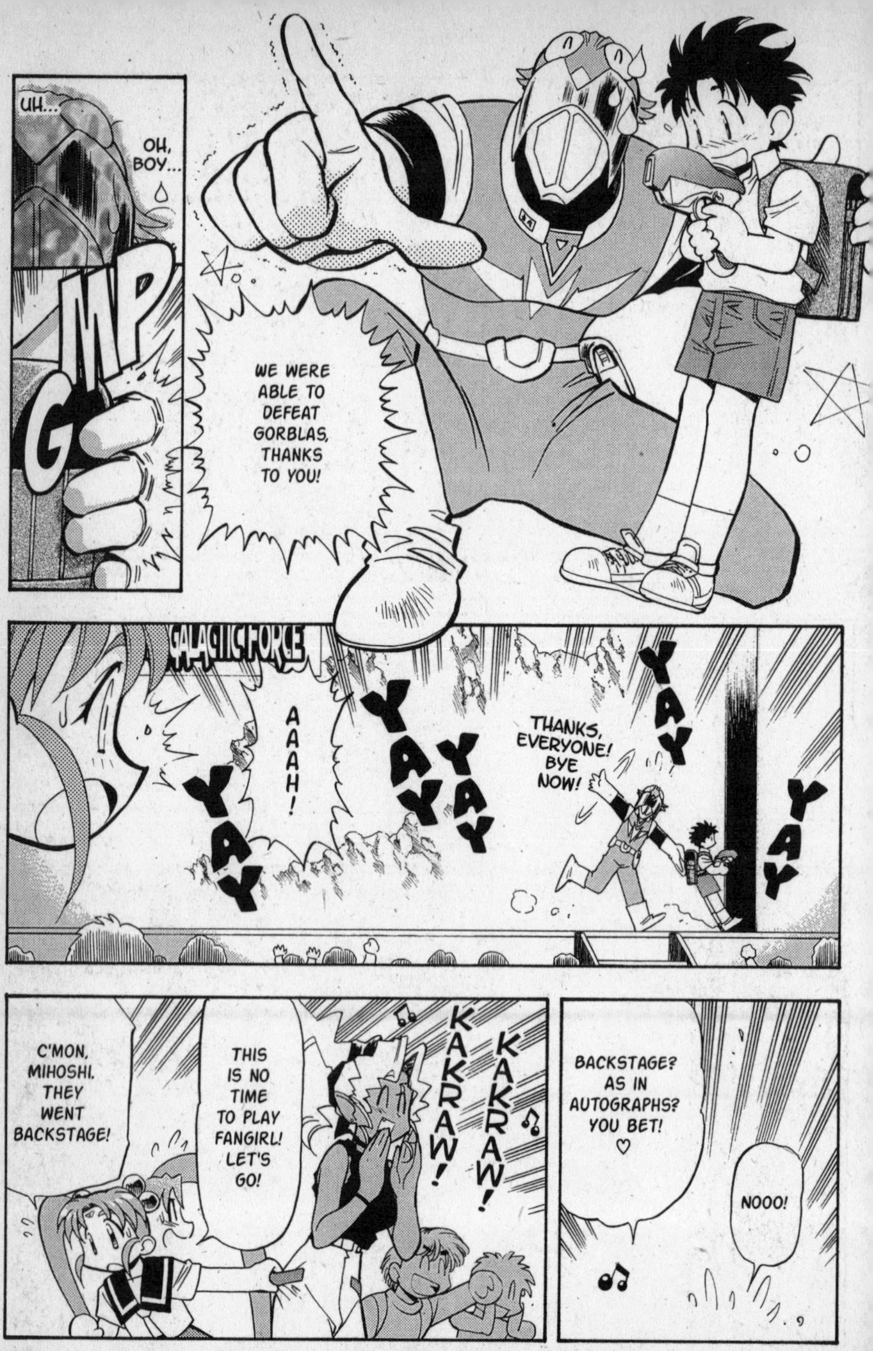
UH...
OH, BOY...
GMP
WE WERE ABLE TO DEFEAT GORBLAS, THANKS TO YOU!
GALACTIC FORCE
YAY
AAAH!
YAY
YAY
THANKS, EVERYONE! BYE NOW!
YAY
YAY
C'MON, MIHOSHI. THEY WENT BACKSTAGE!
THIS IS NO TIME TO PLAY FANGIRL! LET'S GO!
KAKRAW!
KAKRAW!
BACKSTAGE? AS IN AUTOGRAPHS? YOU BET! ♡
NOOO!

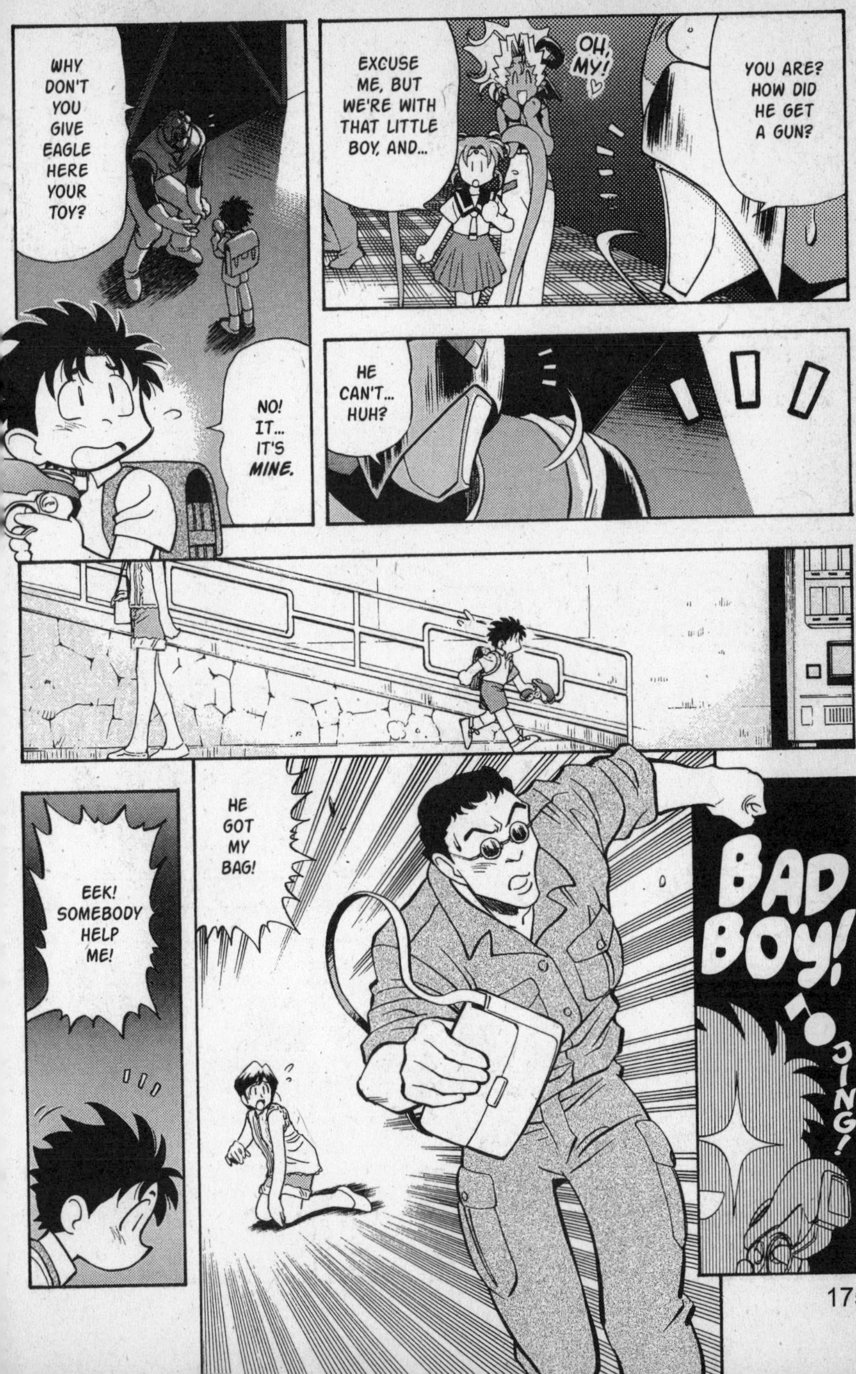
WHY DON'T YOU GIVE EAGLE HERE YOUR TOY?
EXCUSE ME, BUT WE'RE WITH THAT LITTLE BOY, AND...
OH, MY! ♡
YOU ARE? HOW DID HE GET A GUN?
NO! IT... IT'S *MINE.*
HE CAN'T... HUH?
EEK! SOMEBODY HELP ME!
HE GOT MY BAG!
BAD BOY!
JING!

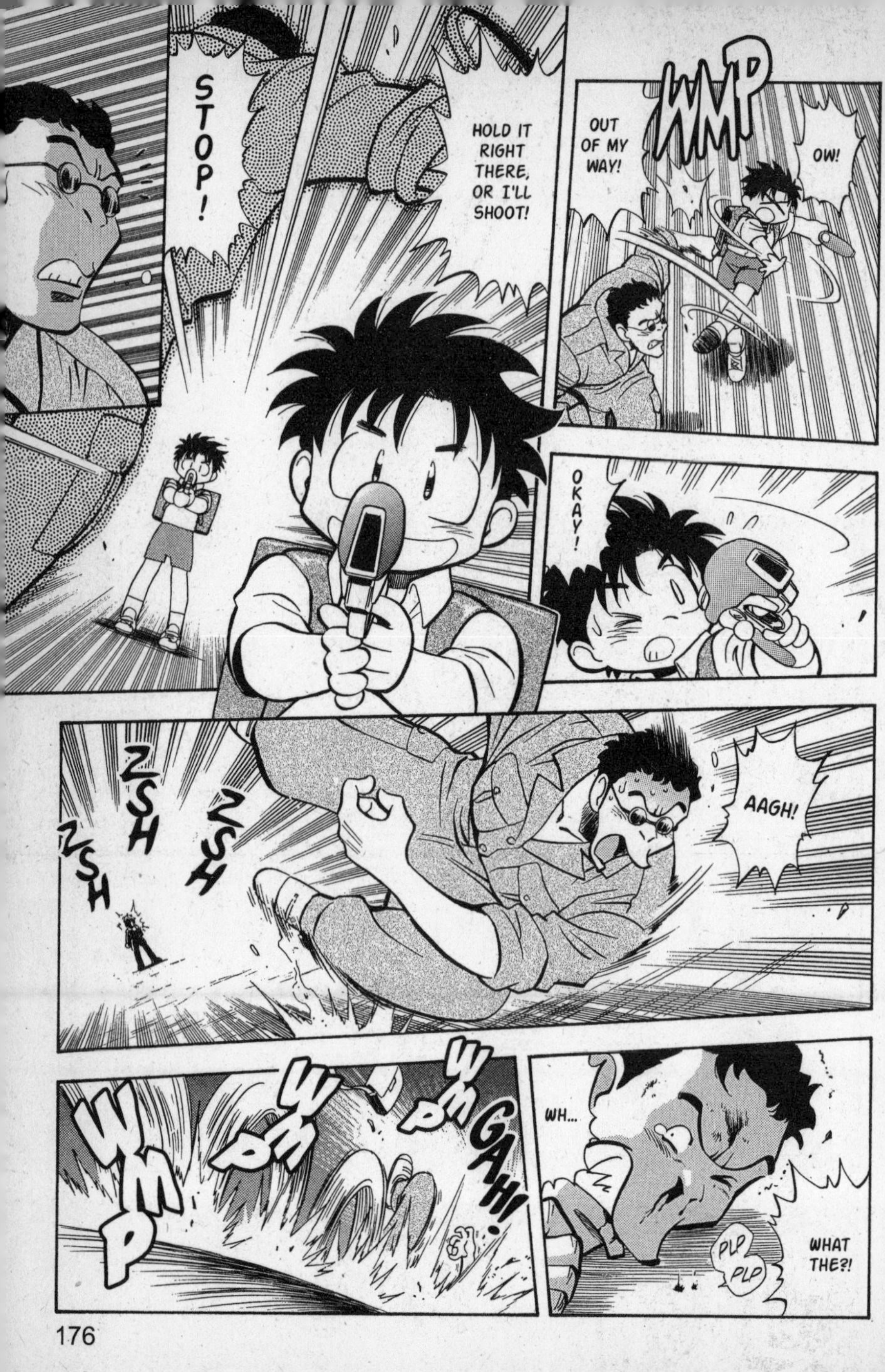
STOP!
HOLD IT RIGHT THERE, OR I'LL SHOOT!
WMP
OUT OF MY WAY!
OW!
OKAY!
ZSH
ZSH
ZSH
AAGH!
WMP
WMP
WMP
GAH!!
WH...
PLP PLP
WHAT THE?!

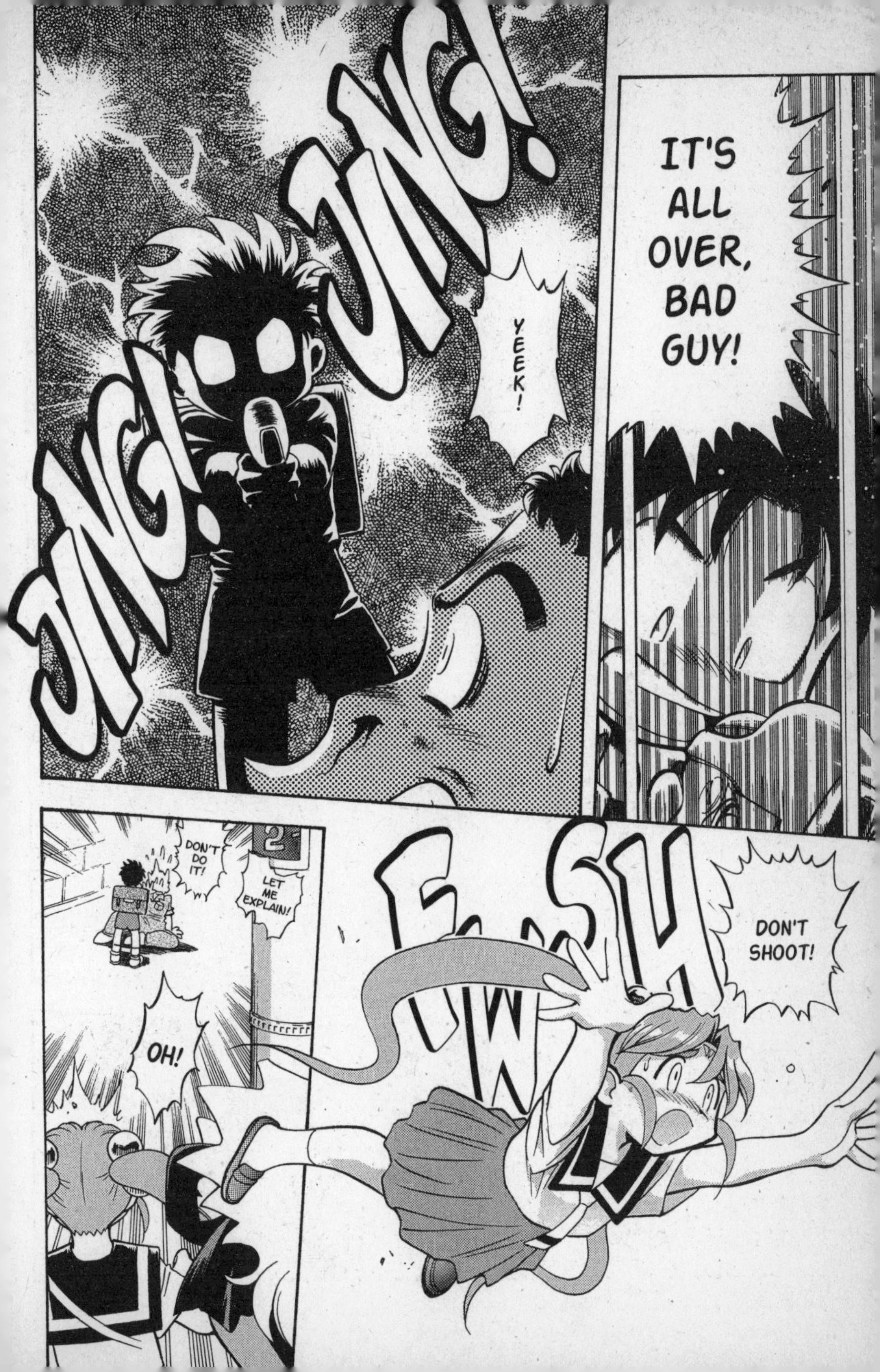
JING! JING!
YEEK!
IT'S ALL OVER, BAD GUY!
DON'T DO IT!
LET ME EXPLAIN!
OH!
DON'T SHOOT!

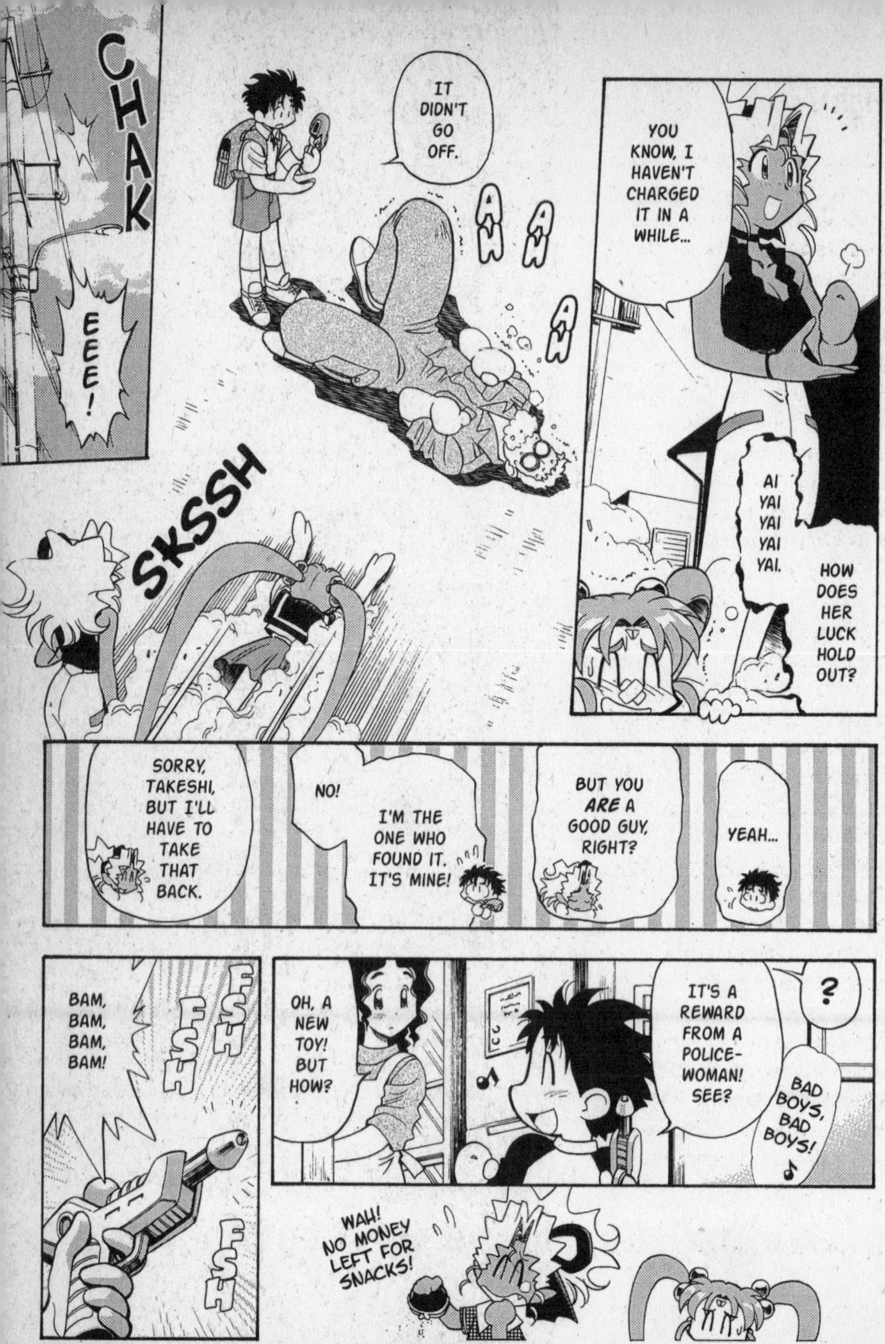
CHAK
EEE!
IT DIDN'T GO OFF.
AH AH AH
SKSSH
YOU KNOW, I HAVEN'T CHARGED IT IN A WHILE...
AI YAI YAI YAI YAI.
HOW DOES HER LUCK HOLD OUT?
SORRY, TAKESHI, BUT I'LL HAVE TO TAKE THAT BACK.
NO!
I'M THE ONE WHO FOUND IT. IT'S MINE!
BUT YOU ARE A GOOD GUY, RIGHT?
YEAH...
BAM, BAM, BAM, BAM!
FSH FSH
FSH
OH, A NEW TOY! BUT HOW?
IT'S A REWARD FROM A POLICE-WOMAN! SEE?
?
BAD BOYS, BAD BOYS!
WAH! NO MONEY LEFT FOR SNACKS!

TO BE CONTINUED IN VOLUME 8!

Fight!

VIZ editor Jason Thompson once said a very wise thing: "In the manga industry, *anything* can become a fighting tournament." As the man in charge of the English versions of *Yu-Gi-Oh!* And *Dragonball Z*, Jason knows fighting, and he's right on the money. In this volume of **All-New Tenchi**, we witness high drama and ideological battles raging in the rough-and-tumble world of children's-book illustration. To write her book, Yae has to conquer writer's block, fight a sleazy editor, win the trust of a goddess, and learn how to walk. The commercial-art business is tough.

Did Hitoshi Okuda put a little of his own experiences into Yae's story? I have my suspicions. As loyal readers will recall, the previous volume of **All-New Tenchi!** included the tragic death of Ayeka's adorable pet Mitsu. In this volume, Sleazy Editor Guy declares, "These days readers prefer to have an animal die to get the story really going." Coincidence? Only Okuda and his editors know for sure. And surely only a manga artist can appreciate Yae's creative struggle and give it the dramatic treatment it deserves.

At any rate, the Editor's Recommendations in this volume focus on the working world. All of them feature fighting, intense competition, and the struggle for success. Because it's a jungle out there...

Shaenon K. Garrity
Editor of **The All-New Tenchi Muyô!**

Like Tenchi?
Love Tenchi?

If so, here are some other books the editor thinks you'll enjoy:

© Hiromu Arakawa/SQUARE ENIX

Fullmetal Alchemist

In a childhood laboratory accident, young alchemists Edward and Alphonse Elric suffered serious injuries. Edward lost an arm and a leg—and Alphonse lost his entire body! Now Edward (fitted out with prosthetic limbs) and Alphonse (currently a soul inhabiting a suit of armor) are state alchemists, using their skills to carry out government orders. But they're secretly on the lookout for the legendary Philosopher's Stone, which may give them the power to set things right. One of the most popular manga in Japan today.

© 2004 Yellow TANABE/Shogakukan Inc.

Kekkaishi

Yoshimori is still in high school, but he's training to take over the family business. He's a novice *kekkaishi*, a master of barrier magic, charged with the task of protecting ordinary people from the supernatural. By day, Yoshimori sleeps through his classes; by night, he patrols a sacred—or cursed—plot of land that attracts ghosts and demons. Working the night shift is wearing him out, and not just because every evening is a life-or-death battle. The girl next door is a *kekkaishi*, too...and she's way more skilled than he is!

© 1996 Masahito SODA/Shogakukan Inc.

Firefighter!

Here's a job as dangerous as alchemy or magic...but real. When hyper-enthusiastic young firefighter Daigo is assigned to Fire Company M, he's instantly disillusioned: his teammates seem to be weak, lazy, rude, or all of the above! But when the fire alarm sounds, the seasoned firefighters spring into action...and rookie Daigo panics at the worst possible moment. Now Daigo has to learn the ropes and figure out what makes the other firefighters put their lives on the line, so that he can become the hero he's always wanted to be.

LOVE MANGA? LET US KNOW!

☐ Please do NOT send me information about VIZ Media products, news and events, special offers, or other information.

☐ Please do NOT send me information from VIZ Media's trusted business partners.

Name: _____

Address: _____

City: _____ **State:** _____ **Zip:** _____

E-mail: _____

☐ **Male** ☐ **Female** **Date of Birth** (mm/dd/yyyy): ___ / ___ / _____ (Under 13? Parental consent required)

What race/ethnicity do you consider yourself? (check all that apply)

☐ White/Caucasian ☐ Black/African American ☐ Hispanic/Latino

☐ Asian/Pacific Islander ☐ Native American/Alaskan Native ☐ Other: _____

What VIZ Media title(s) did you purchase? (indicate title(s) purchased) _____

_____

What other VIZ Media titles do you own? _____

_____

Reason for purchase: (check all that apply)

☐ Special offer ☐ Favorite title / author / artist / genre

☐ Gift ☐ Recommendation ☐ Collection

☐ Read excerpt in VIZ Media manga sampler ☐ Other _____

Where did you make your purchase? (please check one)

☐ Comic store ☐ Bookstore ☐ Grocery Store

☐ Convention ☐ Newsstand ☐ Video Game Store

☐ Online (site:_____) ☐ Other _____

How many manga titles have you purchased in the last year? How many were VIZ Media titles?
(please check one from each column)

MANGA

- [ ] None
- [ ] 1 – 4
- [ ] 5 – 10
- [ ] 11+

VIZ Media

- [ ] None
- [ ] 1 – 4
- [ ] 5 – 10
- [ ] 11+

How much influence do special promotions and gifts-with-purchase have on the titles you buy?
(please circle, with 5 being great influence and 1 being none)

1   2   3   4   5

Do you purchase every volume of your favorite series?

- [ ] Yes! Gotta have 'em as my own
- [ ] No. Please explain: _____

What kind of manga storylines do you most enjoy? (check all that apply)

- [ ] Action / Adventure
- [ ] Comedy
- [ ] Fighting
- [ ] Artistic / Alternative

- [ ] Science Fiction
- [ ] Romance (shojo)
- [ ] Sports
- [ ] Other_____

- [ ] Horror
- [ ] Fantasy (shojo)
- [ ] Historical

If you watch the anime or play a video or TCG game from a series, how likely are you to buy the manga? (please circle, with 5 being very likely and 1 being unlikely)

1   2   3   4   5

If unlikely, please explain: _____

Who are your favorite authors / artists? _____

_____

What titles would like you translated and sold in English? _____

_____

THANK YOU! Please send the completed form to:

NJW Research
42 Catharine Street
Poughkeepsie, NY 12601